Is God A Chauvinist?

Is God A Chauvinist?

The Bible and Women
A Complete Look

◆

Elreta Dodds

Press Toward The Mark Publications
Detroit Michigan

Is God A Chauvinist?

ISBN: 0-9660390-2-5
LCCN: 2002090413

Editor: Noreta Dennard

This book is dedicated to my mother, Octavia Katrina Dodds, who successfully raised me under much adversity, commended me in all of my accomplishments, and supported me in all of my endeavors. She is my hero.

Acknowledgements..........

A Very Special Thanks to my Editor, Noreta Dennard, for her attention to detail, for her support throughout the years, and just for being there.

Special Thanks in alphabetical order to Noreta Dennard, Ovella Maples-Davis, Pastor Emery Moss Jr., Sister Mary Moss, and Christine Warren-Holley, for their written critiques. Their time, energy, and effort are greatly appreciated.

Special Thanks to Jean Schroeder and Kathy King of Sheridan Books for all of their expertise, assistance, and patience throughout the years.

Special Thanks to Leisia Duskin for her front cover design and to Barb Gunia of Sans Serif Inc., for her back cover design and for her service throughout the years.

TABLE OF CONTENTS

INTRODUCTION

This book was mainly written so that women who reject the Bible, because they believe it supports chauvinism, can investigate the matter completely to see if what they believe is actually the case. It was also written for women who might not necessarily reject the Bible but who may feel that God favors men over women. Of course, men are encouraged to read the book as well. No stone has been left unturned. This book is not for the squeamish. The chapters cover virtually *everything* that the Bible says about *anything* that concerns women.

Each chapter in this book can basically be read independently of the others. So the reader is at liberty to "jump around." But due to the fact that a single verse of scripture has the potential of addressing a variety of concerns and subjects, the topics that are presented have a tendency to overlap. Because of this, some verses of scripture are quoted in more than one chapter and some explanations are reiterated.

Many women believe that the Bible teaches women to be subservient to men and that it does not advocate for equal opportunity for women when it comes to social issues, domestic roles, religious duty, career opportunities and the like. They believe that the God of the Bible has double standards for men and women, that stricter rules are placed on women regarding certain issues than are placed on men regarding those same issues. They especially believe that God has set a higher standard for women than he has for men when it comes to societal roles. They feel that women are expected to be perfect mothers, perfect housekeepers, perfect wives and the like while the societal standard of this "perfection" doesn't seem to apply to men as to their role of provider, father, and husband. And they hold God responsible for these discrepancies.

Women who believe these things may not readily admit it, nor be completely cognizant of it, but they essentially believe that God is a chauvinist, if they believe in God at all. Since the Bible and Christianity go hand in hand, many of them reject Christianity because they feel it fits into the definition of what some refer to as "organized religion." These women particularly feel that Christianity is not only organized in general, but that the religion itself is organized against them, as women.

Indeed the Bible is not lax in instructing men and women in areas of marriage, sex, singleness, raising children, working, church attendance, serving God, and so forth. The problem, as stated before, is that many women believe that God is not fair to women when it comes to women's roles in relation to men's roles and that the Bible gives men more privileges than it does women.

This book is aimed at dispelling the beliefs that God is a chauvinist and that the Bible is a chauvinistic/sexist book. It is also aimed at dispelling the belief that the Bible does nothing but add to the oppression that women experience to some degree in almost every society of the world.

There are two definitions of a chauvinist. The original definition describes a person who is overly proud and supportive of his or her country to the point of unreasonable, irrational advocacy and combative, hostile patriotism. The word *chauvinist* was actually derived from the name of a man named Nicholas Chauvin who was a soldier in Napoleon's army. Chauvin was infamous for his militant and unrelenting endorsement of imperialism. Imperialism is the mechanism by which one country sets out to control and dominate the natural resources and economic capital of other smaller countries by invasion, colonialism, market exploitation, and similar means.

The use of the word *chauvinist* is used more loosely in the English language and a second meaning has developed over the years. The second definition of a chauvinist describes a person who is dedicated to putting one's own gender on a pedestal. It combines together an irrational advocacy and love for one's own sex. Not only is there the love and glorifying of one's own sex but along with it comes the minimization, status declassification, putting down, and belittling of the opposite sex as a whole. Therefore, some of the original meaning of the word applies to this definition as well.

A man or a woman can be a chauvinist but chauvinism is most commonly thought of as associated with men. Male chauvinists tend to think, or at least allude to, the belief that they are better, smarter, more apt, more deserving, more able, more entitled, more fitting, more suited for roles that merit greater status and more spiritual, than women, simply because they are men. Male chauvinists also believe that menial and mundane tasks belong to women or that the tasks that women do are menial and mundane and they often believe that men are superior to women.

Chauvinism is often times confused with sexism. The two are very similar but are not quite the same. While chauvinism is generally defined as the thought or belief that men are superior to women and while male chauvinists often advocate for and endorse chauvinistic thought and policy, sexists are the ones who implement the actual discrimination against women. This sexist discrimination is of course the culmination of what began as chauvinistic thought. Chauvinism therefore often leads to sexism. The two work hand in hand. And while male chauvinists see themselves as intellectually and spiritually superior to women, sexists are the ones who stereotype women and implement double standards against them.

Despite the subtle differences in definition, most people fuse chauvinism and sexism together when defining the two terms. Since this is so, and since the definition of a chauvinist has developed into a term mostly associated with men, the operative definition of chauvinism for the purposes of this book will incorporate both definitions of what a chauvinist and a sexist are and the general term itself (*chauvinist*) along with variations of it, will be basically used to refer to male chauvinism (gender specific to men).

Many women believe that the Bible is a chauvinistic book and that it discriminates against women. Because of this, as stated earlier, there are those women who reject the Bible thereby rejecting the message of Jesus Christ and ultimately rejecting salvation. This is a spiritually dangerous thing because the Bible teaches that it is only by the name of Jesus that people can be saved. To be saved means to live eternally in heaven with God. Not to be saved means to live eternally in hell. So, if to reject the Bible means to reject Christ, and rejecting Christ prevents one from obtaining the gift of salvation, then to reject the Bible is a serious matter indeed. Christians believe that the Bible (the canonized Old and New Testaments) is the authentic word of God and that it is the only book which truly represents what God has said. Christians believe this because they believe the miraculous accounts of Jesus and of others that the Bible documents and they believe that the Bible is a miraculous piece of literature itself seeing that it was written by 40 different authors, on 3 different continents (Africa, Asia, Europe) over a span of 1500 years and does not contradict itself.

But we cannot discuss whether or not God is a chauvinist without first identifying who God is. The book of Genesis tells us that *"in the beginning God created the heavens and the earth."* Genesis 1:26 teaches us that God made mankind in his own image. It says, *"And God said, let us make man in our image, after our likeness...."* Therefore "God" (singular) is identified in plural form ("us" and "our"). 1st John 5:7 tells us that *"there are three that bear record in heaven, the Father, the Word, and the Holy Ghost, and these three are one."* Orthodox Christian theologians have concluded that there is therefore one God who represents himself in three persons (beings): the Father, the Son, and the Holy Spirit. They hold different offices but are equal in authority to one another. The Son is Jesus Christ. Scripture identifies Jesus as the Son of God and also identifies him as The Word in John 1:1-14.[1] The Word is identified as God himself, which makes Jesus God. John 3:16[2] identifies Jesus as God's only begotten Son. This means that Jesus was the only person that was born directly of God. Jesus is the Word that was with God in the beginning. John 1:14 tells us that the Word was made flesh. This means that Jesus was manifested in human form since he is the Word. He is the Son of God and God the Son at the same time. In Isaiah 44:6 God is quoted as saying that there is no other God besides him. When Moses asked God his name, God replied by saying that his name is "I AM THAT I AM."[3] As recorded in John 8:58, Jesus also identified himself as "I AM" which is why the Jews set out to kill him because they knew he was making himself equal with God by identifying himself as he did.[4]

To explain further, during Old Testament times, the blood offering of an animal was needed to atone for sin. However, when Jesus came, he atoned for the sins of all of us by shedding his blood on the cross. Therefore, he is also referenced in the Bible as the Lamb of God. Jesus was the ultimate sacrificial lamb. Since he became the ultimate sin offering, a person needs only to confess his or her belief in the lordship of Jesus Christ and sincerely believe that he rose from the dead, in order to be saved. This is conveyed in Romans 10:9 which says, *"if thou confess with thy mouth the Lord Jesus, and shalt believe in thine heart that God has raised him from the dead, thou shalt be saved."* As stated earlier, to be saved is to be saved from eternal hellfire. To be saved is to

---

[1] See Appendix
[2] See your Bible.
[3] Moses said to God, "Suppose I go to the Israelites and say to them, 'The God of your fathers has sent me to you,' and they ask me, "What is his name?' Then what shall I tell them?" God said to Moses, "I AM WHO I AM. This is what you are to say to the Israelites: "I AM has sent me to you.' (Exodus 3:13-14 NIV) The King James Version translates I AM WHO I AM as I AM THAT I AM.
[4] John 8:42-59 (see your Bible).

have everlasting life in the kingdom of God. Acts 4:12 teaches us that there is no other name, besides the name of Jesus, by which mankind can be saved.

In this book there will be no less than nine different English Translations of the Bible used when quoting scripture. The King James Version is used sparingly. The following are a list of the other biblical translations that are used along with their acronyms. No acronym is used for the King James Version.

> *New International Version* (NIV)
> *New Living Translation* (NLT)
> *New American Standard Bible* (NASB)
> *New King James Version* (NKJV)
> *Contemporary English Version (CEV)*
> *New Revised Standard Version* (NRSV)
> *Good News Translation (GNT)*
> *Amplified Bible* (Amp.)
> *King James Version*

The translations teach the same doctrine but sometimes one translation might present the scripture in a more understandable or contemporary way than another translation. Therefore, different translations are used according to the style of the translation and the subject being discussed.

In this book there is much talk of dispensationalism. Dispensationalism is the theory that the work of God has been divided into seven different God-ordained time periods since the beginning of the creation of man. God has established certain rules by which mankind is to live, but there are those rules that only apply during a particular dispensation and then there are those rules that apply across all seven dispensations. According to *Holman's Bible Dictionary*, the dispensations are as follows:

The dispensation of Innocency: This is the period of time when Adam and Eve lived in the Garden of Eden before they fell prey to the serpent.[5] They were innocent and had not yet come against God. During that time, life was simple and the earth's soil was fertile and gave forth abundantly.

---

[5] Genesis 2:8-25 and Genesis 3:1-19 (see your Bible)

God gave Adam and Eve everything they needed in the Garden. They did not lack anything.

The dispensation of Conscience: This is the period that follows Adam and Eve's expulsion from the Garden of Eden. Whereas they were not conscious of good and evil before eating of the forbidden fruit, they were conscious of it after their fall into temptation.

The dispensation of Human Government: Because mankind had become very evil and went against God, God destroyed mankind with a flood. But he spared Noah and his family due to the righteousness of Noah. After the flood, God promised Noah that he would never again destroy all living creatures and curse the ground because of man.[6] This ushered in the beginning of human government.

The dispensation of Promise: Noah had three sons, Ham, Shem, and Japheth. Abraham is a descendant of Shem. God promised Abraham that Abraham's descendants would become a great nation. His descendants are the Jews. God not only promised to make Abraham into a great nation but he also promised to give land to the nation.[7] God confirmed his promises with Abraham after he tested Abraham's faithfulness. Abraham was willing to kill his own son as a sacrifice to the Lord to prove his faithfulness to God.[8] Therefore, not only would God promise the descendants of Abraham a certain stretch of land (then called the land of Canaan, now called the land of Israel, which includes Jerusalem) but God would also enable them to "take possession of the cities of their enemies."[9]

The dispensation of the Law: Moses was instructed by God to lead the Jews from under the oppressive slavery of the Egyptians. Once he led them out of slavery, God established certain laws that the Jews had to follow. These laws are often times called the Mosaic laws because it was Moses who instructed the Jews concerning these laws. Many of the laws that applied then do not apply today. However, some of the laws were upheld by Jesus and therefore apply today. The biblical documentation of the laws that God set forth is documented in the 19th chapter of the book of Exodus through the 40th chapter and includes the Ten commandments. The laws instructed the Jews on what to do in cases of personal injury,

---

[6] Genesis 8:20-21 (see your Bible)
[7] Genesis 12:1-7, Genesis 13:18 (see your Bible)
[8] Genesis 22:1-18 (see your Bible)
[9] Genesis 22:1-18 (see your Bible)

protection of property, burnt offerings, social responsibilities and so forth. There is further documentation of the Mosaic Law in the book of Leviticus. These laws cover the procedures mandated for burnt offerings, grain offerings, sin offerings, peace offerings, guilt offerings, what to eat and what not to eat, procedures regarding contagious diseases, procedures regarding contaminated clothing, laws surrounding bodily discharges, laws surrounding sexual conduct, laws surrounding personal conduct, punishment for disobedience, laws regarding slaves, laws regarding the redemption of property, laws regarding the poor, and other laws.

The dispensation of Grace: This is the time period that began after the death and resurrection of Jesus Christ. It is the dispensation that we are currently living in today. During the dispensation of the Law, those who worshipped the Lord could only atone for their sins by going to the priest and giving him an animal to sacrifice as a sin offering. But Jesus became the ultimate sacrificial sin offering when he died on the cross. This is why he is called the sacrificial Lamb of God. Now all people have to do is confess that Jesus is Lord and believe in his resurrection from the dead,[10] and their sins will be forgiven. They will also have a place in the Kingdom of heaven when they die.

The dispensation of Kingdom: The first coming of Christ (the Messiah) is represented by the birth of Jesus and his earthly ministry thereafter. The Bible tells us that there will be a Second Coming of Christ and this is when the dispensation of Kingdom will be ushered in. At the first half of the Second Coming, Jesus will be seen in the clouds. Those who have believed on Jesus and confessed that belief will be caught up with him in the air. The dead in Christ will rise first and then those Christians who are living will be caught up in the clouds to meet the Lord.[11] This will happen suddenly without warning.[12] Those who are left behind (those who are not saved) will endure an earthly seven-year tribulation during which time the antichrist will rule.[13] But, after the seven years are gone, Jesus will come back in the clouds again (second half of the Second Coming) this time as a warrior and will defeat the

---

[10] Romans 10:9 (see your Bible)

[11] 1 Thessalonians 4:13-18 (see your Bible)

[12] 1 Corinthians 15:50-58 (see your Bible)

[13] Revelation 13:5-8 then verses 11-18 along with Daniel 9:27 (see your Bible)

antichrist and the devil himself in a battle known as Armageddon.[14] After this battle, Jesus will establish his earthly Kingdom and a New Jerusalem will descend from heaven. Those who followed Christ (Christians) will reign with Christ on earth for a thousand years.[15]

It should be mentioned that certain terms are interchangeable. A Christian is a person who follows Christ and believes in Jesus as Lord and Savior. The church is not only a building where Christians worship, but is the body of people all over the world identified as Christians. A saint is also any person who is a Christian. These four terms: *Christian, saint, believer,* and *the church* refer to the same thing and have been used interchangeably throughout this book.

The words *Jew, Israel, Israelites,* and *Hebrew* are also used interchangeably. The Jews are the Israelites and the Israelites are often times referred to as Israel (the nation). The twelve tribes of Israel that are documented in the Bible are Reuben, Simeon, Levi, Judah, Issachar, Zebulun, Joseph (who produced the sub-tribes of Ephraim and Manesseh), Dan, Benjamin, Naphtali, Gad, and Asher.[16] Each tribe is named after the man who originally fathered the tribe.

It should also be clarified that although God refers to himself as the God of Abraham, Isaac, and Jacob, he is a God to everyone who will accept him. The Jews (Abraham's descendants) are the "chosen people" only because of the promises God made to Abraham due to Abraham's righteousness. But Romans 2:28-29 makes it clear as to who the Jews really are. It says, *"For you are not a true Jew just because you were born of Jewish parents or because you have gone through the Jewish ceremony of circumcision. No, a true Jew is one whose heart is right with God. And true circumcision is not a cutting of the body but a change of heart produced by God's Spirit."* The Bible teaches that those, whose hearts are right with God, are those who have confessed that Jesus is Lord and believe in their hearts that he rose from the dead. They are the true Jews. Hence, all Christians are Jews and accordingly, anyone can become a Jew and inherit the title of being one of God's children, if they choose to confess and believe in Jesus.

---

[14] Revelation 19:11-16 then verses 19-21 (see your Bible)
[15] Revelation 20:1-6 (see your Bible).
[16] Revelation 7:1-8 (see your Bible). Theologians are not certain why the tribe of Dan is omitted from the list of tribes in Revelation 7:8.

Although this book was primarily written for women who are not Christians, the book is also intended for Christian women and Christian men as well. It is intended to encourage Christian women who may be struggling with some of the biblical passages that speak about women's issues and it is intended to help Christian men look at the other side of things, who believe that the Bible teaches that a woman's primary purpose in life is to serve, or be subservient to, men.

In order to believe in the Bible as the absolute and only word of God, certain beliefs that prevent some from accepting the Bible as true, need to be examined. The beliefs that say that the Bible is a chauvinistic book, that say that the God of the Bible is a chauvinist or a sexist, and that say that God is not fair to women, are barriers that must be torn down because those beliefs are getting in the way of the salvation of many women. The aim of this book is to aid in tearing down those barriers in order that certain women might be saved.

1.

GREAT WOMEN OF THE BIBLE

It stands to reason that if God were truly a chauvinist then there would be no biblically recorded incidences whereby women were deemed powerful, faithful, or able to appropriately serve God. Not only does the Bible give historical documentation of powerful, faithful, and God-fearing women, but the documentation is given so that lessons can be learned. God uses women as well as men as tools for his mighty works. If God were a chauvinist then women would never be used to carry out his missions. Only men would be used. But as this chapter will point out, women have played a vital role in aiding to propagate and uphold the doctrines of the Holy Scriptures.

When most people think of great women of the Bible, they immediately envision, Mary (mother of Jesus), Elizabeth (mother of John the Baptist), Eve,[1] and other more popular female biblical historical figures. However, there are many more great women of the Bible whose fame is not as aggrandized as the aforementioned, but are still distinguished women.

The women profiled in this chapter are but a few of the women who are made notable in the Bible. To summarize all of the accomplishments of all of the women the Bible specifies would constitute an entire book itself. Therefore, we will only look at a few of the women, this author, and many others, deem great.

WOMEN OF POSITION

Deborah

Deborah is spoken of in the book of Judges. The book of Judges is part of the Old Testament of the Bible and gives the historical account of Israel's settlement in the Promised Land[2] from the time of Joshua's death

---

[1] Mary, Elizabeth, and Eve will be spoken of in detail in later chapters.
[2] The land God promised to Abraham for his faithfulness. Historical accounts are located in Genesis 12:1-7 and Exodus 3:4-10 (see Appendix)

1

through the period in which God placed certain Judges over Israel. Theologians have had difficulty in calculating the exact period of time when the Judges were leaders over the Israelites during the Israelites' stay in the Promised Land. Some have estimated, however, with some reservation, that the time was between 1380 and 1050 B.C.

Before expounding on the historical life of Deborah, some background information about Joshua's reign must first be given. Joshua became the leader of Israel after Moses died. During Joshua's reign, other nations confronted Israel for occupation of the Israelites' land. The Canaanites, Amorites, and Hittites, were a few of the nations that battled with Israel regarding land. Eventually Israel strengthened its position and was able to defeat and enslave the Canaanites and the Amorites. Because of the enslavement, the opposing nations were never really driven out of the land of the Israelites.[3] During the time of Joshua's reign over Israel, the Israelites did what was right and worshipped the Lord God. But when Joshua died, the generation of those who followed did not know the Lord and did not worship God, as they ought to have. They began to worship false gods, so God allowed them to be enslaved by their enemies.[4] Then God began to raise up Judges in Israel, as the following verses of scripture attest to:

> [16]Then the LORD raised up judges, who delivered them out of the power of those who plundered them. [17]Yet they did not listen even to their judges; for they lusted after other gods and bowed down to them. They soon turned aside from the way in which their ancestors had walked, who had obeyed the commandments of the LORD; they did not follow their example. [18]Whenever the LORD raised up judges for them, the LORD was with the judge, and he delivered them from the hand of their enemies all the days of the judge; for the LORD would be moved to pity by their groaning because of those who persecuted and oppressed them. [19]But whenever the judge died, they would relapse and behave worse than their ancestors, following other gods, worshiping them and bowing down to them. They would not drop

---

[3] Judges 1:27-36 (see your Bible)
[4] Joshua 2:6-15 (see your Bible)

any of their practices or their stubborn ways. (Judges 2:16-19 NRSV)

Deborah was one of the judges that the Lord raised up to lead the people during this time. She was a woman whom God used to govern men, make all of the major decisions concerning Israel, and lead a nation (Israel) that God has had his hands on since the time of Abraham. Certainly, a chauvinistic God would not have allowed a woman to be in such a powerful position. Deborah was the judge of Israel during the time of King Jabin's terrible reign over Israel. The following verses of scripture give an account of just how much power and position God gave Deborah:

> [1]After the death of Ehud, the Israelites again started disobeying the LORD. [2]So the LORD let the Canaanite King Jabin of Hazor conquer Israel. Sisera, the commander of Jabin's army, lived in Harosheth-Ha-Goiim. [3]Jabin's army had nine hundred iron chariots, and for twenty years he made life miserable for the Israelites, until finally they begged the LORD for help.
>
> [4]Deborah the wife of Lappidoth was a prophet and a leader of Israel during those days. [5]She would sit under Deborah's Palm Tree between Ramah and Bethel in the hill country of Ephraim, where Israelites would come and ask her to settle their legal cases.
>
> [6]One day, Barak the son of Abinoam was in Kedesh in Naphtali, and Deborah sent word for him to come and talk with her. When he arrived, she said:
>
>> I have a message for you from the LORD God of Israel! You are to get together an army of ten thousand men from the Naphtali and Zebulun tribes and lead them to Mount Tabor. [7]The LORD will trick Sisera into coming out to fight you at the Kishon River. Sisera will be leading King Jabin's army as usual, and they will have their chariots, but the LORD has promised to help you defeat them.

[8]"I'm not going unless you go!" Barak told her.

[9] "All right, I'll go!" she replied. "But I'm warning you that the LORD is going to let a woman defeat Sisera, and no one will honor you for winning the battle."

Deborah and Barak left for Kedesh, [10]where Barak called together the troops from Zebulun and Naphtali. Ten thousand soldiers gathered there, and Barak led them out from Kedesh. Deborah went too.

[11]At this time Heber of the Kenite clan was living near the village of Oak in Zaanannim, not far from Kedesh. The Kenites were descendants of Hobab, the father-in-law of Moses, but Heber had moved and had set up his tents away from the rest of the clan.

[12]When Sisera learned that Barak had led an army to Mount Tabor, [13]he called his troops together and got all nine hundred iron chariots ready. Then he led his army away from Harosheth-Ha Goiim to the Kishon River.

[14]Deborah shouted, "Barak, it's time to attack Sisera! Because today the LORD is going to help you defeat him. In fact, the LORD has already gone on ahead to fight for you."

Barak led his ten thousand troops down from Mount Tabor. [15]And during the battle, the LORD confused Sisera, his chariot drivers, and his whole army. Everyone was so afraid of Barak and his army, that even Sisera jumped down from his chariot and tried to escape. [16]Barak's forces went after Sisera's chariots and army as far as Harosheth-Ha Goiim. Sisera's entire army was wiped out. (Judges 4:1-16 CEV)

Verse 1 tells us that the children of Israel turned against God once more. God punished them by allowing them to be handed over to King Jabin of the land of Hazor. Jabin cruelly oppressed the Israelites and once again the Israelites cried out to God.

The Israelites came to Deborah when there were disputes to be settled and decisions to be made amongst them. Verse 4 identifies Deborah as a prophet and as the leader of Israel at the time.[5] By being a prophet, this means that she received divine revelations from the Lord as well as the ability to discern those revelations. In scripture, to be endowed with the gift of prophecy also means to be able to foretell the future, and in New Testament terms it means to preach the word of God. The fact that Deborah was a prophet puts her in the same category with all the other prophets of the Old Testament including Jeremiah, Nehemiah, Isaiah, and more.

Whenever there were any disputes among the people of Israel or any incident in which a decision had to be made, the people came to Deborah for judgment. Deborah not only had the final say over legislative decisions, and all else, but she also had the final say regarding military decisions. Verse 6 tells of the instruction Deborah gave Barak (per command of the Lord) to deploy ten thousand troops at Mount Tabor in order to defeat Sisera, the commander of Jabin's army. Verse 8 documents Barak's refusal to go into battle against Sisera unless Deborah went with him. Although the scripture does not say why he refused, it appears that from the tone of verse 8, Barak did not believe he could win the battle without Deborah at his side. Deborah had already assured Barak (verse 7) that he would defeat Sisera and his army. But Barak was unwilling to do his duty unless Deborah went with him. It is safe, therefore, to conclude that Barak (despite the assurances he received from the Lord through Deborah that he would be the victor) was afraid of Sisera's army.

Deborah responded to Barak by agreeing to go with him but declared that what was to be his victory would instead become a victory obtained by a woman.[6] Although Barak was powerful in battle, Deborah would get the credit for the victory of this particular battle. Surely, if God were a chauvinist he would not have inspired the writers of the Bible to include this bit of information in the scriptures. Moreover, if God were a chauvinist, he would not have allowed the cowardice of a man to be overshadowed by the courageousness of a woman.

---

[5] Judges 4:4 of the New International Version of the Bible reads, "Deborah, a prophetess, the wife of Lappidoth, was leading Israel at that time."
[6] Deborah's reply in the New Living Translation of the Bible reads, "I will go with you. But since you have made this choice, you will receive no honor. For the LORD's victory over Sisera will be at the hands of a woman."

5

Aside from being the judge of a nation, a prophet, and the Commander in chief of Israel's army, Deborah was also identified as the wife of Lappidoth (verse 4). There is no indication that Deborah consulted with her husband before she made any leadership decisions. God put her, not her husband, in charge of the land. From what we can tell, Deborah's husband had nothing to do with the job God gave to her. This tells us that God is not beyond giving a greater position to the wife of a man than to the man himself. It also gives indication that it is unwise for any man to try to stop or hinder his wife in the ministry or duty that God has ordained for her to have. Chauvinism on God's part is inarguably not apparent here.

Verse 16 tells us that the army of Sisera was wiped out, defeated. To this day, the credit for this defeat goes to Deborah, as she prophesied. She was the one that actually led Israel into battle (verse 14) by her command. Sisera initially escaped death and fled on foot to the tent of Jael.[7] Jael was the wife of Heber the Kenite. As Sisera slept in Jael's tent, she assassinated him by driving a tent peg into the temple of his head. Both the army and the general had been defeated, one by the command of a woman and another by the hand of a woman.

Esther

Esther was responsible for saving the entire nation of Israel from genocide. The account of Esther is found in the Old Testament book of Esther and begins with the historical depiction of King Ahasuerus.

The book of Esther 1:1 tells us that King Ahasuerus[8] reigned over "one hundred and twenty-seven provinces, from India to Ethiopia." During the third year of his reign as king, he celebrated his officials and servants by means of a feast that lasted a week. On the seventh day of the feast, King Ahasuerus decided to summon his wife Queen Vashti before him in order to show off her beauty to the others at the feast. The following verses of scripture give the account:

---

[7] The historical account of Jael is documented in Judges 4:17-24 (see Appendix). Deborah refers to Jael as "most blessed among women" in a song that she sang on the day of Sisera's demise (Judges 5:24-27, see your Bible)

[8] The New International Version of the Bible uses the Greek form of this name which is "Xerxes."

> ¹⁰On the seventh day, when the heart of the king was merry with wine, he commanded Mehuman, Biztha, Harbona, Bigtha, Abagtha, Zether, and Carcas, seven eunuchs who served in the presence of King Ahasuerus, ¹¹to bring Queen Vashti before the king, wearing her royal crown, in order to show her beauty to the people and the officials, for she was beautiful to behold. (Esther 1:10-11 NKJV)

However, Queen Vashti refused to come. The account in the book of Esther does not give the reason why she refused King Ahasuerus' command. Maybe she was insulted. The king was drunk and summoned her for no more reason than to put her on display in front of men. King Ahasuerus was furious at the fact that Queen Vashti did not obey his command. His advisors suggested that Queen Vashti's refusal would incite other women to despise the commands of their husbands as well. After all, she was the Queen and was a role model for many. The following verses of scripture continue the account:

> ¹⁹If it pleases the king, let a royal decree go out from him, and let it be recorded in the laws of the Persians and the Medes, so that it will not be altered, that Vashti shall come no more before King Ahasuerus; and let the king give her royal position to another who is better than she.
> ²⁰When the king's decree which he will make is proclaimed throughout all his empire (for it is great), all wives will honor their husbands, both great and small."
> ²¹And the reply pleased the king and the princes, and the king did according to the word of Memucan.
> ²²Then he sent letters to all the king's provinces, to each province in its own script, and to every people in their own language, that each man should be master in his own house, and speak in the language of his own people. (Esther 1:19-22 NKJV)

Vashti was dethroned as queen. The king's advisors, specifically Memucan, suggested that young virgins be brought to him so that he could find another Queen. The king followed the advice. Esther was one of the young maidens brought to the king's palace. Esther was the first cousin of Mordecai. Mordecai was a descendant of the Jewish Benjamite tribe. Both he and Esther were Jews. Esther had been orphaned at a young age. She was the daughter of Mordecai's uncle. Mordecai took it upon himself to raise Esther as if she were his own daughter. Mordecai instructed Esther not to tell the king that she was a Jew.

Mordecai's great grandfather had been captured and carried away during the reign of King Nebuchadnezzar. Consequently, Mordecai and Esther ended up living among people who were not Jews. Of all the virgins brought to King Ahasuerus, Esther pleased him the most and he made her Queen, as the following verses of scripture attest to:

> [17]The king loved Esther more than all the other women, and she obtained grace and favor in his sight more than all the virgins; so he set the royal crown upon her head and made her queen instead of Vashti.
> [18]Then the king made a great feast, the Feast of Esther, for all his officials and servants; and he proclaimed a holiday in the provinces and gave gifts according the generosity of a king. (Esther 2:17-18 NKJV)

The 2nd chapter of the book of Esther[9] goes on to inform us that one day Mordecai overheard two of the king's doorkeepers plotting to do bodily harm to the king. Mordecai told Queen Esther, who in turn told the king. Queen Esther also told the king that Mordecai was the one who discovered the impending act of betrayal. When the matter was investigated, both of the men who conspired to murder the king were found to be guilty and were executed.

As time went on, King Ahasuerus promoted a man named Haman,[10] making him leader over all of the princes. The king also ordered everyone to kneel down and pay homage to Haman. But because Mordecai was a Jew, he refused to kneel down to Haman. Eventually, the king's attendees and servants questioned Mordecai as to why he refused to adhere to the king's demands regarding Haman. Mordecai had no other choice but to tell them that he was a Jew and that this was the

---

[9] See your Bible.

[10] Esther 3:1-7 (see your Bible).

reason he could not kneel down to Haman. As a Jew, Mordecai would only kneel down to God. Haman became very angry, not only with Mordecai, but also with all of the Jews and sought to destroy them. Haman convinced the king to allow him to kill the Jews. The following is the scriptural account:

> [8]Then Haman said to King Ahasuerus, "There is a certain people scattered and dispersed among the people in all the provinces of your kingdom; their laws are different from all other people's, and they do not keep the king's laws. Therefore it is not fitting for the king to let them remain.
> [9]If it pleases the king, let a decree be written that they be destroyed, and I will pay ten thousand talents of silver into the hands of those who do the work, to bring it into the king's treasuries.
> [10]So the king took his signet ring from his hand and gave it to Haman, the son of Hammedatha the Agagite, the enemy of the Jews.
> [11]And the king said to Haman, "The money and the people are given to you, to do with them as seems good to you." (Esther 3:8-11 NKJV)
>
> [13]And the letters were sent by couriers into all the king's provinces, to destroy, to kill, and to annihilate all the Jews, both young and old, little children and women, in one day, on the thirteenth day of the twelfth month, which is the month of Adar, and to plunder their possessions. (Esther 3:13 NKJV)

The 4th chapter of the book of Esther[11] goes on to tell us that Mordecai was devastated upon hearing the news of the genocidal decree. Esther heard of it as well and sent one of the king's eunuchs to Mordecai in order to get information from him as to why this was happening. Mordecai told the eunuch everything and gave him a copy of the written decree. Mordecai also asked the eunuch to encourage Esther to plead to the king for their lives. The eunuch, whose name was Hathach, returned

---

[11] See your Bible.

to Queen Esther, giving her all of the information that Mordecai gave him. Esther's response to Hathach was as follows:

> [10]Then Esther spoke to Hathach, and gave him a command for Mordecai:
> [11]All the king's servants and the people of the king's provinces know that any man or woman who goes into the inner court to the king, who has not been called, he has but one law: put all to death, except the one to whom the king holds out the golden scepter, that he may live. Yet I myself have not been called to go in to the king these thirty days.
> [12]So they told Mordecai Esther's words.
> [13]And Mordecai told them to answer Esther; "Do not think in your heart that you will escape in the king's palace any more than all the other Jews.
> [14]For if you remain completely silent at this time, relief and deliverance will arise from the Jews from another place, but you and your father's house will perish. Yet who knows whether you have come to the kingdom for such a time as this?" (Esther 4:10-14 NKJV)

Esther was in a position to save Israel. However, in order to do so, she would have to put her own life in danger. Mordecai assured her that her position at the palace was no guarantee of her safety and that the Lord would use another person to deliver Israel if she was not willing. He also expressed to her that God might have put her in the position of being Queen for the very purpose of saving her people. With this, Esther agreed to go to the king and instructed Mordecai as below:

> [16]Go, gather all the Jews who are present in Shushan, and fast for me; neither eat nor drink for three days, night or day. My maids and I will fast likewise, And so I will go to the king, which is against the law; and if I perish, I perish!" (Esther 4:16 NKJV)

Before Esther approached the king she fasted for three days and instructed all of the Jews to do the same. No doubt, she and all of the Jews prayed as well. Their prayers were heard and when Esther approached the king, he did not become angry but instead welcomed her to him, as the following verses of scripture attest to:

> [1]Now it happened on the third day that Esther put on her royal robes and stood in the inner court of the king's palace, across from the king's house, while the king sat on his royal throne in the royal house, facing the entrance of the house.
> [2]So it was, when the king saw Queen Esther standing in the court, that she found favor in his sight, and the king held out to Esther the golden scepter that was in his hand. Then Esther went near and touched the top of the scepter.
> [3]And the king said to her, "What do you wish, Queen Esther? What is your request? It shall be given to you—up to half the kingdom!"
> [4]So Esther answered, "If it pleases the king, let the king and Haman come today to the banquet that I have prepared for him. (Esther 5:1-4 NKJV)

Not only was the king very receptive to Esther but God arranged things so that the king would soon discover who had revealed the plot of the doorkeepers to kill him. Let's take a look:

> [1]That night the king could not sleep. So one was commanded to bring the book of the records of the chronicles; and they were read before the king.
> [2]And it was found written that Mordecai had told of Bigthana and Teresh, two of the king's eunuchs, the doorkeepers who had sought to lay hands on King Ahasuerus. (Esther 6:1-2 NKJV)

Upon discovering that Mordecai was the one who had exposed the doorkeepers, the king realized that nothing special had been done for Mordecai in order to thank him. Consequently arrangements were made so that Mordecai would be celebrated in the streets as he rode horseback adorned in a royal robe. And at the banquet that Esther prepared, the evil plot of Haman was finally exposed, as we see below:

²And on the second day, at the banquet of wine, the king again said to Esther, "What is your petition, Queen Esther? It shall be granted you. And what is your request, up to half the kingdom? It shall be done!"
³Then Queen Esther answered and said, "If I have found favor in your sight, O king, and if it pleases the king, let my life be given me at my petition, and my people at my request.
⁴For we have been sold, my people and I, to be destroyed, to be killed, and to be annihilated. Had we been sold as male and female slaves, I would have held my tongue, although the enemy could never compensate for the king's loss."
⁵So King Ahasuerus answered and said to Queen Esther, "Who is he, and where is he, who would dare presume in his heart to do such a thing?"
⁶And Esther said, "The adversary and enemy is this wicked Haman!" So Haman was terrified before the king and queen. (Esther 7:2-6 NKJV)

What Haman thought was dinner with the king was really a trap that Esther had set. When Esther exposed Haman, he did not have the opportunity to run or hide because she exposed him in the king's presence. In response to Haman's plot against the Jews, the king ordered that Haman be hung on the same gallows that Haman had built for Mordecai to be hung on. After Haman was executed, Esther petitioned the king again:

³Now Esther spoke again to the king, fell down at his feet, and implored him with tears to counteract the evil of Haman the Agagite, and the scheme which he had devised against the Jews.
⁴And the king held out the golden scepter toward Esther. So Esther arose and stood before the king.
⁵and said, "If it pleases the king, and if I have found favor in his sight and the thing seems right to the king and I am pleasing in his eyes, let it be written to revoke the letters devised by Haman, the son of Hammedatha

> the Agagite, which he wrote to annihilate the Jews who
> are in all the king's provinces.
> ⁶For how can I endure to see the evil that will come to
> my people? Or how can I endure to see the destruction
> of my countrymen? (Esther 8:3-6 NKJV)

The king did as Esther asked. He also decreed that the Jews be allowed to protect themselves from anyone who wished to destroy them, as indicated below:

> ¹¹By these letters the king permitted the Jews who were
> in every city to gather together and protect their lives—
> to destroy, kill, and annihilate all the forces of any
> people or province that would assault them, both little
> children and women, and to plunder their possessions.
> (Esther 8:11 NKJV)

After this decree, the Jews went about annihilating all the people who intended to do them harm. Mordecai became a great and feared man who lived in the king's palace. Eventually the Jews ended up killing seventy-five thousand of their enemies. Those who had planned to kill the Jews were instead themselves killed by the hands of those they sought to annihilate. The Jews were able to obtain this victory because of Esther's courage.

Esther saved her people from genocide. Just as God used Moses to deliver the Jews from slavery, God used Esther to deliver the Jews from certain death and annihilation, from a holocaust. Even Esther said that slavery would be preferable than death. If Esther had not put her life on the line to prevent the destruction of the Jews (and if Mordecai had not urged her in doing so), in theory, Hitler's holocaust may never have happened because there would have been no Jews left for him to murder.[12] The Jews would have been annihilated through the instigation of Haman and the decree of King Ahasuerus. But in actuality, according to Mordecai, God would have raised up another to deliver the Jews from annihilation if Esther had not stepped up to the task. Jesus was born

---

[12] By pleading with God, Moses also saved the Jews from destruction. However, if the Jews had been destroyed at that time, God would have continued the Jewish line through Moses (Exodus 32:10-14, see your Bible).

through the Jewish line. Therefore, some might conclude that Satan himself, in an ultimate attempt to stop the birth of Christ, was behind Haman's effort to destroy the human nation through which Christ would be born.

It was God that put a woman in such an honorable position as Esther's. The Bible says that it is God who gives promotion and God who takes it away.[13] God promoted Esther to the position she needed to be in to save her people from genocide. With this in mind, it is apparent that God will not hesitate to use women to get his greatest of works accomplished.

Esther was willing to die for the sake of her people. She risked her life to do a noble deed. God could have chosen a man to deliver his people from the king's murderous decree, instead, he chose a woman. A chauvinistic God would not have selected a woman for such a heroic deed. Neither would a chauvinistic God put a woman in such a great position of power. Furthermore, Esther's deeds were so great in the eyes of God that she is among an elite group of people: those who have a biblical book named after them.

WOMEN OF FAITH

Mary of Bethany

The book of Mark gives the account of a certain woman named Mary[14] who lived in the town of Bethany and served God by anointing Jesus' feet with fragrant oil. She was the sister of Lazarus, the man whom Jesus raised from the dead.[15] Because of how Mary anointed Jesus' feet with oil, Jesus greatly commemorated her. Let's take a look:

[1]After two days it was the Passover and the Feast of

---

[13] "For promotion cometh neither from the east, nor from the west, nor from the south. But God is the judge: he putteth down one, and setteth up another." (Psalms 75:6-7)

[14] Many women were named Mary in those times. This is not the Virgin Mary, the mother of Jesus.

[15] The historical account of Jesus raising Lazarus from the dead is found in John 11:1-45 (see your Bible)

Unleavened Bread. And the chief priests and the scribes sought how they might take Him[16] by trickery and put Him to death.

[2]But they said, "Not during the feast, lest there be an uproar of the people."

[3]And being in Bethany at the house of Simon the leper, as He sat at the table, a woman came having an alabaster flask of very costly oil of spikenard. Then she broke the flask and poured it on his head.

[4]But there were some who were indignant among themselves and said, "Why was this fragrant oil wasted?"

[5]For it might have been sold for more than three hundred denarii and given to the poor." And they criticized her sharply.

[6]But Jesus said, "Let her alone. Why do you trouble her? She has done a good work for Me.

[7]For you have the poor with you always, and whenever you wish you may do them good; but Me you do not have always.

[8]She has done what she could. She has come beforehand to anoint My body for burial.

[9]Assuredly, I say to you, wherever this gospel is preached in the whole world, what this woman has done will also be told as a memorial to her." (Mark 14:1-9 NKJV)

Mary's critics accused her of wasting an amount of oil that was worth three hundred denarii. One denarius (the singular of denarii) was equal to a day's wages for the common laborer. Therefore 300 denarii represented close to a year's wages. The book of Luke gives the following version of the account:

[37]And a woman in the city, who was a sinner, having learned that he was eating in the Pharisee's house brought an alabaster jar of ointment. [38]She stood behind him at his feet, weeping, and began to bathe his feet

---

[16] Jesus

15

with her tears and to dry them with her hair. Then she continued kissing his feet and anointing them with the ointment. [39]Now when the Pharisee who had invited him saw it, he said to himself, "If this man were a prophet, he would have known who and what kind of woman this is who is touching him—that she is a sinner." [40]Jesus spoke up and said to him, "Simon, I have something to say to you." "Teacher," he replied, "speak." [41]"A certain creditor had two debtors; one owed five hundred denarii, and the other fifty. [42]When they could not pay, he canceled the debts for both of them. Now which of them will love him more?"

[43] Simon answered, "I suppose the one for whom he canceled the greater debt." And Jesus said to him, "You have judged rightly." [44]Then turning toward the woman, he said to Simon, "Do you see this woman? I entered your house; you gave me no water for my feet, but she has bathed my feet with her tears and dried them with her hair. [45]You gave me no kiss, but from the time I came in she has not stopped kissing my feet. [46]You did not anoint my head with oil, but she has anointed my feet with ointment. [47]Therefore, I tell you, her sins, which were many, have been forgiven; hence she has shown great love. But the one to whom little is forgiven, loves little." [48]Then he said to her, "Your sins are forgiven." [49]But those who were at the table with him began to say among themselves, "Who is this who even forgives sins?" [50]And he said to the woman, "Your faith has saved you; go in peace." (Luke 7:37-50 NRSV)

The account in Luke goes on to reveal some things that the account in Mark does not, specifically, Mary's worship of Jesus as she poured the expensive oil on Jesus' feet.

Evidently, the Pharisee believed that Jesus should have dismissed the woman because she was a sinner (verse 39). Jesus quickly pointed out that the woman, by anointing him with oil, did far more for him than the Pharisee did during the time he had been at his home to dine with him. Jesus readily forgave the woman's sins because "she showed great love" (verse 47).[17] Jesus also pointed out, through his parable that people who have many sins have a lot to be forgiven for. When Jesus forgives these people, they will love him more than those who don't have as much to be forgiven for. Mary loved the Lord greatly because she knew she had much to be forgiven for and one of her ways of showing her love to Jesus was to weep, kiss his feet, wipe his feet with her hair, and anoint his feet with oil. Mary loved the Lord so much that she put all pride aside and threw herself at the feet of Jesus in front of the religious dignitaries of the land.

In Luke 7:50 Jesus is quoted as telling Mary that her faith has saved her. This does not mean that Mary was able to save herself by her own strength, but that her faith and belief in Jesus Christ and his gospel saved her from her sins.

Mark 14:9 documents the commemoration that Jesus gave to Mary of Bethany for her actions towards him. Jesus said that wherever the gospel is preached in the whole world, "what this woman has done will also be told as a memorial to her." Mary was to be memorialized on earth, in the world.[18] This specific honor that Jesus gave to Mary was not given to any one else. Her deed was documented especially so that she would be memorialized. Most assuredly, a chauvinistic God would have never memorialized a woman.

Rahab

The historical account of Rahab is found in the book of Joshua. Rahab was responsible for assisting the Israelites in their defeat of the city of Jericho. Joshua was the leader of the Israelites at the time.

Jericho was a fortified city that was located roughly five miles from Jordan. Jericho had a gracious water supply and was an oasis near one of

---

[17] Verse 47 of the NLT reads "'I tell you, her sins—and they are many—have been forgiven, so she has shown me much love. But a person who is forgiven little shows only little love.' Then Jesus said to the woman, 'Your sins are forgiven.'"

[18] It should be noted that the 12 apostles will also be memorialized as well. Their names will be written on the foundation stones of the heavenly city of New Jerusalem (Revelation 21:14, see your Bible). The difference is that theirs is a heavenly memorial and Mary's was an earthly memorial.

Palestine's strongest springs.[19] At the time, the city of Jericho was occupied by the Amorites, a nation of idolaters.[20]

Joshua sent two spies from the city of Shittum to infiltrate Jericho. During their assignment, the spies entered the house of Rahab and stayed there. The scriptures identify Rahab as a prostitute. Eventually, the king of Jericho was informed about the spies. The king sent messengers to Rahab instructing her to give up the spies. Rahab hid the men instead. The following gives the account:

> [4]But the woman took the two men and hid them. Then she said, "True, the men came to me, but I did not know where they came from. [5]And when it was time to close the gate at dark, the men went out. Where the men went I do not know. Pursue them quickly, for you can overtake them." [6]She had, however, brought them up to the roof and hidden them with the stalks of flax that she had laid out on the roof. [7]So the men pursued them on the way to the Jordan as far as the fords. As soon as the pursuers had gone out the gate was shut.
>
> [8]Before they went to sleep, she came up to them on the roof [9]and said to the men: "I know that the LORD has given you the land, and that dread of you has fallen on us, and that all the inhabitants of the land melt in fear before you. [10]For we have heard how the LORD dried up the water of the Red Sea before you when you came out of Egypt, and what you did to the two kings of the Amorites that were beyond the Jordan, to Sihon and Og whom you utterly destroyed. [11]As soon as we heard it, our hearts melted, and there was no courage left in any of us because of you. The LORD your God is indeed God in heaven above and on earth below. [12]Now then, since I have dealt kindly with you, swear to me by the LORD that you in turn will deal kindly with my family. Give me a sign of good faith [13]that you will

---

[19] This region of the world was not called Palestine until sometime in the 1st century BC. During the time of Joshua, this region was part of what was called the land of Canaan.

[20] The Amorites were descendants of Canaan.

spare my father and mother, my brothers and sisters, and all who belong to them, and deliver our lives from death." [14]The men said to her, "Our life for yours! If you do not tell this business of ours, then we will deal kindly and faithfully with you when the LORD gives us the land." (Joshua 2:4-14 NSRV)

The scriptures go on to say that the spies escaped Rahab's dwelling by using a scarlet rope to make a descent from her home that she placed at the window.[21] The house Rahab lived in was part of the city wall, so the spies were able to escape easily after climbing down the rope. Rahab instructed the spies to go in the hills and stay in hiding there for three days. The spies informed Rahab that their promise would not be binding to her unless she left the same scarlet rope in the window as a sign for their army not to attack her house at the time of what was to become the Jew's invasion of Jericho. The spies also instructed Rahab to have those that she wanted protected to stay in the house with her during the invasion. If anyone in her house ventured outside during the invasion, then their own blood would be on their own hands and the spies would not be accountable. Rahab agreed to this arrangement and tied the scarlet rope in the window.[22] The historical account of the fall of Jericho is found in chapter 6 of the book of Joshua. Let's take a look:

[1]Meanwhile, the people of Jericho had been locking the gates in their town wall because they were afraid of the Israelites. No one could go out or come in.
[2-3]The LORD said to Joshua:
With my help, you and your army will defeat the king of Jericho and his army, and you will capture the town. Here is how to do it: March slowly around Jericho once a day for six days. [4]Take along the sacred chest and have seven priests walk in front of it, carrying trumpets.

---

[21] For this part of the account read Joshua 2:15-24 (see your Bible)
[22] The full account of the conversation between Rahab and the Israelite spies is documented in the second chapter of Joshua (see your Bible).

But on the seventh day, march slowly
around the town seven times while the priests
blow their trumpets. [5]Then the priests will
blast on their trumpets, and everyone else
will shout. The wall will fall down, and your
soldiers can go straight in from every side.
(Joshua 6:1-5 CEV)

Joshua did as the Lord instructed and he and his army eventually
defeated the city of Jericho. During the siege he instructed his people to
spare Rahab and all of those in her house, as the following verses of
scripture attest to:

[16]Then the priests blew the trumpets, and Joshua yelled:
Get ready to shout! The LORD will let you
capture this town. [17]But you must destroy it
and everything in it, to show that it now
belongs to the LORD. The woman Rahab
helped the spies we sent, so protect her and
the others who are inside her house. But kill
everyone else in the town. (Joshua 6:16-17
CEV)

The scriptural account goes on to inform us that Rahab and those in
her house were spared and that she lived out her life among the
Israelites. Rahab ultimately married an Israeli man named Salmon and
bore him a son that she and Salmon named Boaz. Boaz became the father
of Obed, Obed became the father of Jesse and Jesse became the father of
King David. The lineage of Christ[23] on Joseph's side includes the lineage
of King David. This means that Rahab, a woman who was once a
prostitute, is a part of Jesus' genealogy.

Rahab is also celebrated in Hebrews 11:31 as a woman of great faith.
Let's take a look:

By faith Rahab the prostitute did not perish with those

---

[23] The genealogy of Christ on Joseph's side is documented in Matthew 1:1-16
(see Appendix).

who were disobedient, because she had received the
spies in peace. (NRSV)

Because of Rahab's faith in the God of the Bible, she did not perish
with the Amorites, who worshipped false gods thereby being disobedient
to God. Instead, Rahab lived to become part of Israel and to become
celebrated as a woman of faith among the more popular historical figures
of the Bible, including (as documented in the eleventh chapter of
Hebrews)[24] Abel, Enoch, Noah, Abraham, Isaac, Joseph, Moses, Gidion,
Barak, Samson, and those prophets "who through faith conquered
kingdoms, administered justice, and gained what was promised; who shut
the mouths of lions, quenched the fury of the flames, and escaped the
edge of the sword, whose weakness was turned to strength; and who
became powerful in battle and routed foreign armies."[25]

Rahab is listed among great men such as Noah, Abraham, and Moses
because of what she did to aid the Israelites in their defeat of Jericho and
because of her belief that the God of the Jews[26] is indeed the true God.
She knew that Jericho would be delivered into the hands of the Israelites,
because she knew that God would not fail them. Although she eventually
began to worship the true God and live a moral life, there is no getting
around the fact that Rahab was once a prostitute and that her greatest
deed (the hiding of the spies) was done when she was still practicing
prostitution. This tells us that anyone, regardless of one's past, can serve
God, if their heart is right, if God is willing to use them, and if they are
willing to purge sin from their lives.

Not only is Rahab listed in the Bible among men of great faith, but
she is also listed as being part of Jesus' lineage.[27] To be listed in either of
these respects is a magnificent honor. Certainly, a chauvinistic God
would not have inspired the writer of the book of Hebrews, to include a
woman among the list of men who have exhibited great faith in God.
Certainly a chauvinistic God would not have listed a woman in the same
category as the likes of Moses and Noah. A chauvinistic God would

---

[24] The 11th chapter of Hebrews lists all those who are celebrated for having great
faith and chronicles the reasons why they are celebrated. Rahab is included in
this list. (see your Bible)

[25] Hebrews 11:33-34 NIV

[26] See Introduction

[27] Matthew 1:1-16 (see Appendix)

certainly not have used a prostitute to help Joshua conquer Jericho. But indeed God used Rahab to aid Joshua in defeating Jericho by hiding his spies and inspired Paul to include her name among the men of great faith listed in the book of Hebrews.

The Hemorrhaging woman

This woman is more commonly known as the woman with the issue of blood[28] and is one of the most preached about women of the scriptures. Her name is not recorded and therefore is unknown. The historical account of this woman is given in the book of Mark. Let's take a look:

> [21]And when Jesus had crossed over again in the boat to the other side, a great multitude gathered about Him; and He stayed by the seashore.
> [22]And one of the synagogue officials named Jairus came up, and upon seeing Him, fell at His feet,
> [23]and entreated Him earnestly, saying, "My little daughter is at the point of death; please come and lay Your hands on her, that she may get well and live."
> [24]And He went off with him; and a great multitude was following Him and pressing in on Him.
> [25]And a woman who had had a hemorrhage for twelve years,
> [26]and had endured much at the hand of many physicians, and had spent all that she had and was not helped at all, but rather had grown worse,
> [27]after hearing about Jesus, came up in the crowd behind Him, and touched His cloak.
> [28]For she thought, "If I just touch His garments, I shall get well."
> [29]And immediately the flow of her blood was dried up; and she felt in her body that she was healed of her affliction.
> [30]And immediately Jesus, perceiving in Himself that the power proceeding from Him had gone forth, turned

---

[28] King James Version

around in the crowd and said, "Who touched My garments?"

[31]And His disciples said to Him, "You see the multitude pressing in on You, and You say, 'Who touched Me?'

[32] And He looked around to see the woman who had done this.

[33] But the woman fearing and trembling, aware of what had happened to her, came and fell down before Him, and told Him the whole truth.

[34]And He said to her, "Daughter, your faith has made you well; go in peace, and be healed of your affliction." (Mark 5:21-34 NASB)

The woman with the hemorrhage had been bleeding vaginally for twelve years. Not only was this physically stressful for the woman but emotionally stressful as well. Because of the Mosaic laws in regards to menstruating women,[30] this woman was looked upon as unclean and she was consequently ostracized from society. Verse 26 informs us that the woman had gone to many doctors and spent all that she had in her effort to be treated, but her affliction grew worse and the doctors, although they apparently tried, could not help her.

It could easily be assumed that the woman had heard of Jesus and knew that he had miraculously healed other people. It could also be assumed that although she tried, she couldn't get near him enough, because of the crowd, to tell him about her plight. However, she felt if she could just touch his clothes, she would be healed. Verse 27 tells us that she reached in from the crowd and touched his cloak with the reassurance in her heart and mind (verse 28) that touching his clothes alone would heal her. Verse 29 tells us, that once she touched Jesus' cloak her flow of blood was immediately dried up and that she could feel the blood drying up in her body.

Some believe that it wasn't Jesus who healed her but instead the woman's own faith. They therefore unfortunately fault the sick for not having enough faith to be healed. Verse 34 does indeed document Jesus as saying to the woman that her faith made her well. But it was her faith *in Jesus* that made her well and God's willingness to honor the faith that

---

[30] See Chapter 4.

she had.[31] Paul the apostle also had faith, and he prayed to the Lord three times to take away what he called "a thorn in the flesh"(what many theologians believe was some kind of physical illness). Although Paul had great faith, God did not take away Paul's thorn in the flesh. It was not God's will to do so despite the faith that Paul had.[32] God explained to Paul that power (God's power) is perfected in weakness.[33] With this said, it is safe to say that going to a doctor is a good thing when one is sick, and does not symbolize a lack of faith.

It should further be noted that when Jesus asked 'Who touched my Garments?' that the question was rhetorical. Jesus knew who touched his him (his clothes), for he is part of the Godhead[34] and is therefore all knowing. Likewise, there are many other instances in scripture where God asks questions of men that he already knows the answers to. But he asks the question in order to make a point or script an event. When God asked Cain where his brother Abel was, God knew where he was. God knew that Cain had killed Abel.[35] The question was asked so that his answer would be historically documented and lessons would be learned from it.

The hemorrhaging woman's great faith is considered legendary because of the encouragement it gives. The woman was healed just by taking hold of Jesus' cloak. Theologians agree that the Hebrew word used for *healed* in Mark 5:34 also means that she was saved[36] as well. So, not only was the woman healed but also, Jesus Christ saved her because of her belief in him.

---

[31] 1 John 5:14 (see next footnote)

[32] "This is the confidence we have in approaching God: that if we ask anything according to his will, he hears us." (1 John 5:14 NIV)

[33] And because of the surpassing greatness of the revelations, for this reason, to keep me from exalting myself, there was given me a thorn in the flesh, a messenger of Satan to buffet me—to keep me from exalting myself! Concerning this I entreated the Lord three times that it might depart from me. And He has said to me, "My grace is sufficient for you, for power is perfected in weakness." (2 Corinthians 12:7-9 NASB)

[34] See Introduction.

[35] Genesis 4:1-16 (see your Bible)

[36] See Introduction

WOMEN OF SERVICE

Ruth

Ruth belongs to the genealogy of Jesus Christ on the side of Joseph (Mary's husband). However, her inclusion in the genealogy of Jesus Christ is without question, an honorable inclusion and exists not because of familial hereditary lines, but instead because of Ruth's undying noble service that she gave to her mother-in-law, Naomi. The following verses of scripture set up the historical account:

> [1]In the days when the judges ruled, there was a famine in the land, and a certain man of Bethlehem in Judah went to live in the country of Moab, he and his wife and two sons. [2]The name of the man was Elimelech and the name of his wife Naomi, and the names of his two sons were Mahlon and Chilion; they were Ephrathites from Bethlehem in Judah. They went into the country of Moab and remained there. [3]But Elimelech, the husband of Naomi, died, and she was left with her two sons. [4]These took Moabite wives; the name of the one was Orpah and the name of the other Ruth. When they had lived there about ten years, [5]both Mahlon and Chilion also died, so that the woman was left without her two sons and her husband. (Ruth 1:1-5 NRSV)

The account goes on to say that Naomi decided to go back to her original place of residence, the land of Judah. Ruth and Orpah decided to go back with her. Their original home was the city of Moab, home to the Moabites.[36] In general, the Moabites did not worship the God of Israel, but worshiped the false god, Chemosh. Naomi attempted to encourage both Ruth and Orpah to go back to their mothers' homes respectively in the hopes that they would both eventually marry again. Initially both Ruth and Orpah refused to leave Naomi. But then, after much persuasion from Naomi, Orpah left Naomi. Let's take a look:

---

[36] The Moabites were descendants of Lot who was the nephew of Abraham (Genesis 19:30-38, see your Bible)

6-7When Naomi heard that the Lord had given his people a good harvest, she and her two daughters-in-law got ready to leave Moab and go to Judah. As they were on their way there, 8Naomi said to them, "Don't you want to go back home to your own mothers? You were kind to my husband and sons, and you have always been kind to me. I pray that the LORD will be just as kind to you. 9May he give each of you another husband and a home of your own."

Naomi kissed them. They cried 10and said, "We want to go with you and live among your people."

11But she replied, "No my daughters, why don't you return home? What good will it do you to go with me? Do you think I could have more sons for you to marry? 12You must go back home, because I am too old to marry again. Even if I got married tonight and later had more sons, 13would you wait for them to become old enough to marry? No, my daughters! Life is harder for me than it is for you, because the LORD has turned against me."

14They cried again. Orpah kissed her mother-in-law good-by, but Ruth held on to her. (Ruth 1:6-14 CEV)

In order to comprehend Naomi's distress we have to understand that during the dispensation of the Mosaic Law[38] the following was God's command concerning widows whose husbands died without giving them a son:

5If brothers are living together and one of them dies without a son, his widow must not marry outside the family. Her husband's brother shall take her and marry her and fulfill the duty of a brother-in-law to her. 6The first son she bears shall carry on the name of the dead brother so that his name will not be blotted out from Israel.

7However, if a man does not want to marry his brother's wife, she shall go to the elders at the town

---

[38] See Introduction.

gate and say, "My husband's brother refuses to carry on his brother's name in Israel. He will not fulfill the duty of a brother-in-law to me. [8]Then the elders of this town shall summon him and talk to him. If he persists in saying, "I do not want to marry her," [9]his brother's widow shall go up to him in the presence of the elders, take off one of his sandals, spit in his face and say, "This is what is done to the man who will not build up his brother's family line." [10]That man's line shall be known in Israel as The Family of the Unsandaled. (Deuteronomy 25:5-10 NIV)

During the days of the dispensation of the Law, a widow was to marry her deceased husband's brother if her husband died before giving her a son and if the brother was available for marriage. If her husband's brother were able to give her a son,[39] then the child would be given the name of the dead husband and not the name of the brother-in-law.[40] This was done in order to preserve the name of the dead brother (the husband). The surname was not at issue. The widow's son would be named according to the first name of his dead father. This was part of the Mosaic Law that applied directly to the Jews and does not apply today. A woman does not have to marry her dead husband's brother and neither does a man have to marry his dead brother's wife.

Both Ruth and Orpah wanted to stay with Naomi, but there was no benefit for them to stay since Naomi did not have any more sons for them to marry. Naomi was distressed because she had lost her husband and both of her sons. Despite this, she was concerned for the happiness of her daughters-in-law and told them to leave her so that they could live their own lives. Orpah kissed Naomi and left but Ruth put aside her happiness to stay with Naomi. The account continues:

---

[39] The biological chromosomal composition of a man's sperm at the time of genital intercourse with a woman is the sole determining factor of whether or not a pregnancy will result as a boy or girl. The biological factors that determine gender rest solely with the man and not with the woman. Despite this, there are some cultures today that advocate for the torturing and killing of women who have not reproduced a boy child for their husbands.

[40] This only applied to the first son. Any son born after the first son would take the name of the brother.

> ¹⁵"Look," said Naomi, "your sister-in-law is going back to her people and her gods. Go back with her."
>
> ¹⁶But Ruth replied, "Don't urge me to leave you or to turn back from you. Where you go I will go, and where you stay I will stay. Your people will be my people and your God my God. ¹⁷Where you die I will die, and there I will be buried. May the LORD deal with me, be it ever so severely, if anything but death separate you and me.
>
> ¹⁸When Naomi realized that Ruth was determined to go with her, she stopped urging her. (Ruth 1:15-18 NIV)

Ruth knew that without a husband or sons, Naomi needed help settling down and reestablishing herself among the Israelites. Ruth's loyalty to Naomi was a prime example of selflessness. Eventually Naomi and Ruth arrived in Bethlehem and were well accepted. The townspeople there remembered Naomi from long ago.

During her stay among the Israelites, Ruth would sometimes work the fields and one day found herself working the field of one of Naomi's relatives, a man named Boaz.[41] When Boaz asked about her, the foreman of the field told him who she was. The account continues:

> ⁴When Boaz left Bethlehem and went out to his field, he said to the harvest workers, "The LORD bless you!"
>
> They replied, "And may the LORD bless you!"
>
> ⁵Then Boaz asked the man in charge of the harvest workers, "Who is that young woman?"
>
> ⁶The man answered, "She is the one who came back from Moab with Naomi. ⁷She asked if she could pick up grain left by the harvest workers, and she has been working all morning without a moment's rest."
>
> ⁸Boaz went over to Ruth and said, "I think it would be best for you not to pick up grain in anyone else's field. Stay here with the women ⁹and follow along behind them, as they gather up what the men have cut.

---

[41] Boaz was the son of Rahab.

I have warned the men not to bother you, and whenever you are thirsty, you can drink from the water jars they have filled."

[10]Ruth bowed down to the ground and said, "You know I come from another country. Why are you so good tome?"

[11]And Boaz answered, "I have heard how you've helped your mother-in-law ever since your husband died. You even left your own father and mother to come and live in a foreign land among people you don't know. [12]I pray that the LORD God of Israel will reward you for what you have done. And now that you have come to him for protection, I pray that he will bless you."(Ruth 2:4-12 CEV)

Boaz was impressed with Ruth's loyalty to Naomi, and therefore Ruth found favor in his eyes. When Naomi realized that Ruth was working in Boaz's field, she was very pleased. Naomi identified Boaz as one of her kinsmen-redeemers.[42] If Boaz was the closest male relative to Ruth's former husband then he was required to marry her. The account goes on to inform us that Ruth, in a customary way, expressed to Boaz, her desire to marry him. Boaz was again impressed that Ruth did not go after the younger men who had money and he told her how impressed of her he was.[43] He also told her that he was not the nearest male relative to her husband but that another man was. However, he stated that if that particular man refused to fulfill his responsibilities then he (Boaz) would redeem her. The account continues as follows:

---

[42] The NIV Study Bible has this definition of a kinsman-redeemer: "The kinsman-redeemer was responsible for protecting the interests of needy members of the extended family—e.g. to provide an heir for a brother who had died (Dt 25:5-10), to redeem land that a poor relative had sold outside the family (Lev 25:25-28), to redeem a relative who had been sold into slavery (Lev 25:47-49) and to avenge the killing of a relative (Nu 35:19-21; 'avenge' and 'kinsman-redeemer' are translations of the same Hebrew word)." Taken from The NIV Study Bible 10th Anniversary Edition, Edited by Kenneth Barker, Copyright ©1995 by Zondervan Publishing House, Grand Rapids Michigan (p.364) used by permission of Zondervan.

[43] For the account of Boaz and Ruth's brief courtship, see Ruth 3:1-13 (see your Bible)

[2]Boaz took ten of the elders of the town and said, "Sit here," and they did so. [3]Then he said to the kinsman-redeemer, "Naomi, who has come back from Moab, is selling the piece of land that belonged to our brother Elimelech. [4]I thought I should bring the matter to your attention and suggest that you buy it in the presence of these seated here and in the presence of the elders of my people. If you will redeem it, do so. But if you will not, tell me, so I will know. For no one has the right to do it except you, and I am next in line."

"I will redeem it," he said.

[5]Then Boaz said, 'On the day you buy the land from Naomi and from Ruth the Moabitess, you acquire the dead man's widow, in order to maintain the name of the dead with his property."

[6]At this, the kinsman-redeemer said "Then I cannot redeem it because I might endanger my own estate. You redeem it yourself. I cannot do it." (Ruth 4:2-6 NIV)

[9]Then Boaz said to the elders and all the people, "Today you are witnesses that I have acquired from the hand of Naomi all that belonged to Elimelech and all that belonged to Chilion and Mahlon. [10]I have also acquired Ruth the Moabite, the wife of Mahlon, to be my wife, to maintain the dead man's name on his inheritance, in order that the name of the dead may not be cut off from his kindred and from the gate of his native place; today you are witnesses." (Ruth 4:9-10 NSRV)

Ruth and Boaz were married and became the parents of Obed who was the father of Jesse who was the father of David whose lineage is cited when considering the genealogy of Jesus Christ on the side of Joseph. Because of Ruth's faithful service to Naomi she ultimately became a part of Jesus' genealogy and was the only other woman besides Esther to have a biblical book written in her honor and named after her.

Mary Magdalene

Mary Magdalene was a disciple of Jesus Christ. When Jesus was teaching his gospel in Galilee, Mary Magdalene and Mary the mother of James, Joses, and Salome followed Jesus and tended to his needs. They served Jesus as he ministered.[44] Mary Magdalene was one of the people present during Jesus' crucifixion. The following gives account of Mary Magdalene after Jesus was crucified and buried in the tomb:

[1]Early on the first day of the week, while it was still dark, Mary Magdalene came to the tomb and saw that the stone had been removed from the tomb. [2]So she ran and went to Simon Peter and the other disciple, the one whom Jesus loved, and said to them, "They have taken the Lord out of the tomb, and we do not know where they have laid him." [3]Then Peter and the other disciple set out and went toward the tomb. [4]The two were running together, but the other disciple outran Peter and reached the tomb first. [5]He bent down to look in and saw the linen wrappings lying there, but he did not go in. [6]Then Simon Peter came, following him, and went into the tomb. He saw the linen wrappings lying there [7]and the cloth that had been on Jesus' head, not lying with the linen wrappings but rolled up in a place by itself. [8]Then the other disciple, who reached the tomb first, also went in, and he saw and believed; [9]for as yet they did not understand the scripture, that he must rise from the dead. [10]Then the disciples returned to their homes.

[11]But Mary stood weeping outside the tomb. As she wept, she bent over to look into the tomb; [12]and she saw two angels in white, sitting where the body of Jesus had been lying, one at the head and the other at the feet. [13]They said to her, "Woman, why are you weeping?" She said to them, "They have taken away my Lord, and I do not know where they have laid him." [14]When she had said this, she turned around and

---

[44] Matthew 27:50-56 (see your Bible)

saw Jesus standing there, but she did not know that it was Jesus. [15]Jesus said to her, "Woman, why are you weeping? Whom are you looking for?" Supposing him to be the gardener, she said to him, "Sir, if you have carried him away, tell me where you have laid him, and I will take him away." [16]Jesus said to her, "Mary!" She turned and said to him in Hebrew, "Rabbouni!" (which means Teacher). [17]Jesus said to her, "Do not hold on to me, because I have not yet ascended to the Father. But go to my brothers and say to them, 'I am ascending to my Father and your Father, to my God and your God.'" [18]Mary Magdalene went and announced to the disciples, "I have seen the Lord"; and she told them that he had said these things to her. (John 20:1-18 NRSV)

The entire Christian faith rests on the resurrection of Jesus Christ.[45] Jesus prophesied that after being buried in the grave for three days, he would rise from the dead.[46] He did as he prophesied. The resurrection of Jesus Christ is proof that Jesus is who he said he was: God in the flesh.[47] Mary Magdalene was the first to see Jesus after he rose from the dead. Mary's greatness rests in the fact that she was the first to see the risen Lord and that God chose her to be the first. It is this same Mary whom seven demons had been cast out of. The following verses of scripture affirm this:

[1]After this, Jesus traveled about from one town and village to another, proclaiming the good news of the kingdom of God. The twelve were with him, [2]and also some women who had been cured of evil spirits and diseases: Mary (called Magdalene) from whom seven demons had come out; [3]Joanna the wife of Cuza, the

---

[45] 1 Corinthians 15:12-22 (see your Bible)

[46] Jesus answered and said to them, "Destroy this temple and in three days I will raise it up." The Jews therefore said, "It took forty-six years to build this temple, and will You raise it up in three days?" But He was speaking of the temple of His body. (John 2:19-21 NASB)

[47] See Introduction.

manager of Herod's household; Susanna; and many
others. These women were helping to support them out
of their own means. (Luke 8:1-3 NIV)

Before Mary Magdalene began to follow Jesus Christ, she had been
possessed by seven demons. Jesus had cast the demons out of her.[48] After
the demons were cast from Mary, she began to follow Jesus. Not only
did she follow Jesus but she also helped to support Jesus and his disciples
(along with other women) by giving out of her own financial and
material resources. Mary was apparently grateful to Jesus for what he
had done for her.

With this said, one would be hard pressed to argue in favor of God
being a chauvinist. Undeniably, a chauvinistic God would have made
certain that a man, not a woman, be the first to see the Lord after his
resurrection. A chauvinistic God would not have given a woman that
honor and he certainly would not have given it to a woman who had been
exorcised of seven demons. But a God of grace who saves lost sinners
and esteems both men and women as he chooses, would and did.

The Shunammite Woman

Although there is no biblical record of this woman's name, she is
considered, by many theologians, to be one of the greatest women of the
Bible. The Shunammite woman was a wealthy lady that lived in the land
of Shunem, along with her husband. The following is her account:

> [8]One day Elisha went on to Shunem, where a rich and
> influential woman lived, who insisted on his eating a
> meal. Afterward, whenever he passed by, he stopped
> there for a meal.
> [9]And she said to her husband, Behold now, I perceived
> that this is a holy man of God who passes by
> continually.
> [10]Let us make a small chamber on the [housetop] and
> put there for him a bed, a table, a chair, and a lamp.

---

[48] "It was early on Sunday morning when Jesus rose from the dead, and the first
person who saw him was Mary Magdalene, the woman from whom he had cast
out seven demons." (Mark 16:9 NLT)

> Then whenever he comes to us, he can go [up the
> outside stairs and rest] here. (2 Kings 4:8-10 Amp.)

Here was a rich woman who would insist on feeding Elisha each time
he passed by her house during his journeys as a prophet of God. Verse 9
indicates that Elisha did not reveal who he was to her but that she
perceived that he was a man of God. Because of this, she wanted to do
more for him than just feed him and convinced her husband to make a
special place for Elisha in their home so that he could rest in private
(before continuing along on his journey) for as many days as he liked or
needed to, whenever he was in the city. Let's continue:

> ¹¹One day he came and turned into the chamber and lay
> there.
> ¹²And he said to Gehazi his servant, Call this
> Shunammite. When he had called her, she stood before
> him.
> ¹³And he said to Gehazi, Say now to her, You have
> been most painstakingly and reverently concerned for
> us; what is to be done for you? Would you like to be
> spoken for to the king or to the commander of the
> army? She answered, I dwell among my own people
> [they are sufficient].
> ¹⁴Later Elisha said, What then is to be done for her?
> Gehazi answered, She has no child and her husband is
> old. (2 Kings 4:11-14 Amp.)

Elisha was very appreciative of all of the hospitality the woman had
shown him and his servant, Gehazi, who traveled with him. In order to
express his thanks, Elisha wanted to give the woman something in
return. It is interesting to note that Elisha did not approach the man of
the house in order to reciprocate the service rendered to him. He knew
that the hospitality came from the heart of the woman and that she was
the one, between she and her husband, who had made the arrangements
for his comfort.

When asked what he could do for her in return, the woman basically
indicated that she was fine as she was. Verse 14 says that later on Elisha
asked Gehazi for advice as to how he could return the favors the woman
had bestowed upon them. Elisha wasn't going to give up on his quest to

repay the woman. It was difficult for him to continue to benefit from her hospitality without reciprocating some of her generosity and service.

When Elisha asked of Gehazi what could be done for the woman, Gehazi stated that the woman had no child and that her husband was old (verse 14). This implies that the woman was not able to conceive either because she was barren or because her husband may have been too old to biologically father children, or because her husband might soon die since he was getting along in years. In those times, not being able to conceive a child was an emotional hardship for a woman. The societies then, validated women according to their childbearing abilities. Let's look further at the account:

> [15]He said, Call her. [Gehazi] called her, and she stood in the doorway.
> [16]Elisha said, At this season when the time comes round, you shall embrace a son. She said, No my lord, you man of God, do not lie to your handmaid.
> [17]But the woman conceived and bore a son at that season the following year, as Elisha had said to her.
> (2 Kings 4:15-17 Amp.)

Elisha was able to work miracles.[49] The ability to work miracles is a gift of the Holy Spirit.[50] It is safe to assume, of course, that Elisa appealed to God in order that the woman might conceive, for the woman would not have conceived unless it was God's will for her to do so.[51] The woman did miraculously conceive a son, despite her unbelief that she would. And she bore her son at the time the prophet Elisha said she would. This means that the woman conceived within three months after Elisha had prophesied that she would have a baby. The woman had been compensated in a magnificent and miraculous way for her hospitality. Through the will of God and by the gift that God had given him, Elisha repaid the woman. The way in which he repaid her, and his insistence in doing so says much about the service that the woman gave to him. Her hospitality was no small thing and was greatly appreciated by the

---

[49] 2 Kings 2:1-17 (see your Bible)
[50] 1 Corinthians 12:7-10 (see your Bible)
[51] We must ask God for what we want according to God's will as 1 John 5:14 teaches us (see Footnote 32).

prophet. Not everyone that Elisha met along his journeys could or would be as hospitable as she. During his travels, Elisha was able to stay in the woman's home as long as he wished, whenever he wanted to, and stay in a section of the house that was furnished especially for him. Let's continue looking at the account:

> [18]When the child had grown, he went out one day to his father with the reapers.
> [19]But he said to his father, My head, my head! The man said to his servant, Carry him to his mother.
> [20]And when he was brought to his mother, he sat on her knees till noon, and then died.
> [21]And she went up and laid him on the bed of the man of God, and shut the door upon him and went out.
> [22]And she called to her husband and said, Send me one of the servants and one of the donkeys, that I may go quickly to the man of God and come back again.
> [23]And he said, Why go to him today? It is neither the New Moon nor the Sabbath. And she said, It will be all right.
> [24]Then she saddled the donkey and said to her servant, Ride fast; do not slacken your pace for me unless I tell you. (2 Kings 4:18-24 Amp.)

The woman's child had suffered some sort of illness while he was in the fields. His head began to hurt and he cried out. Not long afterward, the child died. The woman immediately laid the child on the bed of the man of God. The woman placed the dead boy in the bed that was used as a guest bed for Elisha even though there were other beds in the home. After laying her dead child on the prophet's bed, she proceeded to go quickly to see Elisha.

Although the woman's husband questioned her when she told him that she was going to see the Elisha, he did not quarrel with her or try to stop her, or detain her, and she did not ask her husband for permission to go. She did, however, tell her husband where she was going. She also told him that everything would be all right. This was good enough for her husband. The woman's husband had enough discernment to know that there was some meaning in his wife's urgency and he did not get in her way. The woman was being led of the Lord and what she had to do was to be done quickly. Her husband did not interfere and let her go to do what she felt she had to do. Let's continue:

> ²⁵So she set out and came to the man of God at Mount Carmel. When the man of God saw her afar off, he said to Gehazi his servant, Behold, yonder is that Shunammite.
> ²⁶Run to meet her and say, Is it well with you? Well with your husband? Well with the child? And she answered, It is well. (2 Kings 4:25-26 Amp.)

Elisha realized that an emergency was what brought the woman to him. But he didn't know what was wrong. When he saw the woman, he immediately instructed Gehazi to run and meet her. From the tone of the scripture, Elisha was just as driven, as the woman was to solve the problem. However, when Gehazi reached the woman and asked her "Is it well with you, well with your husband, well with the child?" she answered, "It is well."

The woman's answer was as profound as it was perplexing. How could all be well if the child was dead? In her haste to speak with Elisha, the woman may have been trying to avoid conversing with Gehazi about the situation and simply said, "it is well" in order to avoid any further questions. On the other hand, she may have indeed felt that all was well despite her trauma, because she knew that the child was in the hands of God. When considering the latter explanation, the profundity of her answer becomes heightened, for what woman would say that all is well when her child has just died? The fact that she did so has given encouragement over the centuries to many who have found themselves grieving, and this, in addition to the spiritual hospitality she showed the prophet, is what makes her great. Let's continue to look at the account:

> ²⁷When she reached the man of God at the mountain, she took hold of his feet, Gehazi came over to push her away, but the man of God said, "Leave her alone! She is in bitter distress, but the LORD has hidden it from me and has not told me why."
> ²⁸Did I ask you for a son, my lord? She said, "Didn't I tell you, 'Don't raise my hopes?

37

> [29]Elisha said to Gehazi, "Tuck your cloak into your belt, take my staff in your hand and run. If you meet anyone, do not greet him, and if anyone greets you, do not answer. Lay my staff on the boy's face."
> [30] But the child's mother said, "As surely as the LORD lives and as you live, I will not leave you." So he got up and followed her.
> [31]Gehazi went on ahead and laid the staff on the boy's face, but there was no sound or response. So Gehazi went back to meet Elisha and told him, "The boy has not awakened." (2 Kings 4:27-31 NIV)

Initially, Gehazi had no idea what the woman wanted and felt he needed to protect Elisha from her. So, as the woman approached Elisha, Gehazi tried to push her away. But Elisha stopped him from doing so, knowing that she was in distress but not knowing why. As soon as the woman began to ask questions of Elisha (verse 28) he instinctively knew that the child was dead. Elisha instructed Gehazi to run to the child's house with his staff, and lay the staff on the boy's face. Elisha and the woman were not far behind. Gehazi did as Elisha requested, but it didn't work, the boy was still dead.

> [32]When Elisha came into the house, he saw the child lying dead on his bed. [33]So he went in and closed the door on the two of them, and prayed to the LORD. [34]Then he got up on the bed and lay upon the child, putting his mouth upon his mouth, his eyes upon his eyes, and his hands upon his hands; and while he lay bent over him, the flesh of the child became warm. [35]He got down, walked once to and fro in the room, then got up again and bent over him; the child sneezed seven times, and the child opened his eyes. [36]Elisha summoned Gehazi and said, "Call the Shunammite woman." So he called her. When she came to him, he said, "Take your son."[37]She came and fell at his feet, bowing to the ground; then she took her son and left. (2 Kings 4:32-36 NSRV)

Through the power given to him by God, Elisha was able to work a miracle by raising the boy from the dead. But he was not able to do so without the help of the Lord. It took Elisha three attempts to bring the boy back to life. He first had Gehazi use his staff but that didn't work. He then laid upon the boy and the boy's body became warm. However, it appears the boy was not yet alive. Finally, with the third attempt, Elisha paced back and forth across the room (no doubt in fierce prayer to the Lord) and laid upon the boy again. This time the boy opened his eyes. God stepped in and blessed the efforts of Elisha.

Elisha didn't give up. It seems he loved the woman dearly for all that she had done for him and felt personally responsible for her pain. It is because of the great care the woman gave him that Elisha immediately put aside everything to take care of her. The woman's unselfish service is one of the best examples of what serving another really means.

SUMMARY

As stated earlier, to discuss all of the women of the Bible who made significant impacts would constitute an entire book itself. However, the discussion of the female historical biblical figures that have been presented in this chapter supplies the reader with eight examples of women who were mightily used by God, to accomplish his works.

Deborah was a Judge of Israel and therefore was in leadership over all of the people of Israel. This means that men were under her authority and she had the final say in Israel at the time of her jurisdiction. Not only was Deborah a judge, but she was the Commander in chief of the military and a prophet as well. The only other biblical historical figures that have carried all three positions (leader, prophet, Commander in chief) simultaneously are Moses and Samuel. Although Deborah was married, her marriage did not get in the way of the positions that God placed her in. When it came to her fulfilling her God given duties, Deborah did as the Lord led her. There is no biblical indication that she necessarily felt compelled to consult her husband on the matters that God left to her charge or that her husband tried to stand in the way of what the Lord would have her to do. Of course, she may have indeed asked her husband's opinion from time to time, but from what the text teaches us, the Lord spoke directly to Deborah and made clear *to her* what it was that he wanted her to do. This teaches us that God is not against calling a man's wife to a greater position in the Lord than her husband.[51] This teaches us that a woman should heed the call of God, no matter what that calling is, and that her husband should not stand in the way of that calling.

If God were a chauvinist he would never assign great tasks to married women without at least assigning their husbands similar tasks of greatness. If God were a chauvinist he certainly would not put women in roles that are traditionally thought of as roles for men. But in the case of Deborah, he did.

Esther saved all of Israel from total annihilation. Esther's bravery prevented the Jews from being exterminated. Theoretically, if the Jews had been exterminated, they would not exist as a nation today. Esther saved an entire nation by being willing to die for the sake of her people. Certainly a chauvinistic God would never have given the honor of saving all of Israel to a woman. But he did. Some might choose to ignore her great deed, but it can never be minimized.

Mary of Bethany was the only biblical historical figure, man or woman, to be memorialized by Jesus during this dispensation.[52] This is indeed a great honor. As stated before, a chauvinistic God would not have given a woman such great honor.

Rahab was used of God despite the fact that she was a prostitute. God used her to deliver the city of Jericho into the hands of the Israelites. In the eleventh chapter of Hebrews she is listed as having great faith along with Abel, Enoch, Noah, Abraham, Isaac, Jacob, Joseph, Moses, Gideon, Samuel, Samson, Barak, Jephthah, David, and the prophets. She is the only woman who is listed among these great men. A chauvinistic God certainly would not have included a woman with such a sordid past among this hall of fame faith listing. But God did include her. This teaches us that even the most commonplace of women can be called upon by God to do a great service for him.

Ruth's faithfulness to her mother-in-law was such that her loyalties and the reward for her loyalties are given specific attention in the Bible in a book named after her.

---

[51] It is only speculative on this author's part that God called Deborah to a greater position than he did her husband. Actually, we have no knowledge of the calling that God bestowed upon Lappidoth.

[52] The dispensation of Grace. See Introduction.

The Shunammite woman provided the prophet Elisha with so much hospitality that she and her husband were blessed with the birth of a child because of it. Again we have an example of a woman who was called by God to serve and a husband who did not get in the way of her calling but actually supported it. He ended up benefiting tremendously from the blessings that the Lord bestowed upon his wife because of her faithfulness to her calling.

Mary Magdalene was the first to see the risen Lord. The importance of Jesus' resurrection is emphasized by Paul in his writings to the Corinthians when he said "And if Christ is not risen, then our preaching is empty and your faith is also empty."[54] Paul went on to say that Christ has risen from the dead, his point being that the resurrection of Christ is the one most single event that proved the deity of Christ and therefore gives support to Romans 10:9 which says that if we confess that Jesus is Lord and believe that he rose from the dead, we will be saved. Therefore, the fact that Mary was the first to see Jesus after his resurrection means that she was the first to witness the physical proof for the basis of the Christian faith. The honor of being the first to set eyes on the risen Lord was not given to a man, but to a woman. A chauvinistic God would have instead given this honor to a man.

---

[54] 1 Corinthians 15:12-22 (see your Bible)

2.

"KEEP 'EM BAREFOOT AND PREGNANT"

"Keep 'em barefoot and pregnant" is the old Southern chauvinistic cliché that rings a harsh bell in the ears of women today. This old saying is the epitome of chauvinistic rhetoric that has survived through the years. It symbolizes a man's wish to have complete control and dominance over a woman. It's an insulting idiom to women because it tells them that all they're any good for is sex and the breeding of the next generation. The symbolism in "keeping a woman barefoot" means that a man should strive to decrease his wife's ability to go anywhere and do anything, except stay at home and have his babies. How can a woman go anywhere if her most primitive means of travel (her feet) is taken away by the fact that she has no shoes? The symbolism means that a man will only provide his wife with the bare essentials she needs to survive, this way she is totally dependent on him and less likely to express any opinion that is contrary to his. To add to this, if a man keeps his wife pregnant she'll never have a chance to do much outside of the home because she'll be too busy with the children.

This old "barefoot and pregnant" cliché is no longer as popular with the men as it used to be. The reason for this is because of the huge increase of divorce over the last fifty years or so and the recent laws that mandate child support. When a man gets a divorce, his wife usually ends up with custody of the children. If he is working, he will be mandated to pay child support. If he refuses to pay his child support or falls behind on his payments, a warrant will be issued for his arrest. A man must also pay child support to a woman who has custody of his children whether or not he was ever married to her. Thus, a man's financial security rests quite a bit on whether or not he has to pay child support, and if so, how much of it he has to pay, and whether or not he can comfortably pay it.

Most men today expect their wives to work to help support the family. The days of a man single-handedly and properly providing for his family (even if it means that he has to work two or three jobs) is gone, and a man who supports his wife single-handedly without counting on his wife to work also, is rare. So now a more modern-day chauvinistic cliché has surfaced to take place of the "barefoot and pregnant" one. It goes something like this: "I want a wife who's a chef in the breakfast room, a maid in the boardroom, and a whore in the bedroom."

But although one chauvinistic cliché has been replaced with another, the ability that God has given women to carry life in the womb, is still an amazing thing.

THE HONOR OF PREGNANCY

Pregnancy is an honorable condition for any woman to be in as long as she conceived in marriage and as long as the baby she is carrying has been fathered by the man who is or was her husband at the time of conception. A baby conceived in adultery, sex before marriage, or rape has been conceived in sin. In these instances (with the latter not being the fault of the woman) the pregnancy is the *result* of sin but the pregnancy *itself* is not a sin and it is not a sin for the mother to carry the child to term and give birth. Furthermore, the baby is no less a legitimate person than a baby conceived in marriage, even though the baby has unfortunately been given an "illegitimate" title by some and was conceived dishonorably.

There is no better historical account that teaches us about the honor of pregnancy than the account of the Immaculate Conception of Jesus Christ. Let's take a look:

> [26]In the sixth month the angel Gabriel was sent by God to a town in Galilee called Nazareth, [27]to a virgin engaged to a man whose name was Joseph, of the house of David. The virgin's name was Mary. [28]And he came to her and said, "Greetings, favored one" The Lord is with you." [29]But she was much perplexed by his words and pondered what sort of greeting this might be. [30]The angel said to her, "Do not be afraid, Mary, for you have found favor with God. [31]And now, you will conceive in your womb and bear a son, and you will name him Jesus. [32]He will be great, and will be called the Son of the Most High, and the Lord God will give to him the throne of his ancestor David. [33]He will reign over the house of Jacob forever, and of his kingdom there will be no end." [34]Mary said to the angel, "How

43

can this be, since I am a virgin?" [35]The angel said to her, "The Holy Spirit will come upon you, and the power of the Most High will overshadow you: therefore the child to be born will be holy; he will be called Son of God. [36]And now, your relative Elizabeth in her old age has also conceived a son; and this is the sixth month for her who was said to be barren. [37]For nothing will be impossible with God. [38]Then Mary said, "Here am I, the servant of the Lord; let it be with me according to your word." The angel departed from her. (Luke 1:26-38 NRSV)

Mary was pledged to marry Joseph. The scriptures specifically indicate that Mary was a virgin. She had never had sexual intercourse with a man. This fact is even more plausible when taking into account that Mary was approximately fifteen years of age when she was engaged to marry Joseph. She was very young. However, ancient Jewish custom allowed girls to wed at an early age. Current Western law also permits adolescents to marry as long as they have parental consent.

God didn't leave Mary to any surprises. Verses 26 through 32 tells us that God sent the angel Gabriel to Mary to specifically inform her that she would become pregnant and that the child she'd be carrying would be the Son of God. After the angel told her that she would become pregnant, Mary was perplexed and asked the angel how this could be since she was a virgin. The angel Gabriel explained that the spirit of God would overshadow her. There is absolutely no indication here that God had sex with Mary, as some say, but only that God's Spirit overshadowed her. Mary had to be informed of her impending pregnancy so that she would know how she became pregnant and so that she would know the identity of the child she was to carry. This way she could carry Jesus with honor and without shame. The angel Gabriel informed Mary that she was highly favored of God. This is no small honor. Mary probably experienced the greatest honor a single human being could have ever experienced: she gave birth to God incarnate.[1] No man could have

---

[1] Some would argue that Jesus Christ experienced the greatest honor a single human being could have experienced by sacrificing himself to save the world. But Jesus was more than human, he is the second personage of the Godhead. He is deity and is therefore in a class by himself. Mary was a mere mortal, nothing

carried this honor because God did not create men with the ability to become pregnant. Therefore, this honor was given to a woman. Jesus Christ, the Son of God, the everlasting Father and Prince of Peace, lived inside of Mary for nine months. She felt his every move. If God were a chauvinist then he certainly would not have used a woman as the entryway for Jesus to come into the world. He would have found some way to use a man. Actually, God did not have to use a man or a woman to bring Jesus into the world. Surely there are several alternative ways in which God could have accomplished the task without using a human being. But he chose to use a woman. It was part of his plan all along.

After the angel explained things to her, Mary realized that she indeed was highly favored. She did not resist her calling but with all dignity accepted her assignment as a faithful servant to God. However, Joseph also had to be informed. Otherwise, he would have suspected fornication on Mary's part and put her to shame. Let's take a look at how God handled this:

> [18]Now the birth of Jesus the Messiah took place in this way. When his mother Mary had been engaged to Joseph, but before they lived together, she was found to be with child from the Holy Spirit. [19]Her husband Joseph, being a righteous man and unwilling to expose her to public disgrace, planned to dismiss her quietly. [20]But just when he had resolved to do this, an angel of the Lord appeared to him in a dream and said, "Joseph, son of David, do not be afraid to take Mary as your wife, for the child conceived in her is from the Holy Spirit. [21]She will bear a son, and you are to name him Jesus, for he will save his people from their sins." [22]All this took place to fulfill what had been spoken by the Lord through the prophet:
>
> > [23] "Look, the virgin shall conceive and bear a son, and they shall name him Emmanuel," which means, "God is with us."

more. And among mere mortals she has experienced the greatest honor of service to God.

²⁴When Joseph awoke from sleep, he did as the angel of the Lord commanded him; he took her as his wife, ²⁵but had no marital relations with her until she had borne a son; and he named him Jesus. (Matthew 1:18-25 NRSV)

Unlike Mary, Joseph had not been forewarned about Mary's impending pregnancy. Therefore, when Joseph discovered Mary was pregnant he decided to quietly divorce her.[2] Before Jesus' ministry, the punishment for adultery was death. Let's take a look:

²³If a man happens to meet in a town a virgin pledged to be married and he sleeps with her, ²⁴you shall take both of them to the gate of that town and stone them to death—the girl because she was in a town and did not scream for help, and the man because he violated another man's wife. You must purge the evil from among you. (Deuteronomy 22:23-24 NIV)

The above decree is just one command of the Law out of many that God gave to the Jews during the reign of Moses. This law does not apply today because we are in the dispensation of Grace.[3] The indication that the girl consented to the affair has to do with the fact that she did not scream. She did not scream because the man's advances were welcome. Notice, both the girl and the man were both stoned. God made no difference between them.

Upon discovery of Mary's pregnancy, Joseph was unwilling to expose Mary to public disgrace. He decided not to humiliate her and to take care of the matter privately. Furthermore, Joseph apparently loved Mary enough not to risk the possibility that she could have been stoned to death. Let's take another look at Matthew 1:24-25.

²⁴When Joseph woke up he did what the angel of the Lord had commanded him and took Mary home as his

---

[2] During the time that Joseph and Mary were engaged to one another (the dispensation of the Law), an engagement was essentially the same as a marriage.
[3] See Introduction.

wife. [25]But he had no union with her until she gave
birth to a son. And he gave him the name Jesus. (NIV)

Joseph, without hesitation, did exactly what the angel Gabriel told
him to do. He took Mary home with him as his wife. It must be
emphasized that Joseph had no sexual relations with Mary until after the
birth of Jesus. He realized the honorable position both he and Mary were
in. Neither Mary nor Joseph did anything to hinder or tarnish the
miraculous birth of Jesus Christ.

The angel Gabriel not only gave Mary the news of her own
impending pregnancy but also told her of Elizabeth's pregnancy.
Elizabeth, Mary's relative, was in her sixth month of pregnancy when
the angel Gabriel visited Mary. Elizabeth had not been able to have
children and she was old. But the Bible teaches us that "nothing is
impossible with God."[4] Therefore, Elizabeth conceived.

After the angel Gabriel delivered God's message to Mary, she
immediately prepared to visit Elizabeth to tell her the news. The
following is the account of that visit:

> [39]In those days Mary set out and went with haste to a
> Judean town in the hill country, [40]where she entered the
> house of Zechariah and greeted Elizabeth. [41]When
> Elizabeth heard Mary's greeting, the child leaped in her
> womb. And Elizabeth was filled with the Holy Spirit
> [42]and exclaimed with a loud cry, "Blessed are you
> among women, and blessed is the fruit of your womb.
> [43]And why has this happened to me, that the mother of
> my Lord comes to me? [44]For as soon as I heard the
> sound of your greeting, the child in my womb leaped
> for joy. [45]And blessed is she who believed that there
> would be a fulfillment of what was spoken to her by the
> Lord. (Luke 1:39-45 NRSV)

Mary had not told Elizabeth about the message she received from the
angel Gabriel. However, Elizabeth was filled with the Holy Spirit and
she began to prophesy and proclaim what had already been told to Mary
by the angel Gabriel. Therefore, Mary heard the same information from

---

[4] "For with God nothing shall be impossible." (Luke 1:37)

two different sources. Elizabeth knew of Mary's pregnancy because the Holy Spirit revealed it to her.

Mary and Elizabeth were very happy women indeed and it was the honor of their pregnancies that made them happy. Mary was carrying our Lord and Savior, Jesus Christ and Elizabeth was carrying John the Baptist who was to be filled with the Holy Spirit from birth and foretell the ministry of Jesus Christ. Let's take a look at the events surrounding the conception of John the Baptist:

> [5]In the time of Herod king of Judea there was a priest named Zechariah, who belonged to the priestly division of Abijah; his wife Elizabeth was also a descendant of Aaron. [6]Both of them were upright in the sight of God, observing all the Lord's commandments and regulations blamelessly. [7]But they had no children, because Elizabeth was barren; and they were both well along in years.
>
> [8]Once when Zechariah's division was on duty and he was serving as priest before God, [9]he was chosen by lot, according to the custom of the priesthood, to go into the temple of the Lord and burn incense. [10]And when the time for the burning of incense came, all the assembled worshipers were praying outside.
>
> [11]Then an angel of the Lord appeared to him, standing at the right side of the altar of incense. [12]When Zechariah saw him he was startled and was gripped with fear. [13]But the angel said to him: "Do not be afraid, Zechariah; your prayer has been heard. Your wife Elizabeth will bear you a son, and you are to give him the name John. [14]He will be a joy and delight to you, and many will rejoice because of his birth, [15]for he will be great in the sight of the Lord. He is never to take wine or other fermented drink, and he will be filled with the Holy Spirit even from birth. [16]Many of the people of Israel will he bring back to the Lord their God. [17]And he will go on before the Lord, in the spirit and power of Elijah, to turn the hearts of the fathers to their children and the disobedient to the wisdom of the

righteous—to make ready a people prepared for the Lord.

[18]Zechariah asked the angel, "How can I be sure of this? I am an old man and my wife is well along in years."

[19]The angel answered, "I am Gabriel. I stand in the presence of God, and I have been sent to speak to you and to tell you this good news. (Luke 1: 5-19 NIV)

Many of the Jews had turned against God. And John the Baptist would be the one who would bring many of those Jews back to God by preaching a "baptism of repentance for the forgiveness of sins" as attested to in the following passage of scripture:

[1]In the fifteenth year of the reign of Tiberius Caesar—when Pontius Pilate was governor of Judea, Herod tetrarch of Galilee his brother Philip tetrarch of Iturea and Traconitis, and Lysanias tetrarch of Abilene—[2]during the high priesthood of Annas and Caiaphas, the word of God came to John son of Zechariah in the desert. [3]He went into all the country around the Jordan, preaching a baptism of repentance for the forgiveness of sins. [4]As is written in the book of the words of Isaiah the prophet:

"A voice of one calling in the desert,
Prepare the way for the Lord,
   make straight paths for him.
[5]Every valley shall be filled in,
   every mountain and hill made low.
The crooked roads shall become straight,
   the rough ways smooth.
[6]And all mankind will see God's
      Salvation.
      (Luke 3:1-6 NIV)

The ministry of John the Baptist foreshadowed and made way the ministry of Jesus Christ. Elizabeth carried John the Baptist in her womb.

She carried and gave birth to the man that would prepare the way for the Lord. What an honor indeed.

When looking at the accounts of the Virgin Mary and Elizabeth, there is no doubt that it is a blessing for a woman to be pregnant. When a woman is pregnant she carries the life of another human being inside of her. Not only is this a miraculous occurrence but it is a gift from God. Mary, the mother of Jesus, was so excited and honored by her impending pregnancy that she sang a song dedicated to the Lord during her visit with Elizabeth.[5] And the eighth day after the birth of his son (John the Baptist) Zechariah became filled with the Holy Ghost and began to prophesy.[6] Both Mary and Zechariah realized the blessing that had been bestowed upon them to be the parents of Jesus and John the Baptist respectively.

All life that exists in the womb has the potential to accomplish great things in the Lord, once born. This is why pregnancy, in and of itself, is not a sin, no matter what the circumstances behind it are. If a woman becomes pregnant and she has no husband or her husband is not the father of her child, it is not a sin for her to carry the baby. Her pregnancy in and of itself is not a sin. However, her pregnancy is the *evidence* of sin and her pregnancy came about in a dishonorable way. The following is a biblical example of a pregnancy that came about in a dishonorable way.

DISHONORABLE CONCEPTION: THE CASE OF DAVID AND BETHSHEBA

David was the King of Judah and eventually became king over all of Israel. He ruled Israel from 1005 to 965 B.C. David was a mighty king and feared the Lord. However, his greatest recorded downfall was when he slept with Uriah's wife, Bathsheba, and consequently had Uriah killed.

As a result of the adultery committed between David and Bethsheba, Bethsheba became pregnant with David's child. Therefore the pregnancy was not conceived honorably, because adultery is a sin. Here is the beginning of the account:

---

[5] Luke 1:46-56 (see your Bible).
[6] Luke 1:67-80 (see your Bible).

¹In the spring, at the time when kings go off to war, David sent Joab out with the king's men and the whole Israelite army. They destroyed the Ammonites and besieged Rabbah. But David remained in Jerusalem.

²One evening David got up from his bed and walked around on the roof of the palace. From the roof he saw a woman bathing. The woman was very beautiful, ³and David sent someone to find out about her. The man said, "Isn't this Bathsheba, the daughter of Eliam and the wife of Uriah the Hittite?" ⁴Then David sent messengers to get her. She came to him, and he slept with her. (She had purified herself from her uncleanness.) Then she went back home. ⁵The woman conceived and sent word to David, saying, "I am pregnant."

⁶So David sent this word to Joab: "Send me Uriah the Hittite." And Joab sent him to David. ⁷When Uriah came to him, David asked him how Joab was, how the soldiers were and how the war was going. ⁸Then David said to Uriah, "Go down to your house and wash your feet." So Uriah left the palace, and a gift from the king was sent after him. ⁹But Uriah slept at the entrance to the palace with all his master's servants and did not go down to his house. (2 Samuel 11:1-9 NIV)

Verse 3 tells us that David asked about Bathsheba before he decided to seduce her. He probably hoped that Bathsheba wasn't married. However, the man who he sent to get information about her, told David that Bathsheba was the wife of Uriah. David disregarded this information and sent his messengers to bring her to him anyway. She came to him and the two of them had sexual intercourse. From the tone of the scripture, it appears as though Bathsheba was a willing partner, despite her marriage to Uriah. Verse 4 tells us that Bathsheba had purified herself from her uncleanness before sleeping with David.[7] This means that she had just completed her monthly period. If Uriah began his tour of duty during any time of his wife's monthly cycle that month, he'd be aware that she was not pregnant before he left. Therefore, if she became

---

[7] Leviticus 15:19-26 (see Appendix)

pregnant, which she did, Uriah would immediately know that the baby was not his. Remember, during this time, adultery was a sin punishable by death.

In order to cover his sin, David attempted to manipulate events so that Uriah would sleep with Bathsheba as soon as possible. At the time, however, Uriah was on a military tour of duty with the other soldiers in David's army. David sent for Uriah. Verse 7 tells us that David asked Uriah about the war's progress and how the soldiers were doing. Surely Uriah thought that David had sincerely summoned him in order that he may give the king an update. However, David's real motive was to encourage Uriah to go home. His wife, Bathsheba would be waiting. David figured that Uriah would not be able to resist making love to his wife, especially after he had been such a long time away from her. But things didn't go as David planned. Verse 9 tells us that Uriah did not go home but instead slept at the entrance of the palace with all of David's servants.

> [10]When David was told, "Uriah did not go home," he asked him, "Haven't you just come from a distance? Why didn't you go home?"
> [11]Uriah said to David, "The Ark and Israel and Judah are staying in tents, and my master Joab and my lord's men are camped in the open fields. How could I go to my house to eat and drink and lie with my wife? As surely as you live I will not do such a thing!"
> (2 Samuel 11:10-11 NIV)

It had not occurred to David that Uriah might feel disloyal to his comrades if he enjoyed pleasures while they were yet in battlefield mode. In Uriah's eyes it would have been dishonorable to partake in the luxuries of his home while his fellow soldiers were still on duty. Of course, David could not argue against such loyalty. So he instead got Uriah drunk, hoping that in a drunken state Uriah would become uninhibited, throw loyalty out of the window and go sleep with his wife, as the following passage of scripture attests to:

> [12]Then David said to him, "Stay here one more day, and tomorrow I will send you back." So Uriah remained in Jerusalem that day and the next. [13]At

> David's invitation, he ate and drank with him, and
> David made him drunk. But in the evening Uriah went
> out to sleep on his mat among his master's servants; he
> did not go home. (2 Samuel 11:12-13 NIV)

Even though David cajoled Uriah into getting drunk, Uriah,
nonetheless, held on to his loyalties. He still refused to enjoy the
pleasures of his home and make love to his wife. Finally, out of
desperation, David conspired to have Uriah killed. Let's take a look:

> [14]In the morning David wrote a letter to Joab and
> sent it with Uriah. [15]In it he wrote, "Put Uriah in the
> front line where the fighting is fiercest. Then
> withdraw from him so he will be struck down and
> die." (2 Samuel 11:14-15 NIV)

Joab, apparently without question, accommodated the king. David's
instructions were to have the platoon withdraw from Uriah. They were
not to aid him in battle. Just as David had planned, Uriah was killed in
battle.[8] But as the following scripture indicates, God was not pleased.

> [26]When Uriah's wife heard that her husband was dead,
> she mourned for him. [27]After the time of mourning was
> over, David had brought her to his house, and she
> became his wife and bore him a son. But the thing
> David had done displeased the LORD. (2 Samuel 11:26
> NIV)

As much as David and Bathsheba tried to give her pregnancy the
appearance of being an honorable one, God knew that the child was
conceived in sin, in dishonor. Certainly there were others who knew as
well. David abused his position of power in his attempt to cover his sin,
but he needed help in order to cover things up. He knew that Uriah did
not go home while on leave of his tour of duty because he sent servants
to keep watch of Uriah. He specifically told Joab that his aim was to kill
Uriah, knowing that Joab would obey orders without question. It is

---

[8] Read chapter 11 of 2nd Samuel for the full account (see your Bible)

uncertain whether or not Bethsheba ever knew that David was responsible for her husband's death.

Bathsheba finally gave birth to a son. David had quickly covered up his sin. After not being able to manipulate Uriah into sleeping with Bathsheba so that Uriah would think that the baby she was carrying was his, David conspired to have Uriah killed during battle and then afterwards he married Bathsheba as soon as he could. God was angry with David. God sent the prophet Nathan with a message to David. The following is the account of Nathan's message:

> [1]Then the LORD sent Nathan to David.
> And he came to him, and said,
> "There were two men in one city, the one
> rich and the other poor.
> [2]The rich man had a great many flocks
> and herds.
> [3]But the poor man had nothing except one
> little ewe lamb
> Which he bought and nourished;
> And it grew up together with him and his
> children.
> It would eat of his bread and drink of his
> cup and lie in his bosom,
> And was like a daughter to him.
> [4]Now a traveler came to the rich man,
> And he was unwilling to take from his
> own flock or his own herd,
> To prepare for the wayfarer who had
> come to him;
> Rather he took the poor man's ewe lamb
> and prepared it for the man who had
> come to him."

[5]Then David's anger burned greatly against the man, and he said to Nathan, "As the Lord lives, surely the man who has done this deserves to die.
[6]And he must make restitution for the lamb fourfold, because he did this thing and had no compassion."

[7]Nathan then said to David, "You are the man! Thus says the LORD God of Israel, 'It is I who anointed you king over Israel and it is I who delivered you from the hand of Saul.

[8]I also gave you your master's house and your master's wives into your care, and I gave you the house of Israel and Judah; and if that had been too little, I would have added to you many more things like these!

[9]Why have you despised the word of the LORD by doing evil in his sight? You have struck down Uriah the Hittite with the sword, have taken his wife to be your wife, and have killed him with the sword of the sons of Ammon. (2 Samuel 12:1-9 NASB)

The prophet Nathan was given a message by God to give to David. Nathan began by giving David an analogy of a rich man who took the only ewe away from a poor man in order to feed a traveler. The rich man had great many flocks and herds and could have taken any animal from his own resources to kill, cook, and prepare as part of dinner for the traveler. But instead he took the only ewe that the poor man had. David was angered by what the rich man did and felt that the rich man was worthy of death. This is when Nathan revealed to David that the analogy pertained to him and his dealings with Uriah.

Nathan explained to David that the rich man in the analogy was symbolic of David because David was a king with many wives.[9] And Uriah was synonymous with the poor man. Uriah only had one wife whom he cherished very much. Just as the rich man took the only ewe lamb the poor man had, David took the only wife Uriah had.

David had done an evil thing in the sight of the Lord (verse 9). Nathan accused David of killing Uriah. It didn't matter that Uriah was

---

[9]Deuteronomy 17:14-17 (see Appendix) teaches us that God forbade men, especially kings, to have more than one wife. However, it was customary during Old Testament times for kings and men of great wealth to ignore this particular command of God and take on many wives anyway. Although God forbade men to multiply wives unto themselves, God did not cite a punishment for those who went against this command. Basically, God put up with the custom, at least for a time. However, by having more than one wife, a man was ultimately going against the will of God. See Chapter 11 for a complete discussion on Polygamy.

killed in battle and therefore not killed directly by David's hand. As far as God was concerned, Uriah was killed directly by David's hand. David set the stage to have Uriah killed and gave the orders for Joab to make certain that Uriah would be on the front line so that there would be no doubt that he would be killed. In God's eyes, this was murder. God therefore punished David in the following way:

> [11]"Thus says the LORD, 'Behold, I will raise up evil against you from your own household; I will even take your wives before your eyes, and give them to your companion, and he shall lie with your wives in broad daylight.
> [12]Indeed you did it secretly, but I will do this thing before all Israel, and under the sun.'"
> [13]Then David said to Nathan, "I have sinned against the LORD." And Nathan said to David, "The LORD also has taken away your sin; you shall not die.
> [14]However, because by this deed you have given occasion to the enemies of the LORD to blaspheme, the child also that is born to you shall surely die." (2 Samuel 12: 11-14 NASB)

If one is not familiar with Biblical language and the way the Hebrews used to express themselves, then in verse 11 it may appear as if God is saying that he will cause David's wives to commit adultery against him. However, what is actually being said is that God will not stop the impending incidences of adultery that will occur. God did not *cause* the adultery to take place in the sense that today's reader would think of *cause*, but *cause* in the sense that he did not set the stage to stop it. The Lord's prophecy as to a companion sleeping with David's concubines in front of all Israel literally came true not too long after the prediction. Absalom, David's third son, brought the prediction to life. The fifteenth and sixteenth chapters of 2nd Samuel[10] record Absalom's wish to be king and Absalom's plans to overthrow his father's government. In order to do this, Absalom set out to kill his father, David. David fled from Absalom. Let's take a brief look:

---

[10] See your Bible.

> [13] A messenger came to David, saying, "The hearts of
> the Israelites have gone after Absalom." [14]Then David
> said to all his officials who were with him at Jerusalem,
> "Get up! Let us flee, or there will be no escape for us
> from Absalom. Hurry, or he will soon overtake us, and
> bring disaster down upon us, and attack the city with
> the edge of the sword." [15]The king's officials said to
> the king, "Your servants are ready to do whatever our
> lord the king decides." (2 Samuel 15:13-16 NRSV)

Earlier in the 15th chapter of Samuel it is revealed that Absalom was
very clever at getting the people of the land to like him enough to want
him to be king. In order to further influence the people's preference
away from his father, Absalom took the following advice of one of his
aids while he was in pursuit of his father and those with him:

> [20]Absalom said to Ahithophel, "Give us your
> advice. What should we do?"
> [21]Ahithophel answered, "Lie with your father's
> concubines whom he left to take care of the palace.
> Then all Israel will hear that you have made yourself a
> stench in your father's nostrils, and the hands of
> everyone with you will be strengthened." [22]So they
> pitched a tent for Absalom on the roof, and he lay with
> his father's concubines in the sight of all Israel. (2
> Samuel 16:20-22 NIV)

Absalom was the companion that God said he would cause to go
against the house of David and sleep with his wives in broad daylight in
front of all Israel. But God did not actually cause this to happen, again,
he simply did not stop it from happening. God allowed this wicked thing
to occur but the wickedness came from Absalom at the suggestion of
Ahithophel, not from God. This thing was not only wicked because
Absalom went against his father in this manner, but this thing was
wicked because Absalom abused his position of power by having sex
with his father's concubines.

In regards to the punishment that God placed upon David because he
killed Uriah, not only did God allow Absalom to disrespect David's
household by publicly sleeping with his wives, but he also cursed David

and Bethsheba's first born son with an early death. More than likely, besides those closest to David and Bathsheba, people assumed that the boy had been conceived very early in her marriage to David. However, there were certainly those who knew Bathsheba's child had been fathered by David before the death of Uriah and knew that David had therefore sought to have Uriah killed. Since David was a representative of God, this gave God's enemies the excuse to say bad things about God, to blaspheme. Again, 2nd Samuel 12:14 puts it this way, *"However, because by this deed you have given occasion to the enemies of the LORD to blaspheme, the child also that is born to you shall surely die."* 2nd Samuel 12:15 says that God struck the child so that he was very sick. The following is the account:

> [15]Then Nathan departed to his house.
> And the LORD struck the child that Uriah's wife bore to David, and it became ill.
> [16]David therefore pleaded with God for the child, and David fasted and went in and lay all night on the ground.
> [17]So the elders of this house arose and went to him, to raise him up from the ground. But he would not, nor did he eat food with them.
> [18]Then on the seventh day it came to pass that the child died. And the servants of David were afraid to tell him that the child was dead. For they said, "Indeed, while the child was alive, we spoke to him, and he would not heed our voice. How can we tell him that the child is dead? He may do some harm!"
> [19]When David saw that his servants were whispering, David perceived that the child was dead. Therefore David said to his servants, "Is the child dead?" And they said, "He is dead."
> [20]So David arose from the ground, washed and anointed himself, and changed his clothes; and he went into the house of the LORD and worshiped. Then he went to his own house; and when he requested, they set food before him, and he ate.
> [21]Then his servants said to him, "What is this that you have done? You fasted and wept for the child while he

was alive, but when the child died, you arose and ate food."

²²And he said, "While the child was alive, I fasted and wept; for I said, "Who can tell whether the LORD will be gracious to me, that the child may live?'

²³But now he is dead; why should I fast? Can I bring him back again? I shall go to him, but he shall not return to me."

²⁴Then David comforted Bathsheba his wife, and went in to her and lay with her. So she bore a son, and he called his name Solomon. Now the LORD loved him. (2 Samuel 12:15-24 NKJV)

During the dispensation of the Law, there were recorded incidences in which children paid for the sins of their parents. However, during the dispensation of Grace (the dispensation we are now currently in) this is no longer necessarily the case.[11] Verse 24 tells us that God loved the second son of David and Bethsheba (who they named Solomon). This does not mean that he didn't love the first son, but we can safely surmise that God did not like the circumstances under which the first son was born. Despite this, he still blessed David and Bethsheba with a second child after the death of their first child.

It must be emphasized that both David and Bethsheba paid the price for the dishonorable way in which their first son was conceived. As a matter of fact, God seemed to hold David more accountable than he held Bethsheba. After all, David was king over Israel. He abused his position of power in order to sleep with Bethsheba. Bethsheba was not alone in her sin and she was not alone in the shame she suffered. David suffered just as much shame for fathering the child. When looking at the fact that God allowed Absalom to come against David the way he did, David can be said to have actually suffered more shame than Bethsheba did.

In today's society the woman is seen as more accountable for becoming pregnant out of wedlock than a man is for impregnating a woman out of wedlock. Society sees the woman as the one responsible for birth control and the woman is the one frowned upon by others, especially in the church, when she finds herself carrying a baby without being married. However, we can clearly see that God holds the man just

---

[11] John 9:1-3 (see Appendix)

as accountable. As a matter of fact, in the case of David, God held the man more accountable, especially since the sin of adultery led to the sin of murder. We can also see, from our examination of the account of David and Bethsheba, that getting married after impregnation doesn't necessarily make things right. The sin has already been committed and it cannot be undone. Marriage therefore is not always the solution to an unwanted pregnancy and it doesn't necessarily fix things with God.

SUMMARY

Some women may feel that part of their service to God is having children. If they have been called in this manner then they should marry and have children. The Virgin Mary was called in this manner as was her cousin Elizabeth. Both were specifically called to have children. Mary's assignment from God was to carry Jesus Christ, our Lord and Savior, in her womb, to bear him, and to mother him. This was her calling. The same can be said for Elizabeth in regards to her motherhood to John the Baptist. There are other historical biblical female figures whose service to God was to bear great men and women. However, as we will see in chapter 12, this does not mean that all women are supposed to have children.

Although a woman might conceive a child in a dishonorable way, there is no scripture in the Bible that teaches that the pregnancy itself is a sin. God did not punish David and Bethsheba because Bethsheba became pregnant. God punished them because they had both committed adultery and because David had Uriah killed. When examining what the prophet Nathan said to David, God was particularly angry at David because he had slept with another man's wife. The issue of the pregnancy was not included in Nathan's rebuke. It's fair to assume that God would have still been angry with David and Bethsheba had Bathsheba not become pregnant.

Since women are the ones who become pregnant, then there is a higher probability that a woman's sin of fornication will be exposed while men who fornicate will be less likely to be exposed. However, God does not deem a woman any guiltier of fornication because she has become pregnant as a result of fornication, than he does a woman who commits fornication and does not become pregnant or than he does a man who commits fornication. To clarify the point, society looks down on the woman who has five children out of wedlock fathered by five different men. However, she is no guiltier than a woman who has slept with five different men (who were not her husbands) and did not become pregnant by any of them. She is also no guiltier than a man who has slept with five different women (who were not his wives at the time). Pregnancy itself is not a sin regardless of how conception occurred. But pregnancy can be the result of sin. The sin of fornication is not lessened or increased by the result of pregnancy.

As we have seen, a man who impregnates a woman without being married to her is just as responsible for the misdeed as the woman. He is equally accountable in the eyes of God. A chauvinistic God would certainly hold the woman more accountable than the man. But in the case of King David, God held the man more accountable. And in the case of Mary and Joseph, a chauvinistic God would have certainly told Joseph about the wonderful news of the impending birth of Christ before he told Mary. The husband would have been the first to know. But Mary had been given the information before her husband was given the information. Joseph wasn't informed of what was going on until after he discovered that Mary was pregnant. Furthermore, after the angel Gabriel told Mary what her service to God was to be, Mary did not go to her husband and ask him if it was all right with him. God instructed her to do something and she set out to do it. Moreover, when God instructed Mary he did not readily go to Joseph. God didn't ask Joseph for his approval in the matter and neither did Mary. Once God instructed Mary on what to do, she didn't need her husband's approval and God didn't need her husband's approval either. Certainly a chauvinistic God would never instruct the wife of a man without consulting with her husband first.

Overall, a woman's ability to become pregnant and carry life inside of her womb is an honorable thing. Therefore, a woman should never be scorned for carrying a child and if a woman conceives a child by means of consenting sexual sin, then the sexual sin should be scorned but not the pregnancy. Although David and Bethsheba's first child was conceived dishonorably and the child's death was used by God to punish both David and Bathsheba for their adultery, this does not mean that all women who become pregnant in dishonorable ways have the hand of God against them.

3.

MARRIED WOMEN AND SUBMISSION

The scriptures given in the Bible instructing wives to be in subjection to their husbands is one of the main reasons why many women in general believe that God has not been fair to women and that he is a chauvinist. There are those Christian women who struggle with this issue as well.

THE "S" WORD.....SUBMIT

Let's take a look at Ephesians 5:22:

> Wives, submit to your own husbands, as to the Lord. (NKJV)

> Wives, be subject to your own husbands, as to the Lord. (NASB)

Out of all the verses of scripture in the Bible, this particular verse, and verses similar to it, is probably the most discouraging and perplexing for many women. Although the scripture applies to all married women, women who are not Christians may not feel compelled to apply it to themselves while Christian women have no other choice but to apply the scripture to themselves. Therefore, our focus will mainly be on the reaction of the church[1] to this verse of scripture.

In the church, men put great emphasis on this particular verse of scripture when talking about the marriage relationship. Some men even tend to gloat about the fact that women are commanded to submit to their husbands, and say they don't understand why many women become despondent when it comes to this particular passage. One can accept being subject to God because he is God, but being subject to a human

---

[1] See Introduction

being, for no apparent reason other than gender, can understandably cause great concern for the one under subjection.

Many pastors preach on marriage as if the main hindrance of a successful marriage is a non-submissive wife. In this day of great pervertedness, the word, *submit* means many things to many people. There are those men who take the verse of scripture to mean that a wife must submit to her husband in everything (all of his demands, his desires, and his thoughts) and if she does not, then she is not only sinning against him but against the Lord as well.

According to John Temple Bristow, author of *What Paul really said about Women*, the way in which the Greek word for *submit* is used in Ephesians 5:22 lends itself to less of an oppressive meaning than it does in the English language. Let's take a look at what Bristow says:

> In English, verbs can be in the active or passive voice. In the active voice, the subject of the verb is acting. In the passive voice, the subject of the verb is being acted upon. Greek has the same active and passive voices. But it has also a third, middle voice, in which the subject of the verb is acting in a way that affects the subject.
>
> It is difficult for English-speaking persons to grasp the subtle yet important distinction between middle and passive voice in Greek verbs just by reading the definition, and yet we think in ways that the Greek verb forms express. For example, a person may teach—an active verb. And one may be taught—a passive verb. But a person may also teach himself or herself by careful listening, discovering, reasoning, learning. In that sense, the person is both subject and object of the action. That is what the Greek middle voice expresses, a voluntary action by the subject of the verb upon the subject of the verb.
>
> .....However, Paul used *hupotasso* in the middle voice. This way, he was requesting that wives voluntarily, willingly, actively be subject to their husbands. This is the form *hupotassomai* (hoop-O-TASS-o-my). Since it is asking for something that is voluntary in nature, "to be subject to" is an awkward translation at best.

> *Hupotassomai* means something like "give allegiance to," "tend to the needs of," "be supportive of" or "be responsive to." Perhaps the best meaning of *hupuotassomai* is found in a German translation of that word, sich unterstellen, "to place oneself at the disposition of."[2]

To *be subject to* as opposed to placing *oneself at the disposition of* is a significant enough difference to have a huge impact on what Paul was really conveying in the 5th chapter of Ephesians. *To be subject to* implies unwillingness on the part of the one that is commanded to subject his or herself. The word *submit* in the English language implies that the one doing the submitting has no other choice but to succumb to the one making the demands. However, placing oneself at the disposition of another gives a general connotation of willingness. Without the application of the middle voice the word *hupotassomai* is simply translated in English as *to obey* or *to submit*, which lend themselves more to strict obedience than to voluntary support. In colloquial terms, according to Bristow, Paul was instructing the wife to "be in her husband's corner."

Bristow's explanation "softens the blow" a bit but it does not lessen the command that a woman is to submit to her husband. Ultimately, placing oneself at the disposition of another is a form of submission. And whether or not a wife willingly submits or not is immaterial since she is ultimately commanded to submit. So, Let's take another look at Ephesians 5:22:

> Wives, submit to your own husbands, as to the Lord. (NKJV)

> Wives, be subject to your own husbands, as to the Lord. (NASB)

Not only is a woman to submit to her husband but she is to do so *as to the Lord*. The scripture is not saying that a woman's husband *is* the

---

[2] *What Paul said about Women* by John Temple Bristow, copyright © 1988 by John Temple Bristow, published by HarperSanFranciso, New York NY, p. 40, used by permission.

Lord. Neither is the scripture putting a married man on the same level *as* the Lord. The scripture is simply instructing a married woman on the *way* in which she is to "submit." The phrase "as to the Lord" takes on a different connotation when used in conjunction with Bristow's middle voice explanation of the Greek word *hupotassomai.*

When substituting the English word *submit* for the more descriptive phrases "tend to the needs of" or "place oneself at the disposition of," the phrase "as to the Lord" becomes more palatable and less offensive, as Bristow says Paul intended it to be. A woman tending to the needs of her husband as to the Lord is merely tending to the needs of her husband with the same voracity as she would tend to the things of the Lord. She is simply placing herself "at the disposition of" her husband with the same eagerness she has in placing herself at the disposition of the Lord. The implication of oppression is decreased when translating *hupotassomai* more distinctly. However, by instructing women to voluntarily submit, Paul does not eradicate the feeling of oppression that some wives may experience upon submitting but instead makes way for the easing of whatever feeling of oppression might be triggered from the directive to submit. If a wife is willing to submit, or if she can somehow conjure up a willingness to submit, then whatever oppression she may feel as a result of her husband's authority may be lessened. But, it should be understood that if a woman submits because she feels she has to and not because she wants to then her submission is not voluntary.

All Christians are commanded to submit to one another. Let's take a look:

> [15]See then that you walk circumspectly, not as fools but as wise,
> [16]redeeming the time, because the days are evil.
> [17]Therefore do not be unwise, but understand what the will of the Lord is.
> [18]And do not be drunk with wine, in which is dissipation; but be filled with the Spirit,
> [19]speaking to one another in psalms and hymns and spiritual songs, singing and making melody in your heart to the Lord,
> [20] giving thanks always for all things to God the Father in the name of our Lord Jesus Christ,
> [21] submitting to one another in the fear of God.'

[22]Wives, submit to your own husbands as to the Lord.
(Ephesians 5:15-22 NKJV).

Verse 21 specifically instructs all Christians to submit themselves to other Christians in the fear of God. So, this command includes Christian husbands. Therefore, a Christian husband is just as much obligated to submit to his wife as a Christian wife is to her husband. He should tend to her needs, put himself at the disposition of, be in allegiance to, and be supportive of his wife, in the fear of God. Although there is no less of an obligation for a man to "submit" to his wife, the church puts much more emphasis on the command for a wife to "submit" to her husband. This may be so because Paul, the apostle, put a greater emphasis on it as well.

If indeed both husband and wife are to submit to one another, then why the emphasis on the submission of the wife? Emphasis is placed on submission of the wife to the husband because a man has the ultimate decision in a marriage. The fact that a man has the final say in a marriage is disturbing to most women. Why does a man have the final say? Does God think that men are better than women?

Although God has given men the final say in authority over their wives, this does not mean that God deems men superior to women. Furthermore, there is some debate as to whether or not the final-say authority that men have over their wives has more to do with God's curse placed upon Eve in the Garden of Eden than a "birthright" for men. But let's first take a look at some of the verses of scripture that teach that men and women are equal as human beings:

> [28]Faith in Christ Jesus is what makes each of you equal with each other, whether you are a Jew or a Greek, a slave or a free person, a man or a woman. [29]So if you belong to Christ, you are now part of Abraham's family, and you will be given what God has promised. (Galatians 3:28-29 CEV).

There is no question that men and women, who have faith in Christ, are equal as human beings and that men are not superior to women. God will give no more to a man than he will to a woman in regards to what he has promised human beings as a whole. The fact that men and women are equals also holds true when looking at the creation account of man and woman. Let's take a look:

66

[24]And God said, "Let the land produce living creatures according to their kinds: livestock, creatures that move along the ground, and wild animals, each according to its kind." And it was so. [25]God made the wild animals according to their kinds, the livestock according to their kinds, and all the creatures that move along the ground according to their kinds. And God saw that it was good.

[26]Then God said, "Let us make man in our image, in our likeness, and let them rule over the fish of the sea and the birds of the air, over the livestock, over all the earth, and over all the creatures that move along the ground."

[27]So God created man in his own image,
in the image of God he created him;
male and female he created them.
(Genesis 1:24-27 NIV)

Verse 26 tells us that God gave "man" rule over all of the fish, birds, animals, and insects. As a matter of fact the verse specifically says "and let *them* rule...." Verse 27 identifies *them* as "male and female." Therefore, women as well as men initially had rule and equal dominion over all of the fish, birds, animals, insects, and so forth. As a matter of fact, men and women were both made in the image of God and therefore were made equal. The Hebrew word for *man* in verse 26 ("let us make *man* in our own image") really translates in the English as *humans* or *people* and therefore encompasses both men and women. Let's look further:

[18]The LORD God said, "It is not good for the man to be alone. I will make a helper suitable for him."
[19]Out of the ground the LORD God formed every beast of the field and every bird of the air, and brought them to Adam to see what he would call them. And whatever Adam called each living creature, that was its name.
[20]So Adam gave names to all cattle, to the birds of the air, and to every beast of the field. But for Adam there was not found a helper comparable to him.

²¹And the LORD God caused a deep sleep to fall on Adam, and he slept; and He took one of his ribs, and closed up the flesh in its place.
²²Then the rib which the LORD God had taken from man He made into a woman, and He brought her to the man.
²³And Adam said:

"This is now bone of my bones
And flesh of my flesh;
She shall be called Woman,
Because she was taken out of Man."

²⁴Therefore a man shall leave his father and mother and be joined to his wife, and they shall become one flesh.
²⁵And they were both naked, the man and his wife, and were not ashamed. (Genesis 2:19-25 NKJV)

God created Eve so that Adam would have someone to help him tend to the Garden of Eden. Genesis 2:8 says, "Now the LORD God had planted a garden in the east, in Eden; and there he put the man he had formed."[3] So, the Garden of Eden was Adam's home. It was where he lived. Genesis 2:15 says that "The Lord God took the man and put him in the Garden of Eden to work it and take care of it."[4] Adam was the keeper of his home. However, God saw that Adam needed assistance. Verses 19 and 20 indicate that God first brought to Adam the birds and beasts, not only so that Adam could name them, but also so that he may find a suitable helper among them. When Adam found no suitable helper among the birds and beasts, God then created woman.

Despite the fact that God says men and women are equal, the question still remains as to why God gave men the final say in a marriage. Why do women have to ultimately submit to their husbands? Why not the opposite way around? There are two basic trains of theological thought that have been presented in answer to these questions. One train of thought says that the authority that men have over their wives is similar to a "birthright" so to speak, and that God gave men the

---

[3] NIV
[4] NIV

authority over their wives simply because God made man first and women were put on earth to assist men. The following scripture text is what is used to support this argument. So let's take a look at it with special emphasis on verses 8 through 12:

> [4]Every man who has something on his head while praying or prophesying, disgraces his head.
> [5]But every woman who has her head uncovered while praying or prophesying, disgraces her head; for she is one and the same with her whose head is shaved.
> [6]For if a woman does not cover her head, let her also have her hair cut off; but if it is disgraceful for a woman to have her hair cut off or her head shaved, let her cover her head.
> [7]For a man ought not to have his head covered, since he is the image and glory of God; but the woman is the glory of man.
> [8]For man does not originate from woman, but woman from man;
> [9]for indeed man was not created for the woman's sake, but woman for the man's sake.
> [10]Therefore the woman ought to have a symbol of authority on her head, because of the angels.
> [11]However, in the Lord, neither is woman independent of man, nor is man independent of woman.
> [12]For as the woman originates from the man, so also the man has his birth through the woman; and all things originate from God.
> [13]Judge for yourselves: is it proper for a woman to pray to God with head uncovered?
> [14]Does not even nature itself teach you that if a man has long hair, it is a dishonor to him,
> [15]But if a woman has long hair it is a glory to her? For her hair is given to her for a covering.
> [16]But if one is inclined to be contentious, we have no other practice, nor have the churches of God.
> (1 Corinthians 11:4-16 NASB)

Since the custom[5] at the time demanded that women wear headdresses while involved in the things of the Lord, Paul's instruction to women was that they wear a covering as a symbol of authority on their heads. However, no such custom exists in the church in general today, and therefore a woman is not obligated to cover her head while praying, prophesying, or the like.[6]

Some would argue that Paul symbolically applies the custom of women wearing headdresses to women being submissive to their husbands (verse 10) and that in order to justify the symbolism, Paul uses the argument that the first woman was made from a man and was made for man's benefit and that she should therefore cover her head while praying and prophesying as a sign of a man's authority over her. Those who have this view use it to support the position that the authority men have over their wives was there from the very beginning, before the fall of Adam and Eve, and therefore men have always had the final say in marriage.

But, verse 12 teaches the following, "For as the woman originates from the man, so also the man has his birth through the woman; and all things originate from God." In other words, in the big scheme of things,

---

[5] In the days of Paul it was customary for a woman to cover her head as she worshipped in the church congregation. It was also customary for a woman not to shave or cut her hair. Any woman that went against these traditions was said to be dishonoring her husband. Paul writes about these things probably because there was some argument in the church regarding these issues. Clarification was needed. But Paul only defended his position on the issue by proclaiming that there was no other custom in all of the churches. Paul was adhering to the customs of the church. No one could argue with him because the churches were uniform in their customs regarding these things. This implies that if the churches had not been uniform in their customs regarding these things, then the custom could have been argued. A custom is not the same as a command of God. Customs change through generations. And as long as a custom does not go against the word of God, then in the eyesight of man and apparently in the eyesight of Paul through God's directive, there is nothing wrong with practicing it.

[6] Although long hair will always be seen as a mark for beauty where women are concerned, it is not necessary in today's world for a woman to have long hair in order to be thought of as beautiful. Furthermore, customs have changed and it is not a disgrace for a woman to cut her hair. See Chapter 5 for further discussion regarding the custom of women covering their heads.

it doesn't really matter that a woman came from man, because just as a woman came from a man, men come from women because they are born of women and both men and women are created by God. What Paul is saying here is that who came first, the man or the woman, is, when looking at the big picture, irrelevant.

Verse 11 teaches that both men and women, who are in the Lord, are dependent on each other. A woman is no more dependent on a man than a man is on a woman. Although a man has the final say in a marriage, he is just as dependent on his wife as she is on him.

But although some would say that verses 9 and 10 indicate that women are under the authority of their husbands due to the fact that a woman was made in order that she may help a man, others might argue that the scripture does not specifically teach that Eve was automatically born into submission before both she and Adam fell from Grace. Paul only argues that *since* women were made to help men *then* women should be under the authority of men, not that they *always were* under the authority of a man from the beginning of time. This view is backed up by verse 11 that says that "in the Lord" men and women (referring to Christian marriages) are not to be independent of one another. Again, verse 12 goes on to say that although a woman first came from a man, all men who were and are ever born come from the womb of a woman. Some take this to mean that Paul was only trying to emphasize the fact that men and women are equal as human beings, not equal in authority. However, others take this to mean that since the authority of a man is what was being talked about in verse 10, that the plan of God spoken of in verse 11 has more to do with the possibility that women were not born into submission (under a man's authority) but instead that God's original plan was that men and women would share in earthly authority (since they were not initially supposed to be independent of one another) with God being the head of both. The commentators of the NIV Study Bible present both arguments with the following quote:

> *sign of authority*. Understood by some to refer to the woman's authority as co-ruler with man in the creation (Ge 1:26-27). Others take the phrase to refer to the

man's authority as properly recognized by the woman
in her head covering.[7]

This brings us more fully to a second train of thought that says that
men have authority over their wives, not because women were created to
assist men with the things that God has given them to do in the earth and
not because a woman first came from man, but because God cursed Eve
to be ruled by her husband in response to her disobedience to him when
she ate of the tree of good and evil in the Garden of Eden. This train of
thought says that the husband's headship in a marriage is directly
associated with the cursed rule that he now has and that before the fall,
Adam's headship over his wife did not include the rule that a man's
headship now includes. A man's headship has now taken on a different
meaning than it did before the fall and is now associated with a curse. It
is argued that since most English speaking people understand the
definition of headship as meaning that one is in charge, one rules, and
one has the final say, that the husband headship itself, when defining it
this way, is a cursed thing and that this type of headship, if we are to
define headship as such, was not implemented until after the fall of Adam
and Eve. This train of thought says that the symbol of authority that a
woman must wear on her head means that she herself has authority
despite being under her husband's authority. Both trains of thought will
be examined further under the next subheading.

"AND HE WILL RULE OVER YOU"

The position that says that a man's rule over his wife is a curse and
that therefore a man's authority in the home has a curse associated with
it, is rarely presented in the pulpit. But let's take a look at the main
verses of scripture at the brunt of the debate:

> [11]And he said, "Who told you that you
> were naked? Have you eaten from the tree
> that I commanded you not to eat from?"

---

[7] The NIV Study Bible, 10th Anniversary Edition. Kenneth Baker, General
Editor. Copyright ©1995 by The Zondervan Corporation p. 1750. Used by
permission of Zondervan.

¹²The man said, "The woman you put here
with me—she gave me some fruit from the
tree, and I ate it."
¹³Then the LORD God said to the woman,
"What is this you have done?"
The woman said, "The serpent deceived
me, and I ate."
¹⁴So the LORD God said to the serpent,
"Because you have done this,
  "Cursed are you above all the livestock
and all the wild animals!
You will crawl on your belly
And you will eat dust
All the days of your life
¹⁵And I will put enmity
between you and the woman,
and between your offspring and hers;
he will crush your head,
and you will strike his heel."

¹⁶To the woman he said,

"I will greatly increase your pains in
childbearing;
with pain you will give birth to children.
Your desire will be for your husband
And he will rule over you."

¹⁷To Adam he said, "Because you listened
to your wife and ate from the tree about
which I commanded you, 'You must not eat
of it,'

"Cursed is the ground because of you;
through painful toil you will eat of it
all the days of your life.
¹⁸It will produce thorns and thistles for you,
and you will eat the plants of the field.
¹⁹By the sweat of your brow

you will eat your food
until you return to the ground,
since from it you were taken;
for dust you are
and to dust you will return."

[20]Adam named his wife Eve, because she
would become the mother of all the living.
(Genesis 3:11-20 NIV)

As previously discussed, after God created Adam, he placed him in the Garden of Eden to take care of it.[8] Adam was commanded not to eat the fruit from the tree of Knowledge of good and evil, but he could eat from any other tree in the garden.[9] Eventually God made a companion for Adam, a woman (Eve) who was to be his helper. Eve was deceived by the serpent, ate of the tree of the Knowledge of good and evil, and convinced her husband to do the same.

Because of their transgressions, God cursed all three, the serpent, Eve, and Adam (in that order). And the ground was cursed as well. The original Hebrew word used for the word *cursed* in the verses of scripture above, is *arar* which is defined as to *bitterly curse*. A curse is defined in the English language as a severe affliction or torment. It is one of the methods God uses to punish people. Essentially, a curse can be a long lasting or *everlasting punishment*. Adam and Eve were both punished everlastingly. The punishment would last for as long as the two of them lived and also transcend dispensations to effect every man and woman thereafter.[10]

God cursed the serpent for deceiving the woman. God cursed the woman for eating the fruit and encouraging her husband to do the same, and God cursed the man for eating the fruit and allowing his wife to lead

---

[8] For the full historical account of Adam and Eve, read Genesis chapters 2 and 3 (see your Bible).

[9] "And the LORD God took the man, and put him into the garden of Eden to dress it and to keep it. And the LORD God commanded the man, saying, Of every tree of the garden thou mayest freely eat; But of the tree of the knowledge of good and evil, thou shall not eat of it: for in the day that thou eastest thereof thou shalt surely die." Genesis 2:15-17

[10] See Introduction.

him astray. The serpent was cursed to crawl on his belly. The woman's curse was twofold. She was to have increased pain in childbearing and she was to be ruled by her husband. The man was cursed to have to work hard in order to put food on his table because the entire ground which bore forth abundantly was now cursed because of Adam's sin. All of these curses are still in operation today. The curse God placed on the ground was the only curse of the five curses[11] that effected all human beings, men and women alike.[12] The curse that God placed on Adam theoretically effects all men whether they are married or single. The two curses placed on Eve were the only curses that are arguably conditional because they are theoretically only directly applicable to married women. This is not to say that the curses of increased pain in childbearing and husband rule do not apply to single women but that they only apply to single women indirectly since theoretically a single woman must marry in order to feel the direct effect of these curses.

A single woman has no husband who rules over her. She is free to rule over her own life and make her own final decisions about everything: where she lives, where she works, money, friends, career, and so on. A married woman must concern herself with how her husband feels about these things, since he now rules her and therefore gets the final say in all of her affairs. Let's look further:

> [3]But I want you to know and realize that Christ is the Head of every man, the head of a woman is her husband, and the Head of Christ is God. (1 Corinthians 11:3 Amp.)

The scripture teaches us that Christ is the head of every man, that the head of a woman is her husband, and that the head of Christ is God. Of course then, if a woman has no husband, then Christ is her head. Christ is the one whom she submits to. There is no middleman, so to speak. There is no man that rules her life, per se that she must submit to. However, as we will discuss later, the fact that a man is the head of his wife means that he has earthly authority over her but it does not mean

---

[11] The serpent was cursed, Adam was cursed, Eve was cursed twice, and the ground was cursed.

[12] However, one person may more strongly feel the effects of this curse than another, depending upon which area of the world they live in.

that she must submit to his demands if those demands go against the will of God.

It is essential that the Greek word that is used for the word *head* in 1st Corinthians 11:3 be presented in order that we may get a better understanding of what Paul was saying when he said that the head of the woman is her husband. According to Bristow, there are two Greek words that can be translated into the English word *head*. They are *arche* and *kephale*. *Arche* is the Greek word that is used to denote leadership. It signifies someone as being primary and foremost in importance, significance, and power. The word is associated with those who rule, those who are in charge, those who are the boss, and so forth. *Kephale* means *"head (of a body); top (stone in a building); by extension: someone or something in the primary place, the point of origin."*[13]

The Greek word that is used for *head* in 1st Corinthians 11:3 is *kephale*. When using the word *kephale* to denote someone who is the head of something the word *head* does not take on the meaning of ruler, boss, or person in charge but instead is indicative of a primary position someone may be in when looking at a part of a whole. For example, most of us would consider the physical head of one's body as the *kephale* of the body. If everything is working properly then the head and the rest of the body will work agreeably together. The head does not necessarily rule the body but instead sits in a primary position of a well functioning unit. The head is the primary extension of the body. Some would argue that it is in this sense that Adam was the head of Eve before the fall just as they would argue that it is in this sense that God is the head (again, *kephale* is the Greek word used here) of Christ and Christ is the head of man and man is the head of his wife. Bristow puts it the following way,

> It [*kephale*] was never used to mean "leader" or "boss" or "chief" or "ruler." Kephale is also a miltiary term. It means "one who leads," but not in the sense of "director." *Kephale* did not denote "general," or "captain," or someone who orders the troops from a safe distance; quite the opposite, a *kephale* was one who went before the troops, the leader in the sense of

---

[13] Zondervan NIV Exhaustive Concordance, Second Edition, edited by Edward W. Goddrick , John R. Kohlenberger III, James A. Swanson, copyright © 1999. 1990 by The Zondervan Corporation, p. 1564, Fair use.

being in the lead, the first one into battle. Therefore, the two words in Greek can both be translated into one English word *head*. One word means "boss" the other means "physical head" (or, sometimes, "the first soldier into battle"). Unfortunately, an English-speaking person who reads that the husband is head of his wife will normally conclude that this means the husband is to rule over his wife.[14]

Most men indeed equate headship to ruling over. But it appears that being the head and being in charge are two different things. Some argue that a man's headship simply has to do with position while his being in charge has to do with the cursed rule. The two are not really the same, but many men speak as if they are. Others argue that since the headship of the Father over Christ is a good thing then the headship a man has is a good thing, since both were spoken of in the same verse. This would be true if men did not lump being the head and being the ruler together. But they often times do. They go on to argue that since the Father has always been the head of the Son, then Adam was the head of Eve before the fall. They believe that since the two headships are compared they must be alike in every way. But the main point has less to do with the headship, and more to do with the rule that is now encompassed within that headship. This rule is what scripture tells us is a cursed thing for a wife.

There is no scripture that teaches us that God's headship over Christ has any cursedness about it. As a matter of fact, when taking into consideration Bristow's explanation of things and the fact that *kephale* is the Greek word that is used for the word *head* when speaking of the Father's headship to Jesus, it appears that the Father's headship is not one in which he is "the ruler," per se, but one in which he is in a primary position as his part in a whole. The Orthodox Church has always understood the Father, Son, and Holy Ghost (one God represented in three beings/persons) to hold different offices but be equal in authority. Some would argue that Adam and Eve fit into a similar mode (but of course only on a human level) before the fall and that they were equal in authority but held different positions. Therefore, when looking at the fact

---

[14] *What Paul really said about Women*, by John Temple Bristow, copyright © 1988 by John Temple Bristow, published by HarperSanFransico, a division of Harper Collins publishers. pp.36-37. Fair use.

that God is God and men are mere mortals, there is a huge difference between the Father's headship over Christ and a man's headship over his wife. The difference being that scripture teaches us that a man's rule over his wife is now a cursed thing for a woman and that this rule is now intertwined with a man's headship. But God's headship over Christ is not associated with any cursed rule as man's headship now is. Therefore, some would further argue that since a man's headship in the home is now accompanied by a cursed rule that the headship itself (which is a different headship than before the fall) is now a cursed thing as well.

Many men attempt to minimize the fact that there is a curse associated with the rule that men have over their wives. In their attempts to minimize the curse, they turn to the scripture we read in 1st Corinthians 11:8-12. Let's take a look at it again:

> [8]For man does not originate from woman, but woman from man;
> [9]for indeed man was not created for the woman's sake, but woman for the man's sake.
> [10]Therefore the woman ought to have a symbol of authority on her head, because of the angels.
> [11]However, in the Lord, neither is woman independent of man, nor is man independent of woman.
> [12]For as the woman originates from the man, so also the man has his birth through the woman; and all things originate from God. (NASB)

Men who cite this scripture to defend their attempt at minimizing the fact that the type of rule men have over their wives today is a curse for women, shrug their shoulders and say "See, wives were under the authority of their husbands from the beginning. This is the way God set things up. So what's the problem? Why focus on the curse?" The rebuttal is: "Saying that husbands had authority over their wives from the beginning does not minimize the fact that the authority (rule) men now have since the fall of Adam and Eve is an authority that is a cursed thing for wives. The scripture (Genesis 3:16) tells us that it is. And even if we were to say that Adam had authority over Eve before the fall of the two of them, we would then say that when before, a man's authority over his wife was not a cursed thing to a woman, that *now* it is. There is now a difference between what used to be a man's authority over his wife before the fall of Adam and Eve and the authority that a man has over his wife after the fall in today's time. The latter authority is a grievous thing because it is now synonymous with the cursed rule. And this cursed rule is applicable to all women who are married."

If we say that Adam had authority over his wife before the fall, we can safely assume that there was nothing cursed about his authority, there was no cursed rule that was encompassed within his authority, and that his authority was non-oppressive. However, after the fall, God cursed Eve to be ruled by her husband. Therefore, a man's authority now has a cursed rule attached to it. It has a negative aspect that wasn't there before. Since this cursed rule is now embodied in the husband's authority, then his authority has some cursedness about it. And if this authority is to be made synonymous with a man's headship (as many men do) then the headship would also have to have some cursedness about it.

Again, some would argue that a man's authoritative headship over his wife did not exist before the fall of Adam and Eve and that the two were equal in authority before the fall. They'd argue further that if Adam *did* have headship over his wife it was only the *kephale* type of headship that he had. They'd say that the authoritative headship that exists now exists is a result of or is synonymous with the rule that Eve was cursed to bear.

To support their position, they might argue that scripture implies that prior to Eve's curse, her husband had no rule over her since Genesis 3: 16 documents that God said to Eve, "your desire will be for your husband and he *will* rule over you." Their argument here is that Adam had not ruled over Eve prior to this, otherwise, it would seem that the verse would read that Adam would *continue* to rule over Eve, or rule over her with more vigor. They might further their argument by pointing out that the same reasoning could be used when looking at the curse of the serpent as well as the curse of the ground due to Adam's sin. The assumption is that before the serpent was cursed to crawl on his belly that standing upright had been his original and normal state of being. The serpent was not crawling prior to the curse. Similarly, the ground gave forth abundantly before the fall of Adam. God's original intent was for Adam to eat comfortably from the produce of the ground, not from the sweat of his brow. They would therefore conclude that likewise, Eve's original normal state was to be equal in authority with Adam, and not to be ruled by him. They may argue further by saying that if authority of the husband over the wife is how things were supposed to be in the beginning, and if the curse of husband rule simply did nothing but bring out the original or "normal" scheme of things, so to speak, then the same must be said for the curse that the serpent had to endure as well as for the curse that Adam had to endure (which includes the ground being cursed). But the same cannot be said for either. The curses placed upon the serpent, Adam, and the ground went against the original and normal scheme of things and therefore it can be argued that the curses placed upon Eve went against the original and normal scheme of things as well.

Those who believe that the man's headship over his wife in the marital home is itself the curse of Genesis 3:16, might also point to the Hebrew meaning of the word *rule* that is used in the verse of scripture in question. The Hebrew word used for *rule* in the phrase "and he will rule over you" is *masal* and means, according to the Zondervan NIV Exhaustive Concordance *to rule, govern, control; make one a ruler, dominion, gain control, has right, in charge, made ruler, master.*[15] The argument here is that the headship a man now has over his wife encompasses some of the same meanings. Therefore, if God cursed wives by putting their husbands in charge of them, then it stands that their husbands were not in charge of them previously. Otherwise, the curse was there all the time. The advent of the curse implies that there was a change from one state to another. And the implication is that the state of the woman changed from her husband not being in charge of her to her husband being in charge of her. Otherwise, where is the curse? Some would argue that the authoritative headship was there before the fall but now after the fall the rule under that headship can be oppressive and this is where the curse comes in.

Some might also argue against the premise that since Eve was created as a helper she was automatically under Adam's authority, by arguing that although Eve is described as a "help meet" in Genesis 2:18, the Hebrew that is used for the word *help* in this text is *ezer* which means *to aid, to help* and is the same Hebrew term used in Psalms 33:20 when describing God as "our *help* and our shield." God is our help, but this does not mean we have authority over him. Instead he has authority over us. Therefore, to be a help to someone doesn't necessarily mean that the person providing the help is under the authority of the person he or she is

---

[15] Zondervan NIV Exhaustive Concordance, Second Edition, edited by Edward W. Goddrick , John R. Kohlenberger III, James A. Swanson, copyright © 1999. 1990 by The Zondervan Corporation, p. 1447, Fair use.

helping. They would therefore conclude that it was possible for Eve to be Adam's "help meet" without Adam having authority over her or without Adam having an *arche* type of headship over her. Again, some might also argue that the verses of scripture found in 1st Corinthians 11:8-12 (discussed previously) do not concretely indicate that from the beginning of time men had authority over women.

There are revered theologians of times past that have commented on Eve's second curse, which has to do with the rule of her husband over her. We will briefly take a look at the comments of three of these revered biblical scholars: Adam Clarke, Robert Jamieson, and Matthew Henry. Henry's comments appear to agree more with the position that says a man's authority over his wife was the way God arranged things in the beginning, whereas the comments of Clarke and Jamieson appear to agree more with the position that says that a man's authority over his wife is synonymous with a husband's rule and is therefore, itself, a cursed thing and was not there before the fall.

Adam Clarke was born in Ireland in 1762 and died in 1832. He began work on his commentary of the Bible in 1825. His commentary was published in 1826 and has been heralded as one of the most authoritative commentaries ever. This is what he says about the curse that women must bear:

> *Unto the woman he said.* She being second in the transgression is brought up the second to receive her condemnation, and to hear her punishment: I will greatly multiply, or "multiplying thy sorrows, and multiply those sorrows by other sorrows, and this during conception and pregnancy, and particularly so in parturition or childbearing. And this curse has fallen in a heavier degree on the woman than on any other female. It is added farther, *Thy desire shall be to thy husband*—thou shalt not be able to shun the great pain and peril for childbearing, for thy desire, thy appetite, shall be to thy husband; and he shall rule over thee, though at their creation both were formed with equal rights, and the woman had probably as much right to rule as the man; but subjection to the will of her husband is one part of her curse; and so very capricious is this will, often that a sorer punishment no human

81

being can well have, to be at all in a state of liberty, and under the protection of wise and equal laws. [16]

Clarke is basically saying that neither Adam nor Eve initially had rule over the other but that both had equal rule and equal rights. He is therefore saying that there was no husband authority before the fall of Adam and Eve.[17] He continues by saying that the subjection of a woman to the will of her husband is indeed part of her curse that she must suffer. Clarke goes even further and says that a man's rule over his wife is so capricious that a human being could be under no worse a punishment than a woman who is under the cursed rule of her husband. He concludes that because she is now under the subjection of her husband's capricious will that a wife is no longer free as a human being; she is no longer in the state of liberty that she once was in before the curse.

Robert Jamieson was born in Scotland in 1802 and obtained a doctorate of Divinity from the University of Glasgow in 1848. His commentaries are from the books of Genesis through Esther. This is what he says about the curse that women must bear:

> *Unto the woman he said, I will greatly multiply thy sorrow*—She was doomed as a wife and mother to suffer pain of body and distress of mind. From being the help-meet of man and the partner of his affections, her condition would henceforth be that of humble subjection.[18]

Jamieson doesn't mince words. He says that the woman was doomed as wife and mother to suffer pain of body (childbirth) and distress of mind (as a result of her husband's rule). It appears as if Jamieson, like Clarke believes that the rule of the husband (the authority of a man over his wife) did not exist before the fall of Adam and Eve, at least not this kind of authority. Jamieson describes the condition of the wife before the

---

[16] The Bethany Parallel Commentary. Copyright ©1983 by Bethany House Publishers. p. 17, used by permission of Bethany House.

[17] Whether or not he separated the two types of headship and would have agreed that although no *arche* type of headship existed a *kephale* type of headship may have existed, is questionable.

[18] Ibid., p. 17, used by permission.

curse as a helper and partner and then describes the condition of the wife after the curse as one who would now be in humble subjection, which he associates with doom.

Matthew Henry was born in England in 1662 and died in 1714. He began writing his commentary of the Bible in 1704 and completed it in 1714. Of all the commentaries, his has been the one that is most widely used worldwide. He says the following about Eve's curse:

> *Wives, be in subjection to your own husbands*; but the entrance of sin has made that duty a punishment, which otherwise it would not have been. If Eve had not eaten forbidden fruit herself, and tempted her husband to eat it, she would never have complained of her subjection; therefore it ought never to be complained of, though harsh; but sin must be complained of, that made it so. Those wives, who not only despise and disobey their husbands, but domineer over them, do not consider that they not only violate a divine law, but thwart a divine sentence.[19]

Henry agrees that the rule of a man over his wife is a cursed thing but believes that initially it wasn't. He believes that Adam's authority over Eve was there all along, before the fall and that his authority was not a negative thing until both Adam and Eve fell into sin. Afterwards, Adam's authority became part of Eve's curse. Thus he says that the woman's mandate to submit to her husband is punishment for her and implies that a man's authority over his wife is now a harsh and cursed thing. Henry goes even further to say that a woman should not complain about being under subjection since it was the woman's sin in the beginning that has resulted in the curse of her husband's harsh rule over her.

Henry also says that a domineering wife violates what he calls a "divine law' (initial authority before the fall) as well as thwarts a divine sentence (the punishment of submission that all wives must now forever endure). The second of Eve's curse stated in its entirety says that Eve will *desire* her husband and he will rule over her. There are some theologians today who interpret, as Henry did, this *desire* to mean that

---

[19] Ibid, pp.16-17, used by permission.

women, for the most part, will want to control and domineer their husbands and in return their husbands will rule over them. They believe that this *controlling behavior* (desire) triggers the cursed rule, and that the rule is not there without the controlling behavior (desire). But this is like saying that the curse God placed upon the nation of Canaan, wherein the Canaanites were sentenced to be the slaves of the nations that would come from Shem and Japheth, did not exist as long as the slave masters were kind and the slaves were obedient.[20] No matter how cordial the relationship between a slave and his slave master was, and no matter how willingly the slave submitted to the slave master, the cursedness of enslavement still existed. And no matter how cordial the relations are between a husband and his wife (whether this means she willingly submits all of the time or he makes certain not to oppress her), the cursedness of his rule still exists. The NIV Study Bible has this to say about the desire of a wife for her husband and the rule of a husband over his wife:

> Her sexual attraction for the man, and his headship
> over her, will become intimate aspects of her life in
> which she experiences trouble and anguish rather than
> unalloyed joy and blessing.[21]

Most people cannot fathom a woman not initially desiring her husband (after all, Genesis 3:16 says that the woman will desire her husband as if she had not previously desired him before the fall), so they figure that the word *desire* must really mean something other than *desire*. Consequently many theologians teach that the word *desire* that is used in the text really doesn't mean desire at all, but means *to control*. With this, the blame of the cursedness of a man's authority in the home is put on the woman (just like Adam tried to blame Eve for his transgressions). The thinking is, if she wasn't so busy trying to control her husband then her husband wouldn't be so busy trying to rule over her and if she'd just voluntarily submit to his will, then he wouldn't *have to* rule over her. These men don't see the cursed rule, in and of itself, as being present in

---

[20] Genesis 9:18-29 documents the account of the curse of the Canaanites. (see your Bible).
[21] NIV Study Bible, 10th Anniversary Edition, Kenneth Baker, Editor. Copyright ©1995 by Zondervan Corporation. p.11 Fair use.

a marriage regardless as to whether or not the woman is submissive and/or controlling. But it is.

In the following quote, one of the 20th century's most renowned theologians, John MacAuthor Jr., argues in favor of the word *desire* being translated as *to control*. This is what he says:

> The Arabic root for the word translated "desire" means "to seek control." So, the curse is this: The man is installed as the ruler, but the woman is going to seek to control him.[22]

The Bible was written in Hebrew, some Aramaic, and Greek. Many Hebrew and Aramaic words originate from Arabic. However, each language still has its separate meanings for words used. Although the root word for the Arabic word *desire* might indeed be *to control*, this does not automatically mean that the Arabic word for *desire* was what was used in Genesis 3:16 or that the Hebrew word for *desire* automatically means *to control* simply because the etymology of the word may have originated in the Arabic language. We can make the same argument for the meaning of many English words today. Many English words are derivatives of Greek and Latin words. But despite the original meaning of an English word in Latin or Greek, a particular English word today can have a new meaning or additional meaning than the word had when first derived from the Latin or the Greek. Take for instance the word *apology*. The Greek root for the word *apology* means *to defend*. So the word *apologetic* has developed to have a double meaning in English. An apologetic piece of literature is a piece of writing that defends a certain way of thinking. However, an apologetic person is one whom expresses remorse. Same word, two complete different meanings. This happens quite a bit with languages. Languages are always changing and evolving.

When we investigate as to whether or not other notable theologians agree with MacAurthor's translation of the word *desire*, we see that many of them don't.

Edward W. Goodrick, John R. Kohlenberger lll, and James A. Swanson, the translators responsible for the Second Edition of the

---

[22] Jesus' Teaching on Divorce. Study Notes. John MacAuthor Copyright © 1983 by Word of Grace Communications. p. 27, Fair use.

Zondervan NIV Exhaustive Concordance,[23] and Thomas L. Thomas, TH.D, the General Editor of the *New American Standard Exhaustive Concordance* translate the word *desire* in Genesis 3:16 from the Hebrew word "*t'suqa*," which means *to long after, to desire* in the Hebrew. With this rendering, some would argue that, when the scripture says that the woman will desire her husband and he will rule over her, there is no indication from the original Hebrew that this desire actually means that she will try to control her husband. As a matter of fact, it would be safe to conclude that the husband is the one who will seek to control his wife which will come along with the oppressive rule that he now has, but despite this, she will still desire him, want to be with him, and long after him.

In their book, *Hard Sayings of the Bible*, Walter C. Kaiser Jr., Peter H. Davids, F.F. Bruce, and Manfred T. Brauch offer the following explanation:

> The meaning of the second part of the woman's penalty centers around two very important words that have a most amazing translation history, "desire" and "will rule." Seldom has so much mischief been caused by a translation error that became institutionalized....
>
> The Hebrew word *t'suqah*, now almost universally translated as "desire," was previously rendered as "turning." The word appears in the Hebrew Old Testament only three times: here in Genesis 3:16, in Genesis 4:7 and in Song of Songs 7:10. Of the twelve known ancient versions (the Greek Septuagint, the Syriac Peshitta, the Samaritan Pentateuch, the Old Latin, the Sahidic, the Bohairic, the Ethiopic, the Arabic, Aquila's Greek, Symmachus's Greek, Theodotion's Greek and the Latin Vulgate), almost every one (twenty-one out of twenty-eight times) renders these three instances *t'suqah* as "turning," not "desire."
>
> Likewise, the church fathers (Clement of Rome, Irenaeus, Tertullian, Origen, Epiphanius and Jerome, along with Philo, a Jew who died about A.D. 50) seem

---

[23] Winner of the Gold Medallion Book Award.

to be ignorant of any other sense for this word *t͡suqah* than the translation of "turning." Furthermore, the Latin rendering was *conversio* and the Greek was *apostrophe* or *epistrophe,* words all meaining "a turning....."

It is time the church returned to the real meaning of this word. The sense of Genesis 3:16 is simply this: As a result of her sin, Eve would turn away from her sole dependence on God and turn now to her husband. The results would not at all be pleasant, warned God, as he announced this curse.....

The Hebrew reads, "You are turning away [from God!] to your husband, and [as a result] he will rule over you [take advantage of you]."[24]

To *turn to* one's husband and *to desire* one's husband are not exactly the same but do have similar meanings. Both imply a longing after. However to control one's husband and to long after or turn to (desire) one's husband have two different meanings altogether. It appears that the arguments against the position that the text is actually saying that a woman will want to control her husband, is actually stronger than the arguments given in favor of such a translation.

We cannot ignore the fact that after the fall of Adam and Eve a man's rule over his wife became part of the function of his headship in the home. Therefore now a great part of a man being the head is to be in charge, to rule, to have ultimate authority. This authority or rule is now a grievous thing. This is not to say that marriage itself is a curse or that marriage itself is a grievous thing overall. But this is to say that the rule that a husband now has over his wife in the context of his headship within his marriage is most certainly a curse for women. It must be understood that no man's rule over his wife is void of some cursedness. Since, according to Genesis 3:16, every woman who marries is automatically cursed by her husband's rule, then it can be logically concluded that the rule of every husband brings with it a curse.

[24] *Hard Sayings of the Bible* by Walter C. Kaiser Jr., Peter H. Davids, F.F. Bruce, Manfred T. Brauch. Copyright © 1996 of *one volume edition* by Walter C. Kaiser, Peter H. Davids, F.F. Bruce, and Manfred T. Brauch, published by Intervarsity Press. pp. 97-98. Fair use.

However, how strongly a woman feels the cursedness of her husband's rule depends on the personality of her husband and whether or not he loves her the way the Bible directs him to. Some wives feel the effects of this curse everyday, while other wives hardly feel it at all.

This is a difficult thing for many men to accept. It is not to their advantage for their authority in the home (which encompasses the rule) to be recognized as cursed, even if only in part. They find it hard to look at their rule as something negative. They want to feel that it is a positive thing. And so, there is some resistance on the part of some men to accept the fact that their authority in the home will at some point afflict their wives. Along with this resistance comes the tendency to minimize the negativity of the rule. One way of minimizing negativity is to blame the person who is the receiver of negativity for the negativity itself. Hence, many men are drawn to the view that says *desire* means *to control*.

Again, although the rule a man has over his wife is a cursed thing in a marriage, this does not mean that marriage itself is cursed. Marriage is a blessing for many despite the curse of the man's rule within the home. Similarly, increased pain in childbearing is most certainly a curse for women, but not the child itself. In general, children are a blessing for many despite the pain of childbirth.

The fact that a man's rule over his wife is a cursed thing for any woman who is married, is certainly a humbling realization for men and the more men there are who accept this fact, hopefully the more men there will be who will endeavor to treat their wives in a non-oppressive way (if they are not already).

Whether or not Eve was born into submission is really not the issue here. It has no bearing as to whether or not husband rule is a cursed thing. According to Genesis 3:16, it is, simple as that. There are those that have preached entire sermons on the subject of women submitting in marriage without inclusion of the fact that women are cursed by the rule of their husbands.

The fact that there is now something grievous about the authority a man has in the home may be the main reason that the apostle Paul spelled out and emphasized how a man is to treat his wife. It must be understood that God has given men rule over their wives not because men are wiser, better, stronger, smarter, or more spiritual than women, and not because men deserve it, or have earned it. It is a curse. If men follow the guidelines that the apostle Paul set forth in this dispensation of Grace,[25] then the grievousness of the curse of a man's rule over his wife will decrease in each individual marriage thus making marriage more tolerable for men and women alike. The discussion under the following subheading takes a look at the guidelines the apostle Paul gives men regarding how they are to treat their wives.

THE OTHER "S" WORD.....SACRIFICE

When it comes to how married couples should treat one another, many preachers tend to put the greatest emphasis on wives "submitting" to their husbands. But although women are instructed to submit to their husbands, there are also certain instructions that God gave as to how men are to treat their wives. The tide is changing a little and preachers are increasingly beginning to present this side of the marital relationship with the same vivaciousness as they present the side that says wives are to submit to their husbands. Let's take a look at how the Bible says men are to treat their wives:

> [25]Husbands, love your wives, just as Christ also loved the church and gave Himself for her, [26]that he might sanctify and cleanse her with the washing of water by the word.
> [27]that he might present her to Himself a glorious church, not having spot or wrinkle or any such thing, but that she should be holy and without blemish.
> [28]So husbands ought to love their own wives as their own bodies; he who loves his wife loves himself.
> [29]For no one has ever hated his own flesh, but nourishes it and cherishes it, just as the Lord does the church.
> [30]For we are members of His body, of His flesh and of His bones.
> [31]"For this reason a man shall leave his father and mother and be joined to his wife, and the two shall become one flesh."

---

[25] See Introduction.

[32]This is a great mystery, but I speak concerning Christ and the church.
[33]nevertheless let each one of you in particular so love his own wife as himself, and let the wife see that she respects her husband. (Ephesians 5:25-33 NKJV)

Since there is quite a bit to consider when examining the verses of scripture just quoted, the verses will be broken down into subheadings in order to systematically examine the text.

Ephesians 5:25-26

Verses 25 and 26 say, *"Husbands, love your wives, just as Christ also loved the church and gave Himself for her, that He might sanctify and cleanse her with the washing of water by the word."* These verses emphasize how important it is for husbands to love their wives, not only in words, but in deeds as well. Paul specifically instructs men to love their wives "as Christ loved the church and gave Himself for her." This then, is not just any kind of love, but a specific kind of love. It is a sacrificial love. A man who truly loves his wife will sacrifice himself for her. When we look at how much Christ loved the church, we see that Christ died for the sake of the church. He sacrificed himself totally for the sake of the church.[26] By doing so, he disregarded his own wants and desires and put the needs of the church above himself. The following verses of scripture give credibility to this:

[32]Then they came to a place which was named Gethsemane; and He said to His disciples, "Sit here while I pray."
[33]And he took Peter, James, and John with Him, and He began to be troubled and deeply distressed.
[34]Then He said to them, "My soul is exceedingly sorrowful, even to death. Stay here and watch.

---

[26] Jesus Christ died to atone for our sins. Anyone who therefore accepts him as Lord and Savior, thus repenting of their sins, is henceforth a member of the church, the body of Christ. See Introduction.

90

³⁵He went a little farther, and fell on the ground, and prayed that if it were possible, the hour might pass from Him.

³⁶And He said, "Abba, Father, all things are possible for You. Take this cup away from Me: nevertheless, not what I will, but what You will."

³⁷Then He came and found them sleeping, and said to Peter, "Simon, are you sleeping? Could you not watch one hour?

³⁸"Watch and pray, lest you enter into temptation. The spirit indeed is willing, but the flesh is weak."

³⁹Again He went away and prayed, and spoke the same words.

⁴⁰ And when He returned, He found them asleep again, for their eyes were heavy; and they did not know what to answer Him.

⁴¹Then He came a third time and said to them, "Are you still sleeping and resting? It is enough! The hour has come; behold, the Son of Man is being betrayed into the hands of sinners.

⁴²Rise, let us be going. See, My betrayer is at hand."

⁴³And immediately, while He was still speaking, Judas, one of the twelve, with a great multitude with swords and clubs, came from the chief priests and the scribes and the elders. (Mark 14:32-43 NKJV)

Verse 32 tells us that Jesus' intent while he was in Gethsemane was to pray. He asked the majority of his disciples to wait for him and took Peter, James, and John with him into a particular place in Gethsemane.

Jesus expressed to the three that he was very sad, even to the point of death. Jesus asked the three to stand guard while he went a little ways to pray. In his prayer, Jesus asked the Father to "take this cup" from him. In other words, Jesus did not want to suffer on the cross. He prayed that the Father would take the assignment away from him. Jesus knew that what he was asking of the Father was not impossible for the Father to do.

Although it was Jesus' desire to be free from the pains of the cross, Jesus knew that the Father's will was what should come first. Therefore when Jesus prayed, he prayed with the respectable inclusion of the understanding that the Father's will be what was to be done, and not his own will (the will of Jesus) concerning this. After praying, Jesus returned to where he left Peter, James, and John but found them asleep. Jesus scolded the three for falling asleep when they should have been watching, and then he went away to where he was before, and prayed the same prayer as he prayed earlier. But the Father's response to Jesus was not as Jesus would have preferred. Jesus was destined to bear the cross.

At the third time that Jesus caught his disciples sleeping, he woke them up and told them that the hour had come. At that point, Judas, along with several armed people and many officials surrounded Jesus in order to take him away to be tried and crucified. The Father allowed Jesus to be delivered into the hands of his enemies despite Jesus' request to the contrary.

The point is that Jesus loved us so much that he sacrificed his life for us even though he did not want to go through the suffering and degradation that it took to do so. If submission of a wife to her husband is to be emphasized and re-emphasized in the pulpit, then the kind of love that a man is commanded to show his wife should be emphasized and re-emphasized as well. A man is supposed to have the same kind of sacrificial love towards his wife that Jesus had towards us. Apparently this kind of sacrificial love is the kind in which a man puts the needs and desires of his wife before his own needs and desires, even if he doesn't necessarily want to or even if it pains him to do it. This is just what Jesus did. Because he loved us, he put us before his own needs and desires, even though it pained him to do so. Just as Jesus showed us how much he loves us by sacrificing his life for us, a man should show his wife how much he loves her by making sacrifices for her. This is how he is commanded to love his wife. And just as there is suffering in submission, there is suffering in sacrifice. A man should be willing to suffer in sacrifice to his wife no less than a woman should be willing to suffer in submission to her husband.

Just as Paul teaches, in his letter to the Ephesian Church, that all Christians are to submit to one another, while it is specifically emphasized that women are to submit to their husbands, Jesus taught that all Christians are to love one another as Christ loved the church, while it is specifically emphasized that men are to love their wives as Christ loved the church. Let's take a look at what Jesus said concerning this:

> [12]"This is my commandment, that you love one another as I have loved you. [13]No one has greater love than this, to lay down one's life for one's friends. [14]You are my friends if you do what I command you. [15]I do not call you servants any longer, because the servant does not know what the master is doing; but I have called you friends, because I have made known to you everything that I have heard from my Father." (John 15:12-15 NRSV)

Jesus was specifically talking to the twelve disciples, but what he said applies to all Christians. If Christians are to love one another as Christ loved his friends (by dying for them), then certainly the generalization applies to married Christians as well. They are to love their spouses in the same sacrificial way.

Again, men are specifically instructed to love their wives as Christ loved the church just as women are specifically instructed to submit to their husbands. So just as the specification for a woman to submit to her husband makes married women more accountable (than their husbands) to submit to their spouses, the specification for men to love their wives as Christ loved the church, makes married men more accountable (than their wives) to love their spouses.

With this in mind, it would be negligent not to present the detailed definition of love that is found in the book of 1st Corinthians. Of course the instructions on how to love that are presented in 1st Corinthians apply to all Christians. But since a man has specifically been instructed to love his wife as Christ loves the church, then he must always make certain to show his wife the kind of love that is described in the word of God. Let's look at that definition of love cited in 1st Corinthians:

> [1]Though I speak with the tongues of men and of angels, but have not love, I have become sounding brass or a clanging cymbal.
> [2]And though I have the gift of prophecy, and understand all mysteries and all knowledge, and though I have all faith, so that I could remove mountains, but have not love, I am nothing.

³And though I bestow all my good to feed the poor, and
though I give my body to be burned, but have not love,
it profits me nothing. (1 Corinthians 13:1-3 NKJV)

The verses of scripture above teach us that if a man (or woman) has
great status and great gifts, but has no love for his fellow man, then he is
ineffective. He does not gain anything by the good deeds that he does,
because he does not do what he does in love. Despite his great status and
the gifts that he has, he is nothing because he has no love for people. The
same then, can be applied to husbands. If a man does not love his wife,
as he should, then his headship in the home profits him nothing. Even if
he is doing everything to take care of her, if he does not love her as
commanded then the success of his marriage is at stake. Let's look
further:

⁴Love is patient, love is kind. It does not envy, it does
not boast, it is not proud. ⁵It is not rude, it is not self-
seeking, it is not easily angered, it keeps no records of
wrongs. ⁶Love does not delight in evil but rejoices with
the truth. ⁷It always protects, always trusts, always
hopes, always preserves. ⁸Love never fails.....
(1 Corinthians 13:4-8 NIV)

To love someone means to show patience and to be longsuffering
(verse 4). A man who is not patient with his wife is not showing her that
he loves her.

Love is kind (verse 4). A man who truly loves his wife will treat her
with kindness. In doing this, he will restrain himself from criticizing her
(unless it is truly constructive), from complaining, from nagging her.

Love does not envy (verse 4). Therefore, a man who loves his wife
will not become jealous of the relationship his wife has with her friends
and family nor will he become jealous of the relationship that his wife
has with God. He will not become jealous of the gifts that God has given
her in order that she may more perfectly serve the Lord. He will not try
to hold her back in doing what the Lord has burdened her heart to do in
serving Him. If a man loves his wife, he will not compete with her. It is
a true saying that competition breeds contempt. No man competes with
his wife unless he is jealous of her. And any man who competes with his

wife on a continuous basis will most likely begin to have contempt for her.

If a man truly loves his wife, he will not act rudely towards her (verse 5). He will not be demanding of her. He will not behave dogmatically towards her. He will always greet his wife warmly. He will not take advantage of his position in the home. He will not mock her, beat her, or verbally abuse her. He will not do any inconsiderate thing towards his wife or purposely hurt her feelings.

A man who loves his wife will not insist that his wife do anything that is sinful nor will he insist that she do anything that she thinks is a sin, because if she thinks it is a sin, then whether it is a sin or not, it is a sin for her.[27] If he does otherwise then he is guilty of being self-seeking (verse 5) and putting his own wants and desires above those of his wife's.

A man who loves his wife will not become easily angered towards her. This is not to say that he will never become angry with her, but instead to say, that when and if he does, he will have good reason to be. A man who's easily angered gets angry over anything, over trivial matters. A person who becomes angry with another person, even for good reason, is instructed to resolve his or her anger quickly. Therefore, the same applies when a man becomes angry with his wife. Even if he is angry for good reason, he should resolve his anger with his wife quickly.[28]

A man who loves his wife will never bring up his wife's past transgressions (verse 5). He will keep neither a written record nor mental record of her past wrong doings. This means that a man who loves his wife will be truly forgiving towards her. He will forgive his wife just as Christ has forgiven the church.

A man who loves his wife will always look to protect her (verse 7). This means that he will always endeavor to protect her from anything that may hurt her. This does not only mean protecting her from physical harm but from anything that can be psychologically damaging as well.

A man who loves his wife will always trust her (verse 7). He will not interrogate his wife or give her the third degree as to her every move and whereabouts. Of course, exception to this comes with a man scorned by

---

[27] Romans chapter 14 (see your Bible)

[28] "Be angry and sin not: let not the sun go down upon your wrath: Neither give place to the devil." (Ephesians 4:26-27)

a wife who has committed adultery. In this case, trust must be something re-earned and he has the option to divorce her.[29] However, in general, a man who does not trust his wife does not love her, as he should.

A man who loves his wife will seek to preserve her (verse 7). He will handle her with care as with anything that needs preserving. To preserve something means that special care is given in order that what is being preserved may be kept for a longer period of time than would otherwise be. A man who preserves his wife does not set out to overwork and overburdened her. Instead he assists her in whatever he can so that he can preserve her for a lifetime.

Verse 8 says that love never fails. Since a man is commanded to love his wife and since love never fails, then a man, who truly loves his wife, should have a successful and happy marriage, barring any serious backsliding from his wife.

Ephesians 5:27-28

Verses 27 and 28 go on to say that a husband must love his wife as Christ loved the church in order, *"that he might present her to Himself a glorious church, not having spot or wrinkle or any such thing, but that she should be holy and without blemish. So husbands ought to love their own wives as their own bodies; he who loves his wife loves himself."*

A man should love his wife's body as much as he loves his own body. He then, should treat her no worse than he treats himself. If he doesn't beat himself up, then he should never beat her up. This does not mean that a man with masochistic tendencies has a right to beat or hurt his wife. The command for men to love their wives as they love themselves is God's way of ensuring that a married woman is never physically or mentally abused by her husband. The majority of men who abuse their wives physically would never do to themselves what they have done to their wives.[30]

A man is to treat his wife so that she will have no mark on her physically or emotionally. It is no small matter that God commanded men to love their wives as Christ loved the church and that a man is to make certain that he does not hinder his wife from being as glorious as she can possibly be. A man must honor his wife and treat her well. This

[29] See Chapter 8.
[30] See Chapter 8 for detailed discussion on abuse in marriage.

means more than just not beating her and being a provider, but it also means that he should listen to her,[31] consider her needs and desires, and respect her. The Bible tells us that if a man does not honor his wife and does not treat her right, then God will not hear his prayers. The following verses of scripture attest to this. Let's take a look:

> [7]In the same way, you husbands must give honor to your wives. Treat her with understanding as you live together. She may be weaker than you are, but she is your equal partner in God's gift of new life. If you don't treat her as you should, your prayers will not be heard. (1 Peter 3:7 NLT)

There is no doubt about it; God will turn a deaf ear to a man who dishonors and mistreats his wife, because in essence, a man who dishonors his wife has turned a deaf ear to her.

Ephesians 5:29-31

Ephesians 5:29-31 reads as follows: *For no one ever hated his own flesh, but nourishes it and cherishes it, just as the Lord does the church. For we are members of His body and of His flesh and of His bones. "For this reason a man shall leave his father and mother and be joined to his wife, and the two shall become one flesh."*

The apostle Paul continues in his instruction to men that they treat their wives as they would treat themselves. He goes on to say that a man should nourish and cherish his wife's body the same way he nourishes and cherishes his own. A man should be careful to make certain that his wife has everything she needs to be physically comfortable, when she is in good health as well as when she is in poor health. He should not demand anything from his wife physically (or mentally), that he would not be willing to do or undergo himself. He must treat her body as he would treat his own.

Christians are metaphorically the members of the body of Christ just as a man and a woman are metaphorically one body. Verse 31 says that a man should leave his father and mother for his wife. Therefore, a man

---

[31] In Genesis 21:12, God instructs Abraham to listen to his wife (see your Bible).

must put his wife first, above all others, except God. No one can come before his wife. He must consider her first in all things and above all people.[32]

Ephesians 5:33

Verse 33 says the following: *Nevertheless let each one of you in particular so love his own wife as himself, and let the wife see that she respects her husband.*

A man is specifically commanded to love his wife while a woman is specifically commanded to respect her husband. This implies that the success of a marriage will be hindered if a man does not show his wife love and if a woman does not respect her husband. This is not to say that a woman is not to love her husband and that a man is not to respect his wife. But as stated before, although all Christians are commanded to love one another[33] just as all Christians are commanded to submit to one another, men are specifically commanded to love their wives while wives are specifically commanded to respect and submit to their husbands. Therefore, the ultimate responsibility to show love in a marriage is assigned to the man while the ultimate responsibility to show respect and submit in a marriage is assigned to the woman. A woman can respect her husband without loving him because it is not necessary to love someone in order to respect him or her. But as we have seen, a man cannot love his wife and disrespect her at the same time. If he does not respect her, then he does not love her.

Since a husband is the head of the house and is specifically commanded to love his wife as Christ loved the church, then he has the greater challenge in a marriage than his wife and he is more accountable than she is if his marriage fails. After all, he's in charge and leaders have

---

[32] Including children. Notice when reading the book of Job (see your Bible) that God allowed Satan to destroy Job's entire household (including his children) except for his wife. In the end God gave Job more children, thereby replacing them. God could have just as well allowed Satan to take Job's wife, and replace her. But Job and his wife were one flesh (according to Ephesians 5:31 which says, "for this cause a man shall leave his father and mother, and shall cleave to his wife; and the two shall become one flesh" NASB). It is therefore speculated that because of this reason, she was not to be replaced.

[33] "This is my commandment, that you love one another as I have loved you." (John 15:12 NKJV)

more accountability than followers for the Bible teaches us that to whom much is given much is required.[34] Since husbands, have been given ultimate charge of the home, then it is ultimately their responsibility to keep their home together. Therefore, it behooves a man to keep his wife happy.

HAS GOD REALLY COMMANDED THAT A WIFE SUBMIT TO HER HUSBAND IN EVERYTHING?

The phrase "in everything" is the main focus of concern here. Let's take a look at the verse of scripture that gives this command:

> Now as the church submits to Christ, so also wives should submit to their husbands in everything. (Ephesians 5:24 NIV)

Taken alone, The verse of scripture gives the impression that a woman must submit to her husband no matter what. However, when this verse of scripture is examined alongside other verses of scripture, it becomes apparent that there are certain exceptions to the rule. One exception is discussed in the book of Romans. Let's take a look:

> [1]Accept him whose faith is weak, without passing judgment on disputable matters. [2]One man's faith allows him to eat everything, but another man, whose faith is weak, eats only vegetables. [3]The man who eats everything must not look down on him who does not, and the man who does not eat everything must not condemn the man who does, for God has accepted him. [4]Who are you to judge someone else's servant? To his own master he stands or falls. And he will stand, for the Lord is able to make him stand. (Romans 14:1-4 NIV)

---

[34] ".....For unto whomsoever much is given, of him shall be much required: and to whom men have committed much, of him they will ask the more." (Luke 12:48)

[14]The Lord Jesus has made it clear to me that God considers all foods fit to eat. But if you think some foods are unfit to eat, then for you they are not fit.

[15]If you are hurting others by the foods you eat, you are not guided by love. Don't let your appetite destroy someone Christ died for. [16]Don't let your right to eat bring shame to Christ. [17]God's kingdom isn't about eating and drinking. It is about pleasing God, about living in peace, and about true happiness. All this comes from the Holy Spirit. [18]If you serve Christ in this way, you will please God and be respected by people. [19]We should try to live at peace and help each other have a strong faith.

[20]Don't let your appetite destroy what God has done. All foods are fit to eat, but it is wrong to cause problems for others by what you eat. [21]It is best not to eat meat or drink wine or do anything else that cause problems for other followers of the Lord. [22]What you believe about these things should be kept between you and God. You are fortunate, if your actions don't make you have doubts. [23]But if you do have doubts about what you eat, you are going against your beliefs. And you know that is wrong, because anything you do against your beliefs is sin. (Romans 14:14-23 CEV)

During the Dispensation of the Law[35], the Jews were commanded not to eat certain meat.[36] However, at Jesus' ministry, the Dispensation of Grace[37] took effect, and Jesus taught that all meat is clean.[38] Paul also taught that all food is clean as long as it is eaten with thanksgiving unto God.[39] The verses of scripture just cited, inform us that although Jesus

---

[35] See Introduction.

[36] Leviticus chapter 11 (see your Bible).

[37] See Introduction.

[38] Matthew 7:18-19 reads, "Are you so dull?" He asked. "Don't you see that nothing that enters a man from the outside can make him 'unclean'? For it doesn't go into his heart but into his stomach, and then out of his body." (In saying this, Jesus declared all foods "clean.")

[39] 1 Timothy 4:1-5 (see Appendix)

declared all meat to be clean, there were some Jews that still held on to the Mosaic Law regarding the abstaining from certain meat. To those Jews, eating meat of any kind, was a sin. They could not adjust to the change. They could not adjust to the grace that God gave them through the ministry of Jesus concerning these things. They held on to the Old Testament laws that forbid the consumption of certain foods. They believed that eating meat was a sin, although it wasn't, Therefore, according to verse 23, it was a sin for those who believed it to be a sin. And it was a sin to eat meat in front of anyone who felt that eating meat was a sin (vs. 20-21).

It should be noted that verse 1 instructs us not to pass judgment on matters that are disputable. To eat meat or not to eat meat is a disputable and trivial matter. As the scripture says, one's salvation does not depend on what one eats or drinks (verse 17). However, this in no way gives leeway to those who would sin against God by doing indisputable acts. Murder, theft, lust, fornication, and the like are indisputable sins. Therefore, the "meat analogy" of Romans chapter 14, does not apply to these sins.

When applying this reasoning to a husband's rule over his wife, there is no question that a wife is only obligated to submit to her husband as long as what he is asking her to do does not go against her beliefs. If he asks her to do something that she feels is a sin or that she has doubts about, then she should not do it, because for her it is sin (verse 23). If her husband knows that she has doubts or that she believes what he is asking her to do is a sin, and persists in his demands anyway, then he is sinning. He has abused his position of authority in the home and has grieved the Lord. He is guilty of wrongdoing if he demands anything of her that would cause her to have problems (verse 20) or cause her to "stumble" as the New International Version of the Bible puts it.

Stumbling blocks within a marriage seem to become existent when spouses disagree in certain areas, those areas being sex, money, religion, and child-rearing, to name a few. To cite some examples: a man who desires oral sex but has a wife who looks at oral sex as dirty or disgusting, must learn to live without oral sex. It is a disputable matter. He should not submission-bully his wife into performing felatio. A man who drinks a little wine now and then, but has a wife who looks at drinking as a sin, must learn to live without wine. It is a disputable matter. A man who does not want his wife to pay tithes to the church but has a wife that thinks it is a sin not to pay tithes, should not try to stop her from paying tithes. A man who does not mind having sex with a menstruating woman, but has a wife who has doubts about whether or not it is unholy to do so, should learn to get used to not having sex for five to seven consecutive days of every month. A man, who does otherwise, in all of the aforementioned examples, is sinning against his wife according to the verses of scripture contained in Romans chapter 14.

Again, a woman is not obligated to submit to anything her husband asks her to do that she *thinks* is a sin. To do so would go against her very nature as a Christian. A woman should not go against her moral conscious in order to appease her husband. Her husband does not have that kind of authority over her.

Another exception to Ephesians 5:24 that instructs wives to submit to their husbands *in everything* is that which is contained in the following verse of scripture:

> Wives, be subject to your husbands, as is fitting in the
> Lord. (Colossians 3:18 NASB)

The key phrase is "as is fitting in the Lord." This phrase can be taken two ways. It can be taken to mean that it is fitting in the Lord for a woman to submit to her husband. Or, it can be taken to mean that if her husband demands that she do something unfitting in the Lord (against his word) then she is not obligated to do it.

We have just seen that anything that a man asks his wife to do that goes against her beliefs is a sin for her and therefore it would not be fitting in the Lord for her to do whatever it is. To take things further, a wife does not have to submit to her husband if he insists that she do something that is *clearly* a sin. For example: a woman does not have to comply with her husband if he asks her to cheat a little on their income tax. It is a sin to steal money from the government[40] and therefore to do so is not fitting in the Lord.

A wife is not bound to submit to any sin that her husband asks her to commit. The same applies to all Christians. Christians are commanded to abide by authority. However, there is an exception with this mandate when anyone in authority (including the government) mandates sinful practices or mandates practices that go against one's beliefs. The

---

[40] Mark 12:13-17 (See Appendix)

following verses of scripture instructs Christians to abide by authority and governmental rule:

> [13]For the Lord's sake accept the authority of every human institution, whether of the emperor as supreme,
> [14]or of governors, as sent by him to punish those who do wrong and to praise those who do right.
> (1 Peter 2:13-14 NRSV)

> [1]Let every person be in subjection to the governing authorities. For there is no authority except from God, and those which exist are established by God.
> [2]Therefore he who resists authority has opposed the ordinance of God; and they who have opposed will receive condemnation upon themselves. (Romans 13:1-2 NASB)

The above verses of scripture plainly teach that Christians are to abide by the governing authorities, just as women are ultimately subject to the rule of their husbands. However, the Bible also teaches that when those governing authorities give ungodly mandates, then Christians are no longer obligated to abide (as it is with wives in respect to their husbands). This is made evident in the following verses of scripture, which give an account of Peter and the other apostles standing for God instead of abiding by ungodly rule:

> [17]But the high priest rose up, along with all his associates (that is the sect of the Sadducees), and they were filled with jealousy
> [18]and they laid hands on the apostles, and put them in a public jail.
> [19]But an angel of the Lord during the night opened the gates of the prison, and taking them out he said,
> [20]Go your way, stand and speak to the people in the temple the whole message of this Life."
> (Acts 5:17-20 NASB)

²⁵But someone came and reported to them, "Behold, the men whom you put in prison are standing in the temple and teaching the people!"
²⁶Then the captain went along with the officers and proceeded to bring them back without violence (for they were afraid of the people, lest they should be stoned).
²⁷And when they had brought them, they stood them before the Council. And the high priest questioned them,
²⁸saying, "We gave you strict orders not to continue teaching in this name, and behold, you have filled Jerusalem with your teaching, and intend to bring this man's blood upon us."
²⁹But Peter and the apostles answered and said, "We must obey God rather than men.
³⁰The God of our fathers raised up Jesus, whom you had put to death by hanging Him on a cross,
³¹He is the one whom God exalted to His right hand as a Prince and a Savior, to grant repentance to Israel, and forgiveness of sins.
³²And we are witnesses of these things; and so is the Holy Spirit, whom God has given to those who obey Him." (Acts 5:25-32 NASB)

Emphasis is drawn to verse 29 when Peter explains to the governing authorities that he and the apostles must obey God before they obey men. Therefore, if man's ordinances goes against God's ordinances then man's ordinances cannot be obeyed. It is the same in a marriage. A wife must obey God rather than her husband, if her husband has asked her to submit to ungodly deeds.

This brings us to another area that is a thorn of contention for some Christian marriages. It is the area of service to the Lord. Contentions that develop between husbands and wives about spiritual gifts don't seem to surface as long as the wife is doing no more than occasionally baking cookies for the church choir. But if God has called her to preach, teach, and the like,[41] she might find herself in a struggle at home, especially if

---

[41] See Chapter 5.

her husband has not been called to do these very visible things. Many a man get in the way of his wife's ministry that the Lord has called her to, either by stopping her from doing it altogether, limiting her activities in it, trying to control it, or sabotaging it. Since the Bible says that a husband is the head of his wife and the Lord is the head of the husband,[42] many men take this to mean that the Holy Spirit of God does not directly guide married women. But the Bible tells us that God has given us all gifts (men and women), and for those of us that are Christians, those gifts are to be used for the Lord in order to edify the body of Christ.[43]

When it comes to headship, some men feel that they are in charge of their wives to the point where they have the final say in the ministry that God has called her into. But if God calls a woman to a ministry then God is the one who instructs her in it. As discussed in Chapter 1, the Lord called Deborah to a mighty position without calling her husband to that same position. Also, as we saw in Chapter 1, Deborah made major decisions in regards to the position God placed her in, apparently without necessarily consulting her husband.[44] Many men feel that God will not call their wives to a ministry that is more visible, powerful, or influencing than what God has called them to do. But there is no biblical text that supports this. As we have seen, when examining the life of Deborah and even when looking at the life of Esther, a woman can be called to a more visible ministry in the Lord than her husband.

A man has no jurisdiction over his wife when it comes to what God has ordained her to do. And if a woman's husband is trying to control her ministry, limit her ministry, or take it over himself, and his demands are contrary to what she believes the Lord has placed on her heart regarding the ministry that the Lord has given her, then she is not obligated to heed to her husband's demands regarding her ministry because she must obey God rather than man.

This is not to say that a man is not at liberty to give his wife some advice about her ministry, he is. And a woman is at the same liberty to

---

[42] "But I want you to know and realize that Christ is the Head of every man, the head of a woman is her husband, and the Head of Christ is God." (1 Corinthians 11:3 Amp.)

[43] See Chapter 5.

[44] This is speculative. There is no proof that she did not consult her husband. However, there is no historical account of her consulting him either. This certainly is not to say that she never did.

give her husband advice about his ministry. But a woman is not obligated under the rules of submission to heed her husband's advice if she feels that God is not leading her in her ministry the way her husband has advised.

Not only is a husband not at liberty to control, limit, sabotage, or take over his wife's ministry that the Lord has given her, but he should also not try to coerce or convince his wife that God has called her to do something that she does not feel led of the Lord to do.

God can make room in a marriage for a man and a woman to each acknowledge the call of one another's ministry. A husband should support his wife in the ministry the Lord has given her just as a woman should support her husband in the ministry the Lord has given him.

It is unfitting for a man to discourage his wife from using the gifts that God has given her, no matter what gifts they might be. God knows what he is doing. If he has given a woman a gift then he has made enough room in the marriage whereby she can exercise her gift. If indeed her husband says there is no room for her gift in the marriage then he is going against the Spirit of the Lord. Why would God give a woman a gift that she is not at liberty to use?

MARRIED WOMEN AS SLAVES?

Many women believe that the Bible compares being a wife to being a slave. They're right, it does. Let's take a look:

> [18]Slaves accept the authority of your masters with all deference, not only those who are kind and gentle but also those who are harsh. [19]For it is a credit to you if, being aware of God, you endure pain while suffering unjustly. [20]If you endure when you are beaten for doing wrong, what credit is that? But if you endure when you do right and suffer for it, you have God's approval. [21]For to this you have been called, because Christ also suffered for you, leaving you an example, so that you should follow in his steps.
> [22]"He committed no sin,
> and no deceit was found in his mouth."
> [23]When he was abused, he did not return abuse; when he suffered, he did not threaten; but he entrusted

himself to the one who judges justly. [24]He himself bore our sins in his body on the cross, so that, free from sins, we might live for righteousness; by his wounds you have been healed. [25]For you were going astray like sheep, but now you have returned to the shepherd and guardian of your souls. (1 Peter 2:18-25 NRSV)

[1]In the same way, you wives must accept the authority of your husbands, even those who refuse to accept the Good News. Your godly lives will speak to them better than any words. They will be won over [2]by watching your pure, godly behavior.

[3]Don't be concerned about the outward beauty that depends on fancy hairstyles, expensive jewelry, or beautiful clothes. [4]You should be known for the beauty that comes from within, the unfading beauty of a gentle and quiet spirit, which is so precious to God. [5]That is the way the holy women of old made themselves beautiful. They trusted God and accepted the authority of their husbands. [6]For instance, Sarah obeyed her husband, Abraham, when she called him her master. You are her daughters when you do what is right without fear of what your husbands might do.

[7]In the same way, you husbands must give honor to your wives. Treat her with understanding as you live together. She may be weaker than you are, but she is your equal partner in God's gift of new life. If you don't treat her as you should, your prayers will not be heard. (1 Peter 3:1-7 NLT)

Peter begins his comparison by discussing the plight of Christian slaves.[45] He instructs Christian slaves to endure unfair treatment of their masters because ultimately such uncharacteristic human behavior to endure unfair harsh treatment is a strong testimony to the strength God gives to those who follow him and ultimately to the fact that there is a God.

---

[45] For a full discussion on the issue of slavery, see the book by this same author titled, *What the Bible really says about Slavery.*

If a slave suffers a beating from his master, the brutality of the master is increased if the slave has done no wrong and the slave takes the beating without complaint. Paul goes on to explain that God is pleased with those who endure blows (suffer) for doing what is right. His directive to suffer blows for doing what is right is both meant in a literal and figurative way. There are those Christians who are called in a position by God whereby they may be more likely to suffer than others. Paul, himself was called to such a position. Paul was often beaten and imprisoned for preaching the gospel of Jesus Christ.

God knows how to use any circumstance as a tool to bring those who are lost into a saving knowledge of Jesus Christ. Therefore, he inspired Paul to instruct Christians to endure, with a patient attitude, difficult situations. This is not to say that there does not come a time when the suffering must end. There was even a limit to Jesus' suffering.

Paul gives the example of how Christ suffered for us. He takes his point further by saying that Jesus neither sinned nor deceived anyone. In other words, Jesus did not do anything to deserve such suffering as he endured on the cross. But, despite the fact that Jesus was perfect, that he never sinned, that he never deceived anyone, and that he didn't do anything to deserve such suffering on the cross, it was his lot in life to suffer the pain of the cross anyway because the lost sheep needed a Shepherd.

Paul then takes all of what he said about slaves and Jesus and applies it to married women. He begins by saying "in the same way." So, in the same way, women must accept the authority of their husbands just as slaves are to accept the authority of their masters. But Paul never said that women *are* slaves of their husbands. The comparison Paul makes between a wife and a slave is not an absolute one because Paul did not say that a woman must accept the authority of her husband "in the exact way" a slave must accept the authority of his master, but only "in the same way." As a matter of fact, even though Paul speaks of wives being obedient to their husbands, he emphasizes how important it is that women do what is right without fear of what their husbands might do (verse 6). In other words, when the righteousness of a woman is challenged in any way by the authority of her husband, that woman has the go-ahead from God to choose to be righteous over the command to be obedient to her husband, no matter if her husband becomes angry or difficult, or no matter what he might do. She should not let his anger or unreasonableness sway her from doing what is right or from what she thinks is right. There is a limit to a man's authority over his wife. His authority does not go beyond God's authority.

The words *wife* and *slave* are not synonymous. But Paul *did* say that a woman must submit to the authority of her husband the way a slave is to submit to the authority of his master. By saying this Paul is teaching that there is suffering in submitting to authority. So, just as a slave suffers when submitting to his master, especially to a harsh one, so does a woman suffer when submitting to her husband, especially an unbelieving one. Paul ties submitting in with suffering. Suffering is not an easy thing to do. As we've seen earlier in this chapter, Jesus did not want to suffer and asked the Father to remove the yoke of the cross from him. However, it was not the Father's will to remove the yoke and Jesus went on to endure the suffering on the cross. He submitted to the Father's will.

Since Paul has tied the act of suffering to the act of submitting, then it stands to reason that submitting is not an easy thing to do. So, a woman suffers much more in a marriage than a man does, because she is the one who must suffer through the authority of her husband. She is the one who must ultimately submit. This suffering in submission also ties in to the fact that a husband's rule over his wife is indeed a curse for women, for if it were not a curse then it follows that there would be no comparison of a wife's submission to her husband with that of a suffering slave's submission to his master.

Paul says that wives must accept the authority of their husbands in the same way that slaves must accept the authority of their masters. This is not to say that wives must accept the authority of unreasonable and harsh husbands who beat them. We can safely come to this conclusion because Paul uses the marriage of Abraham and Sarah (verse 6) as an example of a marriage in which a woman accepted the authority of her husband. And we know from looking at the historical account in Genesis of their marriage that Abraham was easy-going and tried to please Sarah in every way.

These verses of scripture that compare wives with slaves do not give men a license to beat and mistreat their wives because the verses of scripture do not even give masters the go-ahead to beat their slaves. Paul used the example of slavery in order to teach how important it is to endure unfair treatment patiently, because in doing so others can see holiness and therefore might be impressed enough to consider the gospel of Jesus Christ. Paul used the example that he did regarding the beating of a slave *in the case of* a slave being beaten not to *make a case* for a slave to *be* beaten.[46] Again, Ephesians 5:28-29[47] teaches us that a man should treat his wife's body as he would treat his own body. We can be certain that a man would not beat himself up and therefore, he should not beat his wife up either. However, it should be noted that just as God has made a way out for the mistreated slave,[48] he has also made a way out for the mistreated wife.[49]

With all of what Paul said about these things, he did not leave men out of the equation. Verse 7 continues by teaching that "in the same way" husbands should honor their wives. So, in the same way that a woman is to accept the authority of her husband, a man is to honor his wife. He is to honor her no less than she is to submit to him. If a man truly honors his wife in this way then his wife will seldom experience suffering that can result from the curse of her husband's rule upon her.

Jesus gave us an example of how those in charge are to treat people under their authority. Let's take a look:

> [1]Now before the festival of the Passover, Jesus knew that his hour had come to depart from this world and go to the Father. Having loved his own who were in the world, he loved them to the end. [2]The devil had already put it into the heart of Judas son of Simon Iscariot to betray him. And during supper [3]Jesus, knowing that the Father had given all things into his hands, and that he had come from God and was going to God, [4]got up from the table, took off his outer robe, and tied a towel around himself. [5]Then he poured water into a basin and began to wash the disciples' feet and to wipe them with the towel that was tied around him. [6]He came to Simon Peter, who said to him, "Lord, are you going to wash my feet?" [7]Jesus answered, "You do not know now what I am doing, but later you will understand." [8]Peter said to him, "You will never wash my feet." Jesus

---

[46] It is the same for a wife submitting to her husband. Paul makes a case for submission even in cases where a wife has an unbelieving husband.

[47] See your Bible and see Chapter 8.

[48] See book by this same author titled, "What the Bible really says about Slavery."

[49] See Chapter 8.

answered, "Unless I wash you, you have no share with me." [9]Simon Peter said to him, "Lord not my feet only but also my hands and my head!" [10]Jesus said to him, "One who has bathed does not need to wash, except for the feet, but is entirely clean. And you are clean, though not all of you." [11]For he knew who was to betray him; for this reason he said, "Not all of you are clean."

[12]After he had washed their feet, had put on his robe, and had returned to the table, he said to them, "Do you know what I have done to you? [13]You call me Teacher and Lord—and you are right, for that is what I am. [14]So if I, your Lord and Teacher, have washed your feet, you also ought to wash one another's feet. [15]For I have set you an example, that you also should do as I have done to you. [16]Very truly, I tell you, servants are not greater than their master, nor are messengers greater than the one who sent them. [17]If you know these things, you are blessed if you do them. (John 13:1-17 NRSV)

Jesus taught his disciples a lesson in humility. Although Jesus was their Teacher and their Lord (their God) he served them by washing their feet as an example of how they should serve others. Jesus was the head, but humbled himself to serve those under his authority. A man who rules his home should have the same kind of humility towards his wife. He should be willing to humble himself and serve her, not only in ways that are expected of him, but also in ways that are not expected of him, in the most humble of ways. This is what Jesus did when he washed the disciples' feet. He served them in a way that they did not expect. He served them in a way that most would think was beneath him. This is the way a man should serve his wife. A man should not think that it is beneath him to wash the dishes, or cook, or change diapers. For a man to do these things for his wife is analogous to the foot washing Jesus gave the disciples. A leader is not really humble if he is not willing to do the things that are deemed as "beneath" him. As Jesus depicted, the best leaders are humble leaders. With this being the case, it is safe to say that humble men make the best husbands.

111

In getting back to our examination of 1 Peter 3:1-7, Peter teaches (verse 7) that a wife is equal to her husband even though she is physically weaker and that a man must treat his wife with understanding. If a man does not do this then his prayers will not be heard. Therefore, again, a man has the greater challenge in a marriage. It is difficult for many people to treat those under their authority, honorably. It is easier to boss someone around and treat them badly. If a woman does not submit to her husband, the scriptures do not say that she is in danger of provoking the wrath of God to the point where he will not listen to her prayers. But if a man does not honor his wife, if he does not show her love, if he does not treat her with understanding, God will not hear his prayers. Therefore, women who don't do well in submitting to their husbands have more grace from God than do men who abuse their authority in the home. Certainly then, the latter condition is worse than the former. And therefore the greater instruction rests with husbands, as it should, since they are the ones in authority.

SUMMARY

As soon as a woman gets married she automatically directly falls under the rule of her husband which is identified in Genesis as a cursed thing for these times. But, as we have seen, the fact that she falls under the authority of her husband does not make him superior to her. Both men and women were made in the image of God. Therefore, they were made on equal grounds. Consequently a man is no more superior to a woman than a woman is to a man.

According to Galatians 3:28, as cited earlier in the chapter, all who are in Christ are really the same, despite the roles or gender they may be assigned to here on earth.[50] Slaves are equal to those who are free, Gentiles are equal to Jews, and women are equal to men (which of course means that wives are equal to their husbands). All of those who are children of God will inherit all of God's promises.

The fact that the rule of a husband over his wife is now a grievous thing is part of the punishment women must suffer because of Eve's transgressions. This is one simple fact that most theologians often

---

[50] "Faith in Christ Jesus is what makes each of you equal with each other, whether you are a Jew or a Greek, a slave or a free person, a man or a woman." (Galatians 3:28 NASB)

attempt to minimize or ignore when emphasizing the role women play in a marriage as it pertains to submission.

The fact that a woman will experience multiplied pain in childbirth, is also part of a woman's punishment. It is part of the curse she must endure due to the sins of Eve. Men must also endure a curse. Every man must "work the fields" so to speak in order to earn a living.

Theoretically, if a woman does not marry she is still to feel the brunt of the curse because she would become a burden to her family or a burden to society since there were no man to take care of her besides her father. However, this is not the case today. Women work and take care of themselves. But this could be seen as taking on the curse of the man by "working the fields." However, a married woman lives directly under the two curses which God prescribed for her (the curse of increased pain in childbirth and the curse of her husband's rule over her) and often times endures her husband's curse (toiling the field) as well by working outside of the home.[51]

All women who get married will, at some point in their marriage directly feel the effects of the cursedness of their husband's rule, by reason of the fact that the cursedness of the rule exists in every marriage. However, as stated earlier, some wives will more strongly feel the effects of the curse than other wives will. Whether or not a married woman feels the cursedness of her husband's rule as strongly as another married woman depends on the temperament and personality of her husband and whether or not he loves her sacrificially, the way the Bible instructs him to. On the other hand, single women, since they have no husbands, will not first handedly feel the direct effects of the curse of husband rule as opposed to married women. But they will indirectly feel the effects of the curse. If they remain single then they will, more than likely, have to "toil the fields" in order to take care of themselves (unless their families take care of them or unless they are rich), when theoretically they would not have to do this if they were married. Therefore, the fact that they must toil the fields thereby taking on the man's punishment, is one of the indirect ways in which they experience these curses as well. But many single women would rather "work the fields" than to risk being directly under a man's rule and many women who are married and are directly under a man's rule, have found themselves "working the fields" anyway.

---

[51] See Chapter 6.

Both genders can feel the effects of each other's punishment. If women decide not to marry because they don't want to live under the rule of a man, then there are fewer women to marry and theoretically, there are fewer children being born into the world. If enough women decide that it is better not to marry, it will surely effect men in a negative way. Statistics show that men in general are happier in marriage than women. This is not a surprising statistic since societal trends have eased the burden of the man's curse. Most men enter into a marriage *expecting* women to work. They no longer enter into a marriage expecting to do "whatever it takes" to provide a decent home for their wives and children. In their estimation, "whatever it takes" includes a working wife or at least a wife who has money.

As we will see in Chapter 12, Paul said that a woman is happier being single. Thus, in general, when women get married they risk their happiness more so than men do when they get married. It is therefore essential that a woman examine the man she is about to marry in order to determine, as best as she possibly can, whether or not he will honor her and love her sacrificially as God has instructed him to, or whether or not he will abuse his authority in the home. A man is supposed to create such a loving environment in his home that his wife will not feel the effects of the curse of his rule and will therefore, when need be, submit to him without feeling as though she is suffering or as though she is oppressed.

Some would say that God is a chauvinist because the Bible teaches that married women are to submit to their husbands and that the man is the head of his wife. Indeed, it would seem as if God were a chauvinist if God had instituted, from the beginning, this cursed and grievous rule that a man has over his wife. But he did not. He instituted it as a punishment after Eve disobeyed him. Eve is the guilty party, not God. Furthermore, God has "softened the blow" so to speak, in this dispensation of Grace by instructing men on how to love their wives. Additionally, if God were a chauvinist he would have labeled women as inferior to men because of the rule that men have over their wives. But he didn't. Also, God did not punish Eve alone, but he punished Adam and the serpent for their transgressions as well. Moreover, theoretically a woman will directly experience the effects of Eve's curse only if she gets married and theoretically a man will directly experience the curse of Adam all of the days of his life, married or not. In this respect, neither gender was cursed worse than the other, and therefore when looking at the issue of married women and submission, there is no chauvinism with God.

4.

"FEMALE PROBLEMS"

MONTHLY PERIODS.....THE THIRD CURSE?

In jest, menstruation has been referred to by women, their mothers before them, and their mothers' mothers as "the curse," and not surprisingly so. Each month the uterine lining of a woman's uterus becomes thicker to prepare for the possibility of pregnancy. However, when pregnancy does not occur, the excess uterine lining is no longer needed. Consequently, mechanisms in the body cause the additional lining to be eliminated from the uterus through the vaginal wall. This elimination is what has been termed as the menstrual period and it is always accompanied with blood.

Although menstruation is not really a curse, many women, for good reason, have mockingly labeled it as such. A woman's menstrual period can last from three to seven days. During this time, she is constantly bleeding. Some women experience severe cramping and nausea to go along with this monthly event. Unfortunately, it hasn't been until recently (the last thirty years or so) that menstrual cramping was taken seriously by physicians. Formerly, the women who did not cramp and experience adverse effects were compared with those who did. The latter were indirectly labeled as "cry babies," not only by men, but also by non-empathetic women. Finally, the medical world took the plight of menstrual cramping, nausea, and bloating seriously and began to produce effective medication to relieve some of these unpleasant symptoms, much to the delight of the women who suffer from them.

To complicate things, there are a majority of women who experience adverse premenstrual symptoms (PMS) about a week or two before their actual period begins. Pre-menstrual symptoms can include irritability, bloating, depression, and the like. The irritability and depression can be the result of the chemical changes that are taking place to prepare the body for the upcoming period or can be the result of a woman's reaction to the fact that yet another period, full of cramping, bloating, blood, and nausea, is incumbent.

In addition to all of the cramping, nausea, and PMS, menstrual periods are very inconvenient. Many women are constantly trying to plan around them, especially if they suffer from any of the unpleasant symptoms. No woman wants to be bleeding heavily while she's on a camping trip, or participating in a sports activity, or presenting a statistical analysis to a board of directors. Many women plan their wedding dates (to the best of their ability) around the estimated arrival of their period. Who wants to bleed and cramp during the honeymoon? No wonder some women refer to the menstrual period as a curse. And there are those women that even go further than that. They're upset with God about it. They ask themselves (and others): why did God let men off so easy? They conclude that this menstrual thing is one of the reasons why they think God is a chauvinist. They feel that God must think less of women than of men since he has designed a woman's body to suffer through this madness every month. But let's take a look at what the word of God says about a woman's menstrual cycle:

> [19]When a woman has her regular flow of blood, the impurity of her monthly period will last seven days, and anyone who touches her will be unclean till evening.
> [20]Anything she lies on during her period will be unclean, and anything she sits on will be unclean. [21]Whoever touches her bed must wash his clothes and bathe with water, and he will be unclean till evening. [22]Whoever touches anything she sits on must wash his clothes and bathe with water, and he will be unclean till evening. [23]Whether it is the bed or anything she was sitting on, when anyone touches it, he will be unclean till evening.
> [24]If a man lies with her and her monthly flow touches him, he will be unclean for seven days; any bed he lies on will be unclean. (Leviticus 15:19-24 NIV)

Similar rules that applied to menstruation applied for women who suffered from vaginal bleeding not caused by menstruation, but from some illness that brought on hemorrhaging. Let's take a look:

> [25]When a woman has a discharge of blood for many days at a time other than her monthly period or has a

> discharge that continues beyond her period, she will be unclean as long as she has the discharge, just as in the days of her period. [26]Any bed she lies on while her discharge continues will be unclean, as is her bed during her monthly period, and anything she sits on will be unclean, as during her period. [27]Whoever touches them will be unclean; he must wash his clothes and bathe in water, and he will be unclean till evening.
>
> [28]When she is cleansed from her discharge, she must count off seven days, and after that she will be ceremonially clean. [29]On the eighth day she must take two doves or two young pigeons and bring them to the priest at the entrance to the Tent of Meeting. [30]The priest is to sacrifice one for a sin offering and the other for a burnt offering. In this way he will make atonement for her before the LORD for the uncleanness of her discharge.
>
> [31]You must keep the Israelites separate from things that make them unclean, so they will not die in their uncleanness for defiling my dwelling place which is among them. (Leviticus 15:25-31 NIV)

Upon initially reading the above scriptural verses that speak on menstruation and vaginal bleeding, one would be hard pressed not to believe that there is some chauvinism involved in the laws God set regarding a woman's period. First, we must remember that the laws contained in Leviticus were the laws that God gave Moses to give to the Jews. Furthermore, these laws were for that specific dispensation[1] and do not apply today. Moreover, the laws only applied to the Jews and not to the Gentiles.[2] Despite this, when looking at the Mosaic Law[3] regarding a woman's menstruation, we can safely speculate about how God feels about it.

A hemorrhaging woman had to bring two doves or pigeons to the priest so that he could make atonement (verses 29 and 30)[4] for her by

---

[1] See Introduction.
[2] Those who were not Jews and who did not worship God.
[3] The Law handed down to the Jews by God through Moses. See Introduction.
[4] To make amends for the sins of others.

offering one bird for a sin offering and the other bird for a burnt offering. This does not mean that by bleeding she was sinning. It was not her fault that she bled. However, the priest had to make atonement before the Lord for her because of her blood flow. She was unclean.

A woman's menstrual flow has never been considered by society (nor by women, for that matter), as being something that is clean. And any kind of blood flow that is not contained in some way is generally considered unsanitary.

Although we can all agree that a woman's menstrual flow is unclean and needs to be contained, it may be more difficult to agree that during a woman's monthly flow the woman *herself* is unclean. But during the dispensation of the Law, this was exactly the case. However, if we say God is a chauvinist because of this, we would also have to say that a man's discharges were never considered unclean and that a man was never considered unclean due to any discharge he may have expelled. But as the following scripture quote proves, this was simply not the case. God also considered men to be unclean when they discharged semen. Let's take a look:

> [16]When a man has an emission of semen, he must bathe his whole body with water, and he will be unclean till evening. [17]Any clothing or leather that has semen on it must be washed with water, and it will be unclean till evening. [18]When a man lies with a woman and there is an emission of semen, both must bathe with water, and they will be unclean till evening.
> (Leviticus 15:16-18 NIV)

The ejaculation of semen was considered by God to be just as unclean as a woman's blood flow during her menstrual period. The man himself was unclean after the ejaculation just as a woman was unclean during the flow of her menstrual period. Furthermore, the uncleanness of a man's semen pertained to any time he ejaculated despite whatever circumstances may have led up to it. He was unclean until the next evening. However, the only discharge that made a woman unclean was a vaginal flow of blood. To take things even further, any time a man had sex with his wife which resulted in an ejaculation of semen, *both* the man and the woman were made unclean by his ejaculation just as both partners were made unclean if they had sex while the wife was menstruating. A woman's sexual secretions were not categorized as unclean. Let's look further:

> [1]The Lord said to Moses and Aaron, [2]"Speak to the Israelites and say to them: 'When any man has a bodily discharge, the discharge is unclean. [3]Whether it continues flowing from his body or is blocked, it will make him unclean. This is how his discharge will bring about uncleanness:
> [4]Any bed the man with a discharge lies on will be unclean, and anything he sits on will be unclean. [5]Anyone who touches his bed must wash his clothes and bathe with water, and he will be unclean till evening. [6]Whoever sits on anything that the man with a discharge sat on must wash his clothes and bathe with water, and he will be unclean till evening.
> [7]Whoever touches the man who has a discharge must wash his clothes and bathe with water, and he will be unclean till evening.
> [8]If the man with the discharge spits on someone who is clean, that person must wash his clothes and bathe with water, and he will be unclean till evening.
> [9]Everything the man sits on when riding will be unclean, [10]and whoever touches any of the things that were under him will be unclean till evening; whoever picks up those things must wash his clothes and bathe with water, and he will be unclean till evening.
> [11]Anyone the man with a discharge touches without rinsing his hands with water must wash his clothes and bathe with water, and he will be unclean till evening.
> [12]A clay pot that the man touches must be broken, and any wooden article is to be rinsed with water.
> [13]When a man is cleansed from his discharge, he is to count off seven days for his ceremonial cleansing; he must wash his clothes and bathe himself with fresh water, and he will be clean. [14]On the eighth day he must take two doves or two young pigeons and come before the LORD to the entrance to the Tent of Meeting and give them to the priest. [15]The priest is to sacrifice

them, the one for a sin offering and the other for a burnt offering. In this way he will make atonement before the LORD for the man because of his discharge." (Leviticus 15:1-15 NIV)

As we can plainly see when looking at verses 14 and 15, a man experiencing a discharge whether it was promoted by sickness or some other occurrence, had to do the same as a woman suffering from continuous bleeding. He had to take two doves or two pigeons to the priest so that the priest could sacrifice one as a sin offering and the other as a burnt offering to make atonement before the Lord for the man because of the man's discharge. God is an equal opportunity God. Any excessive discharge on the part of a man or a woman required that they go to the priest for ceremonial cleansing. A chauvinistic God would have declared any discharges from a woman as unclean but would not have declared discharges from a man as unclean.

But as we have seen, discharges from men, including the ejaculation of semen, were deemed just as unclean by God as blood flow from a woman's monthly menstrual cycle. This doesn't sound like a chauvinistic God. As a matter of fact, there's more than one way to look at this: As we recall, Leviticus 15:19 says that a woman's period will last for seven days and during this time anyone who touches her will be unclean until the evening. Verses 20 through 22 go on to say that anything she lies on or touches will be unclean, that anyone who touches her bed will be unclean, and that anyone who touches anything she sits on will be unclean. Verse 24 says that if her husband lies down with her to have sex and her monthly flow touches him, then he is unclean. Everything and everybody a woman touched during her menstrual period was made unclean. This meant that more than likely, someone else did all the housekeeping chores during those seven days. What a benefit. Moreover, a woman was not obligated to have sex with her husband during her menstrual period. Let's take a look:

Do not approach a woman to have sexual relations during the uncleanness of her monthly period. (Leviticus 18:19 NIV)

[29]Everyone who does any of these detestable things—such persons must be cut off from their people. [30]Keep

my requirements and do not follow any of the detestable customs that were practiced before you came and do not defile yourselves with them. I am the LORD your God. (Leviticus 18:29-30 NIV)

Men were commanded by God not to have sex with a woman during her period, no matter if the woman he wanted to have sex with was his wife. No exception was made for his wife. This law included all women. Certainly there were those wives that may not have been pleased with such a law, but surely there were some wives who may have seen this as a welcome break from the sexual advances of their husbands. However, as we have seen earlier, a man who disregarded the Law by having sex with a menstruating woman was unclean for seven days, just as she was.

The command for a man to refrain from having sexual relations with a woman during her monthly period is among a long list of commands cited in Leviticus chapter 18[5] and therefore is in the same category as the other commands that are cited. The other commands include the forbidding of a man to have sexual relations with his mother, his stepmother, his sister, his granddaughter, his aunt, his sister-in-law, his daughter-in-law, his step daughter, his neighbor's wife, and another man. These are the things that verse 29 above says are detestable to God. It is interesting to note that having sex with a woman while she is on her period is included in this list. Although these commands were given to the Jews during the Dispensation of Law, the commands against incest and homosexuality still apply today during the Dispensation of Grace.[6] So then, it would also seem that the command for a man to refrain from having sex with a menstruating woman should apply today as well. This point is emphasized even further by the following verses of scripture:

> [5]Suppose there is a righteous man
> who does what is just and right.
> [6]He does not eat at the mountain
>   shrines
> or look to the idols of the house
>   of Israel.
> He does not defile his neighbor's wife

---

[5] See your Bible.
[6] See Introduction

> or lie with a woman during her
>   period.
> [7]He does not oppress anyone,
> But returns what he took in a
>   pledge for a loan.
> He does not commit robbery
> but gives his food to the hungry
> and provides clothing for the
>   naked.
> [8]He does not lend at usury
> or take excessive interest.
> He withholds his hand from doing
>   wrong
> and judges fairly between man
>   and man.
> [9]He follows my decrees
>   and faithfully keeps my laws.
> That man is righteous;
>   he will surely live,
> declares the sovereign LORD.
> (Ezekiel 18:5-9 NIV)

God, the sovereign Lord is speaking here through Ezekiel. He has described what makes a righteous man. A righteous man is a man who does not worship idols, who does not have sex with his neighbor's wife, who does not oppress anyone, who does not steal, who gives to the poor, who does not charge excessive interest, who stops himself from doing wrong, who judges fairly between men, and who does not have sexual intercourse with a woman during her menstrual period.

It seems fair that God would give a man a "hands off" command in regards to a menstruating woman, since many women experience adverse symptoms during their cycles and therefore are not really in the mood for sex at that time. This certainly doesn't sound like a God who only thinks about the welfare of men.

Despite the fact that God gave men a "hands off" command when it comes to a menstruating woman, it can be argued that this command only applied during the dispensation of the Law and does not apply today. The following scripture is used to argue that point:

122

> Let marriage be held in honor among all, and let the
> marriage bed be undefiled; for fornicators and
> adulterers God will judge. (Hebrews 13:4 NASB)

Many have interpreted the above scripture to mean that the marriage
bed can be defiled by fornication (which includes sex before marriage) or
adultery. However, there are those who also interpret the above scripture
as meaning that there are no sexual limits between husband and wife and
that therefore no sexual act between the two of them can defile their
marriage bed. So, according to those who choose the latter
interpretation, in this current dispensation of Grace, it is permissible for
a man to have sex with his menstruating wife. However, if this
interpretation is used, sex with one's menstruating wife is only
permissible if she believes it is not sinful and if she feels comfortable
having sex with her husband during her period. If she believes it is sinful
for her to have sex with her husband during her menstrual period, then
for her it is a sin and it would therefore be a sin for her husband to try to
force the issue (as discussed in Chapter 3).[7] If her husband insists, then
he is not holding the marriage bed in honor as he and his wife (as well as
others) have been directed to do. Furthermore, the Bible instructs men to
honor their wives.[8] A man is dishonoring his wife if he insists that she
do something sexually that she feels uncomfortable doing or that she
believes is a sin to do.

ON BEING BARREN

A barren woman is a woman who is unable to conceive children.
Barrenness was considered to be a curse in Old Testament society. But it

---

[7] "It is best not to eat meat or drink wine or do anything else that causes
problems for other followers in the Lord. What you believe about these things
should be kept between you and God. You are fortunate, if your actions don't
make you have doubts. But if you do have doubts about what you eat, you are
going against your beliefs. And you know that is wrong, because anything you
do against your beliefs is sin." (Romans 14:21-23 CEV)

[8] "If you are a husband, you should be thoughtful of your wife. Treat her with
honor, because she isn't as strong as you are, and she shares with you in the gift
of life. Then nothing will stand in the way of your prayers." (1 Peter 3:7 CEV)
The strength spoken of here is physical strength.

is no more a curse than any other bodily dysfunction. We will take a more in depth look at the biblical perspective of barrenness, beginning with the following verses of scripture:

> [20]See, I am sending an angel ahead of you to guard you along the way and to bring you to the place I have prepared. [21]Pay attention to him and listen to what he says. Do not rebel against him; he will not forgive your rebellion, since my Name is in him. [22]If you listen carefully to what he says and do all that I say, I will be an enemy to your enemies and will oppose those who oppose you. [23]My angel will go ahead of you and bring you into the land of the Amorites, Hittites, Perizzites, Canaanites, Hivites and Jebusites, and I will wipe them out. [24]Do not bow down before their gods or worship them or follow their practices. You must demolish them and break their sacred stones to pieces. [25]Worship the LORD your God, and his blessing will be on your food and water. I will take away sickness from among you, [26]and none will miscarry or be barren in your land. I will give you a full life span. (Exodus 23:20-26 NIV)

In the verses of scripture just cited, God is speaking to the Jews after he delivered them from slavery in Egypt. He sets an angel before them to guide them into the land that he promised them.[9] He instructs the Israelites to do as the angel says. God tells his people that he will bring them into the land of certain nations who have a history of worshipping false gods. He warns the Jews not to follow the practices of these nations and orders them to destroy the idols of these nations. He then commands the Israelites to worship him and tells them that he will bless them for their worship by supplying them with enough food and water, and delivering them from sickness. God's blessings also included his eradication of miscarriages and barrenness.

---

[9] "....and so I have come down to rescue them from the Egyptians and to bring them out of Egypt to a spacious land, one which is rich and fertile and in which the Canaanites, the Hittites, the Amorites, the Perizzites, the Hivites, and the Jebusites now live." Exodus 3:8 (GNT)

As we can see, miscarriages and barrenness are not necessarily put in the same category as sickness. In the New Living Translation of the Bible, the word *barren* is translated as *infertility*. The Hebrew word for *barren* that is used in verse 26 is *aqar* which applies to both male and female and translates more specifically as the word *sterile* in the English. Barrenness then, does not just apply to women but can also apply to men. Although God has not associated being barren with being cursed, God certainly did indicate that to be able to produce offspring is a blessing as well as having a healthy body and having enough food and water. Let's look further:

> [11]"Therefore you shall keep the commandment, the statutes, and the judgements which I command you today, to observe them.
> [12]Then it shall come to pass, because you listen to these judgments, and keep and do them, the LORD your God will keep with you the covenant and the mercy which He swore to your fathers.
> [13]And He will love you and bless you and multiply you; He will also bless the fruit of your womb and the fruit of your land, your grain and your new wine and your oil, the increase of your cattle and the offspring of your flock, in the land of which He swore to your fathers to give you.
> [14]You shall be blessed above all peoples; there shall not be a male or female barren among you or among your livestock. (Deuteronomy 7:11-14 NKJV)

In verse 14, The word *barren* is applied to men as well as to women. It is the same Hebrew word cited above that translates into the English word for *sterile*. Often times when a husband and wife have difficulty conceiving, it is automatically assumed that the woman is the one who is sterile. But as biblically attested to, it could be either the husband or the wife who is infertile, who is barren. It is not necessarily always the woman.

God's blessings include the ability to produce offspring. However, this does not mean that people who are sterile are not blessed. They are blessed in many other ways. But many barren women, whether they are barren due to their own inability to have children or due to their husband's inability, find it particularly distressing that they cannot conceive. A woman who is barren often times believes that God has cursed her or that he has forsaken her. But as scripture points out, this is generally not the case. However, there is a certain biblical account that tells us of a particular incident in which God caused the women of a certain household to become barren. The women belonged to the household of a man named Abimelech. Abimelech's entire household suffered because of his indiscretions. The following is the account:

> [1]And Abraham journeyed from there to the South, and dwelt between Kadesh and Shur, and stayed in Gerar.
> [2]Now Abraham said of Sarah his wife, "She is my sister." And Abimelech king of Gerar sent and took Sarah.
> [3]But God came to Abimelech in a dream by night, and said to him, "Indeed you are a dead man because of the woman whom you have taken, for she is a man's wife."
> [4]But Abimelech had not come near her; and he said, "Lord, will You slay a righteous nation also?
> [5]Did he not say to me, 'She is my sister?' And she, even she herself said, 'He is my brother.' In the integrity of my heart and innocence of my hands I have done this."
> [6]And God said to him in a dream, "Yes, I know that you did this in the integrity of your heart. For I also withheld you from sinning against Me; therefore I did not let you touch her.
> [7]Now therefore, restore the man's wife; for he is a prophet, and he will pray for you and you shall live. But if you do not restore her, know that you shall surely die, you and all who are yours. (Genesis 20:1-7 NKJV)

Before commenting on the above verses of scripture, some background information is necessary in order to understand why Abraham moved his family to the city of Gerar. Biblical accounts[10] tell of

---

[10] Found in Genesis 12:10-20 (see your Bible).

the time Abraham took refuge in Egypt because a famine had developed in the land in which he was living. He took with him all those in his household including his wife Sarah.[11] Sarah was very beautiful and Abraham was fearful that if the men in Egypt knew that she was his wife they'd try to kill him for her. So he thought that if he deceived them by saying she was his sister they'd be nice to him in an effort to get close to her. This is indeed what happened. The Pharaoh of Egypt set out to marry her. But the Lord put a terrible plague upon Egypt because the Pharaoh was about to marry a woman who was already married.[12] When the Pharaoh discovered that Abraham and Sarah had been deceitful about their relationship to one another he sent them out of the country. So Abraham eventually moved his family to the city of Gerar, which was not far from Egypt. But once again he and Sarah deceived people telling them that the two of them were siblings instead of telling them that they were husband and wife. Unaware of this deception, a man named Abimelech began to pursue Sarah. Again the Lord intervened and revealed the real truth before any sin was committed. This time instead of a plague, God gave warning in a dream. Let's continue with the account of Abimelech:

> [8]Abimelech got up early the next morning and hastily called a meeting of all his servants. When he told them what had happened, great fear swept through the crowd. [9]Then Abimelech called for Abraham. "What is this you have done to us?" he demanded. "What have I done to you that deserves treatment like this, making me and my kingdom guilty of this great sin? This kind of thing should not be done! [10]Why have you done this to us?"
> [11]"Well," Abraham said, "I figured this to be a godless place. I thought, 'They will want my wife and will kill me to get her.' [12]Besides, she is my sister—we both have the same father, though different mothers—and I married her. [13]When God sent me to travel far

---

[11] Initially, Sarah's name was Sarai.

[12] Sarah would be the woman who would eventually carry Isaac in her womb. It was through Isaac in which God's covenant to the Jews was to be made.

from my father's home, I told her, 'Wherever we go, have the kindness to say that you are my sister. '"

[14]Then Abimelech took sheep and oxen and servants--both men and women--and gave them to Abraham, and he returned his wife, Sarah, to him. [15]Look over my kingdom, and choose a place where you would like to live." Abimelech told him. [16]Then he turned to Sarah, "Look," he said, "I am giving your 'brother' a thousand pieces of silver to compensate for any embarrassment I may have caused you. This will settle any claim against me in this matter."

[17]Then Abraham prayed to God, and God healed Abimelech, his wife, and the other women of the household, so they could have children.

[18]For the LORD had stricken all the women with infertility as a warning to Abimelech for having taken Abraham's wife. (Genesis 20:8-18 NLT)

Although Abraham deceived the men of Egypt as well as the men of Gerar into thinking that he and Sarah[13] were not married, God thwarted the eagerness of the men of those cities who wanted to marry Sarah (and thus, if any of them had done so, they would have unknowingly committed adultery with her) by cursing Egypt with a plague and warning Abimelech in a dream. We do not know how far Abraham and Sarah would have taken this deception. Apparently Sarah was beautiful to the point that both she and Abraham believed that Abraham's life would be in danger had they spoken the truth about their relationship in the beginning. God knows the heart of men and in looking at God's way of handling the deception, God was not meek in his approach. Apparently intervention from God was necessary in order to stop what was about to happen in both incidences. God did not punish Abraham or Sarah for their deception, which leads one to believe that the men of the city of Egypt and Gerar may have indeed killed Abraham for the opportunity to make advances towards Sarah. However, once the men learned of their misdeeds through the strong arm of the Lord, they knew better than to

---

[13] Abraham's marriage to his sister, Sarah, took place before the dispensation of Law in which God forbid such incestuous unions.

harm neither Abraham nor his wife, because they knew that the Lord was with them both.

Aside from warning Abimelech in a dream to cease involving himself with Sarah, God also struck Abimelech's entire household with barrenness. Abimelech himself was sterile because of his involvement with Sarah. So, not only were the women of the household cursed with barrenness but the man of the house was too. God was not going to let any man defile Sarah. No one was to impregnate her aside from her husband, Abraham. The misguided courtship between Abimelech and Sarah must have lasted quite some time in order for everyone in Abimelech's household to eventually realize that they were all infertile.

When Abimelech learned of Abraham's deception he must have realized that the reason he and all of the women in his household were sterile was because of the unholy alliance that he (Abimelech) had formed with Sarah. Abraham realized it as well and immediately prayed and asked God to heal Abimelech's household of the sterility. God, who is just and fair, removed the curse from the household and restored the fertility of all that lived there.

The historical account of Abimelech gives us an example of how barrenness can be the result of God's will.[14] Abimelech was able to figure out the reason why his household was barren. But often times God might not reveal his reasons for allowing a man or a woman to be barren. Despite this, we must realize that God knows what he is doing and that there is always a reason for what he does.

In looking at the lives of certain female biblical figures, we learn that in order for a particular purpose to be fulfilled at a particular time, God might have a woman to be barren for a set duration only to bless her with a child later on. Such is the case when looking at the lives of Elizabeth, Sarah, Rachel, and the wife of Manoah, Let's first look at the account of the wife of Manoah:

> [1]Again the children of Israel did evil in the sight of the
> LORD, and the LORD delivered them into the hand of
> the Philistines for forty years.

---

[14] Jesus teaches in John 9:1-11 and John 11:1-4 (see your Bible) that there are some who suffer illness, not because of anything they have done, but so that God can show his glory through them. Such was the case of Elizabeth who was barren for many years but eventually became the mother of John the Baptist.

> [2]Now there was a certain man from Zorah, of the family of the Danites, whose name was Manoah; and his wife was barren and had no children.
> [3]And the Angel of the LORD appeared to the woman and said to her, "Indeed now, you are barren and have borne no children, but you shall conceive and bear a son.
> [4]Now therefore, please be careful not to drink wine or similar drink, and not to eat anything unclean. (Judges 13:1-4 NKJV)

> [24]So the woman bore a son and called his name Samson; and the child grew, and the LORD blessed him.
> [25]And the Spirit of the LORD began to move upon him at Mahaneh Dan between Zorah and Eshtaol. (Judges 13:24-25 NKJV)

Samson was the son that was born to Manoah and his wife. Although a woman from the valley of Sorek, (whose name was Delilah), eventually helped Samson's enemies to defeat him, he was a man of great strength and he rescued his people from the Philistines just as an angel of the Lord had foretold he would.[15]

Samson was to be born at a specific time, at a specific place, and to a specific couple in order to be in the position that God needed him to be in at the right time to rescue the Israelites. Although, Manoah's wife was barren for a while, God opened her womb at a certain time to fulfill a certain purpose. In light of this, her barrenness was not the result of some curse or punishment. It was simply God's will that her time to bear children be delayed for a specific reason. Although Manoah's wife had been barren, she ended up carrying in her womb a person who would one day become one of the men in Israel's history that would deliver the Jews from oppression. What a great honor it was then, for her to have had carried Samson in her womb. A similar thing occurred with Elizabeth. Let's look at her account:

---

[15] The account of Samson and Delilah is found in the 16th chapter of Judges (see your Bible).

⁵In the days of King Herod of Judea, there was a priest named Zechariah, who belonged to the priestly order of Abijah. His wife was a descendant of Aaron, and her name was Elizabeth. ⁶Both of them were righteous before God, living blamelessly according to all the commandments and regulations of the Lord. ⁷But they had no children, because Elizabeth was barren, and both were getting on in years.

⁸Once when he was serving as priest before God and his section was on duty, ⁹he was chosen by lot, according to the custom of the priesthood, to enter the sanctuary of the Lord and offer incense. ¹⁰Now at the time of the incense offering, the whole assembly of the people was praying outside. ¹¹Then there appeared to him an angel of the Lord, standing at the right side of the altar of incense. ¹²When Zechariah saw him, he was terrified; and fear overwhelmed him. ¹³But the angel said to him, "Do not be afraid, Zechariah, for your prayer has been heard. Your wife Elizabeth will bear you a son, and you will name him John. ¹⁴You will have joy and gladness, and many will rejoice at his birth, ¹⁵for he will be great in the sight of the Lord. He must never drink wine or strong drink; even before his birth he will be filled with the Holy Spirit. ¹⁶He will turn many of the people of Israel to the Lord their God. ¹⁷With the spirit and power of Elijah he will go before him, to turn the hearts of parents to their children, and the disobedient to the wisdom of the righteous, to make ready a people prepared for the Lord."(Luke 1:5-17 NSRV)

As discussed earlier in chapter 2, Elizabeth and Zechariah were the parents of John the Baptist. John the Baptist prepared the way for the arrival of the Messiah, Jesus Christ, by proclaiming that the Christ would soon be coming and by baptizing with water.[16] John the Baptist was to be filled with the Holy Spirit and he was to persuade many

---

[16] For more on John the Baptist see Matthew 3:1-6 (see Appendix)

Israelites to return to the Lord their God. John the Baptist was a foreshadow of Jesus.

God had not blessed Elizabeth and Zechariah with a child until they were old in age. However, there was a reason for this. In looking at verse 6, we see that Elizabeth and Zechariah were righteous in the eyes of God and obeyed all of his commandments. One might conclude then that God wanted John the Baptist to be born of righteous parents. However, in order to foreshadow the ministry of Jesus, John had to be born at a certain time, to a certain couple, and at a certain place. Consequently, even though she was a righteous woman, Elizabeth was barren for a long time and was not able to conceive until late in her life. Her barrenness was not the result of any sin of hers. Let's look further into the account:

> [18]Zechariah said to the angel, "How can I know this will happen? I'm an old man now, and my wife is also well along in years."
> [19]Then the angel said, "I am Gabriel! I stand in the very presence of God. It was he who sent me to bring you this good news! [20]And now, since you didn't believe what I said, you won't be able to speak until the child is born. For my words will certainly come true at the proper time."
> [21]Meanwhile, the people were waiting for Zechariah to come out, wondering why he was taking so long. [22]When he finally did come out, he couldn't speak to them. Then they realized from his gestures that he must have seen a vision in the Temple sanctuary.
> [23]He stayed at the Temple until his term of service was over, and then he returned home. [24]Soon afterward his wife, Elisabeth, became pregnant and went into seclusion for five months. [25]"How kind the Lord is!" she exclaimed. "He has taken away my disgrace of having no children!" (Luke 1:18-25 NLT)

The disgrace that Elizabeth felt at having no children was not a disgrace put upon her by God, but a disgrace put upon her by society. Even today, when a woman marries, other women have a tendency to ask her when she is going to have a baby. This of course is a very personal issue that many women only want to discuss with their husbands. Despite this, not only do women feel the pressure from other women to have a baby, but many women are pressured by their own parents to have babies, because their parents want to become grandparents. There are also those women who are pressured by friends or people whom they associate with, to have a baby, if they are, by the estimate of others, taking "too long" to have children after they have married. These friends and associates often times begin to think that "something is wrong" and will often begin to ask questions of a prying nature. Of course, if the woman or her husband is infertile, this may cause a feeling of disgrace, shame, or even anger at God, which is often brought on by the societal and cultural expectations of others. Surely, Elizabeth felt this same pressure. The pressure for a woman to have children once she gets married was even more severe then than it is now. However, the pressure today can still be quite overwhelming.

Verse 18 tells us that Zechariah questioned the prophecy of the upcoming pregnancy given to him by the angel. Zechariah did not really believe that he and his wife were going to become parents. He felt they were too old. Because of his doubt, the angel struck Zechariah with the inability to speak until the child was born. This tells us that God is a God of miracles and does not want his miraculous powers to be doubted. If it is God's will, a barren woman or a barren man can eventually have children. But it must be God's will. It must be in his plan. Sometimes, it is God's will for certain men and women to remain barren.

We see another example of someone doubting the prophetic message given by an angel of the Lord, of an upcoming pregnancy, when looking at the account of Sarah. The account is as follows:

> [29]Then Abram and Nahor took wives: the name of Abram's wife was Sarai, and the name of Nahor's wife, Milcah, the daughter of Haran the father of Milcah and the father Milcah and the father of Iscah.
> [30]But Sarai was barren; she had no child. (Genesis 11:29-30 NKJV)

> [15]God also said to Abraham, "As for Sarai your wife, you are no longer to call her Sarai; her name will be Sarah. [16]I will bless her and will surely give you a son

by her. I will bless her so that she will be the mother of nations; kings of peoples will come from her."

[17]Abraham fell face down; he laughed and said to himself, "Will a son be born to a man a hundred years old? Will Sarah bear a child at the age of ninety?" [18] And Abraham said to God, "If only Ishmael might live under your blessing!"

[19]Then God said, "Yes, but your wife Sarah will bear you a son, and you will call him Isaac. I will establish my covenant with him as an everlasting covenant for his descendants after him. [20]And as for Ishmael, I have heard you; I will surely bless him; I will make him fruitful and will greatly increase his numbers. He will be a father of twelve rulers, and I will make him into a great nation.[21]But my covenant I will establish with Isaac, whom Sarah will bear to you by this time next year." (Genesis 17:15-21 NIV)

Sarah was barren. She was not able to have children. However, at a specific time in her life, God spoke directly to her husband Abraham[17] and told him that he and his wife would have a son whose name was to be Isaac. God's covenant promises[18] would come through Isaac. However before God promised Abraham and Sarah a son, Sarah thought she would never conceive so she abused her authority in the home by insisting that her house slave, Hagar, sleep with her husband in order to produce an heir for him.[19] Abraham went along with it to appease Sarah. But once Hagar gave birth to the child, Ishmael, Sarah began to despise Hagar and mistreat her. Hagar therefore ran away, but God was with Hagar. He knew how Sarah had mistreated her and he increased the descendants of Ishmael as well as those of Isaac (verse 20).

Not only did Abraham laugh when God told him directly that he and Sarah would have a child, but when Sarah overheard the news, she also laughed. Let's take a look:

[1]The LORD appeared to Abraham near the great trees

---

[17] God changed Abram's name to Abraham, Genesis 17:3-8 (see Appendix)
[18] Genesis 17:9-22, with specific attention to verse 19 (see your Bible)
[19] Genesis chapter 16 (see your Bible)

of Mamre while he was siting at the entrance to his tent in the heat of the day.

²Abraham looked up and saw three men standing nearby. When he saw them, he hurried from the entrance of his tent to meet them and bowed low to the ground. (Genesis 18:1-2 NIV)

⁹"Where is your wife Sarah?" they asked him.

"There, in the tent," he said.

¹⁰Then the LORD said, "I will surely return to you about this time next year, and Sarah your wife will have a son."

Now Sarah was listening at the entrance to the tent, which was behind him. ¹¹Abraham and Sarah were already old and well advanced in years, and Sarah was past the age of childbearing. ¹²So Sarah laughed to herself as she thought, "After I am worn out and my master is old, will I now have this pleasure?"

¹³Then the LORD said to Abraham, "Why did Sarah laugh and say, 'Will I really have a child, now that I am old?' ¹⁴Is anything too hard for the LORD? I will return to you at the appointed time next year and Sarah will have a son."

¹⁵Sarah was afraid, so she lied and said, "I did not laugh."

But he said, "Yes, you did laugh."

(Genesis 18:9-15 NIV)

Despite the initial doubt that both Abraham and Sarah had in God's promise of blessing them with a child, God kept his promise anyway and did not punish them for doubting him.

The emphasis here is that nothing is too hard for the Lord. If it is God's will for a woman to bear a child then she will conceive at some point in her life while she is married to her husband.

Proverbs 30:15 says the following: *"The leech has two suckers that cry out, "More, more!" There are three other things--no, four!--that are never satisfied: the grave, the barren womb, the thirsty desert, the blazing fire."*

Proverbs tells us that a barren womb is never satisfied. In other words, a woman who is barren usually longs desperately to have children. But although many women look upon barrenness as a curse, the Bible tells us that there will be a time when barrenness will actually be a blessing for women. Let's take a look:

> [26] As they led Jesus away, Simon of Cyrene, who was coming in from the country just then, was forced to follow Jesus and carry his cross. [27]Great crowds trailed along behind including many grief-stricken women. [28]But Jesus, turning to them, said, "Daughters of Jerusalem, do not weep for Me, but weep for yourselves and for your children. (Luke 23:26-28 NLT) [29]For indeed the days are coming in which they will say, 'Blessed are the barren, wombs that never bore, and breasts which never nursed!'
> [30]Then they will begin to say to the mountains, "Fall on us!" and to the hills, "Cover us!" (Luke 23:29-30 NKJV)

In times of war and suffering women who do not have children and are barren are considered fortunate because they will not have to worry about the suffering that their children will go through, since they don't have any. In regards to the verses cited above, there are those theologians who believed that Jesus was speaking of a time when Jerusalem would be defeated by the Romans and destroy the temple. This occurred in 70 A.D. During that time the people of Jerusalem experienced great suffering and stress. This defeat occurred some 40 years after Jesus prophesied about the coming of the time when childless women would be looked upon as blessed. However, Jesus spoke of another time when being without a child will be looked upon as more of as a blessing than as a curse, and that is the time that he described as the "abomination of desolation." Let's take a look:

> [14]And this gospel of the kingdom will be preached in all the world as a witness to all the nations, and then the end will come.

[15]Therefore when you see the 'abomination of desolation,' spoken of by Daniel the prophet, standing in the holy place" (whoever reads let him understand),
[16]then let those who are in Judea flee to the mountains.
[17]let him who is on the housetop not go down to take anything out of his house.
[18]And let him who is in the field not go back to get his clothes.
[19]But woe to those who are pregnant and to those who are nursing babies in those days!
[20]"And pray that your flight may not be in the winter or on the Sabbath.
[21]For then there will be great tribulation, such as has not been since the beginning of the world until this time, no, nor ever shall be.
[22]And unless those days were shortened, no flesh would be saved; but for the elect's sake those days will be shortened.
[23]Then if anyone says to you, 'Look, here is the Christ! or 'There!' Do not believe it.
[24]For false christs and false prophets will rise and show great signs and wonders to deceive, if possible, even the elect.
[25]See I have told you before hand. (Matthew 24:14-25 NKJV)

Jesus is the one speaking in the verses just quoted above. The abomination of desolation refers to when the antichrist (whose number is 666) will enter the temple and establish peace in the world for 3 and 1/2 years, then in the fourth year (and during another 3 and 1/2 years immediately after) the antichrist will claim to be God (7 years altogether). Those who have accepted Jesus as Lord and Savior will be persecuted and many of them will be beheaded. These events are accounts of the end time tribulation. Scriptures[20] that address the end time tribulation are found in 2nd Thessalonians 2:1-12, Daniel 9:24-27, Daniel 11:36-45, Daniel 12:1-4 Revelation 13:11-18, and Revelation 20:1-10. The antichrist will be able to perform many miracles and he

---

[20] See your Bible for these scriptures.

137

will come against the people of God. The people of God will be heavily persecuted during that time. This is why Jesus indicated that in those days to come, childless women will have a better time of things as opposed to women with children. And those days to come will be the times when women will wish that they were barren.

SUMMARY

As we have seen, menstruation is not a curse and in general, neither is barrenness, although many women speak of menstruation in jest, as a curse, and many women, unfortunately often times mistakenly consider any woman who is barren to be cursed. We must be reminded that the specific curses associated with women are increased pain in childbearing and the rule that husbands have over their wives. Menstruation is a natural physical process that women experience during the course of their lives. Infertility is a physical condition. Although infertility compromises the reproductive ability of a man or woman, it is not something to feel disgraced about and could be the result of God's will as we have seen in our discussion while looking at the lives of Elizabeth, Manoah's wife and Sarah.

In regards to a childless couple, society has a tendency to first speculate that the woman is the one who is infertile. However, the Bible clearly indicates that it could just as well be the man who is infertile. Furthermore a barren woman may be barren, not because she herself is infertile, but because her husband is.

In Romans 4:19 Paul used the word *dead* to describe the barrenness of Sarah's womb. A woman's womb can be desolate or dead for three reasons: because she consciously chooses not to have children (which is all right with God[21]), because she herself is infertile, or because her husband is infertile. God does not hold a woman who is infertile to any shame just as he doesn't hold a man who is infertile to any shame, unless they are cursed with infertility because of some sin that has been committed, as was in the case of Abimelech. There is no biblical command that says all women must have children, just as there is no biblical command that says all men must have children.[22]

---

[21] See Chapter 12.
[22] See chapter 12.

Some would say however, that God has commanded all human beings to procreate because God has commanded each of us to be fruitful and multiply. But the command given to humans to be fruitful and multiply was specifically given by God to certain people in order that they would either replenish the earth with people or birth nations.[23] The command to be fruitful and multiply does not apply to all people in general.

God is reasonable. He never commanded anyone to do something that he or she did not have the ability to do. We are commanded to love our neighbors as ourselves. We all have the ability to do that. We are commanded to abstain from fornication, drunkenness, homosexuality, adultery, slander, stealing, greed[24] and the like and we all have the ability to abstain from these things. But an infertile woman does not have the ability to conceive and neither does an infertile man. When God gave the command to be fruitful and multiply (in regards to having children) he gave this specific command to specific people.

When considering physical inability we have but to look at Paul the apostle. Paul prayed three times to the Lord asking him to heal his body but it was not God's will to do so. God responded to Paul by telling him that his (God's) power is made perfect in weakness. This means that God's power is shown through someone who has an illness or difficulty but keeps working for the Lord regardless of his or her limitations or distresses. Paul therefore took pleasure in his difficulties.[25] Again, it is Paul who said, as quoted in Philippians 4:11[26] that he had learned to be content in whatever condition or situation he was in. Therefore, women who are barren should strive to be content in the state that they are in, love the Lord, and serve the Lord with gladness of heart. This is how God would want them to respond because God's power is made perfect in weakness and in distresses. It is no different for a man. God would want a man to also be content in his state of infertility until the time God

---

[23] Genesis 9:1. Genesis 17:20, Genesis 28:1-3, Genesis 48:3-4, Exodus 1:7, (see your Bible)

[24] "Don't you know that those who do wrong will have no share in the Kingdom of God? Don't fool yourselves. Those who indulge in sexual sin, who are idol worshippers, adulterers, male prostitutes, homosexuals, thieves, greedy people, drunkards, abusers, and swindlers—none of these will have a share in the Kingdom of God." (1 Corinthians 6:9-10 NLT)

[25] 2 Corinthians 12:6-10 (see Appendix)

[26] See your Bible.

chose to heal him of it, if he chooses to at all. Although society may respond differently to a woman who has no children than it does to a man, God does not. God does not make a difference between a barren woman and a barren man. He does not make a difference between a woman who has no children and a man who has no children. Neither men, nor women, are mandated to have children. Therefore there is no chauvinism on God's part concerning these matters.

5.

WOMEN IN THE CHURCH

Over the years there have been questions among Christians as to whether or not God has given women the same opportunities to serve in particular functions as he has given men, especially when it comes to being appointed to certain positions in the church. Most of the functions in question are addressed in the books of Ephesians and 1st Corinthians. Before beginning our discussion we will take a brief look at what certain verses of scripture in Ephesians say about these things:

> [4]There is one body and one Spirit, just as also you were called in one hope of your calling;
> [5]one Lord, one faith, one baptism,
> [6]one God and Father of all who is over all and through all and in all.
> [7]But to each one of us grace was given according to the measure of Christ's gift.
> [8]Therefore it says,
> "WHEN HE ASCENDED ON HIGH,
> HE LED CAPTIVE A HOST OF CAPTIVES
> AND HE GAVE GIFTS TO MEN."
> [9](Now, this expression, "He ascended," what does it mean except that He also had descended into the lower parts of the earth?
> [10]He who descended is Himself also He who ascended far above all the heavens, that He might fill all things.)
> [11]And He gave some as apostles, and some as prophets, and some as evangelists, and some as pastors and teachers,
> [12]for the equipping of the saints for the work of service, to the building up of the body of Christ;
> [13]until we all attain to the unity of the faith, and of the knowledge of the Son of God, to a mature man, to the measure of the stature which belongs to the fullness of Christ.

> ¹⁴As a result, we are no longer to be children, tossed here and there by waves, and carried about by every wind of doctrine, by the trickery of men, by craftiness in deceitful scheming;
> ¹⁵but speaking the truth in love, we are to grow up in all aspects into Him, who is the head, even Christ,
> ¹⁶from whom the whole body being fitted and held together by that which every joint supplies, according to the proper working of each individual part, causes the growth of the body for the building up of itself in love. (Ephesians 4:4-16 NASB)

The above verses of scripture are specifically addressing those who are Christians. Verse 8 says that God gave "gifts to men." The Greek word for the word *men* used in the verse is a derivative of the Greek word *anthropos. Anthropos* refers to mankind in general, human beings, both men and women. Therefore, the gifts and callings that are spoken of are gifts that God may choose to impart and callings that God may choose to convey, to mankind as a whole. This, of course, includes women. The main focus here is what is taught in verses 11 and 12 which tells us that God gave some Christians the abilities (gifts), or callings to function as apostles, prophets, evangelists, pastors, and/or teachers. Some teach that prophesying and teaching are better defined as gifts whereas doing the work of an apostle, pastor, or evangelist fits more into the category of a function or a position. However, for our purposes, all five functions that are listed in verse 11 will be referenced as gifts that God has given to the church for the edifying of the church (verse 12) since it appears that verse 7 (which speaks about gifts) connects with verse 11.

The New Living Translation of the Bible puts it this way: *"He is the one who gave these gifts to the church: the apostles, the prophets, the evangelists, and the pastors and teachers. Their responsibility is to equip God's people to do his work and build up the church, the body of Christ."* Either way, the verses of scripture do not gender-specify either of the five functions (which can be looked at as gifts to the church as a whole, or can be looked at, as some do, as gifts in and of themselves that are imparted to men and women of the church individually) which were cited.

To those whom God has led to operate in the function of apostle, prophet, evangelist, pastor, and/or teacher, God has led them as such in order that they might build up the body of Christ (the church).

Not all that are in the church will be led of the Lord to serve in these functions and not all will possess these gifts. Some Christians will possess other gifts aside from that of being an apostle, prophet, evangelist, pastor, or teacher. And God may give one gift to one Christian that he does not give to another, as evidenced in the following verses of scripture:

> [27]Now you are Christ's body, and individually members of it.
> [28]And God has appointed in the church, first apostles, second prophets, third teachers, then miracles, then gifts of healings, helps, administrations, various kinds of tongues.
> [29]All are not apostles, are they? All are not prophets, are they? All are not teachers, are they? All are not workers of miracles, are they?
> [30]All do not have gifts of healings, do they? All do not speak with tongues, do they? All do not interpret, do they?
> [31]But earnestly desire the greater gifts.
> And I show you a still more excellent way.
> (1 Corinthians 12:27-31 NASB)

Again, there are those in the church that believe certain gifts (or appointed functions as others might call them) are not meant for women, but only for men. Consequently, the church has a history of disallowing women to operate in certain positions in the church. But, women who operate in these gifts anyway, despite what any man might do or say to discourage them, do so because they feel that they are called of God to do so. Their steadfastness and determination incite debate in others. This chapter will take a look at what are the most central points of interest that trigger this debate.

WHY WERE THERE NO FEMALE APOSTLES?

Who says there weren't? But before beginning our discussion as to whether or not there were any female apostles, we will first examine the definition and role of an apostle.

The English word *apostle* is derived from the Greek word *apostolos,* the meaning of which is *messenger* or *ambassador.* An ambassador is a person who represents a country or a kingdom. An apostle is a representative of the gospel of Jesus Christ. Jesus Christ has a kingdom. His is a heavenly kingdom in which all are welcome who worship him as Lord and Savior. More specifically the word *apostolos* means to send on behalf of another. Jesus sent the original twelve apostles to preach the gospel on behalf of him and his gospel.

When Jesus first began his ministry he appointed twelve specific men to help him in its establishment. The original twelve were Simon Peter, James (son of Zebedee), John (brother of James), Andrew, Philip, Bartholomew, Matthew, Thomas, James (son of Alphaeus), Thaddaeus, Simon (the Canaanite), and Judas Iscariot. Let's take a look:

> [13]And He went up on the hillside and called to Him [for Himself] those whom He wanted and chose, and they came to Him.
>
> [14]And he appointed twelve to continue to be with Him, and that He might send them out to preach [as apostles or special messengers]
>
> [15]And to have authority and power to heal the sick and to drive out demons:
>
> [16][They were] Simon, and He surnamed [him] Peter;
>
> [17]James son of Zebedee and John the brother of James, and He surnamed them Boanerges, that is, Sons of Thunder;
>
> [18]And Andrew, and Philip, and Bartholomew (Nathaniel), and Matthew, and Thomas, and James son of Alphaeus, and Thaddaeus (Judas, not Iscariot), and Simon the Cananaean [also called Zelotes],
>
> [19]And Judas Iscariot, he who betrayed Him.
> (Mark 3:13-19 Amp.)

Judas Iscariot eventually betrayed Jesus by turning him over, in exchange for thirty pieces of silver, to the authorities to be imprisoned and ultimately to be crucified. Afterwards, Judas hung himself, as the following verses of scripture attest to:

> [1]Early the next morning all the chief priests and the nation's leaders met and decided that Jesus should be put to death. [2]They tied him up and led him away to Pilate the governor.
> [3]Judas had betrayed Jesus, but when he learned that Jesus had been sentenced to death, he was sorry for what he had done. He returned the thirty silver coins to the chief priests and leaders [4]and said, "I have sinned by betraying a man who has never done anything wrong."
> "So what! That's your problem," they replied. [5]Judas threw the money into the temple and then went out and hanged himself. (Matthew 27:1-5 CEV)

After Judas committed suicide only eleven apostles were left. A replacement was needed. Matthias was selected to replace Judas.[1] Later on, after the death, burial, and resurrection of Jesus, Paul, the man who wrote most of the books of the New Testament, identified himself as an apostle of the Lord. Before his conversion to Christianity while traveling to Damascus, Paul was one of the great persecutors of Christians during his day. Paul, was also known as Saul and is referred to as Saul in the historical account of his conversion.[2]

It was Jesus who confronted Paul while he was on the way to Damascus . Let's take a look:

> [3]As he was nearing Damascus on this mission, a brilliant light from heaven suddenly beamed down upon him! [4]He fell to the ground and heard a voice saying to him, "Saul! Saul! Why are you persecuting me?"
> [5]"Who are you, sir?" Saul asked.
> And the voice replied, "I am Jesus, the one you are persecuting! [6]Now get up and go into the city, and you will be told what you are to do." (Acts 9:3-5 NLT)

---

[1] Acts 1:15-26 (see your Bible)
[2] Acts 9:1-31 (see your Bible)

Paul obeyed the voice of the Lord and began doing the Lord's work. At this point, Paul considered himself just as much of an apostle as the original twelve because not only had Jesus called him specifically, but Paul had seen Jesus with his own eyes. In other words, just as Jesus had appeared to the twelve as well as to others after his resurrection, Jesus had also appeared to Paul. Paul's defense of his apostleship is documented in the following verses of scripture:

> [1]Do I not have as much freedom as anyone else? Am I not an apostle? Haven't I seen Jesus our Lord with my own eyes? Isn't it because of my hard work that you are in the Lord? [2]Even if others think I am not an apostle, I certainly am to you, for you are living proof that I am the Lord's apostle. (1 Corinthians 9:1-2 NLT)

Paul's aim was to convince the Corinthian church that he was indeed an apostle. The position of apostle was a unique one. The apostleship of the twelve was unquestionably an honorable position. The names of the twelve apostles will be written on foundation stones in Heaven. Let's take a look:

> [1]I saw a new heaven and a new earth. The first heaven and the first earth had disappeared, and so had the sea. [2]Then I saw New Jerusalem, that holy city, coming down from God in heaven. It was like a bride dressed in her wedding gown and ready to meet her husband. (Revelation 21:1-2 CEV)

> [10]Then with the help of the Spirit, he took me to the top of a very high mountain. There he showed me the holy city of Jerusalem coming down from God in heaven.
> [11]The glory of God made the city bright. It was dazzling and crystal clear like a precious jasper stone. [12]The city had a high and thick wall with twelve gates, and each one of them was guarded by an angel. On each of the gates was written the name of one of the twelve tribes of Israel. [13]Three of these gates were on the east, three were on the north, three more were on

the south, and the other three were on the west. [14]The city was built on twelve foundation stones. On each of the stones was written the name of one of the Lamb's twelve apostles. (Revelation 21:10-14 CEV)

The New Jerusalem is the eternal heavenly city wherein Christians will dwell with Jesus forever in the afterlife. The 21st chapter of Revelation describes the overwhelming beauty of this city. Not only will the names of the twelve tribes of Israel be written on the gates of the city but also the names of the twelve apostles will be written on the foundation stones that support the wall of the city. It goes without saying that this is a great tribute to the twelve apostles.

Some would say that God is a chauvinist since there will be no names of women written on these stones because all of the apostles were men. However, the names of the twelve tribes of Israel will be written on the gates of the city and those gates will be guarded by twelve angels, conclusively, one angel for each gate. Only those human beings that were believers in Christ during their earthly life will be able to enter the city. In light of this, it is just as great an honor for the names of the twelve tribes of Israel to be written on the gates as it is for the names of the apostles to be written on the foundation stones. Women belonged to the twelve tribes of Israel just as men did. There are men and women today whose descendants are from one of the twelve tribes. As explained in the Introduction, the Nation of Israel is a nation of people who actually descended from a man named Israel (whose original name was Jacob). Israel's twelve sons became known as the twelve tribes of Israel. Each of the twelve sons, through their children, children's children, and so on, developed into a tribe. Israel (Jacob) was the son of Isaac, who was the son of Abraham. God promised Abraham that his descendants would be blessed, because of Abraham's great loyalty to God. The Nation of Israel is the offspring of Abraham that God promised would be blessed.

Since the twelve tribes of Israel include women as well as men, the tribal names on the heavenly gates will not only exalt the men who were and are members of those tribes, but will also exalt the women who were and are members of those tribes. In this sense, God has not excluded women when it comes to this particular reward that will be bestowed upon Israel.

When it comes to the foundation stones, although the names on each of the stones will be names of men, not all of the male apostles will be rewarded in this way. Essentially, there were more than twelve apostles. Judas was the twelfth apostle but he hung himself and was replaced by Matthias. We can safely assume that Judas' name will not be on one of the stones.

Upon his conversion during his travel on the road leading to the city of Damascus, Paul became an apostle of the Lord. But Paul was not one of the original twelve. It is therefore questionable, despite all of the contributions Paul has made to the gospel of Christ, whether or not his name will be on one of the foundation stones. Furthermore, as verse 7 of the following text of scripture reveals, there were more apostles than the original twelve. As we have seen Matthias and Paul were apostles. But Barnabus was also an apostle. Let's take a look:

> [1] Paul and Barnabas spoke in the Jewish meeting place in Iconium, just as they had done at Antioch, and many Jews and Gentiles put their faith in the Lord. [2] But the Jews who did not have faith in him made the other Gentiles angry and turned them against the Lord's followers.
>
> [3] Paul and Barnabas stayed there for a while, having faith in the Lord and bravely speaking his message. The Lord gave them the power to work miracles and wonders, and he showed that their message about his great kindness was true.
>
> [4] The people of Iconium did not know what to think. Some of them believed the Jewish group, and others believed the apostles. (Acts 14:1-4 CEV)

Barnabus is identified as an apostle (verse 4). Theologians basically make a difference between the original twelve and those who were apostles thereafter. The Twelve were unique in that they were appointed together as a group to spread the gospel of Jesus Christ. Others were called to be apostles but they were called outside of the Twelve. However, their charge remained the same as the Twelve. They were to spread the gospel of Jesus Christ and were no less of an apostle than the Twelve were.

Many theologians believe that the apostolic office is closed today and that no one in today's world can really be an apostle. They believe this because of Paul's implication of what qualifies one to be an apostle.[3] Paul implies that in order to be an apostle one must work diligently for the Lord and one must have also seen Jesus Christ, specifically the resurrected Lord. In today's world, no one has seen the resurrected Jesus. Of course, it is possible for Jesus to appear to anyone, but it is questionable and it seems unlikely since the Father has sent the Holy Spirit to help Christians[4] until the return of Christ.

Adronicus and Junias who were relatives of Paul and suffered with him in prison are also listed as apostles. We can safely surmise however, that their names, as well as Barnabas' name, will also not be included on the foundation stones in heaven, since there is only mention of twelve stones with twelve names. Therefore, speaking in assumption, God has not only limited the names on the stones to the original Twelve (with the inclusion of Matthias) but has also eliminated certain men, in general, that most of us would assume would automatically be included (i.e. Paul, Moses, David, Abraham, etc). When looking at it this way, God has given no more reward to men than he has given to women.

Let's take a look at the text that identifies Adronicus and Junias as apostles. We will also see that the text identifies women who are fellow workers in Christ as well:

> [1]I commend to you our sister Phoebe, a servant of the church of Cenchrea. [2]I ask you to receive her in the Lord in a way worthy of the saints and to give her any help she may need from you, for she has been a great help to many people, including me.
> [3]Greet Priscilla and Aquila, my fellow workers in Christ Jesus. [4]They risked their lives for me, not only I but all the churches of the Gentiles are grateful to them.
> [5]Greet my dear friend Epenetus, who was the first convert to Christ in the province of Asia.

---

[3] Am I not an apostle? am I not free? have I not seen Jesus Christ our Lord? are not ye my work in the Lord? If I be not an apostle unto others, yet doubtless I am to you: for the seal of mine apostleship are ye in the Lord. (1 Corinthians 9:1-2)

[4] "But the Helper, the Holy Spirit, whom the Father will send in My name, He will teach you all things, and bring to your remembrance all things that I said to you." (Jesus is speaking here, John 14:26 NKJV)

[6]Greet Mary, who worked very hard for you.

[7]Greet Andronicus and Junias, my relatives who have been in prison with me. They are outstanding among the apostles, and they were in Christ before I was.

[8]Greet Ampliatus, whom I love in the Lord.

[9]Greet Urbanus, our fellow worker in Christ, and my dear friend Stachys.

[10]Greet Apelles, tested and approved in Christ. Greet those who belong to the household of Aristobulus.

[11]Greet Herodion, my relative. Greet those in the household of Narcissus who are in the Lord. Greet Tryphena and Tryphosa, those women who work hard in the Lord.

[12]Greet my dear friend Persis, another woman who has worked very hard in the Lord.

[13]Greet Rufus, chosen in the Lord, and his mother, who has been a mother to me, too.

[14]Greet Asyncritus, Phlegon, Hermes, Patrobas, Hermas and the brothers with them.

[15]Greet Philologus, Julia, Nereus, and his sister, and Olympas and all the saints with them.

[16]Greet one another with a holy kiss. All the churches of Christ send greetings. (Romans 16:1-15 NIV)

Theologians have assessed that Paul is the author of the book of Romans and that the book of Romans is actually a letter that Paul wrote to the church in Rome. At this juncture we want to pay particular attention to verse 7 that speaks of Andronicus and Junias and says, *"Greet Andronicus and Junias, my relatives who have been in prison with me. They are outstanding among the apostles, and they were in Christ before I was."* According to the theologians responsible for the authorship and biblical translation presented in the *NIV Study Bible*, Junias is a feminine name. This means that Junias was a woman. This means that a woman has been biblically and historically identified as an apostle. Additionally, the *Holman Bible Dictionary* identifies both Adronicus and Junias as apostles and also indicates that Junias is a feminine name. However, not all would agree that Junias was an apostle.

150

The scholars responsible for the *NIV Study Bible* point out that there are two ways that verse 7 can be interpreted.[5] One, is the interpretation that says that Andronicus and Junias are indeed apostles, but just not of the original Twelve. The other is the interpretation that says that the phrase "outstanding among the apostles" really translates into something like "outstanding according to the apostles" or "outstanding in the opinion of the apostles." The logic used for the latter translation is that the article *the* that is used before the word *apostles* signifies that the word *apostles* represents a group separate from those who are described as *outstanding,* those being Adronicus and Junias. However, one who decides to uphold the latter interpretation may also be exercising an interpretive double standard when it comes to the interpretations of similar scriptural text that have similar sentence structuring. Let's use the following scripture as an example:

> [22]Then the apostles and elders, with the whole church, decided to choose some of their own men and send them to Antioch with Paul and Barnabas. They chose Judas (Barsabbas) and Silas, two men who were leaders among the brothers. (Acts 15:22 NIV)

Our focal point is the part of the verse that says *"Judas and Silas, two men who were leaders among the brothers."* The Greek word for *among* that is used here is the same Greek word for *among* that is used in Romans 16:7 which says *"they* (Andonicus and Junias) *are outstanding among the apostles."* The sentence structure as it translates into English is also the same. Therefore, the interpretation should be the same as long as there are no cultural barriers limiting like interpretation.

Let's face it. We would normally interpret *"Judas and Silas, two men who were leaders among the brothers"* to mean that Judas and Silas are also included as being identified as spiritual brothers along with the other spiritual brothers that were there at the time. Furthermore Judas and Silas are identified as leaders. So the inference here is that Judas and Silas were leaders who were also brothers (in the Lord). We would not normally make emphasis of the article *the* that comes before the word *brothers.* We *would not normally* interpret the phrase to mean that Judas

---

[5] See page 1732 of the NIV Study Bible, copyright © 1995 by The Zondervan Corporation

and Silas were leaders *in the opinion of* the brothers. Of course, we could argue that it is possible that "in the opinion of the brothers" is how the verse really translates since the article *the* is present before the word *brothers*. But most would argue against this interpretation. Most would say that the scripture is *identifying* Judas and Silas as brothers. If then we are to use the same interpretive rules when looking at the identity of Andronicus and Junias that we use when looking at the identity of Judas and Silas, then we must also identify Andronicus and Junias as apostles. If the inference is that the *leaders* (Judas and Silas) were also brothers, then the inference must also be that the *outstanding* (Andronicus and Junias) were also apostles.

Even with all of this said, still, not all scholars and theologians agree that the correct interpretation of Romans 16:7 is that Andronicus and Junias were apostles. To be fair, let's take a look at some of the different translations of Romans 16:7:

> Then there are Andronicus and Junia, my relatives, who were in prison with me. They are respected among the apostles and became Christians before I did. (NLT)

> Greet Andronicus and Junia, my countrymen and my fellow prisoners, who are of note among the apostles, who also were in Christ before me. (NKJV)

The word *countrymen*, an old English word that is used for the Greek word *suggenes* which means *relative* or *kin*, gives the impression that Andronicus and Junia were both men. Let's continue:

> Greet Andronicus and Junias, my kinsmen, and my fellow prisoners, who are outstanding among the apostles, who also were in Christ before me. (NASB)

The word *kinsmen* is another old English word that is used for the Greek word *suggenes* (relative/kin) again giving the impression that Andronicus and Junias were both men. Let's continue:

> Remember me to Andronicus and Junias, my tribal kinsmen and once my fellow prisoners. They are men

held in high esteem among the apostles, who also were
in Christ before I was. (Amp.)

The Amplified Bible totally dismisses the fact that *Junias* is a
feminine name and identifies both Andronicus and Junias as men. While
it is possible that a man was given the name of a woman, it is unlikely.
Just as it is unlikely in today's time to meet a man who has been given
the name of a woman.

When taking a second look at Romans 16:1-15, not only do we
discover that a woman was an apostle, but we also see that there were
many women who assisted Paul in his apostolic ministry. Let's look again
at those verses of scripture:

> [1]I commend to you our sister Phoebe, a servant of the
> church of Cenchrea. [2]I ask you to receive her in the
> Lord in a way worthy of the saints and to give her any
> help she may need from you, for she has been a great
> help to many people, including me.
> [3]Greet Priscilla and Aquila, my fellow workers in
> Christ Jesus. [4]They risked their lives for me, not only I
> but all the churches of the Gentiles are grateful to them.
> [5]Greet my dear friend Epenetus, who was the first
> convert to Christ in the province of Asia.
> [6]Greet Mary, who worked very hard for you.
> [7]Greet Andronicus and Junias, my relatives who have
> been in prison with me. They are outstanding among
> the apostles, and they were in Christ before I was.
> [8]Greet Ampliatus, whom I love in the Lord.
> [9]Greet Urbanus, our fellow worker in Christ, and my
> dear friend Stachys.
> [10]Greet Apelles, tested and approved in Christ.
> Greet those who belong to the household of
> Aristobulus.
> [11]Greet Herodion, my relative.
> Greet those in the household of Narcissus who are in
> the Lord.
> Greet Tryphena and Tryphosa, those women who work
> hard in the Lord.

153

[12]Greet my dear friend Persis, another woman who has worked very hard in the Lord.
[13]Greet Rufus, chosen in the Lord, and his mother, who has been a mother to me, too.
[14]Greet Asyncritus, Phlegon, Hermes, Patrobus, Hermas and the brothers with them.
[15]Greet Philologus, Julia, Nereus, and his sister, and Olympas and all the saints with them.
[16]Greet one another with a holy kiss. All the churches of Christ send greetings. (Romans 16:1-15 NIV)

As cited in verse 1, Phoebe was a servant of the church of Cenchrea. She was a great help to the apostle Paul. Paul commends Priscilla and Aquila (verse 3) for having risked their lives for him. Priscilla and Aquila were married, with Priscilla being the female counterpart. Both Priscilla and Aquila diligently served the Lord and had traveled with Paul during his ministry.[6] Paul describes both Priscilla and Aquila as his fellow workers in Christ Jesus and put Priscilla's name before her husband's name when referring to the two of them in verse 3. To cite the woman first (when making reference to a married couple) was unusual. It is even unusual today.

Mary (verse 6) is described as a hard worker. Tryphena, Tryphosa, and Persis (verses 11 and 12) are cited as three women who worked hard in the Lord. Apparently, they had also traveled with Paul at some time during his apostolic ministry. Rufus' mother is acknowledged as having been like a mother to Paul during his travels. Julia and the sister of Nereus (verse 15) are grouped along with all of the other saints. As we can see women were very instrumental in assisting Paul in his apostolic ministry.

More evidence that women were very instrumental in assisting Paul in his apostolic ministry is seen when considering the following verses of scripture:

[1]Dear brothers and sisters, I love you and long to see you, for you are my joy and the reward for my work. So please stay true to the Lord, my dear friends.

---

[6] For more on Priscilla, look under the subheading of "Teachers" in this chapter.

> [2]And now I want to plead with those two women, Euodia and Syntyche. Please, because you belong to the Lord, settle your disagreement. [3]And I ask you, my true teammate, to help these women, for they worked hard with me in telling others the Good News. And they worked with Clement and the rest of my co-workers, whose names are written in the book of life. (Philippians 4:1-3 NLT)

Euodia and Syntyche worked side by side with Paul in his apostolic mission to preach the gospel of Jesus Christ. Apparently Paul had many co-workers that helped him in his quest to proclaim the gospel of Christ, and many of these co-workers were women. Unfortunately, these two particular women, Euodia and Syntyche had some sort of disagreement between them which apparently effected their ability to work closely together in their duty to the gospel. It can be safely assumed that both women were an attribute to the cause of the gospel and that it was important that they settle their differences because it was important that the two of them continue to work together. Paul specifically asked the two of them to settle their differences and instructed the Philippian church to assist them in their endeavors in Christ.

Not only were there women who accompanied and assisted Paul in his apostolic ministry but many of the apostles were married and their wives accompanied and assisted them in their travels to preach the gospel. The following verses of scripture attest to this:

> [1]Am I not free? Am I not an apostle? Have I not seen Jesus our Lord? Are you not the result of my work in the Lord? [2]Even though I may not be an apostle to others, surely I am to you! For you are the seal of my apostleship in the Lord.
>
> [3]This is my defense to those who sit in judgment on me. [4]Don't we have the right to food and drink? [5]Don't we have the right to take a believing wife along with us, as do the other apostles and the Lord's brothers and Cephas? [6]Or is it only I and Barnabus who must work for a living? (1 Corinthians 9:1-6 NIV)
>
> [11]If we have sown spiritual seed among you, is it too much if we reap a material harvest from you? [12]If

others have this right of support from you, shouldn't
we have it all the more?

But we did not use this right. On the contrary we
put up with anything rather than hinder the gospel of
Christ. [13]Don't you know that those who work in the
temple get their food from the temple, and those who
serve at the altar share in what is offered on the altar?
[14]In the same way, the Lord has commanded that those
who preach the gospel should receive their living from
the gospel. (1 Corinthians 9:11-14 NIV)

Because Paul and Barnabas were not one of the original twelve
apostles, there were some in the church that did not believe in their
apostolic calling. The church supported the ministry of the apostles. The
apostles did not have to earn wages for a living. Instead their job was to
spread the gospel by preaching it from city to city and the church would
take care of them financially. However, Paul had to convince the church
that he and Barnabas should be taken care of in the same way as the other
apostles. Our focus here however, is the fact that the original twelve
apostles, except for Judas, (who had committed suicide) were
accompanied in their ministry by their wives (those of them who had
wives). When we think of the twelve apostles, we often only think of
twelve men traveling from city to city preaching the gospel. But their
wives and probably their children traveled with them as well. Certainly,
it was a great asset for the apostles to have their wives along on the
journey. Furthermore, despite knowing that the wives of these men would
take part in the ministry of his gospel, Jesus did not hesitate to call
married men to the apostleship.

It must also be noted that although the words *apostle* and *disciple* are
often used interchangeably, apostle means *messenger*, while *disciple*
means *follower* or *student*. Although the twelve apostles are also referred
to as the Disciples,[7] there were many people, besides the Twelve, who
were disciples of Jesus, and many of those disciples included women.

---

[7] "And when he had called unto him his twelve disciples, he gave them power
against unclean spirits, to cast them out, and to heal all manner of sickness and
all manner of disease." (Matthew 10:1)

PREACHERS AND PROPHETS

There was a time when a significant number of male clergy in the Christian church stood in the way of women who were called of God to preach. Many male theologians incorrectly taught that women are not supposed to preach. For some reason they decided that preaching was a man's job, not fit for women. And they went about discouraging women away from their calling. A woman intent on preaching regardless of what men thought, would often times encounter difficulties finding a pastor that would allow her to preach the word of God in "his" pulpit. Many of these pastors would suggest to her that she was mistaken in what she thought the Lord had called her to do. Some would even try to convince her that her place was in the home, not the pulpit (as if God does not have the power to make room for both or as if it were every woman's God given duty to get married and have children). However, the last twenty years or so has brought about a change and a new understanding of what the scriptures say about women preachers.

Acts 2:17-18 seems to be the verses of scripture that were particularly ignored or misinterpreted when it came to the question of whether or not God allows women to preach. But in order to examine these verses we must first look at the verses of scripture that lead into them:

[1]And when the day of Pentecost had come, they were all together in one place.
[2]And suddenly there came from heaven a noise like a violent rushing wind, and it filled the whole house where they were sitting.
[3]And there appeared to them tongues as of fire distributing themselves, and they rested on each one of them.
[4]And they were all filled with the Holy Spirit and began to speak with other tongues, as the Spirit was giving them utterance.

[5]Now there were Jews living in Jerusalem, devout, men, from every nation under heaven.

[6]And when this sound occurred, the multitude came together, and were bewildered, because they were each one hearing them speak in his own language.

[7]And they were amazed and marveled, saying, "Why, are not all these who are speaking Galileans?

[8]And how is it that we each hear them in our own language to which we were born?

[9]Parthians and Medes and Elamites, and residents of Mesopotamia, Judea and Cappadocia, Pontus and Asia,

[10]Phrygia and Pamphylia, Egypt and the districts of Libya around Cyrene, and visitors from Rome, both Jews and proselytes,

[11]Cretans and Arabs—we hear them in our own tongues speaking of the mighty deeds of God."

[12]And they continued in amazement and great perplexity, saying to one another, "What does this mean?"

[13]But others were mocking and saying, "They are full of sweet wine."

[14]But Peter, taking his stand with the eleven, raised his voice and declared to them: "Men of Judea, and all you who live in Jerusalem, let this be known to you, and give heed to my words.

[15]For these men are not drunk, as you suppose, for it is only the third hour of the day;

[16]but this is what was spoken of through the prophet Joel:

[17]And it shall be in the Last days, God says,

that I will pour forth of My Spirit upon all
mankind;
And your sons and your daughters shall
prophesy,
And your young men shall see visions,
And your old men shall dream dreams;
[18]Even upon my bondslaves, both men and
women,
I will in those days pour forth My Spirit
and they shall prophesy.
(Acts 2:1-18 NASB)

Verses 17 and 18 teach that God will pour out his Spirit on all people
including daughters and women and that daughters and women will
prophesy just as men will. To prophesy means more than to just tell the
future. The specific Greek word for *prophesy* in the above verses is
propheteuo which has two meanings: to foretell the future and to
proclaim the gospel of Jesus, to preach. However, the church has
unfortunately had a history of only applying the meaning of foretelling
the future when it came to these verses that teach that women will
prophesy. Clergy would say that when the word *prophesy* was applied to
women, it was limited in it's meaning. But the Bible indicates otherwise.
The scriptures indicate that prophesying as applied to a woman has the
same meaning as prophesying as applied to a man. God does not put a
limitation on the meaning of the word *prophesy* when he applies it to a
woman. But men (as well as women who were taught by men of this
train of thought) have put limitations on the word in the past when it was
applied to women. And some still do today.

Verse 11 tells us that the men who experienced speaking in tongues at
the day of Pentecost were miraculously speaking in other languages that
they had never studied and while doing so were "speaking of the mighty
deeds of God." This means they were doing more than telling the future.
They were ministering, proclaiming, and preaching the word of God to
one another. With this in mind, when we look at Peter's address to the
crowd that is noted in verses 14-18, he clearly makes reference to the
speaking of the mighty deeds of God as the gift of prophecy. Therefore,
it is quite obvious that the meaning of the word *prophesy* in this context
is not limited to foretelling the future but particularly means to speak of
the mighty deeds of God, and in doing so, it can be said that one is

preaching. Peter endorses the prophecy of Joel that said men and women (sons and daughters) will receive this gift. Therefore, no one should say otherwise. Let's look further at what the Bible says prophesying is:

> [1]Pursue love and strive for the spiritual gifts, and especially that you may prophesy. [2]For those who speak in a tongue do not speak to other people but to God; for nobody understands them, since they are speaking mysteries in the Spirit. [3]On the other hand, those who prophesy speak to other people for their upbuilding and encouragement and consolation. [4]Those who speak in a tongue build up themselves, but those who prophesy build up the church. [5]Now I would like all of you to speak in tongues, but even more to prophesy. One who prophesies is greater than one who speaks in tongues, unless someone interprets, so that the church may be built up. (1 Corinthians 14:1-5 NSRV)

Again, the Greek word used for *prophesy* in the above verses of scripture is *propheteuo*. It is the same Greek word used in the verses quoted in Acts. Verse 4 above implies that a person who prophesies is a person who speaks to people for their strengthening, encouragement, and comfort, since one who prophesies is one who builds up the church. This is indeed what someone does who is gifted to preach and has been called of the Lord to operate in that gift or serve in that function. Therefore, if "sons and daughters" will prophesy and "men and women" will prophesy, then this means that both genders will be given the capacity by God to preach. Preaching, therefore, is not just limited to the male gender.

There are four women specifically spoken of in the Bible, identified as being prophets of God. They are Miriam, Deborah, Huldah, and Anna. Let's take a brief look:

Miriam

> [20]And Miriam the prophetess, Aaron's sister, took the timbrel in her hand, and all the women went out after her with timbrels and with dancing.

160

[21]And Miriam answered them,
"Sing to the LORD, for He is highly exalted;
The horse and his rider He has hurled into the sea."
(Exodus 15:20-21 NASB)

Miriam is identified in the Bible as a prophetess. This means that she had the gift of prophecy and used her gift to further edify the people of God. Miriam was the sister of Moses and Aaron. All three were Hebrews (Jews). Miriam was instrumental in helping to hide Moses as an infant when the king of Egypt (Pharaoh) decreed that all Hebrew newborn male children be put to death.[8] As an infant, Moses was hidden in a basket, which was then set to float down the bank of the Nile River. In order to know what would become of Moses, Miriam watched the basket as it traveled down the Nile River. Eventually Pharaoh's daughter discovered the basket with Moses in it, and raised Moses as her own child.

Deborah

[4]Now Deborah, a prophetess, the wife of Lappidoth,
was judging Israel at that time. (Judges 4:4 NASB)

Deborah[9] was a military Commander in chief, the judge and leader of the Israel nation, and a prophet. Deborah gave the order that led the Israeli army into battle against the Canaanites. Israel won the battle. When taking into account her leadership in delivering her people from certain peril and when taking into account the high statuses of appointment God gave her (prophet, judge, and military leader) many theologians consider Deborah to be in the same category as Moses and Samuel because out of all the other people spoken of in the Bible only Deborah, Moses, and Samuel served all three roles as prophet, judge, and military leader.

Huldah

Huldah was a prophet during the time of King Josiah's reign over

---

[8] Exodus chapter 1 and Exodus 2:1-10 (see your Bible)
[9] For a more detailed discussion of Deborah, see Chapter 1.

Israel. The following is her account:

> [11]When the king heard the words of the book of the law, he tore his clothes. [12]Then the king commanded the priest Hilkiah, Ahikam son of Shaphan, Achbor son of Micaiah, Shaphan the secretary, and the king's servant Asaiah, saying, [13]"Go, inquire of the LORD for me, for the people, and for all Judah, concerning the words of this book that has been found; for great is the wrath of the LORD that is kindled against us, because our ancestors did not obey the words of this book, to do according to all that is written concerning us."
>
> [14]So the priest Hilkiah, Ahikam, Achbor, Shaphan, and Asaiah went to the prophetess Huldah the wife of Shallum son of Tikvah, son of Harhas, keeper of the wardrobe; she resided in Jerusalem in the Second Quarter, where they consulted her. [15]She declared to them, "Thus says the LORD, the God of Israel: Tell the man who sent you to me, [16]Thus says the LORD, I will indeed bring disaster on this place and on its inhabitants—all the words of the book that the king of Judah has read. [17]Because they have abandoned me and have made offerings to other gods, so that they have provoked me to anger with all the work of their hands, therefore my wrath will be kindled against this place, and it will not be quenched. [18]But as to the king of Judah, who sent you to inquire of the LORD, thus shall you say to him, Thus says the LORD, the God of Israel: Regarding the words that you have heard, [19]because your heart was penitent and you humbled yourself before the LORD, when you heard how I spoke against this place, and against its inhabitants, that they should become a desolation and a curse, and because you have torn your clothes and wept before me, I also have heard you, says the LORD. [20]Therefore, I will gather you to your ancestors, and you shall be gathered to your grave in peace; your eyes shall not see all the disaster that I will bring on this place." They took the message back to the king. (2 Kings 22:11-20 NRSV)

Josiah was the king of Israel at the time of Huldah. King Josiah was a God fearing man and followed the ways of the Lord. During the eighteenth year of his reign, he assigned men to supervise the work of repair on the temple. At the time, Josiah also sent Shaphan, his secretary, among others, to instruct Hilkiah, the high priest, concerning some money matters.[10] When Hilkiah met with Shaphan, he informed Shaphan that he had found the book of the Law in the temple of the Lord. The book of the Law is the Mosaic Law that was handed down to Moses from God.[11] Shaphan read from the book to Josiah and when Josiah heard the teachings of the book he became distressed. He realized that many of their ancestors had not followed the decrees of the Law and had turned away from God to worship false gods and idols (verse 13). He knew that there was a possibility that the nation of Israel would have to account for this. Josiah sent his officials (Hilkiah the priest, Ahikam, son of Shaphan, Shaphan his secretary, and Asaiah, his attendant) to *"Go, inquire of the Lord for me, for the people, and for all Judah, concerning the words of this book that has been found; for great is the wrath of the Lord that is kindled against us, because our ancestors did not obey the words of this book, to do according to all that is written concerning us."* The person that the four officials (heads of the nation) went to was not a man, but a woman. They went to Huldah, the prophet to "inquire of the LORD" (regarding the plight of Israel) at Josiah's command regarding the book. Huldah's response is quoted above in verses 15 through 20.

Notice, Huldah was the wife of a man named Shallum. Shallum did not get in Huldah's way when it came time for her to exercise the gifts that God had given her. There is also no indication that any of the men felt led to consult with Shallum before they consulted with Huldah. Furthermore, when the four men came to her to inquire of the Lord, Huldah immediately relayed to them the message that the Lord had given her. There is no indication that Huldah consulted her husband first to get his permission to speak with the men or to get his opinion as to whether or not the message that she was about to give them was "on target." She knew what the Lord was telling her and proceeded in her gift independently. Huldah simply and freely exercised her gift and Shallum

---

[10] The entire account leading up to Huldah, is found in 2 Kings 22:1-14 (see your Bible)

[11] See Introduction.

knew better than to get in the way of her doing so, just as Lappidoth knew better than to get in the way of Deborah[12] exercising her gifts in the Lord. To get in the way of these women would have been to get in the way of God since God was using them as a tool to impart knowledge and direction.

God was the one who placed Huldah in this honorable position and gave her the gift of prophecy. Her gift was apparently known throughout the land, because there is no indication in scripture that the men hesitated to consult her. Furthermore, there were other male prophets available in Israel that these men could have sought. Apparently the Lord directed their steps towards Huldah. If God were a chauvinist then there would be no account in scripture whereby we would find men of such status inquiring of a woman as to what the message of the Lord was concerning a nation.

Anna

> [36]There was also a prophetess, Anna, the daughter of Phanuel, of the tribe of Asher. She was very old; she had lived with her husband seven years after her marriage, [37]and then was a widow until she was eighty-four. She never left the temple but worshiped night and day, fasting and praying. [38]Coming up to them at that very moment, she gave thanks to God and spoke about the child to all who were looking forward to the redemption of Jerusalem. (Luke 2:36-38 NIV)

There is not much else said about Anna in scripture. But from the tone of scripture, she was a loyal woman who was very strong in the faith. Apparently, after her husband died, Anna remained unmarried for many years. This enabled her to put all of her energy into serving the Lord. As the scripture says, she lived in the temple and worshipped God endlessly with fasting and praying. The Lord endowed upon her the gift of prophecy. And verse 38 tells us that she preached about Jesus (*"the child to all who were looking forward to the redemption of Jerusalem"*).

There are many men today who feel that women are not equipped to advise or instruct men in any way and that women cannot hear from the

---

[12] See Chapter 1.

Lord before a man does. But as we can see, specifically with the accounts of Huldah and Deborah, this is simply not so. God imparts knowledge and gifts to men and women to an equal degree. It is very possible that a man, even a man who is in a very high position just may find himself inquiring of a woman as to what the message of the Lord is for him. This certainly was the case when looking at the account of Huldah. Josiah held the highest position in Israel. He was the king. His position is synonymous with that of the president of the United States or any other worldly king. However, God placed Huldah in an advisory position over Josiah, by giving her a gift of prophecy. A woman being placed in an advisory position over a man is a hard thing for many men to accept. But with God, if he has placed a woman in an advisory position, then it is simply a matter of fact.

DEACONS

A deacon is a church official. The word *deacon* can be used interchangeably for men and women, however, some prefer to use the word *deaconess* for women. There are those who believe that the office of a deacon is only reserved for men. Before beginning our discussion that addresses whether or not the Bible says women can be deacons, a discussion of what the Bible lists as qualifying characteristics of a deacon must first be discussed.

The duties and characteristics needed to qualify for the office of a deacon are described in the New Testament. Although the word *deacon* stems from the Greek word *diakonos*, meaning to serve or minister, there are a few places in scripture where the noun rendition of the word has been translated as *deacon* instead of *servant* or *minister*. Later on in this chapter, under the subheading of "Pastors", scriptures will be given indicating what kind of character a pastor should have. Those same scriptures lead to the identification of characteristics that deacons should have. Therefore, we must briefly look at what the Bible says are qualifications for a pastor before looking at the qualifications needed to be a deacon:

> [1]The saying is true and irrefutable: If any man [eagerly] seeks the office of bishop (superintendent, overseer), he desires an excellent task (work).

²Now a bishop (superintendent, overseer) must give no ground for accusation but must be above reproach, the husband of one wife, circumspect and temperate and self-controlled; [he must be] sensible and well behaved and dignified and lead an orderly (disciplined) life; [he must be] hospitable [showing love for and being a friend to the believers, especially strangers or foreigners, and be] a capable and qualified teacher,

³Not given to wine, not combative but gentle and considerate, not quarrelsome but forbearing and peaceable, and not a lover of money [insatiable for wealth and ready to obtain it by questionable means].

⁴He must rule his own household well, keeping his children under control, with true dignity, commanding their respect in every way and keeping them respectful.

⁵For if a man does not know how to rule his own household, how is he to take care of the church of God?

⁶He must not be a new convert, or he may [develop a beclouded and stupid state of mind] as the result of pride [be blinded by conceit, and] fall into the condemnation that the devil [once] did.

⁷Furthermore, he must have a good reputation and be well thought of by those outside [the church], lest he become involved in slander and incur reproach and fall into the devil's trap.

⁸In like manner the deacons [must be] worthy of respect, not shifty and double-talkers but sincere in what they say, not given to much wine, not greedy for base gain [craving wealth and resorting to ignoble and dishonest methods of getting it]. (1 Timothy 3:8 Amp.)

Verse 8 specifically defines what must be the characteristics of a man in order for him to become a deacon. The phrase "in like manner" gives indication that a deacon must have a lifestyle synonymous to that of a pastor (bishop, overseer). This does not mean that all of what is required for a pastor is also required for a deacon but that similarities should abound. For example, verse 2 says that a pastor should be a capable and qualified teacher, but this requirement does not necessarily apply to those seeking the office of deacon.

A deacon must be a respectable person. He should not be cunning and deceiving. The scripture says that a man who holds the office of a deacon should not be a double-talker. A person who double-talks is a person who insincerely says things to appease people in order to win friends and influence people. A double-talker is often two-faced and has a tendency to sabotage.

A deacon should not drink much wine. This is the same characteristic that should be found in a pastor (verse 3). This does not mean that a deacon cannot drink wine at all, but that if he does, he should only drink it occasionally and he should never become drunk. Drunkenness is a sin as documented in Galatians 5:19-16 which says, *"The acts of the sinful nature are obvious: sexual immorality, impurity and debauchery; idolatry and witchcraft; hatred, discord, jealousy, fits of rage, selfish ambition, dissensions, factions and envy; drunkenness, orgies, and the like. I warn you, as I did before, that those who live like this will not inherit the kingdom of God"* (NIV). Christians are also commanded not to associate with other people who call themselves Christians and are addicted to alcohol.[13]

Verse 8 goes on to say that a deacon must not be greedy for money and that he must not be prone to try to acquire money by use of dishonest methods. Men are not qualified to be deacons if they want wealth so badly that they will do anything to get it. This is emphasized even further when considering 1st Timothy 6:10 which states, *"the love of money is the root of all evil."* The apostle Paul (the author of the book of Timothy) goes on to describe the characteristics that should be apparent for men who are in the office of a deacon:

> [9]They must possess the mystic secret of the faith

---

[13] "I have written you in my letter not to associate with sexually immoral people—not at all meaning the people of this world who are immoral, or the greedy and swindlers, or idolaters. In that case you would have to leave this world. But now I am writing you that you must not associate with anyone who calls himself a brother but is sexually immoral or greedy, and idolater or a slanderer, a drunkard or a swindler. With such a man do not even eat." (1 Corinthians 5:9-11 NIV)

[Christian truth as hidden from ungodly men] with a clear conscience.

[10]And let them also be tried and investigated and proved first; then, if they turn out to be above reproach, let them serve [as deacons]. (1 Timothy 3: 9-10 Amp.)

The phrase "mystic secret of the faith" is translated in the New American Standard Bible as "holding to the mystery of the faith." Those who would be deacons must understand the basic doctrines of the faith and not be enticed by falsehoods and false doctrines. Verse 10 says that they must also be investigated first before becoming deacons in order that it be proven that they are not currently involved in anything that would be considered disgraceful.

This brings us to our point of interest: whether or not a woman can serve as a deacon. There are those theologians who believe that the scriptures give indication that the office of a deacon is reserved for men only, and then there are those theologians who feel that there is no clear biblical indication that a woman should not be appointed as a deacon. The main focus of the debate has to do with 1st Timothy 3:11-13, which says:

[11]The women likewise must be worthy of respect and serious, not gossipers, but temperate and self-controlled, [thoroughly] trustworthy in all things.

[12]Let deacons be the husbands of but one wife, and let them manage their children and their own households well.

[13]For those who perform well as deacons acquire a good standing for themselves and also gain much confidence and freedom and boldness in the faith which is [founded on and centers] in Christ Jesus. (Amp.)

Verse 11 houses the particular point of debate. In the King James and New International Versions of the Bible, it reads, *"the wives likewise must be worthy......"* Although the translators of the New International Version admit that the Greek for this phrase literally reads *"the women,"* they have opted to use the word *wives* because of the verse of scripture that follows (verse 12) which says that deacons should be the husband of but one wife and manage their children and households well. Of course, being the husband of one wife would apply to a man, not a woman. So theologians have concluded that verse 12 is simply a continuation of verse 11 and therefore further conclude that verse 11 must be speaking about the wives of deacons since verse 12 speaks about wives and also speaks about male deacons who are married (*"let deacons be husbands of but one wife"*).

However, the fact that the literal translation reads, "let the women" indicates that verse 11 could be referring to female deacons (deaconesses). The theologians responsible for the translations presented in the New International Version of the Bible also admit in their footnotes that the Greek for "their wives" simply translates in the Greek to "the women" and could therefore be referring to what they have termed as "female deacons." The New Living Translation of the Bible translates verse 11 as such: *"In the same way, their wives must be respected and must not speak evil of others. They must exercise self control and be faithful in everything they do."* Then in a footnote the New Living Translation translators indicate that the phrase *"their wives"* can also be translated as *"the women deacons."* The bottom line is that no one really knows for sure. The scriptures are not absolutely clear on the matter. Therefore, neither possibility should be ruled out. Verse 11 could be referring to women in general, or to the wives of deacons, and it could also very well be referring to female deacons. To absolutely rule out the very possibility that the verse could be referring to women assigned to the office of deacon is to border on chauvinistic theological interpretation, especially since there is no indication that God ruled it out.

It should also be noted that Paul, who wrote the books of 1ˢᵗ and 2ⁿᵈ Timothy understood the difference between the Greek word used for the word *wives* and the Greek word used for the word *women*. After all, he was the apostle who wrote most of the New Testament literature regarding the relationship between husbands and wives. It would seem, therefore, that Paul would have known to specifically use the Greek word for *wives* if indeed he was referring to the wives of deacons and not to female deacons.[14]

---

[14] Some theologians contend that the New Testament was originally written in Aramaic and later translated into Greek by first century gentiles. They argue that Jesus and the apostles spoke in Aramaic not Greek.

It must also be pointed out that Paul, as we have seen, was never one to mince words. He was very specific about the role of a wife and the role of a husband. He particularly indicated that he did not allow women to teach or have authority over men in the church.[15] We can then safely assume that if Paul felt that women should not be assigned the position of a deacon, he would have come right out and said so.

There's further argument that verse 11 is applying to women in general and not specifically to wives of deacons, when looking at the chapter that precedes chapter 3 of 1st Timothy. In chapter 2,[16] it is very apparent that Paul, when using the words, *women* or *woman,* is speaking about women in general. The Bible was not initially written with the inclusion of chapters and verses. A book of the Bible was simply one long scroll. The chapters and verses were later added in order to assist the reader. Therefore it can be said, that Paul's writing style of referring to women in general in chapter 2 remains consistent when looking at chapter 3 because the chapters were initially actually continuous. This gives more credibility to the argument that the phrase *"the women likewise must be"* is referring to women in general and therefore really refers to female deacons as opposed to referring to wives of deacons.

The argument in favor of women being deacons is strengthened when focusing on the word *likewise* in verse 11. Let's take another look:

> [The] women likewise must be worthy of respect and serious, not gossipers, but temperate and self-controlled, [thoroughly] trustworthy in all things.

Verse 11 must be compared to verse 8 which says, *"In like manner the deacons [must be] worthy of respect, not shifty and double–talkers but sincere in what they say, not given to much wine, not greedy for base gain [craving wealth and resorting to ignoble and dishonest methods of getting it].* As discussed before, the phrase "in like manner" does not mean that a deacon must have the exact same characteristics of a pastor

---

[15] "Let a woman quietly receive instruction with entire submissiveness. But I do not allow a woman to teach or exercise authority over a man, but to remain quiet." (1 Timothy 2:11-12 NASB) It appears that this command had to do with the customs of the time and does not necessarily apply today. It is discussed in detail in the next subheading of this chapter.

[16] 1 Timothy chapter 2, (see your Bible).

but similar characteristics. The same then can be said for verse 11. The word *likewise* does not mean that a female deacon must have the exact same characteristics of a male deacon but similar characteristics. With this said, the argument that says verse 11 cannot be referring to women because verse 2 and 12 (of 1st Timothy chapter 3) says that a pastor and deacon must be the husband of one wife (therefore referring to men only), is made void.

Not only are the verses in 1st Timothy 3:1-13 at issue regarding the theological debate as to whether or not women can serve as deacons, but Romans 16:1-2 is equally at center stage when addressing the issue. Let's take a look at a few different versions. Again, Paul is speaking:

> ¹I commend to you our sister Phoebe, who is a servant of the church which is at Cenchrea:
> ²that you receive her in the Lord in a manner worthy of the saints, and that you help her in whatever matter she may have of you; for she herself has also been a helper of many, and of myself as well. (NASB)

> ¹I commend to you our sister Phoebe, a servant of the church in Cenchrea. ²I ask you to receive her in the Lord in a way worthy of the saints and to give her any help she may need from you, for she has been a great help to many people, including me. (NIV)

> ¹I COMMEND unto you Phoebe our sister, which is a servant of the church which is at Cenchrea.
> ²That ye receive her in the Lord, as becometh saints, and that ye assist her in whatsoever business she hath need of you: for she hath been a succourer of many, and of myself also. (KJV)

> ¹Now I introduce and commend to you our sister Phoebe, a deaconess of the church at Cenchrea,
> ²That you may receive her in the Lord [with a Christian welcome], as saints (God's people) ought to receive one another. And help her in whatever matter she may require assistance from you, for she has been a helper

of many including myself [shielding us from suffering]. (Amp.)

[1]Our sister Phoebe, a deacon in the church in Cenchrea, will be coming to see you soon. [2]Receive her in the Lord, as one who is worthy of high honor. Help her in every way you can, for she has helped many in their needs, including me. (NLT)

Of the five versions cited, the Amplified Version and the New Living Translation are the ones that opt to use the word *deaconess/deacon* instead of the more general term *servant*. However, *diakonos* is the word that is used in the Greek. As discussed earlier, *diakonos* is a word that can be and has been translated either way, as *servant*, *minister*, or *deacon* and in 1st Timothy 3:8-10 (the verses of scripture that describe what the characteristics of a deacon should be) it is translated as *deacons* in all five versions. The point here is that, if *diakonos* can be translated as *deacon*, and it is a word that has been used to describe Phoebe, then it cannot be entirely ruled out that she was a deacon. It is the same argument used, when looking at the Greek word for *prophesy*.[17] If the word *prophesy* has two meanings (to tell the future and to preach the word of God) and it is said that "sons and daughters" will prophesy, then the possibility that daughters (women) will be endowed with the gift of preaching cannot be ruled out.

The definition of the word *prophesy* cannot suddenly become limited in its definition when being referenced to a woman. It is the same with the word *diakonos,* it cannot all of a sudden become limited in its definition when being referenced to a woman. If *diakonos* means *servant, minister*, or *deacon*, and it has been applied to a woman (in this case Phoebe) then it follows that God has allowed women to be servants, ministers, or *deacons*. Moreover, Paul puts Phoebe on the top of the list in his greetings to people that are cited in Romans chapter 16. And he specifically commends her for what she has done in the church and for all of the help she has given, thereby placing her at a particular level of importance. The tone of Paul's salutation to Phoebe sounds as if she is indeed someone functioning in a high position at the Cenchrea church and that she must have worked very closely with the pastor. Paul himself

---

[17] See discussion earlier in the chapter under the subheading "Preachers."

says that she is worthy of high honor. Paul's manner of writing about her lends more towards the probability that Phoebe was in some way part of the administration of the church (a deacon) and less to the generality of servant or minister.

There is no particular job description given in the Bible for a deacon. The office of deacon is not listed along with any of the gifts of the spirit that Paul has listed.[18] It is instead an appointment made by the pastor. The pastor should base his selection on the respectability of the person, as pointed out in 1st Timothy chapter 3 and the abilities that the person possesses. However, there are certain gifts and abilities that it is believed a deacon should possess before being appointed a deacon. Since the word *diakonos* is associated with the words *servant* and *minister*, it is fitting to conclude that a deacon should be willing and able to serve people in various ways and minister to them as well. In Philippians 1:1,[19] just as in 1st Timothy 3:8-10, deacons are put on a similar plane as pastors. With the two being so closely identified in rank, many biblical theologians believe that the main function of a deacon is to serve as a direct assistant to a pastor. This therefore puts deacons at a very high standing in the church, which may be the reason why some pastors are squeamish about appointing women to the position.

If deacons are appointed to serve in assisting the pastor, then what they are really doing is assisting the pastor in carrying out his duties. This means they would assist in very "high status" duties such as assisting in baptism, serving the poor, visiting the sick, assisting with communion, counseling, advising, and the like. In looking at the fact that the majority of Christian churches, at least in America, are comprised of women, it seems practical to have women function in the office of a deacon. And it seems even more practical when there is absolutely no clear-cut biblical indication that a woman should not be appointed as such. Apparently early church leaders were quite aware of this. Church history tells us that women served as deacons in the early church. According to Fred A Grissom's remark cited in the Holman Bible Dictionary, "deaconesses are mentioned prominently in Christian writings of the first several centuries. They cared for needy fellow

---

[18] The gifts are discussed later in this chapter.

[19] "Paul and Timothy, bond-servants of Christ Jesus, to all the saints in Christ Jesus who are in Philippi, including the overseers and deacons" (NASB)

believers, visited the sick, and were especially charged with assisting in the baptism of women converts."[20]

God has given women the same opportunity to serve as deacons as he has given men, and therefore, it cannot be said that, in regards to this matter, that God is a chauvinist.

TEACHERS

Teaching the gospel is high on the list of godly callings and gifts as is evidenced by the following verses of scripture. Let's take a look at them again:

> [28]And God has appointed in the church, first apostles, second prophets, third teachers, then miracles, then gifts of healings, helps, administrations, various kinds of tongues.
> [29]All are not apostles, are they? All are not prophets, are they? All are not teachers, are they? All are not workers of miracles, are they?
> [30]All do not have gifts of healings, do they? All do not speak with tongues, do they? All do not interpret, do they?
> [31]But earnestly desire the greater gifts.
> And I show you a still more excellent way.
> (1 Corinthians 12:28-31 NASB)

> [1]Pursue love, yet desire earnestly spiritual gifts, but especially that you may prophesy.
> [2]For one who speaks in a tongue does not speak to men, but to God; for no one understands, but in his spirit he speaks mysteries.
> [3]But one who prophesies speaks to men for edification and exhortation and consolation. (1 Corinthians 14:1-3 NASB)

---

[20] Taken from the *Holman Bible Dictionary* by Trent C Butler, Ph.D., copyright © 1991 by Holman Bible Publishers, p. 345. Fair use.

1st Corinthians 13:28 places teaching as third on the hierarchy of godly callings and spiritual gifts. Notice, there are no gender qualifications mentioned in any of the verses cited above regarding the calling of, or gift of teaching. This applies to all the other callings and gifts mentioned, as well. Of the gifts that are mentioned, 1st Corinthians 14:1 tells us that Christians should desire spiritual gifts and they should especially desire the gift of prophecy. The specific reference to preaching when speaking of prophesying is made clear by 1st Corinthians 14:3, which says that one should desire to prophesy in order to edify, exhort, and console. Preaching the word of God does those things.

It appears that the callings and gifts have been listed by level of sequential importance when it comes to deciding which appointments and gifts, as used in the church, function as the most influential in getting God's message across and encouraging those who are already in the Lord. Most theologians believe that the office of apostle ended with the Twelve, the later addition of Paul, and a few others. If one takes this as the case, then preaching the word of God is the most influential gift today that God can bestow on a person. Teaching would then come second. This brings us to some of the most debated verses of scripture among theologians: 1st Corinthians 14:34-35 and 1st Timothy 2:11-15. Let's take a look:

> [34]Let the women keep silent in the churches; for they are not permitted to speak, but let them subject themselves, just as the Law also says.
> [35]And if they desire to learn anything, let them ask their own husbands at home; for it is improper for a woman to speak in church. (1 Corinthians 14:34-35 NASB)

> [11]Let a woman quietly receive instruction with entire submissiveness.
> [12]But I do not allow a woman to teach or exercise authority over a man, but to remain quiet.
> [13]For it was Adam who was first created, and then Eve.
> [14]And it was not Adam who was deceived, but the woman being quite deceived, fell into transgression.
> [15]But women shall be preserved through the bearing of children if they continue in faith and love and sanctity with self-restraint. (1 Timothy 2:11-15 NASB)

There are two main trains of thought regarding the above verses of scripture. One says that Paul's instruction to women in the scriptures above had to do with the culture of the time and does not apply now and the other train of thought says that the above verses of scripture apply today as they did then. This author believes that arguments for the former are stronger than arguments for the latter, but both arguments will be presented. Because of the detailed discussion that is about to be presented regarding 1st Corinthians 14:34-35 and 1st Timothy 2:11-15, the particular verses of scripture that compose those references will be broken down into subheadings.

1 Corinthians 14:34

1st Corinthians 14:34 says, *Let the women keep silent in the churches; for they are not permitted to speak, but let them subject themselves, just as the Law also says.*

Most theologians agree that this verse of scripture only applies to women when it comes to how they are to conduct themselves during church services. It needs to be understood that during the time of Paul's ministry, women were not allowed to speak in the church at all. Paul backs up his command that women should keep silent in the churches by saying that the Law confirms this as well. However, there is some question as to what Law Paul was speaking of.

Paul could not have been speaking of the Mosaic Law because there is nothing in the Old Testament Mosaic Law that says that women cannot speak while they are among a congregation of saints in a synagogue. Therefore, some theologians have said that in saying, "the Law also says," Paul must be giving reference to Genesis 3:16 that says husbands will rule their wives. But as we have seen in Chapter 3, God did not define a husband's rule over his wife as a Law but instead as a curse. If we refer to this particular curse as God's Law, then it follows that all of the curses God bestowed upon man must be thought of as Law as well. If there is some godly Law that says that women cannot speak in the church then that Law would transcend any cultural argument and would apply to any Christian woman anywhere.

But the words *law* and *curse* are not interchangeable. Otherwise, the Mosaic Laws would be considered curses, and they were not curses. With this said, it is difficult to attribute the Law that Paul is talking about to the husband rule curse of Genesis 3:16.[21] It is more plausible that Paul may have been referring to some Law of the land at that time or may have been referring to the Mosaic Law indirectly. To be fair, there are some theologians who would say that the verses of scripture in Numbers 30:3-16 is a representation of the Law that Paul was referring to in Corinthians 14:34 since Numbers 30:3-6 is a derivative of Genesis 3:16. Let's take a look:

> [3]When a young woman still living in her father's house makes a vow to the LORD or obligates herself by a pledge [4]and her father hears about her vow or pledge but says nothing to her, then all her vows and every pledge by which she obligated herself will stand. [5]But if her father forbids her when he hears about it, none of her vows or the pledges by which she obligated herself will stand; the LORD will release her because her father has forbidden her.
>
> [6]If she marries after she makes a vow or after her lips utter a rash promise by which she obligates herself [7]and her husband hears about it but says nothing to her, then her vows or the pledges by which she obligated herself will stand. [8]But if her husband forbids her when he hears about it, he nullifies the vow that obligates her or the rash promise by which she obligates herself, and the LORD will release her.
>
> [9]Any vow or obligation taken by a widow or divorced woman will be binding on her.
>
> [10]If a woman living with her husband makes a vow or obligates herself by a pledge under oath [11]and her husband hears about it but says nothing to her and does not forbid her, then all her vows or the pledges by which she obligated herself will stand. [12]But if her husband nullifies them when he hears about them, then none of the vows or pledges that came from her lips will stand. Her husband has nullified them, and the

---

[21] To the woman he said, "I will greatly increase your pains in childbearing; with pain you will give birth to children. Your desire will be for your husband, and he will rule over you." (NIV) The NLT says "and he will be your master."

LORD will release her. [13]Her husband may confirm or nullify any vow she makes or any sworn pledge to deny herself. [14]But if her husband says nothing to her about it from day to day, then he confirms all her vows or the pledges binding on her. He confirms them by saying nothing to her when he hears about them. [15]If, however, he nullifies them some time after he hears about them, then he is responsible for her guilt."

[16]These are the regulations the LORD gave Moses concerning relationships between a man and his wife, and between a father and his young daughter still living in his house. (Numbers 30:3-16 NIV)

During the dispensation of the Law,[22] God allowed men and women to make oaths. However, in the dispensation of Grace,[23] the scriptures warn against making oaths.[24] Oaths were not something that God took lightly. The scriptures cited in Numbers teach that sometimes people would make an oath to God without thinking ("a rash promise") and then they would be bound to that oath for life. But for married women, there was actually a way out of an oath. Her oath would not stand if her husband disagreed with the oath and voiced his disagreement. It was not necessarily the wisest thing to swear an oath unto the Lord. For if one swore an oath to the Lord he had to keep it. Some oaths were not easy to keep.

If a man's wife rashly made an oath to the Lord and did not keep it then her guilt was on her husband's hands (verse 15) if he hadn't already nullified the oath. He, not she, was responsible for her misgiving in the Lord, even if he nullified the oath after the damage was done.

Verses 3-5 also indicate that a father had rule over his daughter while she was living in his house. But this is not a surprising revelation, since the young woman in question was still under her father's roof. Once she left the home, her father no longer had reign over her when it came to any oath she may have made.

---

[22] See Introduction.

[23] See Introduction.

[24] "But above all, my brethren, do not swear, either by heaven or by earth or with any other oath; but let your yes be yes, and your no, no; so that you may not fall under judgment." James 5:2 (NASB)

Although the verses of scriptures in Numbers give an example of a man's rule over his wife, this particular part of the Law documented in Numbers 30:3-16 still says nothing about how a woman is supposed to conduct herself in a church service. The verses only help solidify the fact that, in marriage, men rule women. However, some theologians might use these scriptures to argue that the part of the Mosaic Law, regarding women and oaths, indirectly teaches that a man has rule over a woman in everything and that therefore Paul's position that a woman cannot teach a man or have authority over a man in church, is not just a directive applicable to his times and customs but applies to all times regardless of custom. However, to use the authority that a man had over his wife in regards to oaths and say that this is indicative of the Law that Paul was referring to, does not make for a strong argument since there was no biblical Law that theologians can point to that forbid women to speak in the church.

In continuing to look at the verse in question, 1st Corinthians 14:34 says that a woman must keep silent in the church because she is not permitted to speak. Some would argue that there is even the scriptural suggestion that the instruction for women to keep silent in the church included forbidding them to outwardly pray and worship the Lord during church services. They would use the following verses of scripture to support their view:

> 8I desire therefore that in every place men should pray,
> without anger or quarreling or resentment or doubt [in
> their minds], lifting up holy hands.
> 9Also [I desire] that women should adorn themselves
> modestly and appropriately and sensibly in seemly
> apparel, not with [elaborate] hair arrangement or gold
> or pearls or expensive clothing,
> 10But by doing good deeds (deeds in themselves good
> and for the good and advantage of those contacted by
> them), as befits women who profess reverential fear for
> and devotion to God. (1 Timothy 2:8-10 Amp.)

The men are specifically instructed to pray and lift up holy hands while the women are specifically instructed to adorn themselves modestly. But this is not to say that these verses of scripture are forbidding women to openly worship God, but instead, that during the time Paul wrote this, the societal pressures put upon women were that they be seen and not heard.

In getting back to our verse of scripture in Corinthians, the question becomes: who is not permitting a woman to speak during the assembly of the church, God or man? The fact that women were instructed not to speak is a literal directive. The prohibition goes beyond preaching and teaching but also includes any form of talk. This of course would include praising the Lord. Has God actually commanded that a woman not openly praise him in the assembly of the church? If she is literally commanded to remain silent then she is literally commanded not to vocally praise God. But the Bible directs everyone to praise the Lord.[25] Psalms 150:6 specifically reads, *"Let every living creature praise the Lord. Shout praises to the Lord!"*[26] The Bible instructs every living creature to praise the Lord and in doing so to shout those praises. People are therefore instructed to praise the lord loudly and vocally, not silently. Certainly, "every living creature" includes women. Does Paul's directive for women not to speak in the church mean that women can only praise God outside the assembly of the church? One would think the answer would be, of course not. When taking this into consideration, the only logical conclusion is that Paul must have been writing these things in response to the customs of the times.

What were the customs of the times regarding these things? According to John Temple Bristow author of, *What Paul really said about Women*, the synagogues of the time were built with balconies constructed so that anyone who sat there would be concealed. Those balconies were a place for women and children to sit, out of view from men as they worshipped in the portion of the sanctuary below. Not only were the women hidden but they were mandated to be silent as well. If the women did congregate to worship the Lord it was only among other women.

These drastic measures were taken because sexual activity among parishioners was often a practice that was included in the worship

---

[25] "Kings of the earth and all nations, you princes and all rulers on earth, young men and maidens, old men and children. Let them praise the name of the LORD, for his name alone is exalted; his splendor is above the earth and the heavens." (Psalm 148:11-13 NIV) In addition, read Psalms 148, 149, and 150 (see your Bible).

[26] CEV

services of people that were involved in pagan religions. Therefore in order to avoid any misunderstandings or in order to limit men in any tendency they may have had for perverse thought, the Jews forbade women to be seen among men during the time of worship in the synagogue and rarely allowed a woman to speak in the church. So prevalent was this practice that Paul must have felt that to undermine it at the time may have caused too great a confusion in the church. Bristow tells us that at the time, the city of Corinth was well known for it's partaking in the wicked practice of religious prostitution. He also says the following:

> Now, among conservative Jews in the time of Paul, even social contacts between men and women were restricted. According to the Mishnah, a man might divorce his wife and not have to return her dowery if she were guilty of speaking to another man; and even the act of speaking to a man in the street might be used as evidence of a bride's unfaithfulness to her intended.
>
> Because the Jews were well aware of the obscene orgiastic worship among their pagan neighbors and because the Jews were so concerned with potential contact between males and females, it is a wonder that women were allowed to be present with men during public worship at all. In practice, a compromise had been reached: women might be present during worship, but only if they were silent and out of sight (in a balcony or behind a curtain); women did not count in determining if a congregation were present for worship, for a minimum number consisted of a *minyan*, ten men; and although a woman might be qualified to participate in public worship by reading from Scripture, she was not allowed to "out of respect for the congregation.[27]

Because of these oppressive rules regarding women and worship during the time of Paul, there were many times when the church services

---

[27]*What Paul really said about Women* by John Temple Bristow, copyright © 1988 by John Temple Bristow, published by HarperSanFransicso, A division of HarperCollins Publishers p. 53, used by permission.

were in a state of confusion. Historians have documented that women who attended services would often times talk among themselves in the balcony about what was being preached or taught. This would cause a noisy disruption and they were therefore asked to be silent during the service and to reserve any questions or conversation about the service for their husbands when they returned home with them after attending church service. A balcony with a curtain would provide enough environmental incentive for a private discussion among those who had to sit there. The women could not be seen and it was probably very difficult for them to hear what was going on. Therefore, the temptation for them to talk amongst themselves was great.

Paul did not focus on this cultural and customary injustice to women. He instead focused on what would make an orderly church. In doing so, he wasn't supporting oppression, per se, but instead he was abiding by certain customs in an effort to maintain order. In today's Western society, there is no such custom in the church that separates men from women. Therefore, the command for women to keep silent in the churches simply does not apply today.

Those theologians who argue that the command for women to keep silent in the church is for today would have to have reasons as convincing for their argument as Paul had for his. They'd have to agree that women should be separated in church from men (in order to avoid the possibility of parishioners engaging in outward sexual intercourse during service) by having them sit in a balcony concealed by a curtain, not able to hear what is going on in the service. More than likely, they would not concur with these arrangements. But they cannot have it both ways. Men cannot demand that women keep silent without instituting the customs that triggered the command of that silence in the first place.

If then theologians are to understand this about the physical separation of women that was imposed at that time, then it follows that they should have the same understanding when it comes to the directive for women to keep silent in the church: the directive was only for that time.

If our society today practiced the same customs regarding women in church service that the societies of Paul's time practiced, then it could be said that the directive for a woman to keep silent in the church would apply today. But there is no separation of men and women in today's churches because there is no concern that parishioners will engage in outward sexual conduct during service.

There is also scriptural evidence that the directive to women not to teach men may have only applied to the particular time in which Paul gave the directive and also only applied to the Corinthian church that exercised the custom of disallowing women to speak during church service. The following verses of scripture support this statement.

> Not many of you should presume to be teachers, my
> brothers, because you know that we who teach will be
> judged more strictly. (James 3:1 NIV)

Upon first looking at the verse, it appears that the directive given to Christians to be careful to become teachers, is given only to men. However, when examining the scripture more closely and investigating what the actual Greek says, we discover that the Greek word used for *brothers*, is a general word that encompasses women as well. The New Living Translation therefore translates the verse of scripture as such:

> Dear brothers and sisters, not many of you should
> become teachers in the church, for we who teach will
> be judged by God with greater strictness. (NLT)

There is no question that the directive is given to both Christian men and women. Since this is indeed the case, then the argument supporting the claim that women cannot be teachers in the church is made void. If women cannot be teachers in the church then James would not have included Christian women in this verse. On the contrary, he included all of mankind in his directive, and all of mankind includes women. This tells us that it is not against God's will for women to become teachers in the church.

Some would say then that James 3:1 contradicts 1st Timothy 2:11-12 which again says, *"women should listen and learn quietly and submissively. I do not let women teach men or have authority over them. Let them listen quietly."* [28] Again, there is no contradiction between what Paul says and what James says because Paul was dealing with a specific custom of the Corinthian church and James was not. James was dealing with Christianity as a whole. If Paul had been dealing with Christianity as a whole in what he said, then women would not only be banned from

---

[28] NLT

teaching men in the church today but they would be banned from speaking altogether during their attendance in church service. God uses women no less than he uses men. This is evident when reading Chapter 1 as well as when reading previous portions of this chapter. Paul's instruction for a woman not to teach a man was solely applicable to the Corinthian church, at that time, because of their customs. This particular directive does not apply today, as James has clearly indicated.

Furthermore, the verse tells us that Paul, specifically, did not let women teach or have authority over men. The exact quote is as such, *"I do not let women teach men or have authority over them."* The operative word is *I*. Paul *himself* did not allow women to teach men, probably because of all the potential trouble that doing so would have created in the church at that time. This implies that other leaders of the church may have been letting the women teach and because they were, problems arose. Again, the restriction to prohibit women from teaching men or having authority over them, seems to have been established because of certain concerns that existed during that particular time surrounding the issue of orderly church worship.

1 Corinthians 14:35

1st Corinthians 14:35 says, *And if they desire to learn anything, let them ask their own husbands at home; for it is improper for a woman to speak in church.* (NASB)

As we have seen, it was improper for a woman to speak in the church at the time Paul wrote this because of the customs and concerns then. Again, these customs are not, at least in Western society, in operation today. Therefore it is no longer improper for a woman to speak in the church. To further the point, if we examine Paul's directive that he gave to women regarding hair coverings, we will be able to see another example in which a directive was given (which no longer applies today) in response to the customs of those times. Let's take a look:

> [4]Every man who prays or prophesies with his head covered dishonors his head. [5]And every woman who prays or prophesies with her head uncovered dishonors her head—it is just as though her head were shaved. [6]If a woman does not cover her head, she should have her hair cut off; and if it is a disgrace for a woman to have

her hair cut or shaved off, she should cover her head. [7]A man ought not to cover his head, since he is the image and glory of God; but the woman is the glory of man. [8]For man did not come from woman, but woman from man, [9]neither was man created for woman, but woman for man. [10]For this reason, and because of the angels, the woman ought to have a sign of authority on her head.

[11]In the Lord, however, woman is not independent of man, nor is man independent of woman.[12]For as woman came from man, so also man is born of woman. But everything comes from God. [13]Judge for yourselves: Is it proper for a woman to pray to God with her head uncovered? [14]Does not the very nature of things teach you that if a man has long hair, it is a disgrace to him, [15]but that if a woman has long hair, it is her glory? For long hair is given to her as a covering. [16]If anyone wants to be contentious about this, we have no other practice—nor do the churches. (1 Corinthians 11:4-16 NIV)

The Amplified Bible version of verse 16 gives a bit more clarity to the scripture[29] and reads as follows: *Now if anyone is disposed to be argumentative and contentious about this, we hold to and recognize no other custom [in worship] than this, nor do the churches of God generally.* The phrase in the NIV that says "we have no other practice" is synonymous with the phrase in the Amplified version that says "we hold to and recognize no other custom."

It is clear that Paul's instruction for women to cover their heads during church service (and if not, shave their heads) and for men not to cover their heads during service, was in response to particular customs that were practiced during those times and therefore the directive does not apply today. Paul made it clear that the church had no other practice or custom and therefore his instructions stood. Because of this, Paul said that his position on the matter was not open for debate. This implies that if the church had had other customs contrary to those regarding head coverings, then the instruction for women to cover their heads and for

---

[29] Verses 7-10 are discussed under the next subheading in this chapter.

men not to, would have been open to argument and not necessarily have applied. If then, Paul's instruction that a woman cover her head was only put in place because of the customary practices of the time, then that instruction certainly does not apply today because today neither the church nor Western society keeps such customs.

This is the same argument used when examining 1st Corinthians 14:34-35 which instructs women to be silent in the church and to ask their husbands what was said during service. The verse that comes just before those verses (verse 33) says the following: *"for God is not a God of confusion but of peace, as in all the churches of the saints."* Clearly then, any instruction for a woman to be silent in the churches had to do with maintaining order during the services. But in today's church, women can speak in the church without disrupting the peace and order of the service. Today, women are not causing the kind of confusion in the church that they were causing during Paul's time because today there is no balcony with a veil to shield women from participating in the service. They are therefore not inclined to talk amongst themselves which, of course if they were to do so they'd be disrupting the service and causing confusion. Today's technology has given us the means by which to electronically amplify our voices. Therefore, even if women were to be separated from men during a service, there would be no reason for them to talk amongst themselves and ask questions of each other because they would be able to hear what is being said through the use of modern technology. If then, there is no need for women to talk amongst themselves, be it due to the non-existence of a custom that led to a directive for them to be silent or the innovation of technology that makes way for everyone to hear clearly what is being said, then the directive for them to keep silent becomes null and void. The directive is only there because a problem existed. The problem no longer exists so therefore, the directive is not applicable today.

1 Timothy 2:11-15

1 Timothy 2:11-15 says, *[11]Let a woman quietly receive instruction with entire submissiveness.[12]But I do not allow a woman to teach or exercise authority over a man, but to remain quiet.[13]For it was Adam who was first created, and then Eve.[14]And it was not Adam who was deceived, but the woman being quite deceived, fell into transgression.[15]But women shall be preserved through the bearing of*

children if they continue in faith and love and sanctity with self-restraint. (NASB)

Here is where we come to one of our main points of contention. Should a woman be allowed to teach in the church or not? Paul says that he does not allow a woman to teach or exercise authority over a man but to remain quiet. First of all, Paul is only applying this to the function of the church. This is evident by the phrase "but to remain silent." As we know, when Paul used this phrase before he was specifically referring to a woman's participation in a church service. We have also seen that the instruction for a woman to remain silent during a church service had only to do with the customs of Paul's time.

Paul's instruction for a woman not to teach a man or have authority over a man is accompanied with the instructions for her to remain silent and receive instruction herself, quietly. Therefore, it is apparent that the instruction Paul gave for a woman not to teach a man or have authority over a man had just as much to do with the oppressive male authoritative customs at the time as did the directive for her to remain quiet.

But what Paul says in verses 13 through 15 provokes one to question if whether or not his instruction for women not to teach men or have authority over them only applied then, or applies now as well. Paul explains his directives in verse 13 by implying that a woman is not to exercise authority over a man because man was created first and then woman was created. This is interpreted by some to mean that men are automatically in authority over women because the first woman was made from a man. But as discussed in Chapter 3, Paul is also quoted in 1st Corinthians 11:8-12 as saying, (similar to what is quoted of him above), *For man did not come from woman, but woman from man, [9]neither was man created for woman, but woman for man. [10]For this reason, and because of the angels the woman ought to have a sign of authority on her head. [11]In the Lord, however, woman is not independent of man, nor is man independent of woman. [12]For as woman came from man, so also man is born of woman. But everything comes from God.[30]*

Paul emphasizes that everything (meaning everyone) comes from God (this especially applies for those who are Christians). So again, some would argue that this verse indicates that there is no automatic rank in authority since all men come from the body of a woman just as the first woman came from the body of a man. In other words, when a person,

---

[30] NIV

man or woman, is a Christian ("in the Lord"), then the final authority in their lives ultimately rests in Jesus. They would also argue that the verse supports that men and women are equal since woman came from man and men come from women and neither can really live, as a whole, independently from the other.

On the other hand, others argue that the verse supports the position that the authority that men have over their wives existed before the fall of Adam and Eve. They therefore further argue that this sign of authority is symbolic of what they generally deem as man's authority over women while others argue that it is instead symbolic of an authority that women themselves have. But despite the debate as to whether or not a man's marital authority existed before the fall or is instead a result of it, it appears that the customs of the time was the main factor that triggered Paul's directive for women to refrain from teaching men in the church. And although, a husband's rule over his wife still applies today (which many erroneously generalize to mean that every man has rule over every woman whether married to that woman or not) there is still no custom in today's church that says a woman cannot teach a man.

Paul coupled teaching with authority. Therefore, during the time of Paul, the function of a teacher may have come with a significant amount of authority and may therefore have been another reason why Paul directed women not to teach men. Because of the oppressive customs of the time, Paul probably felt it was wisest not to allow women to teach or have authority over a man (in the church) since, as Bristow tells us, contacts between men and women were restricted and a woman could easily be accused of adultery just by speaking to a man in the street. But today, unless the teacher is also the pastor or a deacon, great authority in the church does not necessarily go hand in hand with teaching and even if teaching does come with some authority, societal customs are more relaxed and women have been given many authoritative functions in the church. Furthermore, women are no longer, in general, at great risk of being falsely accused of some sexual impropriety merely by holding a conversation with a man.

If God imparts the gift of preaching and prophesying to women, which he does, then surely he imparts the gift of teaching, for as we have seen, teaching is secondary to prophesying. Although Paul instructed women not to teach in the church, this does not mean that they were instructed not to teach at all. We can assume that it was acceptable for women to teach other women and for women to teach children. It was also acceptable for women to teach men outside of the church service. Let's take a look:

> [1]After these things Paul departed from Athens and went to Corinth.
> [2]And he found a certain Jew named Aquila, born in Pontus, who had recently come from Italy with his wife Priscilla (because Claudius had commanded all the Jews to depart from Rome); and he came to them. (Acts 18:1-2 NKJV)

> [18]So Paul still remained a good while. Then he took leave of the brethren and sailed for Syria, and Priscilla and Aquila were with him. He had his hair cut off at Cenchrea, for he had taken a vow. (Acts 18:18 NKJV)

> [24]Now a certain Jew named Apollos, born at Alexandria, an eloquent man and mighty in the Scriptures, came to Ephesus.
> [25]This man had been instructed in the way of the Lord; and being fervent in spirit, he spoke and taught accurately the things of the Lord, though he knew only the baptism of John.
> [26]So he began to speak boldly in the synagogue. When Aquila and Priscilla heard him, they took him aside and explained to him the way of God more accurately.
> [27]And when he desired to cross to Achaia, the brethren wrote, exhorting the disciples to receive him; and when he arrived, he greatly helped those who had believed through grace;
> [28]for he vigorously refuted the Jews publicly, showing from the Scriptures that Jesus is the Christ. (Acts 18:24-28 NKJV)

Paul was going about from city to city preaching and teaching the gospel of Christ. After a long stay in the city of Corinth, Paul sailed for Syria. He took Priscilla and Aquila with him. Paul took the two with him in order for them to help him in his quest to preach and teach the gospel of Jesus Christ. Both Priscilla and Aquila were teachers. As mentioned in verse 2, Priscilla was the wife of Aquila. This means that a woman traveled with Paul in order to assist him in spreading the Gospel of Christ. It becomes apparent that Priscilla was a teacher because verse 26 tells us how she and her husband took Apollos aside and explained to him the ways of the Lord more accurately. In other words, Priscilla and Aquila taught Apollos about the gospel of Jesus Christ. Apollos knew that John was baptizing people and knew something about the Lord but did not understand (according to the theological scholars responsible for the New International Version of the Bible) that Jesus was actually the Messiah and that baptism was now in the name of Jesus. However, once schooled on the matter by Priscilla and Aquila, Apollos taught these things more accurately.

The point here is that Priscilla, a woman, taught a man about the things of the Lord. She assisted her husband in teaching Apollos. If indeed women absolutely were not allowed to teach men, then how is it that Paul allowed Priscilla, not only to teach Apollos but to travel with him during his ministry as well? Isn't Paul the one who said, "I do not allow a woman to teach or exercise authority over a man, but to remain silent?" Priscilla did not remain silent. She taught Apollos along with her husband. Paul didn't seem to mind. To add to this, as discussed earlier in this chapter, Paul describes both Priscilla and Aquila as his "fellow workers in Christ Jesus" and at times, mentions her name before her husband's name when referring to the two of them, which implies that she was not under the shadow of her husband as a teacher but was respected as a teacher in her own right.

The account of Priscilla and Aquila gives indication that women can teach men. Had Paul contradicted himself by allowing Priscilla to join him in his ministry of teaching and preaching? No he had not, because his instruction in the book of Timothy only applied to church customs at that time. Priscilla was not an official teacher at a particular church (which is what Paul taught against because of the sinful practices and customs of church assemblies at the time). She was a teacher in the Lord who traveled with her husband and publicly taught the ways of the Lord.

Some would say that Paul only allowed Priscilla to teach because she was accompanied by her husband and that Priscilla was therefore only able to teach under the authority of a man. If this is the case, then a woman should be able to teach in today's church under the authority of any man who is an elder of the church that she attends. And if all a Christian woman needs is a Christian man to be present while she teaches other men, then surely there are plenty of men in the church that can fill this role.

PASTORS

Just as there is disagreement among Christians and biblical theologians as to whether or not the Bible allows women to teach, preach, and hold in the office of deacon, there is also considerable debate about whether or not the Bible says a woman can pastor a church. The main verses of scripture that focus on the qualifications one must have to pastor a church are cited below. These scriptures were cited previously but must be cited again for this discussion:

> ¹The saying is true and irrefutable: If any man [eagerly] seeks the office of bishop (superintendent, overseer), he desires an excellent task (work).
>
> ²Now a bishop (superintendent, overseer) must give no grounds for accusation but must be above reproach, the husband of one wife, circumspect and temperate and self-controlled; [he must be] sensible and well behaved dignified and lead an orderly (disciplined) life: [he must be] hospitable [showing love for and being a friend to the believers, especially strangers or foreigners, and be] a capable and qualified teacher,
>
> ³Not given to wine, not combative but gentle and considerate, not quarrelsome but forbearing and peaceable, and not a lover of money [insatiable for wealth and ready to obtain it by questionable means].
>
> ⁴He must rule his own household well, keeping his children under control, with true dignity, commanding their respect in every way and keeping them respectful.
>
> ⁵For if a man does not know how to rule his own household, how is he to take care of the church of God?
>
> ⁶He must not be a new convert, or he may [develop a beclouded and stupid state of mind] as the result of pride [be blinded by conceit, and] fall into the condemnation that the devil [once] did. [Isa. 14:12-14.]

⁷Furthermore, he must have a good reputation and be well thought of by those outside [the church], lest he become involved in slander and incur reproach and fall into the devil's trap. (1Timothy 3:1-7 Amp).

The term *pastor* is synonymous with *bishop* and *overseer*. The verses of scripture cited above are specifically referring to one who is the chief executive officer of a local church, a pastor. The scriptures imply that all churches need a pastor. The book of Timothy is actually a letter written from the apostle Paul to Timothy. Paul referred to Timothy as his true son in the faith. Paul instructed Timothy as to the duties of church officers. Paul also urged Timothy to stay in the city of Ephesus. Timothy was to monitor the churches that were already established in the city of Ephesus, and it was also expected of him to monitor new churches there once they were established. Some say that Timothy himself was a pastor. This could well have been. But Timothy functioned more in the position of what some would define as Bishop today. He monitored the activities of many churches and therefore the pastors of the churches that he monitored were accountable to him. Paul instructed Timothy to watch over the churches in Ephesus and to make certain that those who sought the office of pastor or deacon were qualified for the position. The following verses of scripture inform us as to how Paul instructed Timothy:

¹Paul, an apostle (special messenger) of Christ Jesus by appointment and command of God our Savior and of Christ Jesus (the Messiah), our Hope,
²To Timothy, my true son in the faith: Grace (spiritual blessing and favor), mercy, and [heart] peace [be yours] from God the Father and Christ Jesus our Lord.
³As I urged you when I was on my way to Macedonia, stay on where you are at Ephesus in order that you may warn and admonish and charge certain individuals not to teach any different doctrine,
⁴Nor to give importance to or occupy themselves with legends (fables, myths) and endless genealogies, which foster and promote useless speculations and questionings rather than acceptance in faith of God's administration and the divine training that is in faith (in

that leaning of the entire human personality of God in absolute trust and confidence)—
⁵Whereas the object and purpose of our instruction and charge is love, which springs from a pure heart and a good (clear) conscience and sincere (unfeigned) faith. (1Timothy 1:1-5 Amp.)

Timothy was assigned to supervise those who would consider themselves called of God to pastor, teach, or preach. Therefore, this assignment was one of great responsibility and was not to be taken lightly.

When looking at what Paul wrote to Timothy concerning the qualifications of a pastor, special attention must be paid to verses 1, 2, 4, and 5 in considering the question as to whether or not the office of a pastor is only reserved for men. Let's take a look at those verses again:

¹The saying is true and irrefutable: If any man [eagerly] seeks the office of bishop (superintendent, overseer), he desires an excellent task (work).
²Now a bishop (superintendent, overseer) must give no grounds for accusation but must be above reproach, the husband of one wife, circumspect and temperate and self-controlled; [he must be] sensible and well behaved dignified and lead an orderly (disciplined) life: [he must be] hospitable [showing love for and being a friend to the believers, especially strangers or foreigners, and be] a capable and qualified teacher, (1 Timothy 3:1-2 Amp.)

⁴He must rule his own household well, keeping his children under control, with true dignity, commanding their respect in every way and keeping them respectful.
⁵For if a man does not know how to rule his own household, how is he to take care of the church of God? (1Timothy 3:4-5 Amp.)

It appears that verse 1 above is not using the word *man* generically to include women as well, but that the verse is addressed specifically to men. However, there is no assuredness of this. Some may argue that the word *man* is being used generically in the text as it is often used in the Bible and therefore the verse applies also to women. But when examining verses 2, 4 and 5 the argument that the office of a bishop (pastor) is reserved only for men, thickens. In verse 2 we learn that one of the qualifications of a pastor is that he only have one wife. As we have seen earlier, many theologians have interpreted this to mean that he cannot have been married more than once. Verse 4 goes on to say that a man seeking the office of pastor should be able to rule his household with dignity, command respect from those in his household, and keep his children under control. This implies that, if a man seeking to be a pastor is married then his wife and children should respect him and his children should be well behaved. The verse also implies that the one seeking an office of pastor is also one who is ruling the house. As we have clearly seen, in marriage, it is the man who has rule of the house. So when putting this altogether, some would conclude that only men should seek the office of a pastor.

However, if we say that only men should seek the office of pastor since (according to verses 4 and 5) men have been given the authority to rule the home (and a man's marital rule is included in defining pastoral eligibility), then we must also conclude that only *married* men should seek the office of pastor, since single men, theoretically, have no children to control and no wives to rule. If we take the verses literally that list the qualifications of a pastor, then we must take the verses literally all the way around. However, there are plenty of single men who pastor churches without being subjected to the conservative interpretation of verses 2, 4 and 5 that many theologians apply when it comes to women. These men are rarely dissuaded from seeking pastoral office even though many of them have never been married and when and if they were, had not been able to keep their households together. Furthermore, many of them have been married a second, or even a third time, which goes against Paul's instruction that a pastor should be the husband of but one wife, which, as stated before, many translations interpret to mean that he can only have been married once.

Some would additionally argue that the office of pastor has been described biblically in terms of a male model (one who rules the household, a man who has had no more than one wife, a man who keeps his children under subjection and so forth) and therefore the role of pastor belongs to men. However, there are other roles in the Bible that are described in terms of a male model, to which many women aspire

194

without much argument from men. For example, although men have been modeled as the ones charged to "work the fields" in order to support the family, most men have no problem with the idea of their wives working to assist with that support. Many men even take it a step further: they have no problem with their wives being the major "breadwinner." And although the office of deacon is described biblically in terms of a male model, Phoebe, a woman, was a deacon. Some might argue that since there is a biblical example of a wife working outside of the home (the virtuous wife)[31] and a biblical example of a female deacon (Phoebe) that these examples make room for exception. What they are then saying is that without an example of a female pastor in the Bible, there can be no exception and that therefore no woman can be a pastor since there is no example of a female pastor in the Bible. But the lack of a biblical example does not mean there were never any female pastors and that there can never be any female pastors, just as the lack of concrete evidence that women may have had a hand in writing the Bible does not mean that they absolutely did not have a hand in it.[32] So, just because the Bible models a role after a certain gender, does not necessarily mean that that particular role is exclusive only to that gender. On a similar note, certainly there have been many that believed that the office of apostle was reserved only for men. However, the fact that Junias, a woman, was an apostle, dissolves the fallacy that being an apostle was exclusively a man's job. As far as God ordained appointments go, being an apostle, of which a woman was one, heads the list. How then can we say that a woman cannot pastor if we have evidence that a woman was put in an even higher position of apostle?

Although verses 4 and 5 might bring some to conclude that the office of a pastor is reserved only for men, there is no direct command given that says a woman should not pastor. Therefore what some believe is an inference that a woman cannot pastor is simply no more than that: a believed inference. There is no absolute in this matter. There is no biblical law or set rule that says a woman can not seek a pastoral office. Therefore, a woman who believes that she is called of God to pastor a church should not be discouraged from it and these scriptures should only be brought to her attention so that she can make certain of her calling.

---

[31] See Chapter 6.
[32] See Chapter 13.

Many theologians would argue that if a woman has been commanded not to teach a man (not that she can't teach at all but that she cannot teach a man) then it follows that she should not pastor a church or preach. But as we have seen, God's word allows women to preach and Paul's directive that women not teach men was his response to the cultural mores of his time. Furthermore, there is no specific or direct command that prevents a woman from becoming a pastor even though the pastoral model is defined in male terms, just as there is no specific or direct command that prevents a single man from becoming a pastor even though the pastoral model is defined in married terms.

THE GIFTS

Although there are varying theological views as to whether or not the word of God allows a woman to preach, pastor, or teach, there is no question that God does not limit women when it comes to all the other callings or gifts. The Bible also clearly states that, although one gift may be greater than another,[33] each gift is just as important as the other, because every gift works together in the mission of spreading the gospel.

As stated before, those who are saved[34] are uniformly referred to as the church, in the Bible. They are also referred to as saints. When it comes to the gifts of the Spirit, there are scriptures that compare the church with a human body, with emphasis on the fact that the human body has many parts but each part is very important to the whole. And although the smaller parts of the body may not have as great of a function as other larger parts, it is still very important for the smaller parts to function properly in order that the larger parts may function properly. For example, the human eye is a small part of the body but if the eyes malfunction, the entire body is seriously affected. The brain, which is one of the greater body parts, if not the greatest, would have to totally readjust itself. Therefore, even the brain is negatively effected if the eyes stop working. And the eyes are negatively effected if the eyelids

---

[33] "Do all have gifts of healing? Do all speak in tongues? Do all interpret? But eagerly desire the greater gifts." (1 Corinthians 12:30 NIV)

[34] Saved from hell and therefore will be in heaven because of their confession in Jesus as God in the flesh (Lord and Savior) and their belief in his resurrection from the dead.

stop working. The Bible says there are similar circumstances when it comes to spiritual gifts. Let's take a look:

> [1]And so, dear brothers and sisters, I plead with you to give your bodies to God. Let them be a living and holy sacrifice—the kind he will accept. When you think of what he has done for you, is this too much to ask? [2]Don't copy the behavior and customs of this world, but let God transform you into a new person by changing the way you think. Then you will know what God wants you to do, and you will know how good and pleasing and perfect his will really is.
>
> [3]As God's messenger, I give each of you this warning: Be honest in your estimate of yourselves, measuring your value by how much faith God has given you. [4]Just as our bodies have many parts and each part has a special function, [5]so it is with Christ's body. We are all parts of his one body, and each of us has different work to do. And since we are all one body in Christ, we belong to each other, and each of us needs all the others. (Romans 12:1-5 NLT)
>
> [6]God has also given each of us different gifts to use. If we can prophesy, we should do it according to the amount of faith we have. [7]If we can serve to others, we should serve. If we can teach, we should teach. [8]If we can encourage others, we should encourage them. If we can give, we should be generous. If we are leaders, we should do our best. If we are good to others, we should do it cheerfully. (Romans 12:6-8 CEV)

Verses 4 and 5 tell us that those who are in the Lord have different things to do. The gifts that are cited are the gifts of prophecy, teaching, encouragement, contributing to the needs of others (giving), leadership, and goodness (or as some call it, the gift of mercy or kindness). Most theologians would agree that it is possible for a woman to have the gift of service, the gift of giving, and the gift of mercy. But then some would question whether or not a woman could have the gift of prophecy, the gift of teaching, and the gift of leadership. However, Paul does not use any gender discrimination when listing these gifts that God gives to the church. The verses cited above are part of the letter that Paul wrote to the church of Rome. Notice that the gift of teaching is included among the list of gifts Paul says that God imparts to people in the church (no matter if the person is male or female). Even though Paul's specific instruction was that women were not to teach men, the fact that women are included as part of those in the church in which the gift of teaching can be given, helps to support the claim that Paul's instruction for women not to teach men was a decision based on customary traditions of the church, not on any erroneous assumption that the gift of teaching is not imparted to women.

Verse 4 warns those in the church (the body of Christ) not to think more highly of themselves than they should when it comes to the gifts God has bestowed upon them. The inference here is that there are some who believe that certain gifts are more honorable than others. Certain gifts may be greater but are no less honorable in the eyes of God. In verses 4 and 5, emphasis is put on the fact that all of the members of the church do not have the same function. They do not all have the same work to do. God has given the saints different functions, different gifts. However, in Christ, they are all one body belonging to one another. Therefore, no one should get to the point where they are cocky or arrogant because of the gift God has bestowed upon them. All the gifts that God gives to the body of Christ work together for the entire body. Therefore, a woman's role in the church is no less honorable than a man's role is.

SUMMARY

When we consider the examples of Anna, Deborah, Huldah, and Miriam, there is no doubt that God endows women with the gift of prophecy. As we have seen, Acts 2:17 teaches us that the sons and daughters of God will prophesy. The gift of prophecy includes the preaching of the word of God. Therefore, it is God's will that women preach the gospel as well as it is God's will that men preach the gospel. He bestows this gift to women just as he does to men.

As we have seen, it is not against the word of God to appoint women as deacons. Phoebe was a deacon and a woman as well. Certainly, if she should not have been in the position of deacon, Paul would have said so.

Things are not as clear when it comes to women teaching and holding the office of pastor. But, the argument that the cultural mores of Paul's time was the main catalyst that triggered Paul's directive for women not to teach a man and to keep silent in the church is a strong one. With this in mind, the argument that female silence in the church and the prohibition of women teaching men is not applicable for today is also a strong one and seems to be the argument that strongly prevails when taking into consideration the cultural history of the Jews. If then, in today's church world, it is not improper for a woman to teach a man and it is not improper for a woman to speak in the church then it would seem that it would also not be improper for a woman to pastor. Paul gave specific commands forbidding women to speak and teach men in the church, yet in most of today's churches, women are allowed to speak and they are allowed to teach men. However, Paul gave no specific command that forbids women to pastor. Yet most Christians do not agree that a woman should pastor unless she has a husband who is a pastor and she is a "co-pastor" with him.

The forbidding of women to function in certain positions in the church seems to have much more to do with custom and legalistic interpretation of the scripture than with God's will. The fact that Pricilla taught a man and that Paul was accepting of this cannot be denied. One can surmise that Paul was not willing to let the traditions of men get in the way of the sound biblical teaching that Apollos was in need of. In looking at all of this, it appears that there are certainly enough examples of God using women as preachers, deacons, and teachers. Although there is no biblical example of a woman in a pastoral position, there is also no biblical scripture that forbids a woman from taking a pastoral position. And we must not forget that there is a biblical example of a woman who was an apostle and that the office of (or gift of, as some may put it) apostle is named first in hierarchy on the list that God has given us regarding his gifts and callings.

With all of this said, one would be hard pressed to present biblical evidence to support limiting a woman's service in the church. God imparts his gifts and makes his callings with no respect of gender. This is not characteristic of a chauvinist.

6.

THE VIRTUOUS WOMAN

The Bible depicts many qualities of a spiritual woman. However, out of all the qualities that the Bible speaks of, none seem to be as popular as those depicted in the 31st chapter of Proverbs (verses 10-31). This particular chapter of the book of Proverbs is a poem and has been labeled as the "Virtuous Woman chapter." Mostly every Christian woman (especially those who are married, were married, or intend to be) has been compared (if not directly, indirectly from Christian men and non-Christian men alike) to the woman in this chapter as a means of determining whether or not she "cuts the mustard" when it comes to being virtuous.

Solomon wrote the majority of the book of Proverbs. He was the first surviving son of King David and Bethsheba and is considered to be the wisest man who ever lived.[1] Solomon ruled Israel approximately forty years beginning about 1000 B.C.

The synonyms for the word *virtuous* include the following: *moral, chaste, effectual, efficient, ethical, noble, principled, righteous, good, blameless, exemplary, innocent, inculpable, irreproachable, pure,* and so on. Therefore, there is no doubt that the woman described in Proverbs 31 was an exceptional woman. She was indeed exemplary. This being the case, she was above average, better than the norm. This however, does not mean that the norm is bad. It does not mean average is sinful. But to many men, after reading Proverbs 31, it does.

What is rarely spoken of is the fact that the virtuous woman depicted in Proverbs 31 had a husband who set up an environment in her home so that it would be easy and even desirable for her to be as virtuous as she was. Many Christian men expect their wives to behave in the same manner as this "virtuous woman", but they themselves don't measure up to the man behind that virtuous woman that is depicted in Proverbs. Actually, the description of the virtuous woman in Proverbs 31 really only applies to a woman who is married. And technically translates as "the virtuous wife."

---

[1] 1 Kings 3:1-28 and 1 Kings 10:1-5 (see your Bible)

THE IDEAL WIFE

Since Solomon is the author of the 31st chapter of Proverbs and since he is considered to be the wisest man who ever lived, his description of the virtuous wife has developed into what men have esteemed to be the ultimate ideal wife. So, let's take a look at this virtuous wife described in Proverbs 31:10-31.

> Who can find a virtuous wife?
> For her worth is far above rubies.
> (Proverbs 31:10 NKJV)

Because the King James Version of the Bible reads "virtuous woman" instead of rendering *woman* as *wife*, modern day Christians have assumed that the description of the virtuous wife in Proverbs 31 applies to all women. However, the operative word is *wife*. Solomon's depiction of the ideal woman is specified to women who are married and taking care of the home. This is not to say that single women are not obligated to be virtuous[2] but only that the virtuousness depicted in the 31st chapter of Proverbs is distinctly applied to a married woman.

A man has a better chance of eliciting virtuousness in his wife, if he is virtuous himself. Interestingly enough, although the 31st book of Proverbs speaks about the ideal wife, the majority of the rest of the book of Proverbs speaks about the ideal man. But often times, this fact is overlooked.

Verse 10 cited above, tells us that it is better to have a wife of virtuous character than to have riches ("her worth is far above rubies"). Let's continue:

> The heart of her husband safely trusts her;
> So he will have no lack of gain.
> (Proverbs 31:11 NKJV)

---

[2] See Chapter 1. Also, Ruth was considered by Naomi to be a virtuous woman. Of Ruth, Naomi said, "And now, my daughter, fear not; I will do to thee all that thou requirest: for all the city of my people doth know that thou art a virtuous woman." (Ruth 3:11)

Her husband trusts her because she is trustworthy. A virtuous woman is practical and sensible when it comes to all matters, including, but not limited to, money and business affairs. Therefore, she will not get in the way of any good thing that her husband might generate. She is trustworthy in all things. She will not spend above her means. The things that she desires will not bankrupt the household financially, emotionally, or spiritually. The Amplified Bible translates the verse this way: *The heart of her husband trusts in her confidently and relies on and believes in her securely, so that he has no lack of [honest] gain or need of [dishonest] spoil.*

Although trustworthiness is one of the characteristics that define a virtuous woman, God has not exonerated men from possessing the same characteristic. Let's continue:

> [13]She seeks wool and flax
> And willingly works with her hands.
> [14]She is like the merchant ships,
> She brings her food from afar.
> [15]She also rises while it is yet night,
> And provides food for her household,
> And a portion for her maidservants.
> (Proverbs 31:13-15 NKJV)

Solomon's virtuous wife[3] had a skill. She had the ability to make fabrics. From the fabrics she would make clothes. Many take these verses to mean that wives should be willing to sew clothes for their family. But, as we will soon see, Solomon's virtuous wife, used her skills at making fabrics and sewing mainly as part of her own business venture. She sold much of what she made. She was an entrepreneur and was in business for herself and her family. In order for her to do this, her husband would have had to be flexible about her establishing her own business. She also would have not been able to establish her own

---

[3] This rendering of her is somewhat ambiguous but more reader friendly than the alternative. This is not to say that Solomon depicted himself as her husband, but that Solomon's literary creation of her gives him ownership of the character just as say, Lewis Carroll's literary creation of Alice (from his children's story "Alice in Wonderland" originally titled "Alice's Adventures in Wonderland") gives him ownership of the character (Carroll's Alice).

business unless her husband was able to amply take care of her so that she could invest comfortably in it. The old motto that says, "it takes money to make money" was just as applicable then as it is now. The wool and the flax had to be purchased. Solomon's virtuous wife needed money to buy her supplies. From the tone of the scripture we can safely assume that she comfortably bought what she needed to further her business. We can also safely assume that her husband made this possible.

Solomon's virtuous wife must have also been very skilled in the art of buying and selling. Such skill requires one to think practically and possess good people skills.

The tone of the verses of scripture also gives us the feeling that Solomon's virtuous wife willingly *chose* to go into business. Her business efforts were not something demanded of her by her husband. Being in business was something that she wanted to do and something he supported her in. She did not live in a household in which her husband requested or insisted that she enter the job market in order to help with the finances of the home. The tone of the scripture that describes this virtuous wife gives the impression that she chose to work outside of the home not necessarily to aid with the economy of the household but because she enjoyed working. She had a business career and her husband did not prevent her from aspiring to achieve what we call in today's world, her career goals. But if she had chosen not to work, that would have been acceptable as well, because it is the duty of the husband to adequately provide for his family,[4] which her husband undoubtedly did thoroughly.

Solomon's virtuous wife worked willingly with her hands and she not only used her gifts to pursue her careers goals but she also used her gifts to advance the household. This added to her virtuousness.

Verse 14 compares Solomon's virtuous wife to the merchant ships who bring their wares from far lands. In other words, she went the extra mile to take care of her household just as the merchants of the merchant ships traveled for miles in order to sell their wares. She is as determined to make sure her family has everything they need, just as the merchants of the merchant ships are determined to arrive safely onto their intended shores with all of their wares intact. The fact that Solomon's virtuous wife brings her food from afar simply means that she does what it takes

---

[4] See discussion in this chapter under subheading "Male and Female Roles in Marriage."

to get the best for her family, or at least the best that her husband can afford. Solomon depicts this virtuous wife's husband as being able to afford quite a bit. Therefore, his wife was very comfortable.

Verse 15 is crucial in giving clarification to the type of environment Solomon's virtuous wife lived in which no doubt contributed to what she was able to do in the home. She provided food for her household but the scripture also says that she provided a portion of food to her maidservants. Maidservants? Yes, she had servants. There were other women in the house who helped her take care of the home. These women were maids. And she had more than one maid. Solomon's virtuous wife would often times rise before dawn (as most wives and mothers do today) to provide food for her household and for her maidservants as well. Then afterwards, she, more than likely, delegated certain duties to her maids (otherwise, what's the use in having them). No doubt, the maids did much of the cooking, the cleaning, and caring for the children. Solomon's virtuous wife was therefore free to concentrate on her entrepreneurial business career and her husband. It is essential that this point is made because many men read the scriptures in Proverbs chapter 31 and expect their wives to do everything that "the virtuous woman" did, without realizing or considering that "the virtuous woman" had a great deal of help at home. The virtuous woman's husband provided her with everything she needed, and then some, which ultimately afforded her the environment and comfort that is required to become this stellar virtuous woman that so many men, when reading the 31st chapter of Proverbs, revere. A man who cannot provide maids, nannies, and/or servants for his wife should not expect his wife to be able to do all the things that this virtuous woman did around the house. A man who wants his wife to be like Solomon's virtuous wife, should be striving himself to be like the husband of this virtuous wife that Solomon depicted. Otherwise he is looking at the splinter in her eye and doesn't see the boulder in his.[5]

There are many women who are as virtuous as this wife that Solomon depicts, but cannot show it because their husbands have not created a climate which gives them an opportunity to show it. A woman who must work to help support the family, who does all of the housework, and is the main caretaker of the children, more than likely will not be able to match up to Solomon's virtuous wife, because she simply doesn't have

---

[5] Matthew 7:1-4 (see your Bible)

time. Solomon's virtuous wife had time to exhibit her virtuousness because there were other people in the house taking care of things. So, she had time to go to the market. She had time to start her own business. She had time to spin thread in order to make fabrics in order to make clothes and tapestry. She had time to use the gifts God gave her to benefit the family because Solomon was wise enough to depict a husband who realized that if a man wants his wife to be all that she can be, he has to provide her with what it takes for her to live to her fullest potential. There's only so much a woman can do by herself.

> [16]She considers a field and buys it,
> From her profits she plants a vineyard.
> (Proverbs 31:16 NKJV)

We saw earlier (verse 11) that Solomon's virtuous wife is described as a trustworthy woman. It appears that she independently makes business decisions without the initial approval of her husband. Remember, verse 11 says that her husband has no lack of gain. So apparently, when it comes to business matters, she is trustworthy and knows how to spend the household money wisely. The husband of this virtuous wife trusts her to make financial decisions independent of him. She has proven herself to be able to do this appropriately because he has no lack of gain. When combining verse 11 with verse 16, we see that her husband trusts her in all things. It appears that he trusts her judgment and that she is free to make business decisions, financial decisions, and many other decisions without necessarily consulting him all of the time before making her decisions. This says as much for her husband as it does for her. This virtuous woman has freedom within her own household. Although her husband is the head of the house,[6] he doesn't "lord it" over her.

The verse goes on to indicate that this virtuous wife is at liberty to spend what she makes as profit and that she is wise in how she does so. The scripture says that with her profits she plants a vineyard. A vineyard is a plantation of grapes. As it is still the case today, fermented grapes are used to make wine. During the era in which the Old Testament was written, wine was a commodity that sold well in the marketplace. So not only did this virtuous wife thrive in her business as fabric maker, but she

---

[6] See Chapter 3.

also invested the money she made from fabrics into another business that had a high profit margin. What she did is comparable to what investors do today with stocks and bonds. She made additional money by investing wisely the money she had already profited. She would not have been able to go into business and then invest in a second business if her husband had not been supporting her endeavors and more than adequately providing for her in the first place.

In order for the virtuous wife to have been free to pursue these business ventures, she would have had to have adequate financial backing and she would have had to live in an environment where she could comfortably spend money and take a loss or gain without jeopardizing the financial security of her family. Therefore, it is safe to assume that her husband was her financier. He took care of her so well, that she was free to take risks in business and still live lavishly with maids and servants who no doubt acted as nannies as well. Her husband provided the environment necessary for this virtuous wife to succeed in business and to be free to pursue an enterprise. This virtuous wife is different from the woman who has to go out and work as a means to help support the family. This virtuous wife was contributing to the finances of her home by manning the businesses she developed. However, if this virtuous wife had never gone into business and had never sold any fabric in the marketplace, and had never invested in a vineyard, the scripture infers that she would have lived just as comfortably in her home because her husband was providing for her exceedingly well. This is not a woman who needed to work. This was a woman who wanted to work.

Again, verse 16 tells us that it is not from her husband's assets that this virtuous wife plants a vineyard (begins her second business). She begins her second business with the profits she made from the first. No doubt her husband is in agreement with what she does with the money, as he should be. Again, the scripture gives us the impression that his wife has a certain independence and freedom to make certain decisions without necessarily consulting her husband. This wife is certainly not submission-bullied.[7] The wisest man who ever lived portrayed a husband who gave his wife the freedom to spend the money he gave her and the money she made in the way she wanted, gave her the room to make business decisions independent of him, and supplied her with all of the help she needed around the house so that she would not feel

---

[7] See Chapter 3.

overburdened and could begin a career doing the things she was interested in doing. Her husband is indirectly depicted as a man who realized and respected the fact that his wife had a need to do more in life besides keep the house and watch after his children. The ideal wife is a reflection of the ideal husband. Certainly then, there is no chauvinism in God's word here. Let's continue:

> [17] She girds herself with strength,
> and strengthens her arms.
> [18] She perceives that her merchandise is good,
> And her lamp does not go out at night.
> [19] She stretches out her hands to the distaff,
> And her hand holds the spindle.
> (Proverbs 31:17-19 NKJV)

She uses the spindle to make thread that she will eventually weave to make fabric which she will ultimately use to make clothes for merchandise.

The distaff is the upper portion of a staff in which wool or flax is wrapped around before being spun into thread. The spindle is the bottom portion of the staff that is used by hand to twist the wool or the flax into thread, which is pulled from the distaff. During the times of Solomon there were no electrical machines, so everything was done by hand. According to verse 18, this virtuous wife made certain that the fabric she weaved for selling was of good quality. She stayed up late in the night tending to her business venture. In order to do this comfortably, her husband had to have left her alone during the night in order for her to tend to her business. Her lamp did not go out at night because it took time to spin the wool in order to make the thread in order to make the fabric in order to make the clothes and tapestry. She was an entrepreneur and her husband didn't discourage her from doing what she was doing. He simply trusted her and let her do it. He did not get in her way or try to take over.

> She extends her hands to the poor,
> Yes, she reaches out her hands to the needy.
> (Proverbs 31:20 NKJV)

This virtuous wife would not be able to extend her hands to the poor if she were poor herself. It would be difficult for her to reach out to the needy if she were needy herself. She's able to give comfortably to those in need because her husband provides her with the ability to do so. Furthermore, her husband does not try to stop her from helping those who need help. He is not a miser and therefore, she is not forced to be one either.

> She is not afraid of snow for her household,
> For all her household is clothed with scarlet.
> (Proverbs 31:21 NKJV)

This verse in the New International Version of the Bible reads, *"When it snows, she has no fear for her household; for all of them are clothed in scarlet.* This verse says more about this virtuous woman's husband than about her. She is not afraid of the snow because her husband has provided so adequately for her that she does not have to be concerned about being cold and she doesn't have to be concerned about those in her household not having enough clothes to be warm. They are clothed with scarlet. Scarlet metaphorically means *high quality*. So, not only is this virtuous wife's household clothed, but her household keeps warm with the best clothes there is to buy. And, her household not only includes her husband and her children, but her maidservants as well. Her household has more than enough to sustain itself because the head of the house (her husband) is no less virtuous than his wife. He more than adequately fulfills his duty as a husband, which helps her to more than adequately fulfill her duty as a wife. This husband makes sure that his wife and his household want for nothing. And he provides them with the best of everything.

> [22]She makes tapestry for herself;
> Her clothing is fine linen and purple.
> [23] Her husband is known in the gates,
> When he sits among the elders of the land.
> [24]She makes linen garments and sells them,
> And supplies sashes for the merchants.
> (Proverbs 31:22-24 NKJV)

This virtuous wife's husband is respected. He has status and sits among the elders of the land. According to the New International Study Bible, the wearing of linen suggests association with royalty or that the person wearing it is of nobility.

Therefore, when husbands compare their wives to this virtuous wife, they must realize that they are comparing their wives to a woman whose husband not only took such good care of his wife that she wanted for nothing and not only supplied his wife with maid service that was available to her twenty-four hours a day but that he was also, more than likely, partaker in nobility. So, if a man wants his wife to be like the virtuous wife of Proverbs 31 then he has no choice but to look at himself and ask whether or not he is the virtuous *husband* of Proverbs 31.

> [25]Strength and honor are her clothing
> She shall rejoice in time to come.
> [26]She opens her mouth with wisdom,
> And on her tongue is the law of kindness.
> (Proverbs 31:25-26 NKJV)

The description of the virtuous wife is included among the proverbs of Solomon. Proverbs are similar to poetry since metaphoric language is frequently used in both. A metaphor is the application of a word to something that would normally be applied to something else. Strength and honor are not clothes, but have been metaphorically symbolized as clothing because clothing is not what makes a person, but instead character. Hence, one should be willing to dress his or herself in good character. The virtuous wife is wise and her tongue is the law of kindness. She is therefore dressed in good character. Her tongue is not literally the law of kindness. There is no law in her tongue, but she is kind to the point where if kindness were legally regulated, then her kindness would be the prime example of what the law of kindness should be. Without these attributes of strength, honor, wisdom, and kindness, the virtuousness of this virtuous wife would not be as profound.

> She watches over the ways of her household,
> And does not eat the bread of idleness.
> (Proverbs 31:27 NKJV)

This wife is described as virtuous because she runs her household well and is not idle. The fact that she is not idle does not mean that she never rests and that her husband expects her to be busy every waking hour. It doesn't mean that she never takes leisure time for herself. Instead, not eating the bread of idleness simply means that this virtuous woman is not lax in tending to the needs of her household and "watches over the ways of her household." This of course includes watching over the children. But let's face it, she has servants. This means she has nannies. This means that there are many people besides her feeding the children, teaching the children, changing the diapers, washing the clothes, cooking the food, and so forth. She watches over these necessary things, but she certainly isn't the only one in the house doing all of this day end and day out. Her servants are the one's doing these chores, and she watches over them to make sure they do things right. When her husband comes home, the food she presents to him was probably prepared by one of her servants. Her husband doesn't expect her to do everything. Her husband adequately provides for her so that she doesn't have to do everything.

> [28]Her children rise up and call her blessed;
> Her husband also, and he praises her:
> [29]"Many daughters have done well,
> But you excel them all."
> (Proverbs 31:28-29 NKJV)

This virtuous wife is appreciated by her children and her husband and they tell her so all of the time. They never take her for granted. Her husband praises her for her good business decisions, for overseeing the ways of the household, for giving to the poor, for her kindness, and so on. If her husband is praising her then he has no time criticize her. Apparently then, a man should compliment his wife, often, and be careful not to nag. This helps to encourage her.

Her husband praises her by telling her that "many daughters have done well, but you excel them all." This verse is very important because it says that although this virtuous wife has exceptional virtue, a woman does not have to be exceptional in her virtue to do well. This virtuous wife exceeds the norm of what virtue is, just as her husband exceeds the norm of what virtue is. Therefore, if a woman has just some of the characteristics that this virtuous wife is described as having, she does well. A woman's virtue does not have to match up the virtue that Solomon's virtuous wife is depicted as having before she can be described as having virtue.

THE IDEAL MAN

Although the book of Proverbs generally applies to both men and women, there are instances when the scriptures seem to target men just as specifically as Proverbs 31 targets married women. When examining the entire book of Proverbs, one can plainly see that there is also a certain standard of Christian living that men should strive for as well as women. God did not exclude men from the equation when it comes to the issue of virtue. A man with no virtue is just as unappealing as a woman with no virtue. All of the virtuous qualities specified for women are the same for men. Men should not be lazy, they should have wisdom, they should strive to be kind, and so on. Let's take a look:

> As vinegar to the teeth and smoke to the eyes
> So is the lazy man to those who send him.
> (Proverbs 10:26 NKJV)

It is a bitter ordeal to give responsibility to a lazy man. It is like smoke to one's eyes. A person who sends a lazy man to relay a message to someone else will probably never get the message through.

> He who tills his land will be satisfied with bread,
> But he who follows frivolity is devoid of
> understanding. (Proverbs 12:11 NKJV)

> The lazy man does not roast what he took in
> hunting,
> But diligence is man's precious possession.
> (Proverbs 12:27 NKJV)

In the days that Solomon wrote the book of Proverbs, it was a man's job to till the fields. Today, working for a living and financially taking care of one's family is synonymous with tending the fields. However, most men today do not work more than eight hours a day whereas, in the days of Solomon, tending the fields and hunting for food was an all-day job just as taking care of the household and tending to the children was then and is now an all-day job.

Solomon speaks against frivolity in a man. A frivolous man is a man who chooses not to toil the field (to work for a living) but to instead focus his attention on things that are not important. Frivolity is associated with laziness because it doesn't benefit anyone. Verse 27 goes on to describe a lazy man as someone who "does not roast what he took in hunting." This figuratively means that he doesn't follow a task through to completion. However, the literal understanding would mean that after he takes the time to hunt the food, he's too lazy to prepare it. If taken literally, the verse of scripture is a plus for women who are married to men who never cook. Let's continue:

> The way of the lazy man is like a hedge of
> thorns,
> But the way of the upright is a highway.
> (Proverbs 15:19 NKJV)

This verse indirectly teaches that an upright man and a lazy man cannot be one in the same. Therefore, laziness is a sign of unrighteousness. There is no virtue in unrighteousness.

> A lazy man will not plow during winter;
> He will beg during harvest and have nothing.
> (Proverbs 20:4 NKJV)

Once again, the measure of whether or not a man is lazy has to do with how willing he is to work. A man who does not work will end up begging others for what he needs. In our society today, they are called moochers. Moochers are men who "will not plow during winter." They would rather live off of their mothers, their wives, or anyone who will let them, rather than work. They would rather ask people for money than look for a job. They are not trying to increase their job skills. They are satisfied to mooch off of people. They are wanderers and have no plans. They're lazy.

> [25]The desire of the lazy man kills him,
> For his hands refuse to labor.
> [26]He covets greedily all day long,

212

But the righteous gives and does not spare.
(Proverbs 21:25-26 NKJV)

Again it is made clear that a lazy man is an unrighteous man and that a lazy man refuses to work for his living. Ironically, even though he refuses to work, verse 26 tells us that he wants what everyone else has. Not only is he lazy, but he is greedy as well. Certainly, there is no virtue here.

He who troubles his own house will inherit the wind,
And the fool will be servant to the wise of heart.
(Proverbs 11:29 NKJV)

A man who makes trouble in his own home is like a fool and will inherit nothing but the wind. The wind is nothing to inherit. One cannot hold on to the wind. It is fleeting and unpredictable.

As charcoal is to burning coals, and wood to fire,
So is a contentious man to kindle strife.
(Proverbs 26:21 NKJV)

It is just as bad for a man to be contentious as it is for a woman. A contentious man is quarrelsome and argumentative and a woman is no better living in a house with a contentious husband than a man is living with a wife of the same character. A contentious man is a man who complains all of the time, argues all of the time, is never satisfied, continually criticizes his wife, puts her down, and is basically a nag. He henpecks his wife and by doing so makes trouble in his own home.

A good man obtains favor from the Lord,
But a man of wicked intentions He will condemn.
(Proverbs 12:2 NKJV)

One test of a good man is whether or not he has obtained favor from the Lord. If he is virtuous then he is good. If he is good then the Lord will openly bless him. People will be able to see that God has given him favor. God will not condemn him.

213

A good man leaves an inheritance to his children's
children,
But the wealth of the sinner is stored up for the
righteous. (Proverbs 13:22 NKJV)

Another test of a good man is determining whether or not he has left
an inheritance to his grandchildren. The inheritance spoken of here has to
do with financial security. If indeed a man is to leave an inheritance then
he must work diligently to do so. A man of noble character therefore,
works for a living and does what it takes to properly support his family.

A quick-tempered man acts foolishly
And a man of wicked intentions is hated.
(Proverbs 14:17 NKJV)

A wrathful man stirs up strife,
But he who is slow to anger allays contention.
(Proverbs 15:18 NKJV)

The discretion of a man makes him slow to
anger,
And his glory is to overlook a transgression.
(Proverbs 19:11 NKJV)

Make no friendship with an angry man,
And with a furious man do not go,
Lest you learn his ways
And set a snare for your soul.
(Proverbs 22:24-25 NKJV)

A man of great wrath will suffer punishment;
For if you rescue him, you will have to do it
again. (Proverbs 19:19 NKJV)

A man with a bad temper should be avoided and not befriended. His
anger is contagious and provoking. Men who are quick-tempered act
foolishly and stir up strife. Eventually a man with a bad temper will get
himself into trouble. He will have to be bailed out of his troubles often.

Because of this, it seems plausible to assume that a virtuous man should be slow to anger.

> [27]An ungodly man digs up evil
> And it is on his lips like a burning fire.
> [28]A perverse man sows strife,
> And a whisperer separates the best of
> friends.
> [29]A violent man entices his neighbor,
> And leads him in a way that is not good.'
> [30]He winks his eye to devise perverse
> things;
> He purses his lips and brings about evil.
> (Proverbs 16:27-30 NKJV)

A virtuous man is a godly man and a godly man does not look to do wrong, is not perverse, does not cause strife among friends, is not violent, does not provoke his neighbor, does not cunningly plot with others to involve himself in perverted acts, and does not say anything that would bring about evil.

> [27]He who has knowledge spares his words,
> And a man of understanding is of a calm
> spirit.
> [28]Even a fool is counted wise when he holds
> his peace;
> When he shuts his lips he is considered
> perceptive. (Proverbs 17:27-28 NKJV)

A virtuous man behaves wisely. He knows how to hold his tongue and say the right things. He is a man of understanding and knows how to speak calmly. He thinks before he speaks and knows when it is best to say nothing.

> A man who has friends must himself be
> friendly,
> But there is a friend who sticks closer than
> a brother. (Proverbs 18:24 NKJV)

What is desired in a man is kindness,
And a poor man is better than a liar.
(Proverbs 19:22 NKJV)

It is good for a man to be friendly. If he is friendly then it follows that he doesn't have a bad temper. It is also desirous of a man to be kind. Part of being virtuous is being friendly and kind.

He who mistreats his father and chases
away his mother
Is a son who causes shame and brings
reproach.
(Proverbs 19:26 NKJV)

A good and virtuous man will not disrespect his mother or his father. He will not mistreat his parents in any way. He will honor his father and mother as commanded in scripture.[8] He will not act in ways that will put his parents to shame.

Most men will proclaim each his own
goodness,
But who can find a faithful man?
(Proverbs 20:6 NKJV)

Every way of a man is right in his own eyes,
But the Lord weighs the hearts.
(Proverbs 21:2 NKJV)

The question is asked, "but who can find a faithful man?" The fact that the question is even asked gives indication that it is difficult to find a faithful man. The same is true when looking at the question about a virtuous wife in Proverbs 31:10. The description of the virtuous wife first begins with the question, "who can find a virtuous wife?" This tells us that finding a virtuous wife that matches up to Solomon's virtuous wife can be just as difficult as finding a truly "faithful" man. A man who proclaims his own goodness and sees all of his ways as right in his own eyes is a self-righteous man who lacks faith. Proverbs 20:6 teaches us

---

[8] "Honour thy father and mother..." Exodus 20:12

that most men are like this (which is why it is difficult to find a truly faithful man).

A self-righteous man does not take well to correction. He feels he has no need for correction. But a faithful man is a righteous man and does his best to live a holy life. He does not applaud his own righteousness and does not appear hypocritical to others. He therefore is a virtuous man. This does not mean that a righteous man doesn't make mistakes. Proverbs 24:16 says, *"For a righteous man may fall seven times and rise again, but the wicked shall fall by calamity."* A righteous man errs and picks himself back up again to keep fighting his temptations until he has corrected his error. A wicked man simply falls by the calamity he has created. The Lord knows the heart of a righteous and faithful man just as he knows the heart of a self-righteous and faithless man. Therefore, although we might not be able to tell the difference, God can. Let's continue.

> A proud and haughty man—"Scoffer" is his name;
> He acts with arrogant pride. (Proverbs 21:24 NKJV)

A man with pride is a man to avoid. He is arrogant, haughty and a scoffer. To scoff at someone means to mock them, demean them, or put them down. These actions should not be confused with men who rebuke or correct others regarding the propagation of false doctrine. The apostle Paul has instructed Christians in 2nd Timothy 4:2 to *"Preach the word; be instant in season, out of season; reprove, rebuke, exhort with all longsuffering and doctrine."* However, a scoffer is different from a righteous man who corrects false doctrine. A scoffer is puffed up, thinks more of himself than he should, and is high-minded. His pride stands in the way of his judgment and because of his pride he is egotistical, self-righteous, and conceited.

> [18]Like a madman who throws firebrands, arrows, and death,
> [19]Is the man who deceives his neighbor,
> And says, "I was only joking!" (Proverbs 26:18-19 NKJV)

Finally, a virtuous man does not set out to play pranks on his fellow man. He takes no part in what is called a practical joke. Practical jokes are used only to humiliate and make fun of those who fall prey to them. Solomon likens those who ascribe to practical joking as madmen.

MALE AND FEMALE ROLES IN MARRIAGE

When it comes to the female role in marriage, most men emphasize a wife's role in the home to include cooking, cleaning, taking care of the children, her sexual duties, and so forth. But when it comes to the male role in the marriage, few men emphasize the fact that the man is supposed to adequately (not marginally, but adequately) take care of his wife and children without her having to work. In taking a look at what God says about these roles, we must revisit the following verses of scripture:

> [4]This is the account of the creation of the heavens and the earth. When the LORD God made the heavens and the earth, [5]there were no plants or grain growing on the earth, for the LORD God had not sent any rain. And no one was there to cultivate the soil. [6]But water came up out of the ground and watered all the land. [7]And the LORD God formed a man's body from the dust of the ground and breathed into it the breath of life. And the man became a living person.
> [8]Then the LORD God planted a garden in Eden, in the east, and there he placed the man he had created. [9]And the LORD God planted all sorts of trees in the garden—beautiful trees that produced delicious fruit. At the center of the garden he placed the tree of life and the tree of the knowledge of good and evil. (Genesis 2:4-9 NLT)

> [15]The LORD God placed the man in the Garden of Eden to tend and care for it. [16]But the LORD God gave him this warning: "You may freely eat any fruit in the garden [17]except fruit from the tree of the knowledge of good and evil. If you eat of its fruit you will surely die." (Genesis 2:15-17 NLT)

[18]And the LORD God said, "It is not good for the man to be alone. I will make a companion who will help him." (Genesis 2:18 NLT)

[21]So the LORD God caused Adam to fall into a deep sleep. He took one of Adam's ribs and closed up the place from which he had taken it. [22]Then the LORD God made a woman from the rib and brought her to Adam. (Genesis 2:21-22 NLT)

Adam lived in the Garden of Eden. The Garden of Eden was his home. He was directed to tend and care for the garden. In other words, God instructed Adam to keep his house up. Therefore, the first housekeeper of sorts, was a man, not a woman.

God created a woman to help Adam because the animals and the birds that God created to help Adam were not suitable.[9] It should be emphasized that the woman (Eve) was created to help Adam tend to the things in the garden, not to tend and take care of the garden all by herself without him. Let's continue:

[17]The LORD said to the man,

"You listened to your wife
and ate fruit from that tree.
And so, the ground
will be under a curse
because of what you did.
As long as you live,
you will have to struggle
to grow enough food.
[18]Your food will be plants,
but the ground will produce
thorns and thistles.
[19] You will have to sweat
to earn a living;
you were made out of soil,
and you will once again

---

[9] Genesis 2:18-20 (see your Bible).

turn into soil.
(Genesis 3:17-19 CEV)

Because Adam ate from the forbidden fruit, the ground was cursed so that Adam would have to work hard to provide for himself and his family. This was God's specific punishment for Adam and it was a curse that would effect all men through the ages to come. Initially, with no effort on Adam's part, food sprouted from the ground in the Garden of Eden.[10] The garden was always producing. However, because of their sins, Adam and Eve were banished from the Garden of Eden and from then on Adam would have to tend cursed soil instead of tending the ever-producing soil in the Garden of Eden. He'd have to work very hard. After the curse, Adam was specifically assigned to toil a ground stubborn in production. The ground was not cursed because of what Eve did. The ground was cursed because of what Adam did. Therefore, a rough terrain was now his, to toil.

Eve's punishment was different than that of Adam's. As discussed previously in Chapter 3, Eve was to endure two different punishments distinct from the punishment that Adam was to endure. Let's take a look at it again in two different translations of Genesis 3:16:

> [16]Then he said to the woman, "You will bear children with intense pain and suffering. And though your desire will be for your husband, he will be your master. (NLT)

> [16]To the woman he said,
> I will greatly increase your pains in childbearing;
> with pain you will give birth to children.
> Your desire will be for your husband,
> And he will rule over you. (NIV)

Both translations virtually say the same thing. The woman's punishment was that her pain in childbearing would be intense and her husband would rule over her thereby being her master. As clearly

[10] Genesis 2:6 and Genesis 2:8-9 (see your Bible)

shown, Eve's punishment did not include toiling the ground. In other words, her curses did not include working hard to make a living. Her husband was cursed with that, not her.

The curses that God brought upon Adam, Eve and the serpent are still in operation for men, women, and serpents today. In general, the serpent is still crawling on his belly, women (for the most part) still have great pain during childbirth, women are still under their husbands' rule in marriages, and men work hard for a living to support their families (or at least they are supposed to).

Since men are the ones that are supposed to work to bring money into the household, they are the ones that are supposed to sweat from their brows in an attempt to provide enough for their family. But in today's Western society, many men seem perfectly content to have their wives work outside of the home in order to make ends meet. Many wives therefore consequently end up working by the sweat of *their* brows in order to help financially support the family. The husband is the one who should endure this "sweat of the brow" curse. The wife has enough curses to endure without having to take on the extra responsibilities of her husband's curse. She has to endure the curse of pain in childbearing and she has to endure the curse of her husband ruling over her.

Of course, if both husband and wife agree that she should work outside of the home then, so be it. But even in an agreement as such, a man who benefits from his wife working outside of the home should realize that his wife is taking on much of the burden of *his* punishment. A man should be cognizant of this and therefore be willing to reciprocate his wife's sacrifice by sharing the burden of the housework and kidswork (to coin a phrase) since his wife is sharing his burden of working to financially support the family. And if he truly loves his wife "like Christ loved the church,"[11] then he would understand this and be willing to do it. Let's look further:

> [8]If anyone does not provide for his relatives, and especially for his immediate family, he has denied the faith and is worse than an unbeliever. (1 Timothy 5:8 NIV)

---

[11] See Chapter 3.

This verse of scripture above is speaking in relation to the care of widows.[12] However, the verse can be applied to a man who is married because, as we have seen, men are supposed to provide for their immediate families. God has charged men to work. God has charged men to be the providers. So, a man who does not provide financially for his family has denied the faith and is worse than an unbeliever.

Just as the Bible has defined a husband's role as that of being a provider, it has defined a wife's role as that of taking care of the home. Let's take a look:

> [1]But as for you, speak the things which are proper for sound doctrine:
> [2]that the older men be sober, reverent, temperate, sound in faith, in love, in patience;
> [3]the older women likewise, that they be reverent in behavior, not slanderers, not given to much wine, teachers of good things—
> [4]that they admonish the young women to love their husbands, to love their children,
> [5]to be discreet, chaste, homemakers, good, obedient to their own husbands, that the word of God may not be blasphemed. (Titus 2:1-6 NKJV)

The word for *homemakers* (verse 5) is derived from the Greek word *oikouros*, which means keeper of the home, or one who is a good housekeeper. It is clear then that part of the wife's role is to keep the house just as it is clear that part of the husband's role is to financially provide for his wife and children. So, often times, when a wife tells her husband she wants a bigger house, what she is really saying is that she wants a better working environment. She is, after all, the keeper of the house. If her husband wants a king's meal for dinner, then his wife needs a queen's kitchen to cook it in. If he wants many children, then she will want a house with room to accommodate. She doesn't want to have to deal with cramped quarters all day. And he wouldn't want to have to deal with cramped quarters all day on his job either. A man is supposed to give his wife the proper provisions she needs to take care of the home. The husband of the virtuous wife did this and more.

---

[12] See Chapter 12.

It is interesting to note, that often times when Christian men speak of women as being the homemakers and housekeepers they usually speak in very conservative terms as if these jobs don't cross any gender lines and only apply to women. They are quick to defend the position that says the role of caring for the house is the role God specifically put women in. Therefore, many of these Christian men are not inclined to share in that role.

However, when men speak of themselves as being the financial provider for the family they usually speak in very liberal terms and have no problem expressing their belief that it's all right for the job of financial provider to cut across gender lines. They don't express the same conservative view about their role as provider as they do about their wives' role as housekeeper. Instead, many of them say that they *want* their wives to work and they are very much inclined to have their wives share in their role as provider. These men are not nearly as quick to emphasize that the role of financial provider is the role God specifically put men in as they are quick to emphasize that the role of housekeeper is the role God specifically put women in. But just as there is nothing in the Bible that prevents women from working outside of the home, there is nothing in the Bible that prevents men from working inside of the home keeping the house. And God has no more specified women to be housekeepers than he has specified men to be providers. Therefore, if men are inclined to be liberal in their thinking when it comes to the provisions made for the family, they should be just as inclined to be liberal in their thinking when it comes to keeping the house.

Furthermore, as we learned by looking at the virtuous wife depicted in Proverbs 31, a woman doesn't necessarily have to physically care for the house herself to be a good housekeeper. Surely, the virtuous wife delegated most of the household chores to her servants and maids. She of course monitored the activities of her house, but she basically delegated the household duties and concentrated quite feverishly on her other interests. There was nothing wrong with this. Since she was managing a fabric business and a vineyard business then she must have been away from the home quite a bit. She must have often left her children with the servants. There is no indication in scripture that in doing so, she was doing anything wrong. Of course, it is conjecture that the virtuous wife left her children often with her servants. But it is logical to conclude that she did since she was a very busy woman with two thriving businesses to run. So, we can safely say that there were other people taking care of her children quite often. This virtuous wife was away from her home a good portion of the time, did what she wanted to do when she wanted to do it, and her husband didn't bother her about it. This virtuous wife ran the house by delegating to others, not by doing it all herself. Her husband took care of her well enough that she was able to pursue her own dreams and ambitions as well as adequately take care of the children and the home through the use of maids and servants that her husband provided for her. This is an important point that many men seem to miss or overlook when comparing their wives to the "virtuous woman." But it is a point that has been inadvertently made by the wisest man who ever lived, King Solomon.

SUMMARY

Solomon was no more lax in his description of the ideal man as he was in his description of the ideal wife. However, it must be emphasized again that the descriptions he laid forth regarding the virtuous wife define someone who is an exception as indicated by Proverbs 31:29 which reads in the King James version as such, *"Many daughters have done virtuously, but thou excellest them all."* With this in mind, it is safe to say that a wife can be virtuous to an acceptable degree without reaching the plateau of virtuousness described in Proverbs 31. It should also be emphasized that the characteristics of virtuousness discussed under the heading of *The Ideal Man* can be applied to women as well.

It bears repeating that the virtuous wife described by Solomon is documented as having a husband who was just as virtuous as she was. Not only does her husband excel in his provision of the home but also, he does not stop her from doing the things that are important to her. He also provides her with the help that she needs around the house in order for her to comfortably keep the house and be the woman that she is. Her exceptional virtuousness is a reflection of her husband's exceptional virtuousness.

Solomon did not discriminate in his description of the ideal wife and ideal man. It takes a great deal of sacrifice for both men and women to excel in virtue. With this being the case, there is no chauvinism in God's word here. Both men and women are encouraged to strive for perfection in the Lord.

We've examined the fact that it is a man's basic responsibility to provide financially for his family. It is also acceptable if a man's wife wants to work, but she should not have to work and a man should not insist that his wife work. In today's Western society, economists have ascertained that a man making no more than minimum wage is earning an annual salary that is below the poverty line if he is caring for three people (himself, his wife, and one child). He will therefore not be able to adequately provide for his family.[13] Consequently, he is faced with either working two jobs or sending his wife to work. Most men would opt to send their wives to work, and most women would want to work in order to help bring the family out of poverty. However, as we have seen, the Bible teaches us that the man was cursed to toil the field, not his wife. Therefore, if anyone has to work like a mule in order for the family to live comfortably, it should be him, not her. If a man's salary does not adequately meet the financial demands of his household then he should consider getting a second job before he considers sending his wife out to work.

His wife already has a job. She has a job at home. For her to work a job outside of the home puts her in a position where she is working two jobs, one outside the home and the other inside the home (actually 3 jobs if one considers the fact that a woman's job in the home does not end at 5:00 if she has children). If a man comes to his wife and asks her to work outside of the home then he is asking her to do what he should be willing to do....work two jobs. If she willingly complies with working outside of the home then she is essentially doing part of his job. She is doing what he's supposed to be doing. She is helping to provide for the family when she shouldn't have to. Her husband should therefore do part of her job, and help around the house. He should help around the house in a way that is comparable to the time that his wife spends away working outside of the home. This means that he should share in the housework and kidswork every day since she is working every day to

---

[13] And with each new additional dependent member added to the family, poverty increases substantially and more household money is needed. A man working two minimum wage jobs who has five children and a wife is still making a salary that is under the poverty line for the amount of people that he must take care of in his home. He is not making an adequate amount of money to care for his family's needs.

help with the finances of the home. There should be an equal trade off. But often times there isn't.

Again, toiling the field used to be a 24-hour job (to use the figure of speech liberally). So everything was equal. Women had a 24-hour day (so to speak) in the home and men had a 24-hour day in the field. But it is not this way anymore. Women have a 24-hour day in the home and men have an 8-hour day at work. Already, there is an imbalance. Therefore, a man should be willing to help his wife in the home (or get her some help) even if she does not work outside of the home.

A woman is supposed to be kept and cared for according to God's word. Despite this, it is not wrong for a wife to work outside the home, as long as she wants to and is willing. We see this with the virtuous wife. But the virtuous wife was kept and cared for in a mighty way and she certainly worked because she wanted to not because she had to.

In regards to the customs of ancient Israel, men were expected to adequately take care of their wives. There was a time when men had many wives and were expected to take care of all of them sufficiently.[14] Dowries were given to the engaged woman's family from the engaged man's family. The dowry was a monetary gift that was to be used for the financial security of a woman in case her husband abandoned her or died, because in such a case, the woman would more than likely return to her father's house. Her father then would have money to take care of her. The inference that this custom makes is that the man was solely responsible for financially providing for his wife. A woman of that time did not enter into a marriage expecting to work for a living. She entered into a marriage expecting her husband to adequately provide for her.

In today's society, women are working and taking care of themselves. It is a good thing that Western culture has changed in that a woman does not have to depend on her father or a husband to take care of her. She can establish her own independence if she likes without feeling pressure to get married in an effort to get away from a father that wants her out of the house so he can stop taking care of her. There is nothing in the Bible that says there is anything wrong with this. As we see, the virtuous wife established her own businesses. However, since there are so many women who are self-sufficient in today's society and so many women who have equal earning power as men (as it should be), men in general, seem to be irritated by women who believe that a man

---

[14] See Chapter 11.

should at least have the ability to properly take care of a woman if he is looking for a wife.

If a woman wants to be taken care of the way the virtuous wife was taken care of, then, when being approached by men, she should not settle for less than what the virtuous wife's husband had to offer. Aside from popular belief, she has the right to decline a man's hand in marriage if she does not feel he can provide for her to the standard that she desires to be provided for. As we have seen in our discussion in Chapter 12, a woman is not commanded to get married. She can stay single if she wants. So if there are certain things that she wants from a man in marriage, she doesn't have to settle for less. She can wait for a man that meets her needs and desires or she can opt not to marry at all. It's her choice. There's no crime and no sin in her desire to marry a man that can meet her wants as well as her needs. Of course, a woman should never marry a man for money, because, as 1ˢᵗ Timothy 6:10 tells us, "the love of money is the root of all evil." But God does not have a problem with a woman adding financial security to her list in determining whether or not a man is right for her. There is nothing wrong with her spirituality and she is no less of a Christian if she doesn't want to marry a man who's broke.[15] After all, once she's married, she will automatically fall under the rule of her husband. So, why shouldn't she want a husband who can at least properly care for her?

Men are not open to marrying women who cannot take care of them the way they want to be taken care of. Most men have a "laundry list" of how they want their wives to be and what they'd like a potential mate to do for them. That seems to be all right. But women are discouraged from having laundry lists when it comes to what they want a potential husband to do for them. If asked, most men would say that they'd want a wife who is willing to work outside of the home in order to supplement the household income as well as be the perfect mother to his kids. To take it further, most men are not even interested in dating women who don't have the ability to add some type of financial security to the home. So basically, men want it all. They want superwoman. But if a woman wants a man with a decent job who can take care of her, she's often times directly or indirectly labeled as one who is shallow, a gold digger, or worse yet—spiritually immature (the erroneous train of thought here is that spiritually mature women should always be willing to consider

---

[15] Slang meaning *penniless*.

marrying men who are struggling financially). The message many women get is that women should be happy and satisfied with a man who is going to make many demands on her but cannot financially supply her with the things she wants or needs.

Again, men who are liberal in their thinking when it comes to women working outside the home and therefore advocate for women to work outside the home should be just as liberal in their thinking when it comes to men working inside the home and should therefore advocate just as strongly for men to work inside the home. Again, if a woman works 8 hours a day just like her husband, then her husband should be willing to put in as much time working in the home as she has to put in working outside of the home. Or he should be willing to do what the virtuous wife's husband did and get her some help inside the home.

Let's face it, most men expect the woman they marry to provide three meals a day for them (no leftovers, eggs have to be cooked a certain way, can't have chicken all of the time, must have fresh vegetables... no canned or frozen), to provide 24 hour care to their children, to provide clean clothes, to provide a clean home, to home-school if need be (doesn't matter if she doesn't have the gift or aptitude to teach), to provide sex on demand, and on and on. And they expect their wives to do all of this without the assistance of a maid, a nanny, or an extended family member. But when a woman insists that her husband provide for her financially on the same level comparable to what he insists she do around the house, she is often labeled as materialistic, lacking in spirituality, or lacking in virtue. These men need to take a look at Proverbs 31 and study what the virtuous wife's husband did for her.

God has not imposed any double standards when it comes to the roles of men and women. Men are supposed to work just as hard to provide for the family, as women are to make sure the house is run well. The mandate for women to work outside of the home as well as inside of the home and do both well, is not a mandate from God but it is a societal mandate that has developed over the years that men have implemented for their own benefit. It is therefore not God, who is the chauvinist, but instead it is the men who insist that a wife work both inside and outside the home, without adequate help inside the home, who are the chauvinists. These men are sorely taking advantage of their wives and abusing the authority they have over them.

7.

WOMEN AND BEAUTY

One might ask the question: If God is not a chauvinist, then why did he design things so women have to be beautiful in order to be validated by men? But this question is based on assumption, not fact.

In America, and even in other countries, especially since the day the movie "Ten" premiered starring Bo Derek,[1] women in general have been overtly subjected to being rated as to their beauty by men in general from a scale of 1 to 10 (with 10 being the highest). However, the old cliché still stands. Beauty is most definitely in the eyes of the beholder and in Western society the standards of beauty change drastically every 40 years or so.

There was a recent time in America, between the 1920s and early 1960s, when voluptuous women were the mark of beauty (e.g. Marilyn Monroe,[2] Jane Russell,[3] Jayne Mansfield[4]) and thinness (e.g. Audrey Hepburn[5]), as a beauty mark, was rare. Marilyn Monroe wore a size 14, which by today's standards is too big. However, since the onset of

---

[1] The movie "10" premiered in 1979 and was a comedy about an aging songwriter who becomes obsessed with a woman he considers a "perfect 10" in physical attributes. Men more brazenly began rating women from 1 to 10 as a result of the movie, with a rating of 10 representing superior beauty.

[2] Voluptuous blonde Hollywood movie star and legendary sex symbol, now deceased. Began a modeling career in the mid-1940s and signed on at Fox studios in 1946. Hollywood exploited and disrespected her.

[3] Voluptuous brunette Hollywood movie star and sex symbol, now deceased. Began her Hollywood career in 1941. Was given her big break by Howard Hughes who ignored her acting talents and would only cast her in films to show off her body.

[4] Voluptuous blonde Hollywood movie star and sex symbol, now deceased. Began her career in the theatre in 1951 which eventually led to her first film for Fox studios in 1956. Hollywood exploited and disrespected her.

[5] Born in Brussells Belgium in 1929, now deceased. Began modeling in London in the 1940s because of her slim figure. Began acting in British movies in the 50s which eventually led to her Hollywood career. She was well respected.

Twiggy,[6] who became a modeling sensation in the sixties, the measure of female beauty has unfortunately included excessive thinness. Twiggy was so thin that she'd probably be labeled anorexic by today's standards. However, in the sixties her thinness was celebrated and beauty became associated with a malnourished look. Women are now pressured into being the size of supermodels that weigh no more than 115 pounds and stand no less than 5'8. This pressure has caused the onset of what the medical society has termed *eating disorders*. These disorders include anorexia nervosa and bulimia.

Anorexia nervosa is an eating disorder in which a person doesn't eat enough food to sustain him or herself because of a fear of gaining weight. Teenaged girls and women mostly suffer from this. A woman who is anorexic sees herself as much heavier than she actually is. The condition, if not treated successfully, will eventually cause hospitalization and often times, death.

Bulimia is an eating disorder in which the person with the disorder forces his or herself to regurgitate meals they've eaten. The regurgitation is done in a quest to become or stay thin. This disorder is also much more prevalent among women than among men. It may be interesting to note that Twiggy was neither Anorexic nor Bulimic. Her metabolism was such that she stayed thin no matter what she ate.

Men are also steadily being pressured to look a certain way. However, they are pressured in the opposite direction of women. A thin man is not considered as attractive as is a weightier man with muscles. But a weighty woman, in general, is considered less attractive than a thin woman is. This is the reason that anorexia nervosa and bulimia are more prominent in women.

Today, discrimination against obese people[7] is more prominent in American society than discrimination against any other group of people,

---

[6] Born in London as Lesley Hornby in 1949, became a supermodel in 1966 at age 16. Her look greatly influenced beauty standards for women. She was exceedingly thin.

[7] People are considered obese if they weigh more than 25% of the maximum suggested weight for their height and bone density. For example, most medical doctors agree that a large boned woman who is 5'5 in height should not weigh more than 155 pounds. 25% of 155 is 39 pounds. Therefore, if she gains 40 pounds (which would put her at 195 pounds and over the 25%) she'd be

including minorities, women, the disabled, and others. Also, the tide surrounding the attractiveness of thin women seems to be changing. Being excessively thin seems to be loosing its appeal somewhat.

WHAT THE BIBLE SAYS ABOUT EXERCISE

Exercise businesses have boomed over the last twenty years. People who don't exercise regularly are frowned upon. Women are more prone to struggle with fat than men because 40% of a woman's body mass is naturally fat as compared to the same 40% of a man's body mass which is naturally muscle.

Exercise takes time and energy. A woman who comes home from work, prepares dinner, washes the dishes, and helps the kids with their homework, might find herself exhausted at the end of the day and too tired to exercise. Or she simply might not have the time to exercise regularly because she's got to get up at four or five o'clock in the morning and start her day all over again. Even a stay at home mom has little time for anything else but child rearing if she has children who are not in school. In order to reap and maintain the benefits of exercise, one must do it consistently...forever.

But what does God have to say about all of this? Let's take a look:

> ¹Now the Spirit expressly says that in latter times some will depart from the faith, giving heed to deceiving spirits and doctrines of demons,
> ²speaking lies in hypocrisy, having their own conscience seared with a hot iron, (1 Timothy 4:1-2 NKJV)

> ⁷But reject profane and old wives' fables, and exercise yourself toward godliness.
> ⁸For bodily exercise profits a little, but godliness is profitable for all things, having promise of the life that now is and of that which is to come. (1 Timothy 4:7-8 NKJV)

---

considered obese, although she wouldn't look obese (large boned women don't look as heavy as small boned women who are the same height and weight).

The Bible tells us that there is some profit in bodily exercise but that bodily exercise should not take priority over exercising spiritual godliness. What good is it to be in great physical shape and at the same time be in poor spiritual shape giving heed to deceiving spirits and doctrines of demons? The message in the above scripture is really directed towards Christians. Rejecting false religions and false teachings is part of what makes one holy. Sculpting one's self spiritually in order to live a holy life should take precedent over sculpting one's physical body. Of course, if there are health concerns, then bodily exercise is needed. But Western societal pressures for a woman to look fit and trim go beyond health concerns. A woman's beauty is measured by how thin she is, how shapely she is, how pretty she is, how she conforms to the Westernized standard of beauty, and so on.

HOW GOD MEASURES BEAUTY

God's definition of beauty differs markedly from man's definition. Let's take a look:

> [3]Your beauty should not come from outward adornment, such as braided hair and the wearing of gold jewelry and fine clothes. [4]Instead it should be that of your inner self, the unfading beauty of a gentle and quiet spirit which is of great worth in God's sight. [5]For this is the way holy women of the past who put their hope in God used to make themselves beautiful.
> (1 Peter 3:3-5 NIV)

In the above scripture, Paul is specifically addressing himself to women in Christ who are married,[8] but what he says basically applies to all women.

The scriptures instruct women not to concentrate on being physically beautiful but instead to concentrate on their inner selves. According to the Bible, a woman's true beauty is revealed by her character and not by her appearance. In God's eyes, a gentle and quiet spirit is part of what makes a woman beautiful, not how she looks. Women are not beautiful

---

[8] See discussion on the same verses of scripture (to include verses 1,2, and 6) in Chapter 3, under the heading "Married women as slaves."

unless they are beautiful on the inside. In other words, they must be spiritually beautiful in order to be really beautiful. Although men are attracted to the physical beauty of a woman, God is attracted to the inner beauty of a woman. The scripture says that it is a woman's inner beauty, not her outer beauty, which is of great worth to God. Surely then, the God of the Bible is not a chauvinistic God. A chauvinistic God would measure a woman by her outer beauty alone as do many men. However, the God of the Bible measures a woman's beauty by the way she carries herself and whether or not she is living a holy life. This is not to say that God does not acknowledge the fact that a woman is outwardly beautiful. This is only to say that outward beauty means nothing to God.

Verse 3 above, teaches that beauty should not come from outer adornment. However, the scripture is not saying that it is a sin for a woman to wear her hair braided, to wear fine jewelry, or to wear fine clothes, but that if she does she should not do so in excess and she should not rely or depend upon these things in an effort to make herself beautiful. A woman should instead strive to master certain traits that make a woman spiritually beautiful. As stated before, those traits include a gentle and quiet spirit. Some might take this to mean that women should not speak or voice an opinion. But as we saw in Chapter 5, scripture commands and encourages Christian women to proclaim the gospel and preach just as scripture commands Christian men to do so. Logically then, women cannot be quiet and proclaim the gospel at the same time. Therefore, Paul must be talking about *the way* in which a woman addresses herself and not the fact that she addresses herself at all. The instruction for women to be gentle and quiet goes along with other scriptures that describe the dissatisfaction God has with women who are quarrelsome and contentious. Therefore, to be quiet does not mean abstaining from voicing one's opinion, but instead it means to abstain from being quarrelsome. Let's take a look:

> A foolish son is his father's ruin,
> And a quarrelsome wife is like a constant
> dripping. (Proverbs 19:13 NIV)

> Better to live on a corner of the roof than
> share a house with a quarrelsome wife.
> (Proverbs 21:9 NIV)

> Better to live in a desert
> than with a quarrelsome and
> ill-tempered wife. (Proverbs 21:19 NIV)

Again, these scriptures are specifically directed towards married women. There is a certain way that a married woman is to act towards her husband. She should not be quarrelsome. This does not mean that she can never quarrel with him. A *quarrelsome woman* is different from a *woman who is quarreling*. A quarrelsome woman is a woman who complains about everything, often. It doesn't take much for her to start grumbling and mumbling. She is very critical of her spouse and is extremely hard to please. She will argue about things that need no argument. She fusses all of the time. She henpecks her husband and bosses him around. Her husband is so oppressed by her that he hates to come home. He'd rather live on the corner of his roof (Proverbs 21:9) or in the desert (Proverbs 21:19) than live in the house with his wife. A quarrelsome woman is a woman who is not in control of her temper (Proverbs 21:19). It doesn't take much to trigger her anger. She is easily irritated. When she becomes angry, which is frequent, she quarrels.

On the other hand, a woman who finds herself in a quarrel with her husband, may have every right to involve herself in that quarrel. If her husband has asked her to do something that is unfitting to the Lord or has asked her to do something that she feels is a sin,[9] then she has no other choice but to express to her husband the reasons why she cannot appease him. Of course, if her husband disregards what his wife is saying, a quarrel could ensue.

Women who express themselves on any view contrary to a man's opinion on the same view are often times seen as quarrelsome while a man who may be just as firm in his opposing viewpoint, is usually seen as merely opinionated.

It would seem, so far in our discussion, that women must be careful not to be more quarrelsome than men. But as the following scriptures attest to, and as previously discussed in Chapter 6, God doesn't really make any distinction between a man and a woman when it comes to his instruction against a quarrelsome personality. Let's take a brief look:

> [20]Without wood a fire goes out;

---

[9] See Chapter 3.

without gossip a quarrel dies down.
[21]As charcoal to embers and as wood to fire
So is a quarrelsome man for kindling strife.
(Proverbs 26:20-21 NIV)

As the scripture tells us, a quarrelsome man stirs up strife. A man is no better for being quarrelsome than a woman is. The book of Proverbs warns against angry quarreling men, as the following verses of scripture attest to:

[18] A hot-tempered man stirs up dissension
but a patient man calms a
quarrel. (Proverbs 15:18 NIV)

[22]An angry man stirs up dissension,
And a hot-tempered one commits many
sins. (Proverbs 29:22 NIV)

As the above scriptures indicate, a quarrelsome man is a hot-tempered man and a hot-tempered man creates disharmony and conflict between himself and others. The scriptures also teach us that a man, who is prone to being quarrelsome because of his impatience, commits many sins. In this sense men are instructed to be as meek and gentle as are women. A gentle nature is an asset to both men and women, as evidenced by the following verses of scripture:

[19]Now the works of the flesh are evident, which are: adultery, fornication, uncleanness, lewdness,
[20]idolatry, sorcery, hatred, contentions, jealousies, outbursts of wrath, selfish ambitions, dissensions, heresies,
[21]envy, murders, drunkenness, revelries, and the like; of which I tell you beforehand, just as I also told you in time past, that those who practice such things will not inherit the kingdom of God.
[22]But the fruit of the Spirit is love, joy, peace, longsuffering, kindness, goodness, faithfulness,
[23]gentleness, self-control. Against such there is no law. (Galatians 5:19-23 NKJV)

As is clearly evident, the mandate for gentleness has no gender discriminations. A cantankerous quarreling man is just as unattractive as a cantankerous quarreling woman is. God has not made a difference.

BEAUTY GONE BAD

In light of the aforementioned, *Beauty* is really an action word. And the ultimate example of physical beauty gone bad is seen when looking at the actions of Lucifer. Let's take a look.

> [12] ....This is what the Sovereign Lord says:
>
> [13] You were the model of perfection,
> Full of wisdom and perfect in beauty.
> You were in Eden,
> The garden of God;
> Every precious stone adorned you:
> Ruby, topaz and emerald,
> Chrysolite, onyx and jasper,
> Sapphire, turquoise and beryl.
> Your settings and mountings were made
> of gold;
> On the day you were created they were
> prepared.
> [14] You were anointed as a guardian cherub,
> For so I ordained you.
> You were on the holy mount of God;
> You walked among the fiery stones.
> [15] You were blameless in your ways
> From the day you were created
> Till wickedness was found in you.
> [16] Through your widespread trade
> You were filled with violence,
> And you sinned.
> So I drove you in disgrace from the
> mount of God,
> And I expelled you, O guardian cherub,
> From among the fiery stones.

> [17]Your heart became proud
> On account of your beauty,
> And you corrupted your wisdom
> because of your splendor. So I threw you
> to the earth;
> I made a spectacle of you before kings.
> (Ezekiel 28:12-17 NIV)

We know that the above scripture text is speaking of Lucifer because of similar reprimands given to him which are represented in the following scripture text:

> [12]How you are fallen from heaven
> Oh Lucifer, son of the morning! How you are
> cut down to the ground,
> You who weakened the nations!
> [13]For you have said in your heart:
> I will ascend into heaven,
> I will exalt my throne above the stars of God;
> I will also sit on the mount of the congregation
> On the farthest sides of the north;
> [14]I will ascend above the heights of the clouds,
> I will be like the Most High.
> [15]Yet you shall be brought down to Sheol,
> To the lowest depths of the Pit.
> (Isaiah 14:12-15 NKJV)

As we can see from our two scripture texts, Lucifer initially had a position in heaven as an angel (cherub) that guarded the Holy Mount of God (Ezekiel 28:14). Lucifer was perfect in beauty (Ezekiel 28:13) and did not sin until one day wickedness was found in him (Ezekiel 28:15). His conceitedness corrupted his wisdom (Ezekiel 28:17). Lucifer became proud because of his beauty and splendor. Lucifer decided that he wanted to be like God (Isaiah 14:14). So God threw him to the earth to be brought down to Sheol, the lowest depths of the Pit (Ezekiel 28:17 and Isaiah 14:15). Once Lucifer was thrown out of Heaven, he was no longer referred to as Lucifer (which means Morning Star) but instead referred to as Satan, which means *adversary*. The following verses of scripture attest to this:

237

[7]And there was war in heaven, Michael and his angels fought against the dragon, and the dragon and his angels fought back. [8]But he was not strong enough, and they lost their place in heaven. [9]The great dragon was hurled down---that ancient serpent called the devil, or Satan, who leads the whole world astray. He was hurled to the earth, and his angels with him. (Revelation 12:7-9 NIV)

God brought Satan down to earth by means of war. Satan fought back but lost. Once Satan decided that he would try to overthrow God, God did not hesitate in throwing him out of heaven. It did not matter how beautiful Satan was. It did not matter that Satan was covered with precious stones. It did not matter that Satan was splendorous. God brought him down anyway.

The fact that Satan was physically beautiful teaches us that outer beauty means nothing to God. God punished Satan despite his beauty. Although beauty is a gift from God[10], it can be a snare as well. Let's take a look:

[23]For these commands are a lamp,
    This teaching is a light,
and the correction of discipline
    are the way to life,
[24]keeping you from the immoral
        woman,
from the smooth tongue of the
        wayward wife.
[25]Do not lust in your heart after her
        beauty
or let her captivate you with her
        eyes,
[26]for the prostitute reduces you to a loaf
        of bread,
and the adulterous preys upon your
        very life.
(Proverbs 6:23-26 NIV)

---

[10] Job 42:12-15 (see your Bible)

The above verses of scripture discourage men from getting involved with a prostitute or adulterous woman (wayward wife). The scripture gives, as one of the first lines of defense against such temptation, the instruction for men not to be enchanted by a woman's beauty. Through no fault of her own, unless she consciously intends to, a beautiful woman provokes lust in a man. God faults the man for his lust, not the woman for her beauty. The scripture teaches us that men become weak at the sight of a beautiful woman. No doubt, Delilah was beautiful.[11]

Beauty can evoke envy or favoritism on the part of others, and narcissism on the part of the one whom is beautiful. It was most certainly a snare for Lucifer. He became puffed up in pride because of his good looks and his conceit lead to his downfall. God does not validate anyone by how beautiful the person is. Character is what is important.

THE BEAUTY OF JESUS

The fact that character is the true measure of one's beauty and not physical attractiveness is most perfectly illustrated in the Bible's description of Jesus. Let's take a look:

> [1]Who has believed our message
> and to whom has the arm of
> the LORD been revealed?
> [2]He grew up before him like a tender
> shoot,
> and like a root out of dry ground.
> He had no beauty or majesty to attract
> us to him,
> nothing in his appearance that we
> should desire him.
> [3]He was despised and rejected by men,
> a man of sorrows, and familiar
> with suffering.
> Like one from whom men hide their
> faces
> he was despised and we

[11] The historical account of Samson and Delilah can be found in Judges chapters sixteen and seventeen (see your Bible).

239

esteemed him not.

[4]Surely he took up our infirmities
and carried our sorrows,
yet we considered him stricken by
God,
smitten by him, and afflicted.
[5]But he was pierced for our
transgressions,
he was crushed for our iniquities;
the punishment that brought us
peace was upon him,
and by his wounds we are
healed.
[6]We all, like sheep, have gone
astray,
each of us has turned to his own
way;
and the LORD has laid on him
the iniquity of us all.

[7]He was oppressed and afflicted,
yet he did not open his mouth;
he was led like a lamb to the
slaughter,
and as a sheep before her shearers
is silent,
so he did not open his mouth.
[8]By oppression and judgment he
was taken away.
And who can speak of his
descendants?
For he was cut off from the land of
the living;
for the transgression of my people
he was stricken.
[9]He was assigned a grave with the
wicked,
and with the rich in his death,

though he had done no violence,
nor was any deceit in his
mouth. (Isaiah 53:1-9 NIV)

There is clear indication that the above verses of prophetic scripture are referring to Jesus Christ. Jesus was despised and rejected by many people during his earthly ministry. So much so, that the Jews finally crucified him. The death, burial, and resurrection of Jesus Christ were predicted by many of the prophets of the Old Testament. The 53rd chapter of Isaiah contains prophetic scripture that foretells the death of Jesus.

Verse 4 is quoted as follows, *"Surely he took up our infirmities and carried our sorrows."* The following verses of scripture indicate that verse 4 is referring to Jesus:

[14]When Jesus came into Peter's house, he saw Peter's mother-in-law lying in bed with a fever. [15]He touched her hand and the fever left her, and she got up and began to wait on him.
[16]When evening came, many who were demon-possessed were brought to him, and he drove out the spirits with a word and healed all the sick. [17]This was to fulfill what was spoken through the prophet Isaiah:

"He took up our infirmities
and carried our diseases." (Matthew 8:14-17 NIV)

The prophet Isaiah predicted that Jesus would heal our infirmities and diseases. The verses quoted in Matthew above back up the prediction. There is no question that the one who took up our infirmities is Jesus Christ.

Verse 5 of Isaiah 53 says, *"but he was pierced for our transgressions."* The following verses of scripture give further indication that the verses quoted in Isaiah 53 above are speaking of Jesus:

[31]Now it was the day of Preparation, and the next day was to be a special Sabbath. Because the Jews did not want the bodies left on the crosses during the Sabbath, they asked Pilate to have the legs broken and the bodies taken down. [32]The soldiers therefore came and broke

241

the legs of the first man who had been crucified with
Jesus, and then those of the other. [33]But when they
came to Jesus and found that he was already dead, they
did not break his legs. [34]Instead, one of the soldiers
pierced Jesus' side with a spear, bringing a sudden flow
of blood and water. (John 19:31-34 NIV)

Verse 34 tells us that one of the soldiers pierced Jesus with a spear.
This goes along with verse 5 of Isaiah 53 that says he was pierced for
our transgressions. Both verses of scripture are referring to the same
person, Jesus Christ.

Verse 9 of the 53rd chapter of Isaiah says, *"He was assigned a grave
with the wicked, and with the rich in his death."* Initially, Jesus was to be
buried in the same burial grounds in which criminals were buried.
However, as prophesied by Isaiah, Jesus was instead buried in a rich
man's tomb, the following verses of scripture attest to this:

[57]As evening approached, there came a rich man from
Arimathea, named Joseph, who had himself become a
disciple of Jesus. [58]Going to Pilate, he asked for Jesus'
body, and Pilate ordered that it be given to him. [59]Joseph
took the body, wrapped it in a clean linen cloth, [60]and
placed it in his own new tomb that he had cut out of the
rock. He rolled a big stone in front of the entrance to the
tomb and went away. (Matthew 27:57-59 NIV)

When looking at the New Testament account in Matthew as to the
historicity of Jesus and comparing it to the prophetic verses in Isaiah 53,
one would be hard pressed to argue against the evidence that the *He* in
Isaiah 53 is Jesus.

With all of this said, special attention is brought to Isaiah 53:2 which
says, *"he had no beauty or majesty to attract us to him, nothing in his
appearance that we should desire him."* In other words, Jesus was not
physically beautiful. There was nothing about his appearance that would
attract someone to him. In colloquial terms, he was an "average looking
guy." If someone were going to follow him, they would do so because
they believed in his Lordship and not because they were overcome by his
looks.

Jesus was not physically beautiful but was perfect in beauty spiritually. Lucifer was perfect in physical beauty but was spiritually blemished and became the biggest adversary of God that there ever was and ever will be, Satan.

God creates many beautiful women, just as he creates many beautiful men. And to be beautiful is a gift and a blessing from God. However, God never set a standard for women based on physical beauty. Eve was not defined by beauty but instead by her ability to help her husband. Mary, the mother of Jesus, was not defined by beauty, but instead by her virtue. And even though Esther was beautiful, her courageousness, not her beauty, is what brought her historical account into the pages of the Bible. There are other great women of the Bible who were not defined by beauty but instead by their character and ability.[12] The following verse of scripture sums this up well:

> Charm is deceitful
> and beauty is passing.
> but a woman who fears the Lord,
> she shall be praised. (Proverbs 31:30 NKJV)

Charm and beauty have no precedence over righteousness. A woman should not be praised for her beauty but instead for her faithfulness to God. It is those women who respect God who should be praised and honored.

SONG OF SONGS

The book of the Song of Songs (the 22nd book of the Old Testament) is a book of lyrics written by King Solomon[13] and set to melody. It is a song. The New International Version of the Bible, New Living Translation, and the Contemporary English Version translates the title of the book as "Song of Songs" while the King James Version, The Amplified Bible, the New American Standard Bible, the Revised Standard Version, and the New King James Version translate the title as "Song of Solomon." The lyrics are poetry in motion and give indication

---

[12] See Chapter 1.

[13] Solomon was the second son of King David and Bathsheba. Solomon succeeded David as King and is consider the wisest man who ever lived.

243

as to the physical sexual attraction newly married men and women should feel towards one another. The song is a love song between a husband and his wife.

The book of Song of Songs must be discussed in this chapter because the entire song has lyrics in which both the lover (the man) and the beloved (the woman) expound upon the beauty of the other. This may lead some to believe that the Bible is teaching that beauty overrides spirituality when considering a lifetime mate. But instead, it appears that the song is actually teaching one of two things or both. The first being that men and women who are in love with one another see the physical beauty in each other that others may not necessarily see. Physical beauty is a very subjective thing when love abounds. The second is that beauty is an added extra thing to all the other positive qualities that a person may possess. The Song of Songs, then, is not teaching that beauty should be the number one priority when selecting a mate but instead teaches that it is an embellishment to the beauty within the person that is already there and that beauty rests in the eye of the beholder. Let's take a look:

[1]Solomon's Song of Songs

Beloved
[2]Let him kiss me with the kisses of his mouth—
for your love is more delightful than wine.
[3]Pleasing is the fragrance of your perfumes;
your name is like perfume poured out.
No wonder the maidens love you!
[4]Take me away with you—let us hurry!
Let the king bring me into his
chambers.

Friends
We rejoice and delight in you;
we will praise your love more
than wine

Beloved
How right they are to adore you!

[5]Dark am I, yet lovely,

244

> O daughters of Jerusalem,
> dark like the tents of Kedar,
> like the tent curtains of Solomon.
> [6]Do not stare at me because I am dark,
> because I am darkened by the sun.
> my mother's sons were angry with me
> and made me take care of the vineyards;
> my own vineyard I have neglected.
> [7]Tell me, you whom I love, where you graze
> your flock
> and where you rest your sheep at
> midday.
> Why should I be like a veiled woman
> beside the flocks of your friends?
> (Song of Songs 1:1-7 NIV)

In verse 5 the beloved says she is dark but lovely. The New American Standard Bible is a translation that is closer to the actual Hebrew and it translates the verse as saying "I am black but lovely." The King James Version of the Bible also translates the word *dark* in verse 5 as *black*. From the earliest days of antiquity, many prejudices have befallen darker skinned people. The darker a person was, the less attractive he or she was considered to be. Even Moses was criticized for marrying an Ethiopian woman.[14] History tells us that this is so and much of this type of thinking, whether overtly expressed or expressed behind closed doors, abounds today.

Discriminatory favor towards lighter skinned women is implicated here and there throughout historical literature just as it is implicated in verse 5 through 6 in the first chapter of the Song of Songs. Because she is dark the beloved must emphasize the fact that she is still beautiful despite her darkness. She also feels compelled to explain why she is so dark. She blames her brothers for making her stay out in the sun too long. But interestingly enough, the beloved's friends refer to her as the

---

[14] "And Miriam and Aaron spake against Moses because of the Ethiopian woman whom he had married: for he had married an Ethiopian woman." (Numbers 12:1) It is not clear why Miriam and Aaron spoke against Moses because of this and it may not have had anything to do with the color of her skin.

most beautiful of women despite the fact that she is dark. Let's look further:

> *Friends*
> [8]If you do not know, most beautiful of
> women,
> follow the tracks of the sheep
> and graze your young goats
> by the tents of the shepherds.
> (Song of Songs 1:8 NIV)

Solomon, the wisest of men who ever lived, describes the beloved fictional character of his song, a black woman, as "most beautiful of women." He does so despite the fact that many others may not have been able to see her beauty because they would automatically have seen the darkness of her skin as a point against her beauty. Physical beauty then, is in the eye of the beholder. The lover and his beloved are beautiful in the eyes of one another partly due to the fact that they have such a great love for each other. However, the beloved (the woman) is beautiful to others as well. As cited, she was the most beautiful of women in the eyes of her friends.

When looking at the Song of Songs, preachers tend to focus on what the lover said about the physical attributes of his beloved. But not only does the lover describe his beloved as beautiful, but also, the beloved describes her lover as handsome, as the following verses of scripture attest to:

> *Lover*
> [15]How beautiful you are, my darling!
> Oh, how beautiful!
> Your eyes are doves.
>
> *Beloved*
> [16]How handsome you are, my lover!
> Oh, how charming!
> And our bed is verdant.
> (Song of Songs 1:15-16 NIV)

If there had been no reference to the lover's (the man's) beauty, and only to the woman's, then one might be able to argue that Song of Songs is a chauvinistic book because it puts pressure on women to be beautiful. However, this is not the case. The lover is described as handsome. Therefore, Solomon's song cannot be put in a chauvinistic category because the same that is said about the beloved by the lover is said about the lover by the beloved. Both the man and the woman are beautiful, or at least both see the other as so. The following verses give further description to the lover's beauty and manliness:

> ³Like an apple tree among the trees of
> the forest
> is my lover among the young
> men.
> I delight to sit in his shade,
> and his fruit is sweet to may taste.
> ⁴He has taken me to the banquet hall.
> and his banner over me is love.
> ⁵Strengthen me with raisins,
> refresh me with apples,
> for I am faint with love.
> (Song of Songs 2:3-5 NIV)

> ⁸Listen! My lover!
> Look! Here he comes,
> leaping across the mountains,
> bounding over the hills.
> ⁹My lover is like a gazelle or a young stag.
> Look! There he stands behind our wall,
> gazing through the windows,
> peering through the lattice.
> (Song of Songs 2:8-9 NIV)

There is no question that the Song of Songs is laced with sexual innuendo. However, it must be emphasized that these expressions of sexual desire are done so between a wife and her husband, as we will soon see.

The man is compared to a gazelle (an antelope) and a stag (a male deer). An antelope is a deer-like animal that is related to the bull. A bull is symbolic of great strength and virility. The lover is described as one who bounds over hills and leaps across the mountains. He is compared to an apple tree by which his fruit is sweet to the taste. And the lover is described as a young man. Of course, if taken literally, then youth and vigor could only produce beauty for a man. However, these descriptions of this virile man with sweet fruit are not literal, but figurative, just as the descriptions of the woman are figurative.

After the woman describes the physical qualities that she adores in her lover, the lover returns her sentiments by saying the following:

> *Lover*
> [1]How beautiful you are, my darling!
> Oh, how beautiful!
> Your eyes behind your veil are
> doves,
> Your hair is like a flock of goats
> descending from Mount Gilead.
> [2]Your teeth are like a flock of sheep
> just shorn,
> coming up from the washing.
> Each has its twin;
> not one of them is alone
> [3]Your lips are like a scarlet ribbon;
> your mouth is lovely.
> Your temples behind your veil
> are like the half of a
> pomegranate.
> [4]Your neck is like the tower of
> David,
> built with elegance;
> on it hang a thousand shields,
> all of them shields of warriors.
> [5]Your two breasts are like two
> fawns,
> like twin fawns of a gazelle
> that browse among the lilies.
> [6]Until the day breaks
> and the shadows flee,
> I will go to the mountain of myrrh

and to the hill of incense.
All beautiful you are, my darling;
there is no flaw in you.

[8]Come with me from Lebanon,
my bride,
come with me from Lebanon......
(Song of Songs 4:1-8 NIV)

The man continues to tell his new bride that she is beautiful. He focuses on certain parts of her body that he feels enhances her beauty and he describes each part metaphorically. His beloved's eyes are described as doves. Doves are visually appealing birds that fly with grace.

The beloved's hair is like a flock of goats descending from Mount Gilead. The implication here is that there was length to her hair since it "descended." Long hair is often times seen as beauty enhancing. However, the beauty enhancing power of long locks applies to men as well as women. Samson's strength was symbolically in his hair.[15] This of course made his hair part of his physical appeal. Although there are many bald men that women look upon as attractive, there is no question that a head of hair adds to a man's physical appeal just as much as it does a woman's.

The beloved's teeth are compared to sheep just shorn coming up from the washing, each tooth having its twin. This means that she had clean, white teeth and that none of her teeth were missing. Certainly tooth decay, plaque, and missing teeth, are no less attractive for a woman than they are for a man.

The beloved's neck is described metaphorically as a tower that is elegantly crafted in which a thousand shields could hang. At first glance, the inference here is that the beloved has a long neck. But, if one's neck is too long, it can actually subtract from one's beauty. It appears that the word *tower* is used throughout the song to emphasize how well sculptured a particular part of the body is and not the size of that body part. This position is further strengthened by the fact that the beloved's

---

[15] Judges 13:1-5, Judges 14:11-15, Judges 16:1-21 (see your Bible)

nose is compared to the tower of Lebanon.[16] If the usage of the word *tower* applies to size, then the implication would be that the woman's nose is extremely large, as it was with Jimmy Durante[17] or the fictional characters Cyrano De Bergerac[18] and Pinocchio.[19] However, in many societies, this type of nose is not seen as attractive. Therefore, the comparison of the beloved's nose with the tower of Lebanon additionally confirms that the usage of the word *tower* is not used to imply size but instead to indicate structure. The beloved's nose is elegantly crafted just as her neck is. This elegant crafting is compared to the elegant crafting of the tower of Lebanon and other towers.

The beloved's breasts are described metaphorically as twin fawns of a gazelle that browse among the lilies. This comparison suggests that the beloved's breasts are youthful breasts since fawns are youthful animals. And although many men fixate on the size of a woman's breasts, there is no indication here that size is a factor in the lover's compliment of his beloved's breasts.

The beloved goes on to describe her lover. Let's take a look:

> *Beloved*
> [10]My lover is radiant and ruddy,
> outstanding among ten thousand.
> [11]His head is purest gold;
> his hair is wavy
> and black as a raven.
> [12]His eyes are like doves
> by the water streams,

---

[16] "Your neck is like an ivory tower. Your eyes are the pools of Heshbon by the gate of Bath Rabbim. Your nose is like the tower of Lebanon looking toward Damascus." (Song of Songs 7:4 NIV)

[17] Lived from 1893 to 1980. Was an American comic known particularly for his large nose.

[18] Character created by French writer Edmond Rostand in his play of the same title. Cryano De Bergerac was loosely based on the life of an actual person who went by the same name. In the play Cyrano believes that he could never win the love of a woman because of his exceptionally large nose. Edmond Rostand lived from 1868 to 1918 and wrote Cryano de Bergerac in 1897.

[19] Character created by Italian author Carlo Collodi (1869-1918) in his book titled, "Pinocchio: the story of a puppet," which he wrote in 1880. In the book, Pinocchio would automatically grow a very long nose every time he lied.

washed in milk,
    mounted like jewels.
[13]His cheeks are like beds of spice
    yielding perfume.
His lips are like lilies
    dripping with myrrh.
[14]His arms are rods of gold
    set with chrysolite.
His body is like polished ivory
    decorated with sapphires.
[15]His legs are pillars of marble
    set on bases of pure gold.
His appearance is like Lebanon,
    choice as its cedars
[16]His mouth is sweetness itself;
    he is altogether lovely.
This is my lover, this my friend,
    O daughters of Jerusalem.
(Song of Songs 5:10-16 NIV)

The man is described just as explicitly metaphorically as the woman is. He is said to be radiant and ruddy. His head is purest gold and his hair is wavy. His eyes are also like doves and his cheeks are like beds of spice yielding perfume. His arms are rods of gold and his body is like polished ivory. His legs are like pillars of marble set on bases of pure gold. He is altogether lovely. The description symbolizes the lover as a gorgeous man with wavy hair who is in great physical shape and has rippling muscles (legs like pillars of marble). However, most of the descriptions of both the lover and his beloved are not literal but figurative.[20] They are poetic depictions between two love-struck newlyweds. The newlyweds are not real people, but exist as fictional characters within the confines of the poetic lyrics of this song composed by King Solomon. Despite this, these characters represent how a man and his new bride should feel towards one another. Verse 16 tells us that the two are not only lovers but friends as well. It is therefore not hard to

---

[20] The description of the wavy hair is probably literal just as the description of the beloved as black, is.

251

understand why they are able to see one another as beautiful. The final chapter of Song of Songs contains the following:

> *Friends*
> [8]We have a young sister,
> and her breasts are not yet grown.
> What shall we do for our sister
> for the day she is spoken for?
> [9]If she is a wall,
> we will build towers of silver on her.
> If she is a door,
> we will enclose her with panels of cedar.
> (Song of Songs 8:8-9 NIV)

> *Beloved*
> [10]I am a wall,
> and my breasts are like towers.
> Thus I have become in his eyes
> like one bringing contentment.
> (Song of Songs 8:10 NIV)

Theologians are not certain as to what the metaphorical usage of the words *wall* and *door* mean. However, both words appear to be positive descriptions since neither description gives indication that a woman is not marriageable if compared as such. The concerns the friends have in verse 8 about their sister, has to do with concerns regarding preparing the young girl for the day she is married. The fact that her breasts are not yet developed is the lyricist's way of indicating that the girl is a child not old enough for marriage. She is still in puberty. The friends answer their own question. If the girl becomes a wall they will adorn her in a different way than if the girl becomes a door. Either way, she will be adorned and prepared for marriage once she leaves puberty and becomes a woman.

During the times of Solomon, marriages were often arranged for young girls at an early age. This might be why Solomon adds the concerns of the friends for their younger sister in his song. They feel a need to find a mate for her. It is interesting to note however, that Solomon's depiction of the marriage between the beloved and the lover is not a marriage that was arranged but instead was a marriage in which a man and woman freely decide to marry and are totally immersed in love for one another. The implication being, that to be free to choose one's lifetime mate is the preferred way to go into matrimony as opposed to being assigned a mate. If one is free to choose one's mate, then more than likely, the love will be there, as it should be.

The Beloved charges that she is a wall and her breasts are like towers. Therefore, she brings contentment to her lover (husband). If one is not careful, because of the visual image that the word *tower* evokes, one could read this to mean that she brings contentment to her husband because she has large breasts. But this is not what the verse is saying. As stated before, the word *tower* is used in this song to represent a part of the body that is elegantly crafted and well sculpted (as is her neck and nose), not to represent size.

The Bible does not applaud women with large breasts any more than it applauds women who are "flat-chested." Furthermore, the Bible does not applaud women with round posteriors any more than it applauds women with "flat" shaped posteriors and the Bible does not applaud women with "pouty" lips any more than it applauds women with thin lips. This is being emphasized because in Western society and especially in America, many small-breasted women, women with flat posteriors, and women with thin lips have had plastic surgery in order to increase their breast size, the roundness of their posterior, and the size of their lips. They do this because of the great emphasis put on breast size, posteriors, and lips as part of a woman's overall sexual attractiveness (not to mention hair, skin color, height, and weight). But breast implants take away nipple sensation and prevent a woman from breast-feeding. This is a high price to pay for the sexual attractiveness approval of men. To loose the sensation in one's nipples is to loose a great part of one's eroticism and sexual satisfaction. It is questionable whether or not a man would be willing to give up his penile function and sensation by surgically increasing the size of his genitals in order to appease women that find a larger size more sexually appealing.[21]

According to the Song of Songs, if a man and a woman love each other then they will love everything about one another, physically and mentally. They will be beautiful in one another's eyes. The word of God does not specifically teach that the size or shape of a woman's breasts, posterior, lips, or any other body part is a measure of her beauty or

---

[21] Contrary to popular belief, size does matter for most women.

sexuality. Just as it doesn't teach that the size or shape of a man's genitals is a measure of his.

The Song of Songs is not a song that standardizes beauty, but instead it is a song that emphasizes the love a husband and wife should have for one another. It is a love song and in this love song the lover describes what he feels is beautiful about his bride and vice versa. Although the lyrics describe two very beautiful people, the song in no way sets a standard of beauty for all women. If this song set beauty standards then a woman could not be looked at as beautiful unless she has an elegantly crafted neck, long hair, elegantly crafted breasts, all of her teeth (no dentures or partials) and black skin. The standards for male beauty would be athletic youthfulness, great strength, agility, virility, black wavy hair, bright white eyes (Song of Songs 5:12), great looking lips (Song of Songs 5:13), and white (ivory colored) skin (Song of Songs 5:14).

The standard that the song sets instead is an attraction standard not a beauty standard. In other words, there is a way a man should feel about the woman he marries and a way a woman should feel about the man she marries. A husband and his wife should be "in love" with one another. They should adore one another the way the lover and his beloved adored each other. They should be physically attracted to one another as well as mentally and spiritually attracted to one another. Physical adoration should not be the only factor in the decision to get married, but it should certainly not be a factor that is absent. And as stated previously, if a man and a woman are truly in love with one another and also consider each other to be friends, then they will automatically be physically attracted to one another. A woman should be no less physically attracted to her groom than a man is to his bride. Song of Songs teaches us that it is just as proper for a woman to be physically and sexually attracted to her groom as it is for a man to be to his bride. Therefore, there is no chauvinism here. What applies to the woman equally applies to the man and vise versa.

SUMMARY

Despite the pressures that society puts on women to be beautiful and despite the fact that societal standards of beauty for women change every 30 to 40 years or so, we have seen that God clearly defines true beauty according to the spiritual maturity of the person and not according to one's physical appearance. Lucifer was exceptionally physically beautiful while Jesus was average looking in appearance. However, Jesus was the one who was really beautiful and Lucifer was the one who was not.

Solomon has taught us that it is wise for people to marry those that they look upon as attractive. He has also taught us that love and friendship between a man and a woman will cause both to see the other as physically attractive. Newlyweds should have sexual attraction towards one another. This type of attraction is a factor that can aid in holding a marriage together. Of course, sexual and physical attraction alone cannot sustain a marriage, but it certainly does help.

In examining the verses in Song of Songs, we see that Solomon's song did not put any more emphasis on the physical attractiveness of the woman than it did on the physical attractiveness of the man. Women are no less captivated by the beauty of an attractive man as are men captivated by the beauty of an attractive woman. To see the beauty in one's spouse is just as important an action for a woman to take as it is for a man.

But although a husband and wife should have a sexual attraction for each other and find one another beautiful, in general, true beauty comes from the inside as far as God is concerned, and not from the outside, no matter how physically beautiful the person is.

God judges the beauty of both sexes from their inner spiritual qualities. So, a woman who is not deemed as physically attractive, but possesses a great spirituality in the Lord and has beauty of character is attractive indeed in God's eyes. She is, for all purposes, most definitely beautiful, even if she doesn't think she is because worldly men have not rated her a "10." But she is a spiritual "10" in God's eyes. The same applies to a man. With God there are no double standards when it comes to the issue of beauty as it applies to men and women.

8.

WOMEN IN ABUSIVE MARRIAGES

There has been great debate over the years within the church as to whether or not a woman can divorce her husband for any reason other than adultery. The problem arises when looking at the words of Jesus quoted in Matthew 19:8-9 which says, *"Moses permitted divorce as a concession to your hard-hearted wickedness, but it was not what God had originally intended. And I tell you this, a man who divorces his wife and marries another commits adultery—unless his wife has been unfaithful."*[1] The majority of theologians[2] agree that this statement applies to women as well as to men, therefore a woman can also divorce her husband if her husband has been unfaithful to her.[3]

Over the years many pastors and theologians have taught that the absolute only reason one can divorce his or her spouse is if the spouse has committed adultery. There is one more very clear exception, which we will discuss in detail later, and that is the exception whereby an unbelieving spouse (one who does not believe in the Lordship of Jesus Christ) leaves a believing spouse. As we will see, a believer is not obligated to stay in a marriage if his or her unbelieving spouse "wants out." However, there is no clear-cut scriptural answer as to whether or not a believer is obligated to stay in a marriage if his or her *believing* spouse "wants out."

If indeed adultery and abandonment are the only exceptions in which one can obtain a divorce without going against the will of God, then the question becomes: what does a woman do who is married to a man who has not committed adultery and is not insisting on leaving her, but is

---

[1] NLT

[2] Catholics believe that all divorce is sin, despite the exception for adultery that Jesus gave.

[3] "Now for those of you who are married I have a command that comes not from me, but from the Lord. A wife must not leave her husband. But if she does leave him let her remain single or else go back to him. And the husband must not leave his wife." (1 Corinthians 7:10-11 NLT)

abusive towards her? Does she stay married to a man who beats her, abuses her verbally, threatens to kill her, threatens to kill her children and/or puts her at risk of death? Is this really what Jesus meant when he said that divorce was only reserved for those who had been cheated on? Although men are also often times the victim of domestic violence, occurrences in which women are victims are substantially higher.

DOMESTIC VIOLENCE

Domestic violence is any kind of violence that is perpetrated against someone wherein the perpetrator intimately knows the victim or is a part of the victim's family. Contrary to popular belief, studies show that the reason the abuser uses violence is not because he or she has difficulty controlling his or her anger but because the abuser has a need to have power and control over the victim. Therefore, one of the main indicators that a man might be abusive is not only that he has a bad temper, but that he is also controlling, no matter how slight.

In order to gain power and control, the abuser must first strive to establish that power and control and then must strive to maintain it. The violence does not only come in the form of physical abuse but can also come in the form of threats of physical abuse, sexual violence, threats of sexual violence, and what has been deemed as economic and/or psychological violence. Most people who have never been the victims of domestic violence do not fully realize or understand the magnitude of the types of violence that is usually associated with it. And then there are those who have been victims of domestic violence but are not aware that they have been, because they only associate domestic violence with physical assault.

The most common professional term used in lieu of the word *abuser* when referring to a perpetrator of domestic violence is *batterer*. However, *batterer* connotes only physical violence whereas *abuser* connotes a much broader range of offenses. Therefore, for our purposes, the word *abuser* will be used and will include those who batter (hit, beat, push, poke, slap, strike in any way, etc.)

According to statistics, 97% of domestic violence victims are women with 97% of the abusers being men. Statistics are always changing and some researchers say that the percentage of men being abused by women is much higher than we think. But on a global level, a 97% victimization of women, is probably a fair assertion. Every 9 seconds a woman in

257

America becomes a victim of domestic violence. Over 50% of women who are murdered in the United States were killed as a result of domestic violence with 42% of these women having been murdered by their husbands or intimate partners. 70% of all assaults that are perpetrated against women is carried out by the victim's husband or boyfriend.

One out of every three women has been the victim of domestic violence at least once in her life. So, if there are 100 couples in a room, statistically speaking, roughly 36 men in that room abuse or have abused their wives/girlfriends and roughly 36 women in that room are being abused or have been abused by their husbands/boyfriends at some point.

Domestic violence effects a huge percent of the female population. It is responsible for most injuries incurred by female adolescents between ages 15 and 17 years, and adult women between the ages of 18 and 44 years.

As stated previously, domestic violence is not only physical assault. A man is guilty of domestic violence against his wife and/or romantic associate, if he is guilty of sexual assault or sexual manipulation of the victim, the destruction or damaging of the belongings of the victim, verbally abusing the victim, humiliating the victim, forcing the victim to become isolated from family and friends, stalking the victim at work, depriving the victim of basic economic resources, threatening the victim, threatening to damage the property of the victim and the like.

In addition to the above, abusive husbands have also been known to prevent their wives from taking prescribed medications, to cancel their wives scheduled doctor's appointments (unbeknownst to the wife), to tell others that their wives are imagining or hallucinating the abuse in an attempt to convince others that she is mentally ill, to intentionally deprive their wives of sleep or to threaten to hurt them while they are asleep, to withhold the car keys from their wives, to withhold access to basic needs such as food and clothing from their wives, and so forth.

Women who are victims or survivors of domestic violence often experience stress, anxiety, and emotional breakdowns. They frequently suffer from severe depression and are five times more likely to kill themselves than women who have not been abused. Abused women have twice as many miscarriages as women who are not abused. They are also more prone to drink excessively and use drugs. Often times they are introduced to drugs by the man who has or is abusing them. They are also more likely to be abusive towards their minor children who are living in the home under their care.

Although 54% of men who abuse women also drink alcohol and/or use drugs, it is a myth that alcohol and drug abuse causes domestic violence. Most abusers who successfully complete drug treatment programs continue to abuse their wives and girlfriends. They need more than therapy that only addresses the addiction. They need therapy that addresses their insatiable need for power and control.

Although drugs and alcohol do not cause domestic violence, they can aggravate the problem. Alcohol decreases inhibitions. So a man who is already abusive when sober will more than likely be more prone to abuse when he is drunk because he is less inhibited.

Many counselors, clinicians, and clergy are under the false impression that marriage/couples counseling and anger management counseling will aid in eliminating domestic violence. However, studies show that a woman's safety is jeopardized further if she is in counseling together with her abusive husband where domestic violence issues are being pursued by the therapist or counselor. It is better for the abuser to be counseled separately from his wife. If not, the abuser may retaliate against his wife when the two of them return home because of something the wife expressed in counseling. Having the abuser and victim in counseling together also gives the abuser plenty of opportunity to blame the victim for his abusive behavior.

Studies also show that many abusive men have confessed to using anger as a tool to manipulate and control their wives but that they are not really angry at all. They are only *expressing* anger in order to frighten the victim and put her under their control. The expression of anger is a part of the abusive and violent tendencies that were already there in the first place. Therefore, because it does not address the underlying reasons for violent and abusive behavior, anger management therapy should not be used as the sole therapeutic venue for domestic violence situations. However, it can be used as an addition to domestic violence counseling.

According to studies, there are many characteristics that profile a man who is abusive. These characteristics include controlling behavior, verbal abuse, sexual abuse, unreasonable jealousy (he is jealous of his wife's or girlfriend's family, friends, work associates, and does everything he can do to sabotage her relationship with them) lying, unreasonable expectations (he expects his wife or girlfriend to be "perfect" and to do everything he wants her to do no matter if necessary resources, such as time and/or money, aren't available or are minimally available) cutting his wife or girlfriend off from friends, family, and associates, blaming, animal cruelty, and pushing his children to achieve beyond their capabilities.

To review all of these characteristics in depth would constitute a book in and of itself. So, three characteristics have been selected for our discussion. They are controlling behavior, verbal abuse, and sexual abuse (marital rape).

Controlling Behavior

A controlling man is a man who wants a woman to do what he says all of the time, and absolutely not make any decision independent of him no matter how small the decision there is to be made. A controlling man will tell a woman where to go, when to go, what time to come back, what to wear, what to eat, what to drink, how much money to spend or not to spend, when to sleep, when to wake up, and even who to vote for. Controlling men will not only try to control a woman's every move but he will also try to control her mind and how she thinks.

Controlling men dictate to their wives exactly how the children are to be handled in every aspect of their lives. A controlling man is bossy. He is relentless, a constant nag, frequently complains to his wife about what she hasn't done, what she has done, or what he thinks she does that she shouldn't be doing. A controlling man hounds his wife. Nothing satisfies him.

Most controlling men will have a tendency to be abusive in some kind of way so it is important that women are able to detect the controlling behavior. Controlling behavior is often times not easy to detect. Often times a man will be careful not to be too bossy when he first meets a woman. But if a woman dates a controlling man long enough he will eventually do or say something that exposes his controlling behavior. However, many times the woman might not see the controlling behavior as controlling. For example, if a woman goes to a restaurant with a man who insists that she order a salad, instead of seeing him as controlling, she might see him as a man who is just simply concerned that she eat healthy. It won't be until she becomes seriously involved with him or married to him that she will realize that he is always telling her what and what not to eat.

Unfortunately, there are just as many men in the church who try to control their wives as there are men in the world.[4] It can even be more difficult to persuade a Christian man who is controlling that he is behaving inappropriately towards his wife. A controlling man who is also a Christian will often try to justify his controlling behavior by emphasizing his wife's role to submit.[5] He believes that his wife's biblical instruction to ultimately submit to him translates into a window of opportunity for him to control. Men like this think that being the head of the house means that they are the one in control all the time in everything regardless of their wife's feelings or ambitions. They abuse and misrepresent the submission scriptures to their own gain and they constantly remind their wives that they are in charge, that they are the head of the house, and that the Bible says the wife is to submit to her husband. They totally disregard the scriptures that tell Christians to submit to one another, that say it is better to obey God rather than men, that deem the authority that the husband has in a marriage as a cursed thing for his wife, that say that women would be happier single, and that say that women will have less trouble and be able to serve God better if they are unmarried.[6]

A controlling man is a contentious man. A contentious man kindles strife as attested to by the following scripture:

> As charcoal is to burning coals, and wood to fire, so is
> a contentious man to kindle strife. (Proverbs 26:21
> NKJV)

A man cannot be controlling without being contentious. A contentious man kindles strife in his home because he sends an ongoing message to his wife that says she can't do anything right. A contentious man kindles strife as quickly as fire burns wood. It doesn't take long for the wood to burn, become charred, and severely damaged. It doesn't take long for a

---

[4] Christians are in the world but not of the world. "When the world hates you, remember it hated me before it hated you. The world would love you if you belonged to it, but you don't. I chose you to come out of the world, and so it hates you." These are the words of Jesus. (John 15:18-19 NLT)

[5] See Chapter 3.

[6] Ephesians 5:21, Acts 5:29, Genesis 3:16, 1 Corinthians 7:28, 34, 38-40 (see your Bible). Also see Chapters 3 and 12.

controlling and contentious man to severely damage his wife, emotionally and otherwise.

A man who is controlling is also often times verbally abusive. This leads us to our next concern.

Verbal Abuse

Most people think of verbally abusive men as men who curse at women and call them names. But verbal abuse comes in many forms. Some forms of verbal abuse are not as obvious as other forms. Let's take a look at what the scripture says about verbal abuse:

> [5]You must put to death, then, the earthly desires at work in you, such as sexual immorality, indecency, lust, evil passions, and greed (for greed is a form of idolatry). [6]Because of such things God's anger will come upon those who do not obey him. [7]At one time you yourselves used to live according to such desires, when your life was dominated by them.
>
> [8]But now you must get rid of all these things: anger, passion, and hateful feelings. No insults or obscene talk must ever come from your lips. [9]Do not lie to one another, for you have put off the old self with its habits [10]and have put on the new self. This is the new being which God, its Creator, is constantly renewing in his own image, in order to bring you to a full knowledge of himself. (Colossians 3:5-10 GNT)

Paul was talking to those who had turned to Christ and away from a life of sin. The men and women to whom Paul was addressing used to be guilty of many sins, which included insults and obscene talk (verbal abuse).[7] But since they had become Christians, Paul warned them against living the same kind of lives they lived before. In reference to verse 8, the NIV translates *insults and obscene talk* as *filthy language* while the NASB translates the same as *abusive speech*.

---

[7] Also note that the word *passions* (v. 5) in the Good News Translation is used instead of the word *lust,* which is the word that most other translations use.

Those who follow God should not use abusive speech towards anyone. Therefore, when a man curses his wife and calls her names, he is sinning against her in the eyes of God. He is also sinning against God. A man who uses filthy language against his wife or insults her is not honoring and loving his wife as scripture commands him to.[8]

Yelling, screaming, threatening, cursing and name-calling are obvious forms of verbal abuse but there are some forms that are not as obvious. Name-calling does not only include using profanity, but can also include using descriptive language that is negative. For instance, the word *dog* is not a curse word but if a man calls a woman a dog he has certainly insulted her and therefore has verbally abused her.

Examples of other descriptively negative abusive words are: ugly, lazy, stupid, idiot, fat slob, dense, looser, crazy, sissy, moron, and the like. These words are very insulting. But there is more to verbal abuse than profanity and name-calling. Verbal abuse includes put downs whether direct or indirect and can also include condescending statements, snide remarks, sarcasm, degrading statements, and the like.

There is some descriptive language that is negative that may indeed correctly describe someone. However, a woman should be very careful if the man she is dating as a tendency to describe her in any negative term. The terms that are negative but not necessarily abusive (simply because the description may be accurate) are words such as *selfish, hostile, self-centered, arrogant, high-minded,* and the like. However, these words can also be used in abusive ways. Sometimes it isn't the words that are used that make a person verbally abusive but the underlying meaning of what is being said indirectly and how it is being said. Snide remarks and sarcasm are all part of verbal abuse. If a man *lovingly* tells his wife, "I was an idiot for not seeing things your way," she will feel as if he really means it. However if the same man says the same thing in a sarcastic or condescending tone, then his wife will perceive that her husband is really indirectly putting her down and that the person her husband is really calling an idiot, is her.

---

[8] "Husbands, likewise, dwell with them with understanding, giving honor to the wife, as to the weaker vessel, and as being heirs together of the grace of life, that your prayers may not be hindered." (1 Peter 3:7 NKJV) "Husbands, love your wives just as Christ also loved the church and gave himself for her." (Ephesians 5:25 NKJV)

Verbally abusive people are very skilled at putting people down either directly or indirectly. A man who teases a woman about how she looks, how she dresses, where she lives, how she thinks, how much education she has or doesn't have, is indirectly putting her down. A man who constantly criticizes his wife's friends is indirectly telling her that she has poor judgment when it comes to her selection of friends. A man who makes his wife feel like she doesn't know anything or is not smart enough to do this or that is putting her down. A man, who talks down to his wife, is putting her down.

Then there are the abusive men who use humiliation and embarrassment as tools of their verbal abuse. Humiliation and embarrassment are usually used to belittle or taunt a person. A man who says something derogatory to or about his wife in front of others, curses her in front of others, makes fun of her in front of others, or "airs her dirty laundry"[9] without her approval, is using humiliation and embarrassment as a tool of verbal abuse against her and anyone else that he does this to. Some men not only humiliate, embarrass, and ridicule their wives, but they do the same to their children.

The Bible talks against verbal abuse. The term for a verbal abuser in the Greek is *loidoros*. It is translated as the word *slanderer* in the New International Version of the Bible and as the word *railer* in the King James Version. Let's take a look:

> [25]It was nine o'clock in the morning when they crucified him, [26]The notice of the accusation against him said: "The King of the Jews." [27]They also crucified two bandits with Jesus, one on his right and the other on his left.
>
> [29]People passing by shook their heads and hurled insults at Jesus: "Aha! You were going to tear down the Temple and build it back up in three days! Now come down from the cross and save yourself!"
>
> [31]In the same way the chief priests and the teachers of the Law made fun of Jesus, saying to one another, "He saved others, but he cannot save himself! [32]Let us see the Messiah, the king of Israel, come down from

---

[9] Figure of speech. To air another's dirty laundry is to expose something about someone that that person would rather keep secret.

the cross now, and we will believe in him!" And the two who were crucified with Jesus insulted him also. (Mark 15:25-32 GNT)

Many of those who had a hand in and supported the crucifixion of Jesus insulted and mocked him as he was being crucified. They made fun of Jesus and put him down. Doing so was part of their verbal abuse. A man who insults, mocks, makes fun of, and puts a woman down is guilty of the same behavior these people exhibited when Jesus was being crucified.

It is interesting to note that even those who were being crucified with Jesus insulted him as well. They felt they had a right to hurl insults at Jesus even though they hung on a cross just as he did. Furthermore, they were guilty and Jesus was innocent. Many men who verbally abuse their wives feel they have a right to do so, even though they are no better than their wives are. Let's look further:

> [11]But now I am writing you that you must not associate with anyone who calls himself a brother but is sexually immoral or greedy, an idolater or a slanderer, a drunkard or a swindler. With such a man do not even eat. (1 Corinthians 5:11 NIV)

A Christian is prohibited from associating with a person who calls himself a Christian and indulges in either fornication, greed, idolatry, drunkenness, swindling and/or slander. So accordingly, if a man takes a woman on a dinner date and during dinner tries to talk her into having sex with him (sexually immorality), orders an overabundance of food for himself (greed), talks about his love of money (idolatry), refers to the waiter as a stupid moron (slander), orders many alcoholic drinks (drunkard), and tries to avoid paying the tip (swindler), she should make certain not to date him again and if at all possible, she should politely leave the table and go home ("with such a man do not even eat").

We will look at this scripture again but this time with an emphasis on the specific instruction not to associate with a slanderer (a verbal abuser). Again, it is easier for a woman to realize she is with an abusive man if he is blatantly abusive than if he is more subtle with his abuse. If the verbal abuse is indirect and masked, then the probability of her recognizing it declines. Furthermore, if a woman's judgment is clouded by an attraction she has for a man, then not only does the probability of her recognizing indirect and masked verbal abuse decline, but the likelihood exists that she will also minimize the abuse if she detects it.

> [8]Finally, all of you, live in harmony with one anther; be sympathetic, love as brothers, be compassionate and humble. [9]Do not repay evil with evil or insult with insult, but with blessing because to this you were called so that you may inherit a blessing. [10]For
>
> > Whoever would love life
> > and see good days
> > must keep his tongue from evil
> > and his lips from deceitful speech.
> > [11]He must turn from evil and do good:
> > he must seek peace and pursue it.
> > (1 Peter 3:8-11 NIV)

Although Peter was specifically addressing himself to Christians, this is good application for all. The Bible tells us that we should strive to live in harmony with one another and be sympathetic and compassionate towards one another. It goes on to say that we should not insult someone who insults us. We should not reciprocate evil for evil or insult for insult. Men who verbally abuse their wives in any way are sinning because they are going against these scriptures that call for compassion, sympathy, and harmony. How can a man expect to live in harmony with his wife if he is always threatening her, calling her names, putting her down, humiliating her, embarrassing her and the like? Where is the sympathy and compassion in such behavior? Let's look further:

> [2]We all make many mistakes, but those who control their tongues can also control themselves in every other way. [3]We can make a large horse turn around and go wherever we want by means of a small bit in its mouth. [4]And a tiny rudder makes a huge ship turn wherever the pilot wants it to go, even though the winds are strong. [5]So also, the tongue is a small thing, but what enormous damage it can do. A tiny spark can set a great forest on fire. [6]And the tongue is a flame of fire.

266

It is full of wickedness that can ruin your whole life. It can turn the entire course of your life into a blazing flame of destruction, for it is set on fire by hell itself. (James 3:2-6 NLT)

[7]We humans are able to tame and have tamed all other creatures—wild animals and birds, reptiles and fish. [8]But no one has ever been able to tame the tongue. It is evil and uncontrollable, full of deadly poison. [9]We use it to give thanks to our Lord and Father and also to curse other people, who are created in the likeness of God. [10]Words of thanksgiving and cursing pour out from the same mouth. My friends, this should not happen! [11]No spring of water pours out sweet water and bitter water from the same opening. (James 3:7-11 GNT)

Verse 4 and 5 describe the tongue as a very small part of the body that has the potential to do enormous damage. A person can damage his or herself with his or her own tongue. We can ruin our own lives just by the things we say. We can also ruin the lives of others by what we say. With what the Bible has to say about the negative effects of the tongue, it is obvious that the Bible does not condone the old adage that names will never hurt. Names do hurt and verbal abuse is very damaging.

Verse 8 teaches us that no one can tame the tongue and that it is an uncontrollable evil while verse 2 says that those who control their tongues can also control themselves in other ways. This is not a contradiction. No one can tame another's tongue and no one can tame his own tongue all of the time. The tongue is uncontrollable in the sense that even a person who has great control of his or her tongue may say something on rare occasion that shouldn't have been said. But the emphasis here is that God wants his people to always strive to be careful of what they say and any slip of the tongue or intentional use of it to insult or hurt another should never be a constant. Furthermore, the scripture tells us that those who are in control of what they say are in control of themselves in other ways as well. This makes sense, because if one is careful of what he or she says, then one is slow to be abusive, one is slow to gossip, one is slow to slander, one is slow to use filthy language, and the list goes on. Furthermore, since the tongue is difficult to control, it follows that those who have a substantial amount of control of it also possess enough willpower to control against other wicked temptations of their flesh.

The following verse of scripture teaches us to live at peace with one another:

> [11]Turn away from evil and do good.
> Work hard at living in peace with others.
> [12]The eyes of the Lord watch over those
> who do right, and his ears are open
> to their prayers.
> But the Lord turns his face
> Against those who do evil."
> (1 Peter 3:11-12 NLT)

If we should work hard at living in peace with one another (verse 11) then we can certainly conclude that a man who verbally abuses his wife is making little effort to live peaceably with her. How could he if he is abusing her?

In her book, *"The Verbally Abusive Relationship,"* Patricia Evans lists the categories of verbal abuse as withholding, countering, discounting, verbal abuse disguised as jokes, blocking and diverting, accusing and blaming, judging and criticizing, trivializing, undermining, threatening, name calling, forgetting, ordering, denial, and abusive anger.

Evans defines withholding as the act of keeping to one's self and rarely expressing emotions. A woman married to such a man never really knows what her husband is thinking. She feels uncomfortable talking to him about her concerns because his response is detached and he is withdrawn. This is not to be confused with a man who is suffering from depression. A man who is depressed is not purposely nonchalant. But a man who is withholding is doing so purposely.

A man who frequently counters his wife is a man who often disagrees with anything she says and often times puts his wife down when she expresses her opinion of things or how she feels.

A man is indulging in discounting behavior when he minimizes the feelings or thought processes of his wife. Discounting the feelings or thoughts of another involves the process of making the person feel that they look at things too intensely, that they are too delicate and emotional, that they make "mountains out of molehills," that they are crying over nothing, or that they are "too sensitive."

Evans defines blocking and diverting as actions that prevent an actual discussion of an issue from taking place, including changing the subject or somehow terminating the conversation.

A man, who is accusatory towards his wife and repeatedly blames her for difficulties in their relationship, sees every problem in the relationship as her fault, including any negative behavior on his part.

A man who judges and criticizes his wife applies negative traits to her. He describes her in negative terms. He doesn't approve of her in some way and he consistently lets her know it. Often times when a man consistently judges and criticizes his wife, he attempts to justify his criticism by telling her that it is for her own good, or for the good of the family. Name-calling is often a part of judging and criticizing.

Trivializing is defined as attributing something that someone says, has done, would like to do, or that is important to them as meaningless, pointless, or unimportant. Evans defines it as "one-upping." To trivialize another's accomplishments or efforts is to indirectly put oneself above that person.

A man undermines his wife when he discourages her in her efforts to do something she wishes to do. Those who undermine sometimes use sabotage as a way of doing so. To sabotage a person's efforts means to deliberately hinder or impede a person's ability to do what he or she is trying to say or do. The saboteur never admits to the sabotage and pretends as if he hasn't done it.

Threatening is a well-known form of verbal abuse. A man who threatens his wife in order to control her might not only threaten to beat her but he might threaten to have an affair, divorce her, move out of the house, force her to move out of the house, and the like. His oppression of her is very direct.

A man who verbally abuses his wife and then later on claims that he can't remember what he did is conveniently "forgetting" what he's done. This method of forgetting is abusive. The victim can never address the abuse if the abuser is always "forgetting" he ever abused her. Another form of verbal abuse that involves forgetting is the breaking of promises. Some men make promises to their wives with no intention of ever keeping the promise. As soon as a man has unfaithfully made a promise to his wife, he has verbally abused her because what he really did was lie to her with intentions of conveniently "forgetting" the promise later on or with the intentions of conveniently changing his mind. He doesn't see how emotionally injurious this can be to his wife. If his wife becomes upset because he broke the promise he'll blame her for not being sympathetic enough towards his forgetfulness.

Ordering is another form of verbal abuse. Many men order their wives around as if their wives are slaves or infantrymen. Ordering another person around is demeaning to the person being ordered and says to them that they are inferior to the one who is doing the ordering. On page 103 of her book, Evans gives examples of ordering phrases that often times come from men who verbally abuse: "Get in here and clean this up," "You're not going to wear that," "We won't discuss it." As one can see, these modes of expression are very condescending. A woman being talked to in this manner could easily feel as if her husband were talking to her as if she were a child. In general, men who speak to their wives like this are controlling.

Verbal abuse frequently involves the act of the abuser denying the abuse ever happened. It is difficult for a man to change a behavior that he denies he has.

Evans says that most verbal abusers are dealing with internal tension, which they express periodically by becoming angry. She defines what she calls *the cycle of anger addiction* in the following way:

> The tension then builds again until the abuser releases it again with another outburst. This build-up of tension and its release become a cyclical pattern of behavior. As soon as the tension is released, it begins to build again. I call this cycle the cycle of anger addiction and the abuser who follows this pattern of behavior an anger addict.[10]

> This cycle carries a double reward for the abuser. The rewards are like a fix for an addict. The first reward is that the abuser feels a sense of relief, a kind of euphoric high after exploding at his partner because he has released the tension built up since the last outburst.

---

[10] *The Verbally Abusive Relationship: How to recognize it and how to respond,* By Patricia Evans, copyright © 1992 by Patricia Evans, published by Adams Media Corporation, Holbrook MA , p. 106, Fair use

The second reward is that he has reasserted his dominance and Power Over his partner. There is nothing she can do and no way she can be to prevent the next attack.[11]

Also, if the partner calmly endures the abuser's behavior, he will feel thwarted. He expects a reaction. He needs his fix of both the release of tension and a sense of Power Over his partner. If he hasn't gotten his partner down, if she shows no signs of losing her enthusiasm, he will increase the abuse. This is probably not a conscious decision. He's just angrier, more tense, and more dependent on his fix of Power Over. This is one of the reasons that verbal abuse increases over time.[12]

The third quote above would seem to contradict Proverbs 15:1 which says, *"a soft answer turneth away wrath but grievous words stir up strife."* If a soft answer turns away anger then it would seem that a woman would be able to deter the verbally abusive antics of her husband by simply ignoring him or by saying something nice to him when the abuse occurs. But according to Evans, this will do nothing but incite his abuse. However, Evans' assessment applies to men who are consistently verbally abusive and Proverbs 15:1 applies to a person who has lost their temper but is not "normally" verbally abusive and isn't on a quest for power and control. Furthermore, as discussed earlier, there is much research that says that an abusive husband is not really angry at his victim but that he uses the expression of anger to gain power and control over his victim. This does not mean that there is never any anger involved. Often times, in the abuser's mind, he really is angry. However, there are those men who are not really angry at all and they *know* that what they are doing is *expressing* anger in order to manipulate. So, there are three types of abusers where anger is a part of the abuse: those who are really angry, those who have convinced themselves that they are angry, and those who feign anger in order to frighten and manipulate their victim (the wife) into submission. Either way, power

---

[11] Ibid, p. 106 Fair use
[12] Ibid, p. 107 Fair use

and control are the goals, just as Evans (along with many other researchers) has stated.

The Bible warns us about angry men and tells us to stay away from them if at all possible. We are not to befriend men who have bad tempers. Not only should we not befriend them but if at all possible, we should not even associate with them. Let's take a look:

> Do not make friends with a hot-tempered man,
> Do not associate with one easily angered,
> (Proverbs 22:24-25 NIV)
>
> A fool gives full vent to his anger,
> But a wise man keeps himself under control.
> (Proverbs 29:11 NIV)

According to the above scripture quote, men who verbally abuse their wives and express their feelings angrily, are fools. They don't keep their anger under control and therefore lack wisdom. Society usually labels women, who are victimized by abusive men, as fools for ever having gotten involved with them. But the word of God identifies the angry and abusive man as the one who is the fool for misbehaving so badly and describes the woman who gets involved with him as vulnerable, as the following verses of scripture indicate:

> [1]Remember that there will be difficult times in the last days. [2]People will be selfish, greedy, boastful, and conceited; they will be insulting, disobedient to their parents, ungrateful, and irreligious; [3]they will be unkind, merciless, slanderers, violent, and fierce; they will hate the good; [4]they will be treacherous, reckless, and swollen with pride; they will love pleasure rather than God; [5]they will hold to the outward form of our religion, but reject its real power. Keep away from such people. [6]Some of them go into people's houses and gain control over weak women who are burdened by the guilt of their sins and driven by all kinds of desires, [7]women who are always trying to learn but who can never come to know the truth. [8]As Jannes and Jambres were opposed to Moses, so also these people

are opposed to the truth—people whose minds do not function and who are failures in the faith. [9]But they will not get very far, because everyone will see how stupid they are. That is just what happened to Jannes and Jambres. (2 Timothy 3:1-9 GNT)

According to verse 6, the profile of a woman apt to become involved with someone who has no self control, who is a slanderer (abusive), who is violent, and so forth, is a woman who is weak. She is weak because she is burdened by many sins and desires. In other words, she is not living a holy life herself and therefore falls prey to people who act holy but really aren't. She can't see through the façade of such people. She can't see through the façade because she is not experienced enough in Christian living herself to be able to quickly identify someone who acts religiously but really isn't. The New Living Translation of the Bible describes her as "vulnerable." The New International Version describes her as "weak-willed" and the New King James Version describes her as "gullible." Certainly, these vulnerable women will also eventually recognize the truth. But by the time they do they will more than likely already be trapped into the abusive relationship and the cycle of violence may have already begun.

The Cycle of Violence theory was developed in 1979 by a woman named Lenore Walker. Walker had worked closely with abused women for many years and in her dealings with them she discovered there was a pattern of behavior that abusers use to keep control of their victims. She documented the pattern and referred to it as the cycle of violence. It should be noted that the cycle of violence does not apply to all abusive relationships, but it does apply to the majority of them in some way.

The pattern of behavior that encompasses this cycle of violence is as such: there is first what is called the "build up phase" between the couple. During this phase, tension mounts between them, usually spurred on by the abuser.

Then comes the "stand-over phase." This is the phase in which the abuser actually becomes abusive toward his wife or girlfriend by using threats, verbal abuse, physical abuse, and the like.

Afterwards, most abusers go into the "remorse phase." In this phase the abuser does not necessarily apologize but instead often times blames his behavior on the victim. Not only does the abuser fault the victim for his own abusive behavior but he minimizes his abusive behavior as well.

One way of minimizing is to say things like, "everyone gets angry now and then," or "I just pushed her a little," or "yeah, I called her names but I didn't use any profanity."

After the remorse phase comes what is called the "buy back phase" or the "pursuit phase." This is the phase where the abuser expects the victim to put aside the abuse, forgive him, and go on as if nothing has happened. In this phase the abuser does what he can to woo the victim. He will tell her how much he needs her, how much he loves her, and so on. He will play on her emotions and her sense of duty to him. This is the phase that is most dangerous to women who are victims of domestic violence. If she does not put her defenses down during this phase, there is a substantial possibility that the situation will become life threatening and that the abuser will murder her. Remember, over 50% of women who are murdered in the United States were killed as a result of domestic violence with 42% of these victims having been murdered by their husbands or intimate partners. And it is usually during a rejected buy back phase, when a woman has decided to separate or is in the process of separating from her abuser, that an abused woman is murdered. Abused women instinctively know the risk that comes along with trying to get away from their abusers, which is one of the reasons why they stay in the abusive relationship.

If the abuser was successful at buying back the affections of his victim then the next and final phase that is entered into is the "honeymoon phase." During this phase intimacy is heightened between the couple and they cleave to one another. There is a great deal of bonding between the couple especially in the realm of sex. This is one of the reasons why some men who abuse their wives want to have sex with them shortly following the abuse. Afterwards the cycle of violence begins all over again.

Depending on the couple, it can take months for this cycle of violence to complete its pattern or the pattern can be completed within hours, even within minutes.

RAPE AND SEXUAL ABUSE IN MARRIAGE

In general, rape is defined, as an act of sexual intercourse between people in which one or more of the persons involved is forced against his or her will to engage in the intercourse.[13] This may include not only genital intercourse but anal and/or oral intercourse. On the other hand, sexual abuse is generally defined as any sexual act, other than sexual intercourse, that is forced upon a person (i.e. unwelcome fondling, unwelcome rubbing, unwelcome patting, unwelcome humping, unwelcome kissing, unwelcome hugging, the tearing off of another's clothes, and the like).[14]

Unfortunately there are many Christian husbands who will be quick to point to the scriptures on submission[15] in an effort to coerce their Christian wives into having sex with them when their wives aren't up to it. A man like this exploits the scriptures that speak about a woman submitting to her husband in order to make his wife feel guilty enough to have sex with him when she really doesn't want to, or when she is too tired, or when she is sick, thereby in essence, exploiting her as well. Some Christian men may also be prone to use the verse of scripture that says that husbands and wives should not refrain from having sex with one another unless it is mutually agreed upon by both of them to abstain for a time for fasting and prayer. Let's take a look at that scripture:

> [5]So do not deprive each other of sexual relations. The only exception to this rule would be the agreement of both husband and wife to refrain from sexual intimacy for a limited time, so they can give themselves more completely to prayer. Afterward they should come together again so that Satan won't be able to tempt them because of their lack of self-control. [6]This is only my suggestion. It's not meant to be an absolute rule. (1 Corinthians 7:5-6 NLT)

For a man to use the verse of scripture above (verse 5) to cajole his wife into having sex with him when she does not, on occasion, want to, is actually a misuse of the scripture and borders on legalism, sexual abuse, and rape. He is essentially insisting that his wife have sex with him under duress and totally ignoring the fact that the scripture teaches that the instruction not to deny sex to one's marital partner, is not an

---

[13] See Chapter 10 for a detailed discussion of what the Bible says on rape.
[14] See Chapter 10.
[15] See Chapter 3.

absolute rule. Sexual abuse and rape are always committed under the duress of the victim. Therefore even if his "persuasion" is "friendly" there is a very thin line between it and abuse.

Verse 5 speaks against a husband and a wife depriving each other sexually, but the inference is that the deprivation should not occur for a long, continuous length of time. The word *deprive* is translated from the Greek word *apostereo*. The definition for *apostereo* is to be *destitute, to keep back by fraud, or to deprive*. All three of these definitions imply a long lasting lack of something. To be destitute means to lack something on a continuous basis. For example, in today's time, when we think of people as being destitute we think of them as living continuously in poverty (although the word *destitute* can apply to the lack of something besides money). In this case, *destitution* would not apply to a person, who say, has plenty of money in the bank but can't get to it on a particular day because of, say, a snowstorm. There might not be any money in the house, but this person is certainly not destitute. In reference to the possession of money, *destitution* applies to a person who basically doesn't have any money at all. It is the same with the word *deprivation*. The synonyms for the word *deprive* are *disinherit, lose, strip, bankrupt*, and the like. All of these words imply a complete and continuous lack of something. Therefore to deprive someone of something is to take that something away completely, for a long period of time. The Greek word *apostereo* also means *to keep back by fraud*. Most fraud is committed on a continuous basis. A person guilty of fraud doesn't usually get caught for a long time. Again, the definition points to a continuous pattern of taking something away. With this said, verse 5 is instructing married couples not to resist each other sexually for long periods at a time. The verse is not addressing an occasional resistance.

The argument that verse 5 particularly pertains to long periods of time, and not to an occasional resistance, is strengthened by the fact that the exception to the rule for a husband and wife not to deprive each other sexually, is an agreement between husband and wife to refrain from sexual intimacy so that they can devote themselves to prayer and fasting. The examples given of prayer accompanied with fasting in the Bible are usually that whereby the prayer and fasting lasted for days, on a continuous basis. Esther instructed the Jews to fast and pray for 3 days.[16]

---

[16] Esther 4:12-16 (see your Bible).

David fasted and prayed for his son for nearly 7 days.[17] Jesus fasted and prayed for 40 days and 40 nights,[18] and the list goes on. The point is that, the exception that is given, is an exception in which a long period of time refraining from sex is allowable. If the solution or the exception to the problem has to do with a lengthy time period then it follows that the problem has to do with a lengthy time period as well. The solution or exception itself implies that Paul was specifically addressing himself to husbands and wives who resist their spouses on a continuous basis, and not addressing those who do so on rare occasion.

No man or woman has the right to withhold sex from his or her marriage partner indefinitely. Withholding sex from one's partner indefinitely is exactly what Paul is speaking against. He is rebuking a man or a woman who intentionally withholds sex from his or her marriage partner for long periods of time on a continuous basis, for no good reason. To do so is a sin. This of course is very different from an occasional refusal.

A man who insists that his wife have sex with him on an occasion when she doesn't want to, is not showing the sacrificial love towards his wife that he is commanded to show towards her when taking into account Ephesians 5:25.[19] The verse says that men should love their wives as Christ loved the church. So, as discussed previously in Chapter 3, a man should love his wife in a self-sacrificing way because that is how Christ loved the church. Christ died on the cross for those who would believe on him. And those who believe on him are referred to as the church.[20] It is not very self-sacrificing for a man to pressure his wife into having sex with him when she doesn't want to or when she's not up to it, or when she is tired, or when she is sick. It is an unloving and selfish act. A man who insists in these matters is putting his wants and desires before those of his wife. According to scripture, he's not supposed to do that.

Taking things a step further, many people feel that a man should not be accused of rape if he forces his wife to have sexual intercourse with him. They justify this by arguing their position that since she is his wife, she is therefore his property. The following verses of scripture are

---

[17] 2 Samuel 12:13-23 (see your Bible).

[18] Matthew 4:1-2 (see your Bible).

[19] See Chapter 3 for more detailed discussion of this verse.

[20] See Introduction.

interpreted by some men to mean that a man has "property rights" over his wife:

> ³The husband should not deprive his wife of sexual intimacy, which is her right as a married woman, nor should the wife deprive her husband. ⁴The wife gives authority over her body to her husband, and the husband also gives authority over his body to his wife.
> (1 Corinthians 7:3-4 NLT)

Again, the scripture is talking about deprivation on a continuous basis. A man is expected to fulfill his sexual obligations to his wife no less than a woman is expected to fulfill her sexual obligations to her husband. So in this sense, a man is just as much the "property" of his wife as a woman is the "property" of her husband. This does not mean that if a man is "not in the mood" his wife has the right to force her husband to have sexual intercourse with her (she really wouldn't be able to anyway because a woman cannot force a man into having an erection). And it doesn't mean the opposite either. If a woman is "not in the mood" her husband doesn't have the right to force her to have sex with him.

The scripture says that neither the husband nor the wife is to deprive the other of sexual intimacy and that both the husband and the wife should, as those who are married, be able to have their sexual urges fulfilled. If then this is the case, then one can assume that sex is something that men and women want and that it is supposed to be something that is pleasurable since neither party should deny the other. Rape is certainly not pleasurable and neither is sexual abuse. Having sex under duress is certainly not pleasurable. No woman wants to feel as if her husband is simply relieving himself by having sex with her. She wants to feel made love to. She does not want to feel that he is using her in the same way he uses the toilet.

Unfortunately, there are some Christian men who have a tendency to be extremely legalistic when it comes to the submission scriptures (and not surprisingly since to do so works to their advantage) [21] and believe that a woman must always submit to her husband sexually (and in everything else) no matter what the circumstance. A man like this will

---

[21] See Chapter 3.

use Ephesians 5:24[22] to insist that his wife submit to his every passion and sexual desire. He believes that the verses of scripture that talk about submission of a woman to her husband outweigh the verses of scripture that command a man to love his wife as Christ loved the church and outweigh the verse of scripture that instructs men to honor their wives. Although a woman must indeed submit to her husband sexually just as a man must submit to his wife sexually, there are occasional extenuating circumstances that may prompt a woman to resist having sex with her husband, that any loving husband should be willing to take into account. There are also circumstances (as discussed in Chapter 3) whereby a woman does not have to sexually submit to her husband. Those circumstances include any time in which her husband is asking her to do something sexually that goes against her spiritual conscious, or in which he is asking her to do something sexually that clearly goes against God's word.[23]

Rape and sexual abuse are acts of violence, control, humiliation, and disrespect and are no less acts of violence, control, humiliation, and disrespect when the perpetrator is the spouse of the victim. The Bible tells us that a man should honor his wife. Let's take a look at that scripture again:

> [7]In the same way, you husbands must give honor to your wives. Treat her with understanding as you live together. She may be weaker than you are, but she is your equal partner in God's gift of new life. If you don't treat her as you should, your prayers will not be heard. (1 Peter 3:7 NLT)

Even though a woman is physically weaker than her husband is, that does not give him the right to mistreat her. This is essentially what Peter is teaching in the verse of scripture cited above. The Bible has basically instructed us to treat others, as we would like to be treated. Ephesians 5:28 says, *"husbands are to love their wives as their own bodies."*[24] It follows then, that if a man would not want to be raped or sexually abused

---

[22] "Now as the church submits to Christ, so also wives should submit to their husbands in everything." (NIV)
[23] See Chapter 3.
[24] NIV

himself, then he does not have the right to rape or sexually abuse his wife.

Marital rape is a criminal act in all of the 50 states of America. Therefore, it is not only a sin but a crime as well. It can be just as devastating for a woman to be raped by her intimate partner or marriage partner as it is for a woman to be raped by a stranger. If rape or sexual abuse is the norm in a marital relationship the woman might be in denial and may not be calling it what it is. Many women who are raped or sexually abused by their husbands are victimized while they are asleep. A man who rapes his wife not only does so for power and control, but feels that he has the right to rape her because he feels he has the right to have sex with her any time he feels like it regardless of how she feels at the time. But even though scripture instructs men and women not to deprive their spouses of sexual intimacy, this instruction should never be used as a tool to sexual abuse or rape a spouse. There is never an excuse for sexual violence or abuse.

BLAMING THE VICTIM

Unfortunately many women who are abused by their husbands are blamed by society for the abuse. Women are either blamed for getting involved with the man in the first place or for not leaving fast enough when he begins abusing her. Regrettably studies show that there are societal myths surrounding domestic violence that don't do much to help in understanding the plight of the victim. One myth is that there are only a few women who experience domestic violence when in actuality, 3 out of 5 women will experience domestic violence sometime in their lifetime.

Another myth is that violent men do not have any control over their behavior, their anger, or their violence. This is not true. Violent men can learn to control their behavior. Furthermore, men who abuse their wives or girlfriends are able to get along with the people they work with on the job, the people they fellowship with in church, and so forth. Their need for control and power is manifested in their relationship with their spouses, girlfriends, and many times their children, but is not manifested in relationships with other people outside of the home. The myth that says that they cannot learn to control their behavior only serves to put more responsibility on the victim to try to control the violence instead of putting the responsibility where it actually lies, with the abuser.

The most damaging myths are the ones that say that women enjoy being abused or that they feel comfortable with it, or that a woman can always leave an abusive situation any time she gets ready, or that a woman has somehow provoked the abuse and that she deserves it. These myths are very prevalent in Western society, so prevalent that it is hard to convince people that these myths aren't true.

When it comes to women being the victims of domestic violence, many of those in Western society will say things like: "well, it's her fault for even being with him." "She should have never got with him in the first place." "That's what she gets for being so stupid." "She married him so now she's stuck with him. Too bad." Accusatory questions are often asked of abused women like "Didn't you see the signs?" or statements such as the following are made, "It's really hard for me to believe that you didn't see the signs." These statements imply that there were all of these "red flags" in place for the woman to see before she became involved with her abuser. However, to assume that every woman who has ever been in an abusive relationship saw the signs of abuse but chose to ignore them, is just that, an assumption. There is nothing in the literature that indicates that this is always the case. Unfortunately, instead of putting the focus upon stopping an abusive man from continuing his abuse, society puts much of the focus on blaming the one who is being abused and getting the woman to leave the abuser. Of course, she should leave her abuser, but this is easier said than done. And while society is steadily giving her the message to leave her abuser, society should also be just as strongly and steadily giving the abuser the message to stop abusing.

Another common misconception surrounding domestic violence is that women who are repeatedly abused have never tried to leave their abusers. This is not true. Statistics reveal that a woman will leave her abuser an average of 6 times before leaving him for good. But as emphasized earlier, each time she tries to leave, the probability that she will be murdered by her abuser, increases substantially. Unfortunately, studies show that a woman has a better chance of surviving domestic violence if she *stays* in the abusive relationship as opposed to if she tries to leave.

According to statistics, the probability that a woman will involve herself in an abusive relationship increases 300 times if, as a girl, she witnessed her mother as a victim of domestic violence. And men are more likely to become abusers if, as boys, they witnessed men abuse women.

Even if a woman becomes involved with a man who is abusive and she was able to see some of the signs before hand, he still has no right to abuse her and she is no more deserving of abuse than any other woman. Most women who have a tendency to involve themselves with abusive men or find themselves attracted to abusive men are not aware of this tendency until they have begun a relationship with an abusive man and then find it difficult to leave. It is not until then that a woman might seek the help of a professional to assist her in ridding herself of this tendency.

Studies have shown that, just as there are many men who look for women to marry who have similar characteristics of their mothers, there are many women who subconsciously look for men to marry who have similar characteristics of their fathers. Women are particularly prone to be attracted to men who fit their "father figures" if the relationship they have had with their own fathers has been strained or severed. Therefore, if a woman's father was abusive to her mother then it is quite likely that she will inevitably get involved with an abusive man. After all, an abusive man is part characteristic of her father figure. This is also true if a woman, as a young girl or adolescent, was beaten, sexually abused, or abused in any other way by her father. She too might look for a man who fits the characteristics of her father. If her father symbolizes beatings, sexual abuse and/or other types of abuse, then she is more prone than other women who have not experienced these things to "look for love in all the wrong places." What she is really subconsciously doing is searching for the love from her father that she never really had or that she thinks she never really had. So, if her father was Frankenstein's monster (or if she perceived him to be), then in adulthood, she may suddenly find monsters attractive.

These things do not excuse a woman from taking some responsibility for involving herself with an abusive man if she saw signs of abuse. However, what society must understand is that many women do not realize they find monsters attractive until they are full fledged into an unhealthy relationship with a monster. By that time the cycle of violence has started and her life is in grave danger each time she attempts to leave.

We must remember that women are 300 times more likely to involve themselves with abusive men if they have witnessed abuse while growing up or were abused themselves while growing up. If men would not abuse women, then women would not be victims of domestic violence. The root of the problem lies with the behavior of men not with the behavior of women. If men would not abuse women, then women would have more positive male role models in their lives and would be less prone to involve themselves with abusive men. Blaming the victim of abuse only serves to exonerate the abuser.

Although it is hard for many people to believe, there are many men who are experts at masking their abusive behaviors. A man who is interested in pursuing the love interests of a woman is usually going to do his best to initially be on his best behavior. As we have seen when examining the "buy back" and "honeymoon" phases of Walker's cycle of violence theory, even an abusive man can be very charming and pleasant when he wants to be. Most men are not going to beat a woman or curse at her on the first date and most women are not experts in picking up on the subtle clues of potential abuse. A man's abusive tendencies might subtly surface while he is dating a woman, but she might not be able to recognize these subtleties or might mistakenly identify them as something else. After all, she's not a psychologist. And even if she were she could still find herself in an abusive relationship if all the pieces to a dysfunctional past are in place.

As stated earlier, there are those who feel that it is a woman's own fault for being abused since "she should have known better" than to get involved with whomever is abusing her. Many feel that all women should be able to pick up on the red flags that an abuser sends before she becomes involved with him. Others feel that women who are in abusive relationships have simply ignored the signs. Some believe that it serves her right to be in an abusive relationship for her lack of judgement and that being abused is "what she gets" for her poor judgement in selection of a mate. But the bottom line is this: if men did not abuse women then 97% of domestic violence would be eradicated, at least on a global level.

The single most prevalent factor in determining whether or not a person will become a victim of domestic violence is gender. No matter how many times the statistics change, there will always be a greater percentage of women being abused by men, as opposed to the reverse.

Most women who remain in abusive relationships have no idea why they stay. But again, for many of them, they instinctively know that to leave will put their lives at great risk and therefore they must choose between life and death. As stated earlier, studies show that a woman has a better chance of surviving domestic violence if she *stays* in the abusive relationship as opposed to if she tries to leave. Five out of seven women, who have been murdered by their abusers, had already left their abuser or were in the process of leaving him when they were murdered.

In order for a woman to leave an abusive situation, she needs a place to go. She is literally trying to get away from her oppressor, her abuser, her torturer, who just happens to be her husband or her boyfriend, and she must plan her escape and plan it well. Her abuser is not going to nonchalantly let her just walk out of the house or walk out of his life. She cannot do this alone. People must be willing to help. Someone must be willing to let her into his or her home. Shelters must be available. She'll need money. If she is working, once she leaves her abuser, she can be sure that he will harass her on her job. An abused woman on the run will often times need a personal protection order. If she has children things are worse. Once she leaves, the abuser may also go after her family members in an attempt to find out where she is. Most women want to leave their abusers but many of them are just plain scared and they have just cause to be.

Many people criticize a woman for not leaving an abusive situation. But the same people who criticize her are rarely willing to offer her a place to stay or a helping hand during this difficult time in her life.

Because of the shame and embarrassment that accompanies domestic violence, there are those women who find themselves the victims of physical abuse perpetrated upon them by their husbands or boyfriends, who opt not to report the abuse to the authorities. This is due to the fact that we still live in a society that has a tendency to blame the victim.

Christian women often times have a more difficult struggle in front of them if they are faced with domestic violence as opposed to women outside of the church, because it can sometimes be very difficult for Christian women to recognize the thin line between husband headship and abuse. This is especially so when a man who is a Christian misuses the fact that he is the head of the house to validate his abuse towards his wife. As stated before, abusive Christian men, in an effort to wield power and control over their wives, will exploit the verses of scripture that instruct women to submit. They will submission-bully their wives by constantly using the submission verses as a trump card. They misuse the scriptures to manipulate and strong-arm their wives and view being the head of the house as synonymous with control and power.

Since pulpit clergy, when speaking on the issue of marriage, seem to more often than not expressly and particularly emphasize the woman's role to submit to her husband, there are many Christian women who have also equated husband headship with control and power. A Christian woman might feel that she doesn't have the right to challenge her controlling and abusive husband. A Christian woman might feel that in challenging her husband, she is sinning.

Not only does a Christian woman have to always be conscious of whether or not she is submitting herself to her husband as the scriptures instruct, but the Bible instructs her, just as it instructs any other Christian, to be forgiving. Let's take a look:

> [3]So watch what you do! If your brother sins, rebuke him, and if he repents, forgive him. [4]If he sins against you seven times in one day, and each time he comes to your saying, 'I repent,' you must forgive him. (Luke 17:3-4 GNT)

Many Christians take this to mean that a woman who leaves an abusive husband has not been forgiving towards him and that as long as he asks her to forgive him, she cannot leave him. But this is not what the scripture says. A person can forgive someone from a distance. Forgiveness comes from the heart. If one neighbor steals from another, the one who was victimized can certainly forgive the one who stole from him. But the act of forgiveness doesn't mean that the victim must have fellowship with the thief in order to prove he forgave him. This doesn't mean that the victim should ask the thief to housesit while the victim goes out of town on a business trip. This does not mean that the victim should leave his door unlocked when he goes to work. Certain precautions should still be taken because the neighbor is a thief. The same applies to an abusive husband. Just because a woman leaves an abusive husband does not mean that she hasn't forgiven him. It only means that she has had to take specific precautions in order to protect herself, one of which may be separating from him, or, if he doesn't get help soon, leaving him for good.

Most abusive men are very resistant to getting psychological counseling and therapy. And even those who decide to get help, or are forced by the court to get help, have a long road to recovery ahead of them. In the meantime, their wives are still targets of abuse until the man sorts through his problems. Therefore, even if a man is receiving domestic violence counseling, this does not mean that a woman is safe at home. She is always at risk until her husband gains control of his behavior. It may take him years to gain control of his behavior. And unfortunately, he may never gain control of his behavior and might always continue to be an abusive man. But although her life could be in jeopardy, a Christian woman might feel that she does not have an option to divorce her spouse and that she must stay with him no matter what. This brings us to our next topic.

"TILL DEATH DO US PART"....THE QUESTION OF DIVORCE IN CHRISTIAN MARRIAGES

Divorce and remarriage is allowed

Many Christians believe that the Bible teaches that it is a sin to get a divorce. Consequently, many Christian women who are in abusive marriages and are the victims of domestic violence are often times encouraged by the clergy not to leave their husbands. Therefore, many Christian women live under the threat of death, in their own homes, everyday. These women never suspected that when they made the vow never to leave their spouses until death do they part that the death of them might be their husbands.

The question becomes whether or not the scriptures teach that a Christian woman must stay in an abusive relationship at risk of death. If so, then there is no way out of a marriage filled with beatings, threats, verbal abuse, and the like for a Christian woman who has made a mistake and married the wrong man. Is this really what God is saying? Is God really saying that there is no way out of a marriage like this and that the woman must endure beatings, disfiguration, emotional trauma, humiliation, torture, embarrassment, and often times imprisonment inside of her own home, for the rest of her life before her husband finally kills her? Let's take a look again at Matthew 19:3-11:

> [3]Some Pharisees came and tried to trap him with this question: "Should a man be allowed to divorce his wife for any reason?"
> [4]"Haven't you read the Scriptures?" Jesus replied. "They record that from the beginning 'God made them male and female.' [5]And he said, 'This explains why a man leaves his father and mother and is joined to his

wife, and the two are united into one.' ⁶Since they are no longer two but one, let no one separate them, for God has joined them together."

⁷"Then why did Moses say a man could merely write an official letter of divorce and send her away?" they asked.

⁸Jesus replied, "Moses permitted divorce as a concession to your hard-hearted wickedness, but it was not what God had originally intended. ⁹And I tell you this, a man who divorces his wife and marries another commits adultery—unless his wife has been unfaithful."

¹⁰Jesus' disciples then said to him, "Then it is better not to marry!"

¹¹"Not everyone can accept this statement," Jesus said. "Only those whom God helps. ¹²Some are born as eunuchs, some have been made that way by others, and some choose not to marry for the sake of the Kingdom of Heaven. Let anyone who can, accept this statement. (Matthew 19:3-12 NLT)

During the time when Jesus made these statements, men were divorcing their wives for any reason (verse 3) just so they could (or at least they thought they could) legitimately marry other women and satisfy their own lusts and wondering eyes. Since Moses permitted divorce (which really meant that God permitted it because Moses was a prophet guided by God and the commands that Moses ordained came from God) these men felt that Jesus had no choice but to agree that a man could divorce his wife for any reason in order to marry his mistress. In asking the question about divorcing their wives they were really asking Jesus to agree that they could divorce their wives for any reason no matter how small and how trivial. But Jesus knew their hearts and knew that they were trying to snag him with this question. So instead of concurring with them, Jesus explained to them that the only reason why Moses allowed them to divorce their wives was because of the wickedness of their hearts and that divorce is not what God had originally intended, although he allowed it (verse 8). He then went on to say (verse 9) that unless a

287

woman is guilty of adultery against her husband, her husband cannot divorce her.[25]

Many Christians believe that, because of verse 9, the only legitimate reason for divorce is adultery. But Jesus never said that adultery is the *absolute only* reason whereby one can seek to get a divorce. Adultery is one of the exceptions but not the only exception, as we will see later.

It should also be emphasized that Jesus' purpose in answering the Pharisees' questions about divorce was to make certain that they understood that divorce was not a trivial matter and it was not what men could use as a tool to give them the opportunity to fulfill the sexual desires they had for other women besides their wives. What better way to bring this point about than to tell these men that even if they divorced their wives and married another they'd still be committing adultery. In other words, they would not be able to legitimize their relationships with their mistresses simply by divorcing their wives and marrying their mistresses. Even by doing such, they would still be committing adultery under the eyes of God.

What Jesus was doing here was protecting the honor of the wives who had been cheated on by their husbands who thought they'd be able to get away with their cheating by simply divorcing their wives and marrying their mistresses. But Jesus made it clear that it doesn't work that way and that the only way that it would work is if their wives were cheating on them in the first place. Apparently not many women were cheating in those days (or at least if they were they must have rarely been caught in the act) because the Pharisees got the message and replied that it was better not to get married (verse 10). Jesus agreed with them but explained to them that the single life isn't for everyone, but only for those who have chosen to remain single to better able themselves to serve God and whom God helps along to be content in an unmarried state (verses 11, 12).

The verses that we have cited and examined in Matthew 19:3-12 need to be taken into account when reading what Jesus said in the following verse of scripture:

---

[25] The NASB translates this to say that a man can divorce his wife is she is guilty of unchasity.

> Anyone who divorces his wife and marries someone
> else commits adultery, and anyone who marries a
> divorced woman commits adultery. (Luke 16:18 NLT)

Many Christians take this to mean that under no circumstances, except in instances of adultery, are men and women allowed to divorce one another. If this scripture is taken alone, then it would appear that the Bible is indeed saying that once a person is married there is no turning back. However, upon examining the scriptures in Matthew 19:3-12 that were discussed earlier, we have learned that the word of God indeed allows divorce. Therefore, the above scripture in Luke should be explored but only in accordance with other scriptures on divorce when investigating the subject. Otherwise, the full picture is not presented.

As we have seen, Jesus said that any one who divorces his wife and marries another is committing adultery. He also said that anyone who marries a divorced woman commits adultery. Most would agree that it is safe to assume that the reverse is true as well. A woman who divorces her husband and marries another man has committed adultery, and a woman who marries man who is divorced, commits adultery. However, as we have seen when discussing Matthew 19:3-12, this only applies if the divorce was pursued for frivolous reasons. Great legalism has been applied to this verse in Luke, but Jesus did not mean it legalistically. He specifically used this line of reasoning to dissuade men from marrying their mistresses. More evidence that Luke 16:18 does not constitute an absolute rule is evident when looking at the following verses of scripture:

> [10]Now, for those who are married I have a
> command that comes not from me, but from the Lord.
> A wife must not leave her husband. [11]But if she does
> leave him, let her remain single or else go back to him.
> And the husband must not leave his wife.
> [12]Now, I will speak to the rest of you, though I do
> not have a direct command from the Lord. If a
> Christian man has a wife who is an unbeliever and she
> is willing to continue living with him, he must not leave
> her. [13]And if a Christian woman has a husband who is
> an unbeliever, and he is willing to continue living with
> her, she must not leave him. [14]For the Christian wife
> brings holiness to her marriage, and the Christian

husband brings holiness to his marriage. Otherwise, your children would not have a godly influence, but now they are set apart for him. [15](But if the husband or wife who isn't a Christian insists on leaving, let them go. In such cases the Christian husband or wife is not required to stay with them, for God wants his children to live in peace.) [16]You wives must remember that your husbands might be converted because of you. And you husbands must remember that your wives might be converted because of you. (1 Corinthians 7:10-16 NLT)

Verses 10 and 11 instruct women not to divorce their husbands. But it also says that if she does (the inference is without just cause) she is to remain single. It doesn't say that if she divorces him that she has lost her salvation. It doesn't say that if she divorces him that God will never forgive her. All it says is that if she divorces him, she is to either reconcile with her husband or remain single.[26] According to Paul, remaining single is not such a bad thing. As a matter of fact, according to Paul, remaining single is a good thing and is preferable to getting married.[27]

Again verses 10 through 11 instruct women not to divorce. If we take the verses alone it would be easy to conclude that this is an absolute command with no alternative. However, when reading further into verse 15, we discover that there is an exception to the directives of verses 10 and 11, the exception being that if a Christian woman is married to a man who is not a Christian, and he insists on leaving her, then she is not obligated to stay with him. She can let him go. If he wants to divorce her, she shouldn't fight it. Some would even interpret this to mean that since there is no indication that she has to wait around for him to divorce her, she can divorce him as well. God wants her to live in peace. She will not be at peace if she tries to stay married to an unbeliever who does not want to be married to her.

Therefore, although men and women are commanded not to marry a divorcee and divorcees are commanded to either stay single or remarry

---

[26] And as we will see, depending on further circumstances that occur in her life and the life of her ex-husband, there is a statue of limitation, so to speak, of the command for her to remain single.

[27] See Chapter 12.

their ex-spouses, there are, so far as we have seen, two exceptions in which these commands do not apply. The first is if the divorcee obtained his or her divorce due to adulterous behavior on the part of the ex-spouse and the second is if the divorcee was the defendant or plaintiff in a divorce action in which a divorce was granted because the ex-spouse wanted to leave.

The concession to divorce a non-believer only applies in a marriage in which the non-believer wants to leave the marriage. If the non-believer chooses to stay married, then, according to verses 12 through 14, the Christian is obligated to remain married. This is because the Christian is the one that brings holiness to the marriage (verse 14). Not only does the Christian bring holiness to the marriage, but also, through the holy behavior of the Christian inside the marriage, the unbelieving spouse might be converted to Christianity. The Christian behavior of the believing spouse might be what it takes to bring the unbelieving spouse to a point of belief in the deity and Lordship of Jesus Christ. It is through this belief that the unbelieving spouse will be saved. It is for this reason the believing Christian is obligated to stay married to the unbeliever unless, as discussed before, the unbeliever wants to leave.

The scripture also teaches that a divorcee can marry again if his or her ex-spouse has remarried, regardless of the reasons why the marriage was dissolved. Let's take a look:

> [1]If a man marries a woman who becomes displeasing to him because he finds something indecent about her, and he writes her a certificate of divorce, gives it to her and sends her from his house, [2]and if after she leaves his house she becomes the wife of another man, [3]and her second husband dislikes her and writes her a certificate of divorce, gives it to her and sends her from his house, or if he dies, [4]then her first husband, who divorced her, is not allowed to marry her again after she has been defiled. That would be detestable in the eyes of the LORD. Do not bring sin upon the land of the LORD your God is giving you as an inheritance. (Deuteronomy 24:1-4 NIV)

291

Although the above commands are part of the Old Testament Mosaic Laws,[28] of which many of those laws do not apply today, specific commands as to what to do if one wants to remarry a previous spouse who is divorced for a second time are only found in the Old Testament. Therefore, we can at least get a relatively good idea of how God feels about the matter even if it is not addressed in the New Testament. From examining the verses of scripture above, it is clear that remarriage of a woman to a man is only allowed if neither remarried someone else in the interim. Here is where the statue of limitations, so to speak, of the command to remain single after divorce, arises. The defilement comes along with the fact that if either married someone else after the divorce, then of course sexual relations occurred in the second marriage and the purity of the first marriage is therefore forever gone and cannot be recaptured. Contrary to popular belief, the second marriage (and all successive marriages thereafter) takes precedent over the first marriage. So, not only is a woman free to remarry another if her ex-husband has remarried, but she is free to remarry another if her ex-husband has had sexual relations with another as well, because by having sexual relations with another woman, he has essentially committed adultery.

How God feels about remarriage when an interim relationship has occurred between either party is even more evident when looking at what God says to the nation of Israel (whom he speaks of often metaphorically as his bride) when combining Jeremiah 2:14-20 with Jeremiah 3:1-5. Let's take a look:

> [14]"Why has Israel become a nation of slaves? Why has she been carried away as plunder? [15]Lions have roared against her. The land has been destroyed, and the cities are now in ruins. No one lives in them anymore. [16]Egyptians, marching from their cities of Memphis and Tahpanhes, have utterly destroyed Israel's glory and power. [17]And you have brought this on yourselves by rebelling against the LORD your God when he wanted to lead you and show you the way!
>
> [18]What have you gained by your alliances with Egypt and Assyria? What good to you are the waters of the Nile and the Euphrates? [19]Your own wickedness will

---

[28] See Introduction.

punish you. You will see what an evil, bitter thing it is to forsake the LORD your God, having no fear of him, I, the Lord, the LORD Almighty have spoken! [20]Long ago I broke your yoke and tore away the chains of your slavery, but still you would not obey me. On every hill and under every green tree, you have prostituted yourselves by bowing down to idols." (Jeremiah 2:14-20 NLT)

"If a man divorces a woman and she marries someone else, he is not to take her back again, for that would surely corrupt the land. But you have prostituted yourself with many lovers, says the LORD. Yet I am still calling you back to me." (Jeremiah 3:1 NLT)

Theologians surmise that the part of Israel that was guilty of adultery (of worshipping other gods, false gods) was the Northern part of the Kingdom (the Nation of Israel) which was destroyed in 721 B.C. and that Judah was the Southern Kingdom. Both Israel and Judah (tribes of the Nation of Israel) turned away from the Lord and were therefore guilty of spiritual adultery. Israel had a habit of worshipping false idols, eventually realizing her mistake, and then returning to God. In Jeremiah 3:1 God is reminding Israel that according to the Law he was not supposed to welcome Israel back. God compared Israel to a woman who had divorced her husband and married another. As far as God was concerned, Israel had ran away to marry another. However, God still called Israel back to him.

[6]During the reign of King Josiah, the LORD said to me, "Have you seen what fickle Israel does? Like a wife who commits adultery, Israel has worshiped other gods on every hill and under every green tree. [7]I thought that after she had done all this she would return to me. But she did not come back. And though her faithless sister Judah saw this, [8]she paid no attention. She saw that I had divorced faithless Israel and sent her away. But now Judah, too, has left me and given herself to prostitution. [9]Israel treated it all so lightly—she thought nothing of committing adultery by worshipping idols

made of wood and stone. So now the land has been greatly defiled. ¹⁰But in spite of all this, her faithless sister Judah has never sincerely returned to me. She has only pretended to be sorry," says the Lord. (Jeremiah 3:6-10 NLT)

Verse 8 tells us that God divorced Israel because of her adultery. Therefore, God has been divorced before. Although the terms are figurative the meaning is the same as it is with men and women. God is very serious about his identification of the Nation of Israel as his bride.[29] Since God has been divorced, then it stands to reason that the stigma that the church puts upon those who are divorced is unfounded. Those who have gotten divorces are not to be judged as long as they obtained divorces for allowable reasons. And even if they erred and did not obtain a divorce for an allowable reason, God will still forgive them if they have repented, just as God forgives all others who repent. Their salvation is not lost and they are no less a Christian than any other Christian.

It is interesting to note that God accused Judah of *pretending* to be sorry for her adultery. Therefore, repentance doesn't come with words but with actions. An abusive man can apologize to his wife a thousand times, pursue her, buy her back, and go through the honeymoon stage as well. But if the cycle of violence continues to occur, then he was never really sorry in the first place. He was only pretending to be sorry. Let's look further:

> ¹¹Then the LORD said to me, "Even faithless Israel is less guilty than treacherous Judah! ¹²Therefore, go and say these words to Israel, "This is what the Lord says: O Israel, my faithless people, come home to me again, for I am merciful. I will not be angry forever. (Jeremiah 3:11-12 NLT)

God is merciful and is not angry forever. Some take this to mean that a man or a woman whose spouse has been unfaithful is entitled to ask for repentance before divorce proceedings are started. Of course, he is entitled. However, when Jesus taught that a man could divorce his wife

---

[29] The Jews are those who belong to the nation of Israel. The Bible defines a true Jew as one who believes in Jesus as the Messiah (Romans 2:29, see your Bible).

for reasons of unfaithfulness, the tone of the scripture indicates that the scorned spouse has the option to pursue a divorce regardless as to whether or not the guilty spouse has repented and asked for forgiveness. As stated before, a person can forgive from a distance.

There is no doubt that the word of God does not allow for divorce except in certain cases. The three exceptions that have been discussed are adultery, the situation in which an unbeliever wants to leave a believer, and the Old Testament prohibition of remarrying an ex-spouse whom has remarried and divorced someone else during the interim of separation. Whether or not these are the only three is questionable.

There are many theologians that still believe, regardless of the exceptions set aside in scripture, that all divorce is sin. But on the other hand, a great number of theologians agree with the exceptions that have been discussed and therefore do not see all divorce as sin. Despite this, since none of the exceptions given for divorce include spousal abuse not much hope is left for a Christian woman who is suffering domestic violence at the hands of her husband. In light of this, it might behoove a Christian woman who is the victim of domestic violence to consider this: if a woman must choose between divorce and death, or choose between divorce and what she deems as a life threatening situation, or choose between divorce and the possibility of great physical harm, or choose between divorce and the possibility of great emotional distress, then it would seem that she would have no other choice but to separate from her husband and get a divorce. The Bible is basically silent on the issue of domestic violence and what a woman is to do if she finds herself married to an abusive man. Since the Bible doesn't specifically address it, many believe it is automatically addressed in the fact that it is not included in one of the three exceptions for divorce. But this is not necessarily the case.

An abused Christian woman should also consider this: if God is really saying that domestic violence is not a good enough reason for a woman to get a divorce, and that if she gets a divorce anyway, the price she must pay is to never remarry again (unless her ex-spouse remarries because in doing so he has sexually defiled his first marriage covenant) then when considering the alternative (great physical/emotional harm or death), remaining single is doable. Living without a man is certainly better than dying at the hands of one.

God is a forgiving God. God held many things against Israel but then always forgave her. So if there are those who believe that God holds against a woman the fact that she has obtained a divorce because she feared for her life, or feared for her sanity, or feared for the life and/or sanity of her children, then they must also believe that God won't hold it against her long, and therefore, neither should society.

"What God has joined together"

When Jesus spoke of marriage and divorce he specified what he taught about marriage and divorce as applying to those whom God has joined together. Let's take a look:

> [4]"Haven't you read," he replied, "that at the beginning the Creator 'made them male and female,' [5]and said, 'For this reason a man will leave his father and mother and be united to his wife, and the two will become one flesh?' So they are no longer two, but one. Therefore what God has joined together, let man not separate." (Matthew 19:4-6 NIV)

Jesus is speaking in the above verses of scripture and teaches us that if God has brought two people together in marriage, then no one should set out to separate them. Some take this to mean that God automatically ordains all marriages. But when taking a closer look at scripture we are hard pressed not to come to the conclusion that God has not joined together all people who are married to one another. In other words, in the case of many marriages, including Christian marriages, God was not the one that drew the two people together. Often times, people come together on their own without the sanction of God. However, most Christians believe that wedding vows automatically make a marriage God-ordained. We will take issue with that kind of reasoning, beginning with the following verses of scripture:

> [14]Don't team up with those who are unbelievers. How can goodness be a partner with wickedness? How can light live with darkness? [15]What harmony can there be between Christ and the Devil? How can a believer be a partner with an unbeliever? [16]And what union can there be between God's temple and idols? For we are the temple of the living God. As God said:

"I will live in them
and walk among them.
I will be their God,
And they will be my people.
[17]Therefore, come out from them
and separate yourselves from them,
says the Lord.
Don't touch their filthy things,
And I will welcome you.
[18]And I will be your Father,
and you will be my sons and
daughters,
says the Lord Almighty.
(2 Corinthians 6:14-18 NLT)

[1]Because we have these promises, dear friends, let us cleanse ourselves from everything that can defile our body or spirit. And let us work toward complete purity because we fear God. (2 Corinthians 7:1 NLT)

The scripture clearly instructs Christians not to team up in any way with those who are not Christians. In other words, those who believe in the Lordship of Jesus Christ and believe that he died on the cross as redemption for sin and also believe that he rose from the dead, should not team up in any way, within reason, with those who do not believe this. The ultimate way of teaming up with or partnering with someone is to enter into a marriage agreement with that person. In today's dispensation of Grace,[30] people choose to marry and they choose who they want to marry. Therefore if a Christian decides to marry an unbeliever, then we can be sure that God has not joined the two of them together in marriage. They chose to get married on their own accord ignoring the word of God that says they shouldn't. Otherwise God would be contradicting his own word. Why would God join a believer and an unbeliever together when he said in his word that they should not be joined together?

---

[30] See Introduction.

It would seem that scripture teaches that the general rule of thumb is that God has no part in joining a believer with an unbeliever. The only exception to this would be if both a married man and his wife were unsaved when they got married and eventually one of them became a Christian while the other remained unsaved. In this case, the following verses of scripture cited previously in 1st Corinthians would apply. Let's look again:

> [12]Now, I will speak to the rest of you, though I do not have a direct command from the Lord. If a Christian man has a wife who is an unbeliever and she is willing to continue living with him, he must not leave her. [13]And if a Christian woman has a husband who is an unbeliever, and he is willing to continue living with her, she must not leave him. [14]For the Christian wife brings holiness to her marriage, and the Christian husband brings holiness to his marriage. Otherwise, your children would not have a godly influence, but now they are set apart for him. [15](But if the husband or wife who isn't a Christian insists on leaving, let them go. In such cases the Christian husband or wife is not required to stay with them, for God wants his children to live in peace.) [16]You wives must remember that your husbands might be converted because of you. And you husbands must remember that your wives might be converted because of you. (1 Corinthians 7:12-16 NLT)

> [17]You must accept whatever situation the Lord has put you in, and continue on as you were when God first called you. This is my rule for all the churches.
> (1 Corinthians 7:17 NLT)

> [20]You should continue on as you were when God called you. [21]Are you a slave? Don't let that worry you—but if you get a chance to be free, take it. [22]And remember, if you were a slave when the Lord called you, the Lord has now set you free from the awful power of sin. And if you were free when the Lord called you, you are now a slave of Christ. (1 Corinthians 7:20-22 NLT)

298

When a person becomes a Christian, they are to continue on as they were when God called them. So if a married woman becomes a Christian, and her husband does not, she is to continue on as she was when God called her (when she became a Christian). She is to remain married as long as her unbelieving husband wants to stay with her. In this sense, God has joined the two of them together.

Jesus said, as documented in Mark 3:25 that *"a home divided against itself is doomed."*[31] If a Christian woman endeavors to marry a man who is not a Christian, then she is endeavoring to live in a house divided against itself and her marriage is doomed for trouble.

Amos 3:3 asks, *"Can two people walk together without agreeing on the direction?"*[32] The question is rhetorical and of course the answer is *no.* Two people cannot walk together without agreeing on the direction. A Christian and an unbeliever are two people who are going in two different directions, because the former is a child of God and the latter is a child of the Devil as attested to in the following verses of scripture:

> [1]See how very much our heavenly Father loves us, for he allows us to be called his children, and we really are! But the people who belong to this world don't know God, so they don't understand that we are his children. [2]Yes, dear friends, we are already God's children, and we can't even imagine what we will be like when Christ returns. But we do know that when he comes we will be like him, for we will see him as he really is. [3]And all who believe this will keep themselves pure, just as Christ is pure.
>
> [4]Those who sin are opposed to the law of God, for all sin opposes the law of God. [5]And you know that Jesus came to take away our sins, for there is no sin in him. [6]So if we continue to live in him, we won't sin either. But those who keep on sinning have never known him or understood who he is.
>
> [7]Dear children, don't let anyone deceive you about this: When people do what is right, it is because they are righteous, even as Christ is righteous. [8]But when

---

[31] NLT
[32] NLT

people keep on sinning, it shows they belong to the
Devil, who has been sinning since the beginning. But
the Son of God came to destroy these works of the
Devil. [9]Those who have been born into God's family do
not sin, because God's life is in them. So they can't
keep on sinning, because they have been born of God.
[10]So now we can tell who are children of God and who
are children of the Devil. Any one who does not obey
God's commands and does not love other Christians
does not belong to God. (1 John 3:1-10 NLT)

Although the word of God teaches us that we all have sinned and
have fallen short of the glory of God,[33] the verses of scripture above
teach us that we must strive not to sin and that the sign of a true
Christian is one who does not purposely and continuously practice sin.
Those who keep on sinning are children of the Devil, not children of
God. Certainly, children of God and children of the Devil are headed in
two different directions. It stands to reason then, that God would not
unite a child of God and a child of the Devil in holy matrimony.

It also stands to reason that a man who continues to abuse his wife
without trying to get help and without trying to stop is continuing to sin.
Furthermore, Jesus told us that we will know who is false and who is
real by the fruits they bear (their deeds). Let's take a look at what he
said:

[15]Beware of false prophets, who come to you in sheep's
clothing, but inwardly they are ravenous wolves.
[16]You will know them by their fruits. Do men gather
grapes from thornbushes or figs from thistles?
[17]Even so, every good tree bears good fruit, but a bad
tree bears bad fruit.
[18]A good tree cannot bear bad fruit, nor can a bad tree
bear good fruit.
[19]Every tree that does not bear good fruit is cut down
and thrown into the fire.
[20]Therefore by their fruits you will know them.
(Matthew 7:15-20 NKJV)

---

[33] "For all have sinned and come short of the glory of God." (Romans 3:23)

Having looked deeply into the issue with the discussions set forth earlier in this chapter, we see that men who are abusive towards their wives practice a multitude of sins on a regular basis. These men are contentious, which goes against the rules set forth in the 26th chapter of Proverbs. They are often angry, full of rage, verbally abusive and many times use profanity and foul language which goes against the rules set forth in the 5th chapter of 1st Corinthians. They go against the command noted in the 3rd chapter of 1st Peter, which instructs all Christians to live in harmony with everyone. A man who abuses his wife is guilty of one or more of these things on a consistent basis. He is therefore guilty of continuous sin.

If a man keeps abusing his wife (continues in the practice of abuse), scripture tells us he is a child of the Devil (1 John 3:9-10 cited previously) and scripture also tells us that abusers will not inherit the kingdom of God.[34] So since he is an abuser, we can safely say that there is a great possibility that he will not inherit the kingdom of God. If he will not inherit the kingdom of God then we can safely say he is not saved. If he is not saved then he is an unbeliever.

One could further argue that a man who wants to stay married to his wife would not abuse her. So then, a woman married to an abusive man and victimized by him is essentially with an unbeliever who says he wants to be with her but really doesn't want to be with her. And when he repents of his deeds he's only pretending to be sorry (since he keeps repeatedly abusing her), just as Israel pretended to be sorry when confronted by the Lord about her adulterous behavior. According to 1st Corinthians 7:15 (cited earlier), a Christian woman is at liberty to divorce an unbeliever who does not want to be with her. When looking at it this way, it becomes very questionable as to whether or not a woman, who has divorced her husband for reasons of abuse, has actually done something wrong. When deeply examining the scriptural text, a continuously abused wife may have the right to pursue a divorce because according to scripture, it is possible that her husband is really an

---

[34] "Don't you know that those who do wrong will have no share in the Kingdom of God? Don't fool yourselves. Those who indulge in sexual sin, who are idol worshippers, adulterers, male prostitutes, homosexuals, thieves, greedy, drunkards, abusers, and swindlers—none of these will have a share in the Kingdom of God. (1 Corinthians 6:9-10 NLT)

unbeliever and, by abusing her, is giving indication that he really doesn't want to be with her.

Christians are specifically instructed not to marry non-Christians, as evidenced by the following verses of scripture that we will take a look at again:

> [14]Do not try to work together as equals with unbelievers, for it cannot be done. How can right and wrong be partners? [15]How can light and darkness live together? How can Christ and the Devil agree? What does a believer have in common with an unbeliever? [16]How can God's temple come to terms with pagan idols? For we are the temple of the living God! As God himself has said,
> > "I will make my home with my people
> > and live among them;
> > I will be their God,
> > and they shall be my people."
> (2 Corinthians 6:14-16 GNT)

Since Christians are instructed not to partner themselves with non-Christians, then we can safely say that God did not bring together a marriage where a Christian knowingly (or unknowingly for that matter) married an unbeliever.[35] God never sanctioned such a marriage in the first place. Why would God ordain the marriage of a Christian with a child of the Devil? A man who continuously abuses his wife is, by biblical definition, a child of the Devil because he is continuing in the sin of abuse. The question therefore becomes: do all of the conservative directives given about divorce in the Bible apply to marriages that God never ordained? Or do the rules regarding divorce and remarriage specifically pertain only to those marriages in which the two people have been "joined together" by God?

Christians are also known by the good fruit that they bear, but abusiveness is a very bad fruit. Not only can we draw the conclusion that

---

[35] "A woman is bound to her husband as long as he lives. But if her husband dies, she is free to marry anyone she wishes, but he must belong to the Lord. In my judgment, she is happier if she stays as she is—and I think that I too have the Spirit of God." (1Corinthians 7:39-40 NIV)

God would not join together a Christian and an unbeliever in marriage but we can also conclude that God would not join a Christian together in marriage with someone who indulges in the sins which keep people from inheriting the Kingdom of God if practiced on a continuous basis. Again those sins are: sexual sin, idol worshipping, adultery, prostitution, homosexuality, stealing, greed, drunkenness/getting high, abusive behavior, pulling scams on people, lying, deceiving, and the like.

With this said, an exception to the argument must be cited here. God specifically told the prophet Hosea to marry a prostitute. Let's take a look:

> ²When the Lord first began speaking to Israel through Hosea, he said to him, "Go and marry a prostitute, so some of her children will be born to you from other men. This will illustrate the way my people have been untrue to me, openly committing adultery against the LORD by worshipping other gods." (Hosea 1:2 NLT)

God not only wanted to express in words how he felt about Israel's adultery towards him but he also wanted to express how he felt by way of illustration. God chose Hosea to be his example and told him to marry a prostitute in order that Israel's adultery may be illustrated through his life. Sometimes people need to see an example of how their own misbehavior is, in order that they might change. Let's look further into the account:

> ¹Then the LORD said to me, "Go and get your wife again. Bring her back to you and love her, even though she loves adultery. For the LORD still loves Israel even though the people have turned to other gods, offering them choice gifts. (Hosea 3:1 NLT)

God used Hosea to illustrate God's love towards Israel despite Israel's continuous and unrelenting desire to worship other gods (false gods). This does not mean that God condones marriages to prostitutes. This does not mean that it is all right with God if a Christian marries an unbeliever. And this does not mean that a Christian cannot divorce an adulterous spouse. The instructions that God gave to Hosea were special instructions meant only for him. They were special instructions for a special purpose and were for Hosea alone.

SUMMARY

God has made it very clear how a man is supposed to treat his wife. Let's look at the verses of scripture again that specifically instruct men how to treat their wives:

> [25]And you husbands must love your wives with the same love Christ showed the church. He gave up his life for her [26]to make her holy and clean, washed by baptism and God's word. [27]He did this to present her to himself as a glorious church without a spot or wrinkle or any other blemish. Instead, she will be holy and without fault. [28]In the same way, husbands ought to love their wives as they love their own bodies. For a man is actually loving himself when he loves his wife. [29]No one hates his own body but lovingly cares for it, just as Christ cares for his body, which is the church. [30]And we are his body. (Ephesians 5:25-30 NLT)

A man is to love his wife like Christ loved the church. He is supposed to make certain that his wife has no blemish on her. A blemish is a scar or a mark. A woman who is being physically abused by her husband, has more than blemishes, she has wounds. If she is being verbally abused then she has psychological wounds. Abusive men are therefore going against the instruction of the above verses of scripture. They do not love their wives like they are supposed to because they are abusing them, which cause their wives to endure physical and mental scars and blemishes. Verse 28 instructs men to care for their wives' bodies as they would care for their own. Certainly no man would beat himself up, or invite someone to sexually abuse him or rape him, or yell at himself or do anything which would hurt his own body. Then he is not to do these things to his wife either. To abuse her in anyway, even a "little bit" is a sin. A man is to treat his wife's body as if it were his own.

The Bible makes it clear that God hates divorce. Let's take a look:

[10]Don't we all have the same father? Didn't the same God create us all? Then why do we break our promises to one another, and why do we despise the covenant that God made with our ancestors? [11]The people of Judah have broken their promise to God and done a horrible thing in Jerusalem and all over the country. They have defiled the Temple which the LORD loves. Men have married women who worship foreign gods. [12]May the LORD remove from the community of Israel those who did this, and never again let them participate in the offerings our nation brings to the LORD Almighty.

[13]This is another thing you do. You drown the LORD'S altar with tears, weeping and wailing because he no longer accepts the offerings you bring him. [14]You ask why he no longer accepts them. It is because he knows you have broken your promise to the wife you married when you were young. She was your partner, and you have broken your promise to her, although you promised before God that you would be faithful to her. [15]Didn't God make you one body and spirit with her? What was his purpose in this? It was that you should have children who are truly God's people. So make sure that none of you breaks his promise to his wife. [16]"I hate divorce" says the LORD God of Israel. "I hate it when one of you does such a cruel thing to his wife. Make sure that you do not break your promise to be faithful to your wife." (Malachi 2:10-16 GNT)

God was specifically upset at the fact that the men of Israel were often disloyal to their wives by committing adultery with other women. He urged them to remain loyal to their wives. God was also upset that many of the men of Israel married women outside of the faith. Although God hates all divorce, when God is quoted above as saying that he hates divorce, God is referring to divorce that results from a man's desire to leave his wife for another woman (verse 16). There are those who read verse 16 and take things a step further. Many believe that God hates people who are divorced. But God never said this. And as we saw earlier, God himself was divorced. Certainly God does not hate himself.

Since God has said he hates divorce there are also those who believe that divorce is unforgivable. But there is no scripture in the Bible that says that divorce is unforgivable.[36]

Not only does God hate divorce but he hates other sins as well, seven sins in particular. Most people have been guilty of at least one of these seven sins at sometime in their lives and therefore are certainly not in a position to judge someone who is divorced. Let's take a look:

> [16]These six things the Lord hates, indeed, seven are an abomination to Him:
> [17]A proud look [the spirit that makes one overestimate himself and underestimate others], a lying tongue, and hands that shed innocent blood,
> [18]A heart that manufactures wicked thoughts and plans, feet that are swift in running to evil,
> [19]A false witness who breathes out lies [even under oath], and he who sows discord among the brethren. (Proverbs 6:16-19 Amp.)

God hates pride, lying, murder, wicked thoughts, evil planning, evil living, and Christians who stir up trouble among other Christians, as much as he hates divorce.

Although God hates divorce, as stated earlier God has called us to peace.[37] It is very questionable as to whether or not God would join one of his female children together in marriage with a man who is set on destroying her peace.

The Bible teaches that Christians will be rewarded in heaven for the good works they have done on earth. Therefore, it stands to reason that many men will loose great rewards in heaven[38] because of the way they

---

[36] According to Matthew 12:31, there is only one unforgivable sin and that is the sin of blasphemy against the Holy Spirit. The scripture reads, "Every sin or blasphemy can be forgiven—except blasphemy against the Holy Spirit, which can never be forgiven." (NLT)

[37] "Yet if the unbelieving one leaves, let him leave; the brother or the sister is not under bondage in such cases, but God has called us to peace." (1Corinthians 7:15 NASB)

[38] "For the Son of man shall come in the glory of his Father with his angels; and then he shall reward every man according to his works." (Matthew 16:27)

have treated their wives. And as stated before, the Bible also tells us that God will not listen to the prayers of men who dishonor their wives.[39] There is no question that when a man is abusive towards his wife in any way, he is dishonoring her. Colossians 3:19 instructs men to love their wives and not to treat them harshly.[40] Surely then, spousal abuse and domestic violence are sins.

In general, women who are not being abused by their husbands are not being abused because their husbands have chosen not to abuse them. Simple as that. Any man has the potential to abuse his wife at any time and vise versa. There are no guarantees. An abused wife has few options. She can encourage her husband to get counseling (which may or may not be effective and must be attended to consistently usually for a lengthy time period before results are seen), leave him and risk being murdered, or stay and keep getting abused which could also result in death. If she tries to physically fight him she won't win unless she plans on seriously disabling him in which case she might find herself in jail.

Although our focus has been on how abusive marriages effect the women who are in them, the same biblical rules apply to men who are victims of spousal abuse. A man being abused by his wife will be faced with the same biblical questions about divorce that a woman is. Should a man risk life and limb for the sake of holding a marriage together? Is it wrong for a man to divorce a woman who is threatening to kill him or his children, since there are only three biblical exceptions (which don't directly include abuse) whereby one can obtain a divorce?

When examining the issue of divorce, God doesn't have a different set of rules for men than he does for women. Therefore, there is no chauvinism on God's part when it comes to the exceptions made for divorce and remarriage. But since a substantially fewer amount of men will ever be faced with the issue of spousal abuse as opposed to women, the conservative stance that the Bible seems to take regarding the subject of divorce has the potential of negatively effecting women more so than men. But this is no fault of God. This is the fault of abusive men.

---

[39] "In the same way, you husbands must give honor to your wives. Treat her with understanding as you live together. She may be weaker than you are, but she is your equal partner in God's gift of new life. If you don't treat her as you should, your prayers will not be heard." (1 Peter 3:7 NLT)
[40] And you husbands must love your wives and never treat them harshly. (Colossians 3:19 NLT)

9.

WOMEN AND SEX

In order to talk about sex, sex must first be defined. For our purposes the operative definition of the act of sex entails one of three activities: genital sexual intercourse between a man and a woman, oral sex, and anal sex. There can be no simultaneous reciprocal genital sexual intercourse between two people of the same sex. It is physically impossible. However, two people of the same sex can engage in oral and/or anal sex.

Kissing and necking are not being included in the definition of sex, although both activities may lead to sex and may be considered sexual contact.

God makes no difference between men and women as far as what is allowed and what is prohibited when it comes to sex. However, during the dispensation of the Law[1] women were under more pressure to maintain their virginity before marriage than men were. Let's take a look:

> [13]If any man takes a wife, and goes in to her, and detests her,
> [14]and charges her with shameful conduct, and brings a bad name on her, and says, 'I took this woman, and when I came to her I found she was not a virgin,'
> [15]then the father and mother of the young woman shall take and bring out the evidence of the young woman's virginity to the elders of the city at the gate.
> [16]And the young woman's father shall say to the elders, 'I gave my daughter to this man as wife, and he detests her.
> [17]Now he has charged her with shameful conduct, saying, "I found your daughter was not a virgin," and yet these are the evidences of my daughter's virginity.'

---

[1] See Introduction

¹⁶And they shall spread the cloth before the elders of the city.

¹⁸Then the elders of that city shall take that man and punish him;

¹⁹and they shall fine him one hundred shekels of silver and give them to the father of the young woman, because he has brought a bad name on a virgin of Israel. And she shall be his wife; he cannot divorce her all his days.

²⁰"But if the thing is true, and evidences of virginity are not found for the young woman,

²¹"then they shall bring out the young woman to the door of her father's house, and the men of her city shall stone her to death with stones, because she has done a disgraceful thing in Israel, to play the harlot in her father's house. (Deuteronomy 22:13-21 NKJV)

In examining the scriptures cited above, during the dispensation of the Law, it appears that men had more sexual freedoms than women did. A woman could be stoned to death if it were discovered that she had lost her virginity before her marriage. But if her husband accused her of such, there needed to be circumstantial evidence to support the allegation. If the parents of the young woman could not convince the elders that the husband was lying or sorely mistaken, then the woman would be taken to the door of her father's house and all of the men of her city would stone her to death. This was not a law that the men of the city thought up themselves, but this was the Law that God set. If indeed the husband had been lying or mistaken,[2] his only punishment was to pay a

---

[2] Proof whether or not a man's wife had been a virgin before he married her had to do with whether or not she bled vaginally during the first time she had intercourse with her husband. If she bled then she was considered a virgin and if she did not bleed then she was not. The bleeding is caused by the breaking of the hymen (during intercourse) within the inner walls of the vagina. However, medical doctors of today have discovered that the hymens of some women are very resistant and elastic and may not break as easily. Therefore, there were certainly women in Old Testament times that were accused of not being virgins who indeed were. The method of "spreading the cloth" in order to see if there was any blood on it, was not foolproof.

fine to the father for trashing her name and to be denied the possibility of ever divorcing her. There is no indication that the same laws applied to men who were not virgins. It should be emphasized that the Mosaic Law is no longer applicable in today's dispensation of Grace[4] and that God has placed men under the same sexual prohibitions that he has placed women under.

SINGLE WOMEN AND SEX

Before the sexual revolution of the 1960s,[5] a woman who had sex before marriage was considered a "loose woman" and men looked upon her in disgust. The stigma associated with a woman who involved herself in premarital sex was similar, if not the same, as the stigma associated with prostitution.

On the other hand, it was acceptable for a man to involve himself in sex before marriage. The male sexual conquest of a woman was looked upon as a badge of honor for men and some fathers even encouraged their sons to seek the service of prostitutes as a right of passage into manhood.

It appears that such societal disparages and double standards between the sexes is what may have been the main trigger for the sexual revolution of the sixties. Society dictated that men should marry "good girls" and that "good girls" don't have sex before marriage. Consequently, a woman who allowed her boyfriend or fiancé to have sex with her often found the man resenting her afterwards and suddenly thinking negatively of her. This type of good girl/bad girl imaging was responsible for ushering in the infamous question: "will you respect me in the morning?" The question was always posed as it related to the woman and was never applied to the man.

Despite the obvious chauvinism that society has played (and still does) regarding female and male sexual roles, the question becomes

---

[4] See Introduction.

[5] It was during the hippie movement of the 1960s that America began experiencing what was called a sexual revolution whereby women and men unashamedly began living together before getting married. The societal pressures regarding women and virginity became very relaxed and women began taking on as many sexual partners and having as many sexual experiences as men were having.

whether or not God has separate expectations for single women as opposed to single men when it comes to the issue of sex. Let's take a look:

> [8]Now to the unmarried and the widows I say: It is good for them to stay unmarried, as I am. [9]But if they cannot control themselves, they should marry, for it is better to marry than to burn with passion. (1 Corinthians 7:8-9 NIV)

The same verses of scripture read in the New Living Translation of the Bible as follows:

> [8]Now I say to those who aren't married and to widows --it's better to stay unmarried, just as I am.
> [9]But if they can't control themselves, they should go ahead and marry. It's better to marry than to burn with lust.

These verses of scripture are addressed to all that are unmarried. This would include men and women who are widowed, divorced, engaged, and/or have never married. The verses particularly mention widows, probably because there may have been some pressure put upon widows[6] for them to remarry since the scriptures command that the church take care of widows (who have no immediate family to care for them) until they remarry.

Paul basically taught that it is better for both men and women to stay single. The only concession he gave for marriage was for those who could not sexually control themselves. Those who are not able to control their sexual desires or "lusts" should marry. Of course, this tells us that sex is reserved only for marriage. Otherwise, Paul would not have

---

[6] 1Timothy 5: 3-16 (see your Bible). Widows are supposed to be taken care of first by their children or grandchildren. However, if a widow has no children and is alone in the world, then she is to be taken care of by the church. One might argue that this decree only applied during Paul's time because of the cultural mores then. In today's world, many women are working and their husbands have left them much support in life insurance, so they might not need the help of the church as they would have then.

instructed those who are having a difficult time abstaining from sex to marry. Since these verses of scripture were addressed to men as well as women, we can easily conclude that the Bible does not have a separate standard for men than it does for women when it comes to premarital sex. A man is just as guilty of fornication as a woman is if he engages in sex before marriage. A woman is no guiltier of sin than a man is if she engages in premarital sex. Any man or woman who finds him or herself unable to resist sexual temptation should get married.

When examining the following verses of scripture, it appears that the decision as to whether one should get married or not has a great deal to do with the willpower one has over one's sexual urges.

> [35]I am saying this for your benefit, not to place restrictions on you. I want you to do whatever will help you serve the Lord best, with as few distractions as possible. [36]But if a man thinks he ought to marry his fiancée because he has trouble controlling his passions and time is passing, it is all right; it is not a sin. Let them marry. [37]But if he has decided firmly not to marry and there is no urgency and he can control his passion, he does well not to marry. [38]So the person who marries does well, and the person who doesn't marry does even better." (1 Corinthians 7:35-38 NLT)

Again we see that the bottom line in regards to whether or not a person should or should not get married depends on whether or not a person has enough self-control to abstain from sexual relations. It is very difficult to abstain from sex when one has romantic affections for a person and is constantly in the company of that person. Along with true romantic affections, true attraction, and love for a person comes the desire to want to make love to that person, as we have seen when looking at the Song of Songs.[7] A man and a woman who have romantic feelings for one another and are dating, are setting themselves up to be tempted of fornication if they do not either marry or stop dating. On the other hand, if they can resist temptation and control their passions then they do better not to marry (verse 38 above).

---

[7] See subheading *Song of Songs* in Chapter 6.

God's prohibition against premarital sex, as shown, applies equally to men as it does to women (verse 36 above). Men get no special consideration when it comes to sex before marriage. Although society has historically placed more pressure on women than men to remain celibate before marriage, God places the same pressures on both men and women when it comes to premarital sex. More specifically, God's command for men and women not to have premarital sex is particularly targeted towards those who are Christians. This is not to say that those who are not believers have been given the go ahead to engage in premarital sex, but the people to whom Paul was specifically speaking to about these sexual matters were Christians. This is evidenced in the following verses of scripture:

> [18]Flee from sexual immorality. All other sins a man commits are outside his body, but he who sins sexually sins against his own body. [19]Do you not know that your body is a temple of the Holy Spirit, who is in you, whom you have received from God? You are not your own; [20]you were bought with a price. Therefore honor God with your body. (1 Corinthians 6:18-20 NIV)

God does not want anyone to engage in any kind of sexual immorality, which includes, as we have seen, premarital sex. However, he specifically forbids it for those who identify themselves as Christians. Christians are those whom God has imparted his Holy Spirit to and to whom the Spirit of the Lord lives within. Therefore, it is essential that a Christian not do anything that is a sin against his or her own body. Of all the sins there are, sexual immorality is the only sin a person can commit that counts as a sin against his own body. Therefore, the word of God tells us that we should run from sexual immorality. As this relates to Christians the command to abstain from sexual immorality becomes even more frank because true Christians have the Spirit of God inside of them and are led by the Holy Spirit.[8] As verse 20 says above, Christians are bought with a price, which is the blood of Jesus.

Jesus died on the cross for all of us. Jesus sacrificed his body for all of us. Therefore we should also be willing to sacrifice our bodies for him, figuratively and literally.

---

[8] Acts 13:4-12 coupled with John 8:42-47 (see Appendix)

Not only are both Christian men and women commanded to abstain from premarital sex, but the word of God takes things a step further and directs Christians not to associate with those who call themselves Christians but at the same time practice sexual sin. Let's take a look:

> [9]When I wrote you before, I told you not to associate with people who indulge in sexual sin. [10]But I wasn't talking about unbelievers who indulge in sexual sin, or who are greedy or are swindlers or idol worshipers. You would have to leave this world to avoid people like that. [11]What I meant was that you are not to associate with anyone who claims to be a Christian yet indulges in sexual sin, or is greedy, or worships idols, or is abusive, or a drunkard, or a swindler. Don't even eat with such people. (1 Corinthians 5:9-11 NLT)

The above verses of scripture apply to both men and women. Both men and women who call themselves Christians and indulge in premarital sex or any other sexual sin are to be avoided. Again, there is no more grace in this area for a man than there is for a woman when it comes to God's word. Therefore, an unmarried Christian woman should no more become romantically involved with a man whom she knows is a fornicator than an unmarried Christian man should. As a matter of fact, according to the above verses of scripture, Christians should not even be friendly with other Christians who are engaging in premarital sex and any other type of sexual immorality. Paul makes it clear in the following verses of scripture that those Christian men and women who commit sexual sin should repent of it:

> I fear that when I come again, my God may humble me before you, and that I may have to mourn over many who previously sinned and have not repented of the impurity, sexual immorality, and licentiousness that they have practiced. (2 Corinthians 12:21 NRSV)

Paul was speaking to the Christians at the church in the city of Corinth. He informed them that he realized that many of them had not repented of the sexual immorality that they had been involved in, nor had they repented of their wantonness and eagerness for sexual pleasure[9] (licentiousness).

When we take into consideration all that has been said regarding premarital sex, we can clearly see that premarital sex is a sin and that both Christian men and women are equally instructed by God to abstain from it.

MARRIED WOMEN AND SEX

Adultery

There is no question that society scorns women who have extra marital affairs more severely than it does men who are guilty of the same offense. Once again, society practices a double standard. Although the tide might be changing a bit, adulterous men are not, in general, as severely scorned for their infidelities as women are for theirs.

The old adage that "boys will be boys" is a hard hitting double standard when it comes to the allowances made for men who are unfaithful to their wives as well as for men who engage in premarital sex. It is expected that men, in general, will engage in such things. However, it is really not expected that women will, or better put, it is not as widely accepted if they do. But let's see what the word of God says about these matters and whether or not God makes a difference between the sexes when it comes to unfaithfulness in marriage.

> [17]Do you not see that whatever goes into the mouth enters the stomach, and goes out into the sewer? [18] But what comes out of the mouth proceeds from the heart, and this is what defiles. [19]For out of the heart come evil intentions, murder, adultery, fornication, theft, false witness, slander. [20]These are what defile a person, but to eat with unwashed hands does not defile. (Matthew 15:17-20 NRSV)

During the dispensation of the Law, God forbid the Jews to eat certain animals.[10] Therefore there was some meat that couldn't be

---

[9] NIV translation of the word *licentiousness*.
[10] Leviticus 11:1-8 (see your Bible)

consumed because God had deemed it unclean. However, when Jesus began his earthly ministry, he counted all animals as clean to eat.[10] The Jews did not have to avoid certain meats or food anymore. But many of the Jews held on to the traditions of the Law. Not only did they feel that certain food was forbidden for them to eat, but customs of the time also dictated that eating with unwashed hands made a person unacceptable to God. Jesus however, emphasized that it was not something as unimportant as eating with unwashed hands that defiles a person, but instead the evil thoughts, evil words, and evil deeds that come from a person is that which instead defiles him or her.

One of the evil deeds cited in scripture is the act of adultery. Again, there are no special allowances given to either gender when it comes to adultery or any other sin, as we see from the verses of scripture cited above. Jesus made it clear that the act of adultery begins with thoughts of adultery which, initially comes from one's heart. Adultery is included in a list of sins that defile a person and make him or her unacceptable to God. Jesus placed adultery in the same league as murder, evil thoughts, all other sexual sin, theft, lying, and slander (verse 19). Let's look further:

> Marriage should be honored by all, and the marriage
> bed kept pure, for God will judge the adulterer and all
> the sexually immoral. (Hebrews 13:4 NIV)

Not only should men and women honor the sanctity of their own marriages, but everyone should honor everyone else's marriage as well. This means that it is a sin for a person to encourage another person to commit adultery. If the marriage bed is to be honored then people should have honor and respect for the marriage bed of others. The scripture says that the marriage bed should be kept pure and that the adulterer will be judged by God. The message here is that the marriage bed should be kept pure from adultery. A man should involve himself sexually with no other woman but his wife and a woman should have no other man sexually besides her husband. There are no double standards here. The command to keep the marriage bed pure applies equally to men and women alike.

During the dispensation of the Law, adultery was punishable by death. The following verses of scripture attest to this:

---

[10] Mark 7:14-23 (see Appendix)

> [10]If a man commits adultery with another man's wife--with the wife of his neighbor--both the adulterer and the adulteress must be put to death.
>
> [11]If a man sleeps with his father's wife, he has dishonored his father. Both the man and the woman must be put to death; their blood will be on their own heads.
>
> [12]If a man sleeps with his daughter-in-law, both of them must be put to death. What they have done is a perversion; their blood will be on their own heads. (Leviticus 20:10-12 NIV)

Although adultery is no longer punishable by death under the eyes of God,[12] it is apparent when reading the above verses of scripture, that God is most definitely opposed to adultery. After all, the seventh commandment given to the Jews following their exodus from Israel was God's forbidding of them to commit adultery.[13] Interestingly enough, although the Old Testament command against adultery applied to both men and women, God's Law specifically addressed men. But we know that these commandments against adultery applied to women as well.

In examining the scriptures we see that God does not tolerate adultery any more readily when committed by a man than when committed by a woman, despite the seemingly double standard of tolerance, in favor of men, that society has.

The right a woman has to sexually pursue her husband

Aside from the high tolerance that Western society has, in general, when it comes to men cheating on their wives as opposed to the low tolerance it has for women cheating on their husbands, it is also generally expected that the husband will pursue sex in the marital relationship, not the wife, and that a wife should never say "no" to her husband if he wants to have sex with her. But let's see what the word of God has to say about this by taking another look at the following verses of scripture:

---

[12] See Chapter 14.
[13] Exodus 20: 1-17 (see your Bible).

[3]The husband should not deprive his wife of sexual intimacy, which is her right as a married woman, nor should the wife deprive her husband. [4]The wife gives authority of her body over to her husband, and the husband also gives authority over his body to his wife. [5]So do not deprive each other of sexual relations. The only exception to this rule would be the agreement of both husband and wife to refrain from sexual intimacy for a limited time, so they can give themselves more completely to prayer. Afterward, they should come together again so that Satan won't be able to tempt them because of their lack of self-control. [6]This is only my suggestion. It's not an absolute rule. (1 Corinthians 7:3-6 NLT)

Married women are instructed not to deprive their husbands of sexual intimacy.[14] However, the reverse is also true. Married men are instructed not to deprive their wives of sexual intimacy, which implies that a woman can initiate sex. If a man cannot deprive his wife of sexual intimacy then it follows that he will not know whether or not he is depriving her unless she is expressing an interest in having sex with him. Therefore, it follows that there is nothing wrong with a woman initiating sex with her husband. There is no chauvinism in God's word here, since what applies to the husband applies to the wife as well.

Although verses 3 and 4 teach that neither a man nor a woman should hold sex back from their spouse, this directive specifically applies in reference to the withholding of sex for long periods of time and does not mean that a man or a woman cannot occasionally refuse the sexual advances of his or her spouse. But not all theologians would agree and a detailed discussion of this is taken up in Chapter 8 under the subheading, *Rape and Sexual Abuse in Marriage.*

Unfortunately many men, when attempting to coerce their wives into having sex with them on a day when she might not want to, look past the scriptures that say that a man should love his wife as Christ loved the church and pull out the scriptures that say a woman is to submit to her husband. In doing so, he is using the verses of scripture that speak of a woman subjecting herself to her husband as a "trump card" of sorts or as

---

[14] For a more detailed discussion of this see Chapter 8.

a weapon against her. He has abused his position of power in the relationship and has established an oppressive rule over his wife in the home when it comes to sex by using the scriptures as a tool to coerce her to make love to him when she doesn't want to. If sex is to be a mutual endeavor between husband and wife, then there is no "rule" in the marital bedroom. In general, both husband and wife are to strive equally to sexually satisfy one another and while neither should deprive the other of sex on a continuous basis, each should try to respect the occasional times when the other may not be up to making love, for whatever the reason.

In getting back to the main point, there is no question that the Bible teaches that women have the same right to sexually pursue their husbands as men do to sexually pursue their wives. Of course we should keep in mind that a woman should also be willing to respect an occasional resistance from her husband, as he should be willing to respect from her. Upon previous examination of the Song of Songs,[15] Solomon depicted the wife as being just as sexually charged as her husband was. Women who desire sex just as much as men are usually labeled nymphomaniacs in American society. As a matter of fact, the term *nymphomaniac* applies only to women and not to men. There is no word that has been coined specifically for men who have excessive sexual drives. Men who have excessive sex drives are said to have a *sexual addiction.* Although the label of *sexual addiction* has been applied to women as well as men, it is mostly associated with men. It is interesting to note that society has labeled a man that has an excessive sex drive as having an "addiction" and a woman with an excessive sex drive as being a "maniac." When looking at this kind of labeling alone it is plain to see that society still has a difficult time accepting the fact that women are just as sexual as men are. The word *maniac* has a much more negative connotation to it than the word *addiction* has. But in the marital bed, there is no such thing as a nymphomaniac because God has allowed a woman to be just as sexually expressive and desirous as he has allowed her husband to be. There is no chauvinism in God's word here.

WOMEN AND MASTURBATION

For the purposes of this book, although not all would agree,

---

[15] See Chapter 6.

masturbation[15] is not included in the definition of sex. Masturbation is in a league of its own. Masturbation is a sexual activity but it is not sex, just as heavy kissing is a sexual activity, but it is not sex. Instead, masturbation is genital stimulation that can bring a person to orgasm, but it is no more sex than a "wet dream"[16] is. How could it be when there is only "one flesh" participating, and not two?[17] In the Bible, all sexual immorality has been described as sinful sexual relations between at least two beings. Again, our operative definition of sex entails one of three activities: genital sexual intercourse between a man and a woman, oral sex, and anal sex. Therefore, masturbation cannot be included in the definition of sex since, in general, only one person is participating and there is no body to body intercourse of any kind. Dr. David Rueben, author of *Everything you always wanted to know about Sex, but were afraid to Ask,* defines masturbation as "sexual stimulation designed to produce an orgasm through any means except sexual intercourse."[18]

The purpose of masturbation is to bring oneself to orgasm instead of having a partner do it. Dr. Rueben says that it is a "substitute form of gratification when sexual intercourse is impossible."[19] However, having an orgasm does not necessarily mean one has had sex. Ask any man who's ever had a wet dream and he'd probably agree. A man or boy who has had a wet dream usually wakes up feeling as if he would like to have sex, not as if he's had sex. He has had an orgasm, but if you were to ask him, he would certainly say that he has not had sex.

---

[15] Genital self stimulation in the quest to achieve an orgasm.

[16] Colloquial phrase used to define involuntary ejaculation while asleep.

[17] And He answered and said to them, "Have you not read that He who made them in the beginning 'made them male and female,' "and said, 'For this reason a man shall leave his father and mother and be joined to his wife, and the two shall become one flesh? (Matthew 19:4-5 NKJV) Do you not know that your bodies are members of Christ himself? Shall I then take the members of Christ and unite them with a prostitute? Never! Do you not know that he who unites himself with a prostitute is one with her in body? For it is said, "The two will become one flesh. But he who unites himself with the Lord is one with him in spirit. (1 Corinthians 6:15-17 NIV)

[18] Taken from *Everything you always wanted to know about Sex, but were afraid to Ask* by David Rueben, M.D., copyright © 1999, original copyright © 1969 by HarperCollins. paperback edition p. 180, Fair use.

[19] Ibid., p. 181. Fair use.

On the other hand, not having an orgasm doesn't necessarily mean that one has not had sex. There are many women who are actively engaging in sexual intercourse who have a difficult time reaching an orgasm. This does not mean that they didn't have sex. It only means that they had sex and for any multitude of reasons, were not sexually satisfied.

It has taken a while for Western society to accept the fact that women are just as sexual as men are. Before the sexual revolution of the sixties, women who actually enjoyed sex were looked down upon. American society (especially between the 1600s and mid 1900s) had labeled it taboo for whom it called "sophisticated women" to enjoy sex. If a man decided to get married, he made every attempt to marry a woman whom society would deem as a "sophisticated woman" or more modernly put, "the girl next door." Again, part of the definition of "the girl next door" was a woman who did not enjoy sex. Since it was taboo for wives to enjoy sex, men did not take the time to try to satisfy their wives. Wives were to engage in sex with their husbands only for reproductive reasons, not for enjoyment. Men were therefore expected to get their steady diet of sex elsewhere, either from their mistresses, a prostitute, or their slaves. Again, it was not until the sexual revolution of the sixties coupled with the 1969 publication of Dr. Rueben's book, that female sexual satisfaction was seen as an important part of love making in the West.

According to Dr. Rueben, almost every person on the earth has masturbated at some point in his or her life. It is very common for children as early as aged 6 to begin masturbating. At this early stage in their lives they begin to have sexual sensations but have not yet reached the point where masturbation brings with it an orgasm. Masturbation that brings about an orgasm usually occurs during puberty.

It is estimated that 70% of adult women masturbate (this includes married as well as single women) and that 55% of women, who are sexually active, fake sexual orgasm on a consistent basis. It is also estimated that 43% of women suffer from some kind of sexual dysfunction. These statistics include married women.

If a woman is masturbating, then more than likely she is not having sex as often as she'd like, and/or she is not being fulfilled during sexual activity, or she is not sexually active at all. The common thought that only those who are celibate masturbate, is a fallacy. There are many sexually active people (including married people) who masturbate and many celibate people who do not.

321

The Bible is silent when it comes to the issue of masturbation. There is no clear indication that masturbation in and of itself is a sin. However, the Bible does speak against lust, and most adults who masturbate must trigger the stimulation they are giving themselves by fantasizing about something lustful. So let's take a look at what the Bible says about lust.

> [27]Ye have heard that it was said by them of old time, Thou shalt not commit adultery:
> [28]But I say unto you, That whosoever looketh on a woman to lust after her committed adultery with her already in his heart. (Matthew 5:27-28)

Jesus is speaking in the above verses of scripture. It was Jesus who said that to even look at someone and lust after him or her is a sin. Of course this was specifically addressed to men who were lusting after married women. Apparently there were those who felt proud in the fact that they had never involved themselves in an adulterous affair with another man's wife. But many of these prideful men, although innocent of committing the act of adultery itself were guilty of having lustful fantasies about certain married women. Jesus told the men that having these fantasies of adultery was just as wrong as committing the act itself. Therefore, lustful thoughts are sinful thoughts and lustful thoughts, in general, almost always accompany the act of masturbation. This in turn makes the act of masturbating a sin in which lust is involved. Let's look further:

> Let no sin therefore reign in your mortal body, that ye should obey it in the lusts thereof. (Romans 6:12)

We should not obey the lustful urges of our bodies. Of course, these urges are often triggered by what we think about in our minds. Our minds are a function of our brain, which is a part of our body. The mind is also what the Bible symbolically refers to as the heart. What one really thinks and how one really feels, is what is in one's heart. Jesus addresses this in the following verses of scripture:

> [13]You cannot be the slave of two masters. You will like one more than the other or be more loyal to one than

322

to the other. You cannot serve God
and money.

[14]The Pharisees really loved money. So when they
heard what Jesus said, they made fun of him. [15]But
Jesus told them:

You are always making yourselves look
good, but God sees what is in your
heart. The things that most people think
are important are worthless as far as
God is concerned. (Luke 16:13-15
CEV)

God knows what is in our hearts. Therefore, he knows what we are
thinking. He is aware of any fantasy we have ever had. We cannot hide
these things from God. Therefore, we should try not to think in lustful or
perverted ways. Job knew this all too well. The Old Testament book of
Job tells about the life of a man named Job who was considered by God
to be blameless. Verse 1 of the first book of Job describes him as
*"blameless, a man of complete integrity. He feared God and stayed away
from evil."*[21]

In regards to lustful thoughts and actions, Job, a man of complete
integrity, said the following:

I made a covenant with my eyes not to look with lust
upon a young woman. (Job 31:1 NLT)

[7]If I have strayed from his pathway, or if my heart has
lusted for what my eyes have seen, or if I am guilty of
any other sin, [8]then let someone else harvest the crops I
have planted, and let all that I have planted be
uprooted.
[9]If my heart has been seduced by a woman, or if I
have lusted for my neighbor's wife, [10]then may my wife
belong to another man; may other men sleep with her.
[11]For lust is a shameful sin, a crime that should be
punished. [12]It is a devastating fire that destroys to hell.
It would wipe out everything I own. (Job 31:7-12 NLT)

---

[21] NLT

In verse 7, Job says that if he lusts in his heart for what he has seen with his eyes then he has committed sin. In verse 9 he takes things even further by declaring that a suitable punishment for one who lusts after another man's wife would be that his own wife run off with other men. Job is not sanctioning adultery on the part of his wife by saying this. He is instead saying that the act of sexually fantasizing about another man's wife is such a shameful thing that if he were to do so, he would deserve the emotional pain of being a victim of adultery if his wife were to involve herself in an extra marital affair.

Verse 1 teaches us that, men should strive not to even look upon a woman with lust in their eyes. Of course, the same would apply for women. With this said, one can safely say that one should not even look lustfully upon pictures of women (or men). It doesn't matter that what is being looked at is in a picture. Looking and lusting, is looking and lusting, no matter if the one doing it is looking at a picture, the television, or an actual person.

There is no difference made between men and women when it comes to the scriptural commands against lusting. Therefore, no difference is made between men and women when examining the subject of masturbation. It would seem that since the Bible is silent on the issue of masturbation itself, that it is arguable whether or not the act of masturbation performed without lust is a sin. Some adults are able to masturbate and bring themselves to orgasm without engaging in lustful or perverted thoughts. For them, the physical stimulation itself is enough. But there is no question that masturbation that involves lustful or perverted thoughts is a sin. Regardless, neither gender is given any greater grace nor latitude when it comes to issues of masturbation coupled with lustful and/or perverted thoughts.

LESBIANISM

A Lesbian is a woman who engages in sexual relations with another woman. She is a female homosexual. Homosexuals are people who are sexually attracted to other people of the same sex. Therefore, homosexuals include men and women. Although society at large has become increasingly accepting of homosexuality, God is not accepting of it at all. Let's take a look:

>²²You shall not lie with a male as with a woman; it is
>an abomination. ²³You shall not have sexual relations
>with any animal and defile yourself with it, nor shall
>any woman give herself to an animal to have sexual
>relations with it: it is perversion.
>
>²⁴Do not defile yourselves in any of these ways, for
>by all these practices the nations I am casting out before
>you have defiled themselves. ²⁵Thus the land became
>defiled; and I punished it for its iniquity, and the land
>vomited out its inhabitants. (Leviticus 18:22-25 NSRV)

After God (through Moses) delivered the Jews from slavery at the hands of the Egyptians, he set forth certain rules that the Jews were to follow. Many of the rules set forth had to do with what God deemed as appropriate and inappropriate sexual behavior. As we can see from the verses of scripture quoted above, men were forbidden to lie down with a man as a man lies down with a woman. In other words, God forbade men to have sex with men. Of course, the command not to engage in same-sex sexual relations applied to women as well. God sees homosexuality as detestable, an abomination.

Not only did God forbid homosexual relations but he also forbid bestiality (the act of having sex with an animal). It is a perversion. God speaks about homosexuality in the same context that he speaks about bestiality. Both acts are an abomination and are detestable to God.

Verse 24 sums up the matter. In this verse, we see that the Jews are commanded not to defile themselves in such ways, neither with homosexual behavior, sexual behaviors involving animals, or in any of the other sexual immoral behaviors that are listed in the 18ᵗʰ chapter of Leviticus.²²

Some would argue that the commands that God gave to the Jews against homosexual behavior were specifically for the Jews and that they only applied during the dispensation of the Law. However, the following verses of scripture refute those arguments:

>¹⁸From heaven God shows how angry he is with all
>the wicked and evil things that sinful people do to crush
>the truth. ¹⁹They know everything that can be known

---

²² Leviticus 18:1-24, Leviticus 20:1-21 (see your Bible)

about God, because God has shown it all to them
[20]God's eternal power and character cannot be seen.
But from the beginning of creation, God has shown
what these are like by all he has made. That's why
those people don't have any excuse. [21]They know about
God, but they don't honor him or even thank him.
[22]They claim to be wise, but they are fools. [23]They
don't worship the glorious and eternal God. Instead,
they worship idols that are made to look like humans
who cannot live forever, and like birds, animals, and
reptiles.

[24]So God let these people go their own way. They
did what they wanted to do, and their filthy thoughts
made them do shameful things with their bodies. [25]They
gave up the truth about God for a lie, and they
worshiped God's creation instead of God, who will be
praised forever. Amen.

[26]God let them follow their own evil desires.
Women no longer wanted to have sex in a natural way,
and they did things with each other that were not
natural. [27]Men behaved in the same way. They stopped
wanting to have sex with women and had strong desires
for sex with other men. They did shameful things with
each other, and what has happened to them is
punishment for their foolish deeds. [28]Since these people
refused even to think about God, he let their useless
minds rule over them. That's why they do all sorts of
indecent things. [29]They are evil, wicked, and greedy, as
well as mean in every possible way. They want what
others have, and they murder, argue, cheat, and are
hard to get along with. They gossip, [30]say cruel things
about others, and hate God. They are proud, conceited,
and boastful, always thinking up new ways to do evil.
These people don't respect their parents. [31]They are
stupid, unreliable, and don't have any love or pity for
others. [32]They know God has said that anyone who acts
this way deserves to die. But they keep on doing evil
things, and they even encourage others to do them.
(Romans 1:18-32 CEV)

The scripture text is referring to all people who are sinful and "crush the truth" (verse 18) and to those who "give up the truth about God for a lie"(verse 25). The New Living Translation of the Bible translates the phrase as "push the truth away from themselves." Therefore these verses apply in this day and time and are referring to people as they are in today's world. Verses 23 and 24 tells us that because men and women insisted on worshipping idols made to look like people or animals God let them go ahead and do whatever they wanted to do. He didn't try to stop these people who insisted on doing wicked things. Eventually their wickedness progressed and they began to involve themselves in homosexual acts.

As is clearly stated in the scriptures, homosexuality is just as sinful an act for a man to engage in as it is for a woman to engage in. It, among other sins listed in verses 29 through 31, is a sin in which those who commit it deserve to die (verse 32). This deserved death is not a death penalty[22] that men enforce through governmental means by way of execution, but instead, a death penalty that refers to the biblical doctrine of death that says that sin will and can eventually lead to physical death and/or spiritual death.[23] But though all of us have deserved death at some point in our lives (because of the sins we have committed), God has been gracious enough to spare us. Here is a final look at what the Bible says about homosexuality, be it a man or a woman (lesbian) who is committing the act:

> [9]Don't you know that evil people won't have a share in the blessings of God's kingdom? Don't fool yourselves! No one who is immoral or worships idols or is unfaithful in marriage or is a pervert or behaves like a homosexual [10]will share in God's kingdom. Neither will any thief or greedy person or drunkard or anyone who

---

[22] See argument against capital punishment in Appendix under Chapter 13.

[23] " In those days, when you were slaves of sin, you weren't concerned with doing what was right. And what was the result? It was not good, since now you are ashamed of the things you used to do, things that end in eternal doom. But now you are free from the power of sin and have become slaves of God. Now you do those things that lead to holiness and result in eternal life. For the wages of sin is death, but the free gift of God is eternal life through Christ Jesus our Lord." (Romans 6:20-23 NLT)

curses and cheats others. ¹¹Some of you used to be like that. But now the name of our Lord Jesus Christ and the power of God's spirit have washed you and made you holy and acceptable to God. (1 Corinthians 6:9-11 CEV)

PROSTITUTION

Prostitution is the act whereby a person has sex for money. Prostitution is also defined as any corrupt action that is carried out in order to achieve financial gain. In society, prostitution is generally associated with women. However, the Bible associates prostitution with men, as well as with women.

The word *gigolo* is used to refer to a male prostitute. *Gigolo* is also used to refer to a man who lives off the income of a woman. Therefore, all gigolos are not necessarily prostitutes, but all male prostitutes are gigolos. Any able-bodied man who refuses to work and instead lives off the income of a woman that he is sexually involved with, is a gigolo. Let's take a look at what the scriptures have to say about prostitution:

> Do not prostitute thy daughter, to cause her to be a whore; lest the land fall to whoredom, and the land become full of wickedness. (Leviticus 19:29)

God specifically commanded men not to prostitute their daughters. It was a sin, and still is a sin, for a man to force or coerce his daughter to have sex for money.

> ¹⁷None of the daughters of Israel shall be a temple prostitute; none of the sons of Israel shall be a temple prostitute. ¹⁸You shall not bring the fee of a prostitute or the wages of a male prostitute into the house of the LORD your God in payment for any vow, for both of these are abhorrent to the LORD your God. (Deuteronomy 23:17-18 NSRV)

During ancient times there were many heathen nations who allowed prostitution to take place within their shrines and places of worship.

These prostitutes were referred to as temple prostitutes or shrine prostitutes. God did not want his people to take on these ways and therefore he commanded the Israelites not to become shrine prostitutes. The money of a prostitute was no good in the house of the Lord. The command not to prostitute oneself was not only given to women but to men. Apparently there were many men who were prostituting themselves just as women were. Let's take a further look:

¹The LORD gave Moses these instructions for Aaron's sons, the priests:

Touching a dead body will make you unclean. So don't go near a dead relative, ²except your mother, father, son, daughter, brother, ³or an unmarried sister, who has no husband to take care of her. ⁴Don't make yourself unclean by attending the funeral of someone related to you by marriage. ⁵Don't shave any part of your head or trim your beard or cut yourself to show that you are mourning. ⁶I am the LORD your God, and I have chosen you alone to offer sacrifices of food to me on the altar. That's why you must keep your selves holy. ⁷Don't marry a divorced woman or a woman who has served as a temple prostitute. You are holy, ⁸because I am holy. And so, you must be treated with proper respect, since you offer food sacrifices to me, the God of holiness.

⁹If any of you priests has a daughter who disgraces you by serving as a temple prostitute, she must be burned to death.

¹⁰If you are the high priest, you must not mess up your hair or tear your clothes in order to mourn for the dead. ¹¹Don't make yourself unclean by going near a dead body, not even that of your own father or mother. ¹²If you leave the sacred place to attend a funeral, both you and the sacred place become unclean, because you are the high priest.

¹³If you are the high priest, you must marry only a virgin ¹⁴from your own tribe. Don't marry a divorced woman or any other woman who has already had sex, including a temple prostitute. ¹⁵In this way, your

descendants will be qualified to serve me. Remember—
I am the LORD, and I have chosen you.

[16]The LORD told Moses [17-18]to say to Aaron: No
descendant of yours can ever serve as my priest if he is
blind or lame, if his face is disfigured, if one leg is
shorter than the other, [19]if either a foot or a hand is
crippled, [20]if he is a hunchback or a dwarf, if an eye or
his skin is deceased, or if his testicles have been
damaged. [21]These men may not serve as my priests and
burn sacrifices to me. [22]They may eat the food offerings
presented to me, [23]but they may not enter the sacred
place or serve me at the altar. Remember—I am the
LORD, the one who makes a priest holy.

[24]Moses told all of this to Aaron, his sons, and the
people of Israel. (Leviticus chapter 21, CEV)

Those who were priests in the nation of Israel were under very strict
rules because all of Israel had to go through the priests in order to offer
up any sacrifices to the Lord God when they wanted to give a burnt
offering for atonement of sin, a grain offering as an act of worship, a
fellowship offering as a way to thank God, a sin offering for
unintentional sins, and a guilt offering for other certain unintentional
sins. The priests were the ones designated by God to offer sacrifices on
behalf of all of the other Israelites.[25] All but the grain offerings were
blood sacrifices. The other offerings required the killing of certain
animals and birds including bulls, rams, goats, and pigeons. God only
allowed men from the tribe of Levite to become priests. The Levite tribe
was the tribe in which Aaron and his descendants belonged. Only the
priests could enter the innermost sanctuary of the temple of God to give
the offerings. This innermost part was called the *Holy of Holies.* Any
Israelite in need of giving an offering to the Lord God had to go through
a priest in order to do so. Therefore, out of all the people in Israel, the
priests were the ones who God allowed to get the closest to him. Because
of this, a priest had to make certain that he was ceremonially clean
before he entered the Holy of Holies to approach God.

Part of the ceremonial cleansing of a priest (verse 1, 2) meant that he
was not to touch any dead body unless it was the body of a close relative

---

[25] Leviticus chapters 1 through 7 (see your Bible).

which could only include his mother, father, son, daughter, brother or virgin sister. The verse explains that what made his sister a virgin was the fact that she had no husband. It is assumed then that if the sister were married, her husband would have been the one to aid in the burial preparation of her body, not the priest. No rule regarding virginity applied to the priest's dead brother.

In order for the priests to be ceremonially clean, it was also forbidden of them to shave their heads or trim their beards. Neither were they allowed to cut their bodies in any way.

The high priest was the chief priest who was in charge of all of the other priests. The high priest could not go near a dead person even if it were his father or mother and he was also not allowed to go to his mother's or father's funeral. While all of the assistant priests could at least marry a widow, the high priest had to marry a virgin. He could not marry a widow, a divorced woman, or any woman that had ever been a prostitute.

When looking at the role of the priest during those days, some women might feel that it was unfair of God to never have called a woman to the priesthood. However, when taking into account the fact that the high priest was very limited in who he could marry and that he was prohibited from attending the funerals of any of his close relatives, it seems to put in perspective any priesthood argument that could be used to label God a chauvinist. There were certain serious consequences to being a priest which many men as well as women in today's world would not really be willing to live up to. Furthermore, only the men from the Levite tribe could be priests. This left out all other men from any of the other 11 tribes. Therefore, most men were left out from obtaining the priesthood, as well.

Our focus is mostly on verse 9 that says that a priest's daughter who became a prostitute was to be put to death. Not only was a priest to maintain a certain character and holiness but his family was also to maintain a certain holiness lifestyle as well. Any priestly family member who committed sin was likely to leave a spiritual blemish on the priest, because God saw the family as a unit and he sees men and women who are married as one flesh. As far as God was concerned, prostitution in the family of a priest left a huge spiritual blemish on the priest and his family. God's way of removing the blemish was to remove the person who was responsible for the blemish: hence the execution of the daughter turned prostitute.

In giving his commands to the priest, God makes his point that he wants neither the priest to have any spiritual defects nor the priest's family to have any spiritual defects. The Levite men who had physical blemishes could not serve as priests. This included those men who were crippled, deformed, facially disfigured, hump backed, or dwarfed. It also included men who had damaged skin, damaged testicles, or one leg shorter than the other. As a whole, no one but the priest could go near God to offer sacrifices and again, the priest could not have any blemish. Although this sounds as if God was being unfair or mean-spirited, he was not. This was God's way of preparing people for the ultimate sacrifice of Jesus Christ who was to die on the cross and who would be referred to in scripture as the unblemished Lamb of God. Jesus was sinless. There was no defect in him. The Old Testament sacrifices and burnt offerings to God were examples of what was to come. And what was to come was the ultimate sacrificial offering, Jesus Christ. Furthermore, Jesus is now considered our High Priest and in order to be cleansed of sin we must go through him.[25] The criteria for the priest was a foreshadowing of what was to be revealed in the life of Jesus. Jesus is the one and only High Priest who could have atoned for our sins because he had no sin and therefore had no blemish. The high priest of Old Testament times was to be an example of the High Priest (Jesus Christ) of New Testament times and therefore, neither the priest nor certain members of his family could have any physical blemish or lingering uncleanness because Jesus was sinless and had no spiritual blemish.

Some might also say that it was unfair of God to single out the daughter turned prostitute for execution when no man was singled out. However, it must be remembered that many of the commands God gave to Moses to give to the Jews after their exodus from Egypt were symbolic representations of what was to ultimately come. Jesus is now our High Priest and we therefore have no need for any other priest. Jesus is now the mediator between God and ourselves. He is our high priest as opposed to the mere men who served priestly functions in days past.[26]

---

[25] Hebrews 4:12-16, Hebrews 5:1-10, Hebrews chapters 7, 8, and 10 (see your Bible)

[26] "And what God wants is for us to be made holy by the sacrifice for the body of Jesus Christ once and for all. Under the old covenant, the priest stands before the altar day after day, offering sacrifices that can never take away sins. But our High Priest offered himself to God as one sacrifice for sins, good for all time.

On the same token, one who practices prostitution (among many other sins) without repentance, whether it is a man or woman, is doomed to burn in the everlasting fires of hell. So the burning of the early Israelite daughter of a priest who became a prostitute represents the ultimate punishment that has been set forth for both men and women who practice such an act. 1st Corinthians 6:9-11 supports this. Let's take a look at these verses again, but this time we'll examine how the verses of scripture are rendered in the New International Version of the Bible:

> 9Do you not know that the wicked will not inherit the kingdom of God? Do not be deceived: Neither the sexually immoral nor idolaters nor adulterers nor male prostitutes nor homosexual offenders 10nor thieves nor the greedy nor drunkards nor slanderers nor swindlers will inherit kingdom of God. 11And that is what some of you were. But you were washed, you were sanctified, you were justified in the name of the Lord Jesus Christ and by the Spirit of our God.

Verse 9 refers to male prostitution. Men and women alike, who are sexually immoral (including those who engage in prostitution, fornication, bestiality, adultery, homosexuality), alcoholics, slanderers (verbal abusers) and scam artists, will not inherit the kingdom of God. And those who don't make it to heaven are going to hell. In today's dispensation of Grace, no difference is made between men and women.

SUMMARY

During Old Testament times there was much pressure for the women of God to remain virgins until marriage. This pressure to remain celibate until marriage did not seem to apply as dogmatically to men as it did to women. However, the Mosaic Laws set forth in the book of Leviticus clearly forbid men from trying to seduce their mothers, step mothers, sisters, granddaughters, step daughters, aunts, daughters-in-law, sisters-in-law, and any one else's wife. Consequently, a man was only to have

Then he sat down at the place of highest honor at God's right hand." (Hebrews 10:10-14 NLT)

sex with his own wife, just as a woman was only to have sex with her own husband.

When it comes to prohibitions against homosexuality, adultery, bestiality, fornication, and the like, God makes no difference between men and women. It is just as sinful for a man to involve himself in these sexual sins as it is a woman.

There is no question that God wants men to be just as sexually pure as he wants women to be. Although ancient Hebrew women were under stricter rules regarding sex, and although today's society (in general) is more lenient when it comes to the sexual sins of men, God has made it clear, that there are no differences in the consequences of sexual sin in today's dispensation of Grace,[28] whether the sinner is a man or a woman. There is no gender discrimination in God's word here and thus, there is no chauvinism on God's part associated with these issues.

---

[28] See Introduction.

10.

FEMALE VICTIMS OF RAPE

By Law, sexual intercourse is defined as male genital to female genital penetration no matter how slight the penetration is. Sodomy and oral sex are classified as deviant sexual intercourse if the acts occur between non-married parties. And sexual contact is defined as including all or one of these three: intimate touching, caressing, and fondling.

A sexual offense occurs if the perpetrator of a sexual act has not obtained consent of the person upon which that act has been carried out. People who are automatically deemed as incapable of consent, when it comes to legalities, are those persons under seventeen years of age, those with a mental defect, those who are mentally incapacitated, those who are physically helpless, those who are hospitalized (whether for physical or mental reasons), and those who are imprisoned.

A man is guilty of rape in the first degree when he engages in sexual intercourse with a woman by force, when he engages in sexual intercourse with a woman who is physically helpless, or when he engages in sexual intercourse with a child ten years of age or younger.[1] A man is guilty of rape in the second degree when he engages in sexual intercourse with a female who is less than fourteen years old, but older than ten years. A man is guilty of rape in the third degree when he engages in sexual intercourse with a woman who is mentally defective or disabled, imprisoned, or hospitalized, or when he being twenty-one years of age or older engages in sexual intercourse with a female who is under seventeen years of age.

A man is guilty of sodomy in the first degree when he engages in deviate sexual intercourse (anal and/or oral sex) with a woman by force, when he engages in deviate sexual intercourse with a woman who is physically helpless, or when he engages in deviate sexual intercourse with a child under the age of eleven.

A man is guilty of sexual abuse in the first degree when he engages in sexual contact with a woman by force, when he engages in sexual contact

---

[1] Laws vary from state to state. These profiles are according to Article 130 of the New York State Laws.

with a woman who is physically helpless, or when he engages in sexual contact with a child who is ten years old or younger.

A man is guilty of aggravated sexual abuse in the first degree when he inserts a foreign object in the vagina, urethra, or rectum of a woman by force and this act causes physical injury to the woman, when he does the same to a woman who is physically helpless and this act causes physical injury to the woman, or when he does the same to a child who is ten years old or younger and this act causes physical injury to the child. A man is guilty of aggravated sexual abuse in the second degree when he inserts his finger into the vagina of a woman by force, when he does the same to a woman who is physically helpless, or when he does the same to a child who is ten years old or younger. A man is guilty of aggravated sexual abuse in the third degree when he inserts a foreign object in the vagina, urethra, or rectum of a woman by force, with no injury resulting, when he does the same to a woman who is physically helpless, with no injury resulting, and when he does the same to a child who is ten years old or younger, with no injury resulting.

Although the legal definition of rape and sexual abuse may vary slightly from state to state, the aforementioned definitions basically encompass general definitions.

For the purposes of our discussion, the operative definition of rape is the same as the definition of both rape and sodomy in the first degree, regardless of the age of the victim. Because rape is a crime in which sexual intercourse is forced upon an unwilling participant, it is the most violating of crimes. It can also be categorized as a sin of fornication. Fornication is any sexual behavior that occurs outside the sanctity of a marriage.[2] The Bible is not silent when it comes to the subject of rape. Let's take a look:

> [23]If there is a girl who is a virgin engaged to a man,
> and another man finds her in the city and lies with her,
> [24]then you shall bring them both out to the gate of that
> city and you shall stone them to death; the girl, because
> she did not cry out in the city, and the man, because he
> has violated his neighbor's wife. Thus you shall purge
> the evil from among you.

---

[2] This is not to say that rape does not occur in marriage. It does. See Chapter 8.

> [25]But if in the field the man finds the girl who is
> engaged, and the man forces her and lies with her, then
> only the man who lies with her shall die.
> [26]But you shall do nothing to the girl; there is no sin in
> the girl worthy of death, for just as a man rises against
> his neighbor and murders him, so is this case.
> [27]When he found her in the field, the engaged girl cried
> out, but there was no one to save her. (Deuteronomy
> 22:23-27 NASB)

During the dispensation of the Law[3] certain sins were punishable by
death. Rape was one of those sins. Verses 23 and 24 are not speaking of
an instance of rape but instead an instance in which two consenting adults
engaged in sexual intercourse. However, the girl who had the sex was
engaged. During these times, an engagement was synonymous to a
marriage. Verse 24 says that the girl was to be stoned to death because
she did not cry out and that the man was to be stoned to death because he
violated his neighbor's wife. The fact that the girl did not cry out gives
indication that the girl was a willing participant in the sexual event.

Verse 25 goes on to give an example of the rape of a girl or woman.
According to God's law at the time, the rapist was to be put to death for
his crime. His crime of rape was compared to that of murder. A man
who rapes his neighbor's wife is just as guilty as a man who murders his
neighbor's wife. By raping her he has violated his neighbor's wife and
has therefore violated her husband as well because scripture says that a
man's body belongs to his wife and a woman's body belongs to her
husband. The two are one flesh.[4]   When considering the verses of
scripture cited above, we see that the rapist was to be put to death, but
the girl who he had raped was deemed innocent. During the rape, she
cried out but there was no one there to save her. In the scenario, God did
not fault the girl for being raped. God does not blame the victim.

There are specific historical accounts of rape documented in the Bible
that gives us a good idea of how God feels about rape and how he
responds to it. We will examine the account of the rape of Dinah, the
rape of the Levite man's concubine, the near rape of Lot's daughters, the
rape of Tamar, and the issue of rape in times of war. The aim is to

---

[3] See Introduction
[4] Ephesians 5:28-31 (see your Bible).

examine biblical events that show that God does not shrug his shoulders at the rape of women and neither does he blame women for having had been raped.

BIBLICAL ACCOUNTS OF RAPE

The rape of Dinah

The rape of Dinah is the first account of rape that is presented in the Bible. Let's take a look at the account:

> [1]Now Dinah the daughter of Leah, whom she had borne to Jacob, went out to visit the daughters of the land.
> [2]And when Shechem the son of Hamor the Hivite, the prince of the land, saw her, he took her and lay with her by force.
> [3]And he was deeply attracted to Dinah the daughter of Jacob, and he loved the girl and spoke tenderly to her.
> [4]So Shechem spoke to his father Hamor, saying, "Get me this young girl for a wife."(Genesis 34:1-4 NASB)

Shechem was a Hivite. The Hivites worshipped pagan gods. Therefore Shechem belonged to a nation of people who turned their faces against God. When reading the verses of scripture above, it appears that Shechem had no remorse about raping Dinah. This may have been because he was a prince and therefore may have been accustomed to getting whatever he wanted. Although the scriptures say that Shechem loved Dinah, he apparently did not know how to show his love. To add insult to injury, he proceeded to try to woo Dinah with tender words after he had raped her. Moreover, he commanded his father to bring Dinah to him so he could marry her. Shechem was indeed an arrogant man who abused the power of his authority. Let's continue with the account:

> [5]Now Jacob heard that he had defiled Dinah his daughter; but his sons were with his livestock in the field, so Jacob kept silent until they came in.
> [6]Then Hamor the father of Shechem went out to Jacob to speak with him.

> [7]Now the sons of Jacob came in from the field when they heard it; and the men were grieved, and they were very angry because he had done a disgraceful thing in Israel by lying with Jacob's daughter, for such a thing ought not to be done.
> [8]But Hamor spoke with them, saying, "The soul of my son Shechem longs for your daughter; please give her to him in marriage.
> [9]And intermarry with us; give your daughters to us, and take our daughters for yourselves.
> [10]Thus you shall live with us, and the land shall be open before you; lie and trade in it, and acquire property in it." (Genesis 34:5-10 NASB)

Jacob was a Jew who was temporarily living in a land inhabited by the Canaanites and Perizzites. These nations worshipped false gods. The reference to intermarrying in verse 9 has to do with the fact that Jacob did not worship the same God as the other nations of people who resided in the city of Shechem (which was in the land of Canaan). The reference to intermarrying had nothing to do with the color of one's skin as it does in today's world but instead had to do with one's religious background, which usually tied into one's nationality. God does not care if men and women of different colors marry one another, but he does not want Christians to marry those who are not Christians.[5] God felt the same way about the matter before the advent of Christ. He did not want those who worshipped him to marry those who worshipped false gods.

In his attempt to make amends for what his son had done and also in an attempt to give his son the woman of his desires, Hamor asked Dinah's brothers to give her to his son in marriage and in return he'd hand his daughters over to them for marriage. Hamor also promised that if the sons of Jacob went along with this arrangement, they could also

---

[5] "Be not unequally yoked together with unbelievers: for what fellowship hath righteousness with unrighteousness? and what communion hath light with darkness? And what concord hath Christ with Belial? or what part hath he that believeth with an infidel? And what agreement hath the temple of God with idols? for ye are the temple of the living God; as God hath said, I will dwell in them, and walk in them; and I will be their God, and they shall be my people." (2 Corinthians 6:14-16)

live in the land permanently, trade in it, and acquire property. From the tone of the scripture, it appears as if Hamor was trying to bribe the sons of Jacob in order that they would be more inclined to give Dinah away. However, verse 7 tells us that the sons of Jacob where very angry and grieved when they heard that Shechem had raped their sister. Let's continue with the account:

> [11]Shechem also said to her father and to her brothers, "If I find favor in your sight, then I will give whatever you say to me.
> [12]"Ask me ever so much bridal payment and gift, and I will give according as you say to me; but give me the girl in marriage."
> [13]But Jacob's sons answered Shechem and his father Hamor, with deceit, and spoke to them, because he had defiled Dinah their sister.
> [14]And they said to them, "We cannot do this thing, to give our sister to one who is uncircumcised, for that would be a disgrace to us.
> [15]Only on this condition will we consent to you: if you will become like us, in that every male of you be circumcised,
> [16]then we will give our daughters to you, and we will take your daughters for ourselves, and we will live with you and become one people.
> [17]But if you will not listen to us to be circumcised, then we will take our daughter and go."
> [18]Now their words seemed reasonable to Hamor and Shechem, Hamor's son. (Genesis 34:11-18 NASB)

Before continuing our account of Dinah, we must first understand how the covenant of circumcision between God and Abraham ties into the outcomes surrounding the rape of Dinah. Abraham was the "father of the Jews." Because of Abraham's faithfulness to God, God made a covenant with Abraham. He promised Abraham that he would be the father of many descendants and that kings would come from the many nations of those descendants. However, God also instructed Abraham to become circumcised as a sign of the covenant between he and God. Furthermore, every male child born to Abraham's line in future generations also had to be circumcised eight days after they were born.[6] Circumcision is the very painful removal of the foreskin from the penis. God warned that any male who had not been circumcised was to be cut off from his people.

Heathen nations were aware of the Jews' practice of circumcising all of their male infants. It was common knowledge that the act of circumcision among the Jews was more than just a custom but was also a sign indicating that the one circumcised belonged to the nation of Israel. Therefore, when the sons of Jacob said they would consent to the request of Hamor but only on the condition that all the men of the city of Shechem become circumcised, this seemed like a reasonable request to Shechem. The account continues:

> [19]And the young man did not delay to do the thing, because he was delighted with Jacob's daughter. Now he was more respected than all the household of his father.
> [20]So Hamor and his son Shechem came to the gate of their city, and spoke to the men of their city, saying,
> [21]These men are friendly with us; therefore let them live in the land and trade in it, for behold, the land is large enough for them. Let us take their daughters in marriage, and give our daughters to them.
> [22]Only on this condition will the men consent to us to live with us, to become one people: that every male among us be circumcised as they are circumcised.
> [23]Will not their livestock and their property and all their animals be ours? Only let us consent to them, and they will live with us.
> [24]And all who went out of the gate of his city listened to Hamor and to his son Shechem, and every male was circumcised, all who went out of the gate of his city. (Genesis 34:19-24 NASB)

Shechem did not hesitate to carry out the conditional request of the sons of Jacob. He and his father commanded that every man in the city of Shechem be circumcised. There was no argument from the men of the

---

[6] Genesis 17:1-14 (see your Bible)

city because, as verse 19 points out, Shechem was even more respected by his subjects, than his father was. Let's continue with the account:

> [24]And all who went out of the gate of his city listened to Hamor and to his son Shechem, and every male was circumcised, all who went out of the gate of his city.
> [25]Now it came about on the third day, when they were in pain, that two of Jacob's sons, Simeon and Levi, Dinah's brothers, each took his sword and came upon the city unawares, and killed every male.
> [26]And they killed Hamor and his son Shechem with the edge of the sword, and took Dinah from Shechem's house, and went forth.
> [27]Jacob's sons came upon the slain and looted the city, because they had defiled their sister.
> [28]They took their flocks and their herds and their donkeys, and that which was in the city and that which was in the field;
> [29]and they captured and looted all their wealth and all their little ones and their wives, even all that was in the houses.
> [30]Then Jacob said to Simeon and Levi, "You have brought trouble on me, by making me odious among the inhabitants of the land, among the Canaanites and the Perizzites; and my men being few in number, they will gather together against me and attack me and I shall be destroyed, I and my household."
> [31]But they said, "Should he treat our sister as a harlot?" (Genesis 34:24-31 NASB)

The sons of Jacob never had any intention to give Dinah to Shechem in marriage and to intermarry with the daughters of the men of the city of Shechem. They tricked Hamor and Shechem into having all of the men of the city circumcised. When Simeon and Levi came to attack the city, the men of Shechem were so weakened in pain by their recent circumcisions that they did not have the physical strength it took to win the battle. Consequently, all the men in the city of Shechem were killed in order that the sons of Jacob could avenge the rape of their sister.

342

When reading on into chapter 35,[7] we see that God did not punish the sons of Jacob for what they did but instead instructed Jacob to take himself and his household and leave the city of Shechem and live in the land of Bethel. Because of the dastardly thing that Shechem did to Dinah, all of those who were under Shechem's rule in the city of Shechem suffered. God allowed the sons of Jacob to avenge the rape of their sister. God did not intervene to stop the sons of Jacob, and God did not blame Dinah at all for the criminal act that Shechem committed against her.

The gang rape of the Levite man's concubine

One of the most disturbing Old Testament biblical accounts of inhumanity and the single mistreatment of a human being is the account of the gang rape of a concubine of a certain Levite man. The account leaves both the woman and her husband nameless. But before we examine the incident and the results thereof, an understanding of what a concubine was and what her function in society was at the time is needed.

Although God has specified that marriages are to remain monogamous, there were many men during Old Testament times, usually wealthy men, or men of great status, who took more than one wife.

Because there were men who took more than one wife, some wives were considered secondary in status. These secondary wives were called concubines. Abraham, King David, Gideon, Saul, and Samson, all had concubines. However, in the Old Testament Mosaic Law,[8] God forbade men, particularly kings, to multiply wives unto themselves. Deuteronomy 17:17[9] attests to this. But there were many men who disregarded this command.[10]

The account of the gang rape of the concubine begins in the 19th chapter of the book of Judges:

---

[7] Genesis 35:1-5 (see your Bible).

[8] See Introduction.

[9] "And he shall not multiply wives to himself, that his [mind and] heart turn not away; neither shall he greatly multiply to himself silver and gold." (Deuteronomy 17:17 Amp.)

[10] See Chapter 11 for full discussion on the issue of polygamy.

¹In those days, when there was no king in Israel, a certain Levite was living temporarily in the most remote part of the hill district of Ephraim, who took to himself a concubine [of inferior status than a wife] from Bethlehem in Judah.

²And his concubine was untrue to him and went away from him to her father's house at Bethlehem of Judah and stayed there the space of four months.

³Then her husband arose and went after her to speak kindly to her [to her heart] and to bring her back, having with him his servant and a couple of donkeys. And she brought him into her father's house, and when her father saw him, he rejoiced to meet him. (Judges 19:1-3 Amp.)

The concubine had been unfaithful to her husband, the Levite. Because of this she went away to live with her father. However, her husband journeyed to his father-in-law's home to forgive her and bring her back home with him. The account goes on to tell us that the Levite man's father-in-law insisted that the Levite man stay at his home awhile. So the Levite man and his wife stayed for five days. On the fifth day the father-in-law attempted to convince his son-in-law to stay another night, but the Levite man decided to depart, as the following verses of scripture attest to:

⁹And when the man and his concubine and his servant rose up to leave, his father-in-law, the girl's father, said to him, Behold, now the day draws toward evening, I pray you stay all night. Behold, now the day grows to an end, lodge here and let your heart be merry, and tomorrow get early on your way and go home.

¹⁰But the man would not stay that night; so he rose up and departed and came opposite to Jebus, which is Jerusalem. With him were two saddled donkeys [and his servant] and his concubine. (Judges 19:9-10 Amp.)

The account goes on to inform us that the Levite man decided to spend the night in the city of Gibeah before continuing the long journey home. This he did, against the advice of his servant. Let's take a look:

> [11]When they were near Jebus, it was late, and the servant said to his master, Come I pray, and let us turn into this Jebusite city and lodge in it.
> [12]His master said to him, We will not turn aside into the city of foreigners where there are no Israelites. We will go on to Gibeah.
> [13]And he said to his servant, Come and let us go to one of these places and spend the night in Gibeah or in Ramah.
> [14]So they passed on and went their way, and the sun went down on them near Gibeah, which belongs to Benjamin,
> [15]And they turned aside there to go in and lodge at Gibeah. And the Levite went in and sat down in the open square of the city, for no man took them into his house to spend the night. (Judges 19:11-15 Amp.)

The nation of Israel consisted of twelve tribes of which the Levite tribe and the tribe of Benjamin were a part.[11] The Levite man, since he himself was an Israelite, assumed that he'd be safer and more welcome staying the night in a city where Israelites resided as opposed to spending the night in a city of foreigners. However, the Levite man, his concubine wife, and his servant began to have trouble as soon as they made camp in Gibeah, as we see when continuing with the account:

> [15] And they turned aside there to go in and lodge at Gibeah. And the Levite went in and sat down in the open square of the city, for no man took them into his house to spend the night.
> [16]And behold, an old man was coming from his work in the field at evening. He was from the hill country of Ephraim but was living temporarily in Gibeah, but the men of the place were Benjamites.

---

[11] See Introduction.

¹⁷And when he looked up, he saw the wayfarer in the
city square, and the old man said, Where are you
going? And from where did you come?
(Judges 19:15-17 Amp.)

Although the Levite man thought it would be best to reside in a city
where people of his own nationality resided, no one in Gibeah offered
him a place to stay the night. Therefore, he, his servant, and his
concubine found themselves about to spend the night outside in the town
square. However, an elderly gentlemen came by and offered his home.
Let's continue with the account:

²⁰The old man said, "You are welcome to spend the
night in my home and to be my guest, but don't stay
out here!"
²¹The old man brought them into his house and fed their
donkeys. Then he and his guests washed their feet and
began eating and drinking.
²²They were having a good time, when some worthless
men of that town surrounded the house and started
banging on the door and shouting, "A man came to
your house tonight. Send him out, so we can have sex
with him!"
²³The old man went outside and said, "My friends,
please don't commit such a horrible crime against a
man who is a guest in my house. ²⁴Let me send out my
daughter instead. She's a virgin. And I'll even send out
the man's wife. You can rape them or do whatever else
you want, but please don't do such a horrible thing to
this man."
²⁵The men refused to listen, so the Levite grabbed his
wife and shoved her outside. The men raped her and
abused her all night long. Finally, they let her go just
before sunrise, ²⁶and it was almost daybreak when she
went back to the house where her husband was staying.
She collapsed at the door and lay there until sunrise.
²⁷About that time, her husband woke up and got ready
to leave. He opened the door and went outside, where
he found his wife lying at the door with her hands on

the doorstep. [28]"Get up!" he said. "It's time to leave."
But his wife didn't move. He lifted her body onto his
donkey and left. [29]When he got home, he took a butcher
knife and cut her body into twelve pieces. Then he told
some messengers, "Take one piece to each tribe of
Israel [30]and ask everyone if anything like this has ever
happened since Israel left Egypt. Tell them to think
about it, talk it over, and tell us what should be done.
(Judges 19:20-30 CEV)

There was a gang of perverted men going about the city who
apparently saw the old man approach the Levite man and his companions
in the square. The gang of men must have followed the old man home.
The men began to pound on the old man's door. They wanted to rape the
Levite man. However, the old man thought it would be disgraceful for
the men to harm the Levite man and instead offered up the women in the
house, including his own daughter. When the men insisted on raping the
Levite man, the Levite man grabbed his concubine wife and pushed her
out to be raped instead of him. Many theologians have tried to defend the
actions of the old man and the Levite man by citing how important the
cultural hospitality mores were regarding houseguests. However, there
was no godly command that said they had to give up the women of the
house in situations such as this and therefore, there is no excuse for
either of these men to have behaved in such a gutless fashion. Both men
could have given themselves up instead. The old man could have initially
offered himself up in place of the Levite man and the Levite man could
have offered himself up instead of giving up his wife. Or, although it
apparently looked hopeless, the old man and the Levite man could have
chosen to fight. The NIV Study Bible commentary describes the tragedy
of this account not only in terms of the perversion of the men of Gibeah
and the vile act that they committed against the woman but also in terms
of the "callous selfishness of men who would betray defenseless women
to be brutally violated for a whole night."[12]

---

[12] Taken from The NIV Study Bible, 10th Anniversary Edition, Kenneth Barker,
General Editor. Copyright © 1995 by The Zondervan Corporation. p.355 Fair
use.

Neither of the men protected the women that were in the house. When the Levite man realized that the men were set on raping him, he took his concubine and "threw her to the wolves" so to speak.

The scriptures describe the men of the gang as worthless. The New International Version of the Bible describes them as wicked. These wicked men raped the woman all night and beat her as well. After the men raped her they let her go at dawn and eventually she came and fell at the doorway of the old man's house at daybreak. This indicates that she must have been taken away from the house during the night and may have stumbled back or crawled back to the home barely alive from her ordeal. She fell at the foot of the door of where her husband[13] was residing who did not know his wife was at the door until he was ready to leave the next morning. Apparently, he had planned to leave without her. When he opened the door and saw her lying at the foot of the door, bleeding, bruised, barely alive and raped, he said to her "get up, it's time to leave." She didn't answer and he realized she was dead.

The Levite man took the corpse of his wife home. While he thought she was alive he had planned to leave her but when he discovered she was dead he took her home. When he got home, he took a knife and cut up her dead body into twelve pieces. He delivered one body part to each of the twelve tribes of Israel.

It took a lot of energy for the Levite man to cut his wife's body into twelve pieces with just a knife. He had to cut through bone and muscle and by the time he got the dead body of his concubine wife home, the body had probably began its transformation into the early stages of rigor mortis[14] which would have made it more difficult to sever.

Most men would not have been able to cut the body of their dead wife into twelve pieces even if they wanted to make a point. Therefore

---

[13]The word in Hebrew is *adon* which means *controller*, (according to the New Strong's Exhaustive Concordance of the Bible). The NASB and NIV translates the word *husband*, as applied to the Levite man, as *master*, which gives indication that the concubine may have been the Levite man's slave as well as his wife and that the Levite man ruled his wife as would a master or controller. See Chapter 3 for an entire discussion of the curse of husband rule.

[14] Rigor mortis is a postmortem stiffening due to the lack of a chemical called adenosine triphosphate which gradually depletes itself in the body after a person has died. The onset of rigor mortis generally begins 4 to 6 hours after death. We can safely assume that it took the Levite man more time than that to get his dead wife back home.

the Levite man's mental state was in question. Did he finally feel a sense of duty to his dead wife? Did he finally get to the point where he was angered? Did he finally feel some profound sadness regarding the incident? Or did he merely want to give an impression of immense distress in order to divert any suspicion that may have been focused on him? We will never really know. The scriptures don't say.

We cannot blame God for the actions of this man or for the actions of the old man. Again, there was no commandment in the Mosaic Law that instructed a man to hand his wife or daughter over to rapists in order to prevent the victimization of the male guests in his home. The Levite man and the old man acted out of their own volition. Neither of them were willing to sacrifice themselves in order to protect the women in the house so they both gave up a defenseless woman. God had nothing to do with this.

But the account doesn't end here. The tribe of Benjamin suffered serious repercussions for the gang rape and murder of the concubine. As quoted above, verse 30 reveals that the Israelites were appalled at the crime committed against this woman and set out to do something about it. Let's continue the account:

> [1]Then all the Israelites came out, and the congregation assembled as one man to the Lord at Mizpah, from Dan even to Beer-sheba, including the land of Gilead.
>
> [2]And the chiefs of all the people, of all the tribes of Israel, presented themselves in the assembly of the people of God, 400,000 men on foot who drew the sword.
>
> [3](Now the Benjamites [among whom the vile tragedy occurred] heard that the [other] Israelites had gone up to Mizpah.) There the Israelites asked, How did this wickedness happen?
>
> [4]And the Levite, the husband of the woman who was murdered, replied, I came to Gibeah which belongs to Benjamin, I and my concubine, to spend the night.
>
> [5]And the men of Gibeah rose against me and beset the house round about me by night; they meant to kill me and they raped my concubine, and she is dead.
>
> [6]And I took my concubine and cut her in pieces and sent her throughout all the country of the inheritance of

Israel, for they have committed abomination and [wicked] folly in Israel.

[7]Behold, you Israelites, all of you, give here your advice and counsel. (Judges 20:1-7 Amp.)

The other eleven tribes of Israel went to the tribe of Benjamin and asked them to give up the men who did this vile thing, as we read below:

[12]Then the tribes of Israel sent men through the entire tribe of Benjamin, saying, "What is this wickedness that has taken place among you?

[13]"Now then, deliver up the men, the worthless fellows in Gibeah, that we may put them to death and remove this wickedness from Israel." But the sons of Benjamin would not listen to the voice of their brothers, the sons of Israel. (Judges 20:12-13 NASB)

Initially the tribes of Israel only wanted to execute the men who had actually been responsible for the rape and murder. However, the Benjamites would not give the men up. Instead the Benjamites rounded up twenty-six thousand men from their own towns along with seven hundred men from the city of Gibeah, to fight against the other tribes of Israel. Let's take a look:

[14]The Benjaminites[15] came together out of the towns to Gibeah, to go out to battle against the Israelites.

[15]On that day the Benjaminites mustered twenty-six thousand armed men from their towns, besides the inhabitants of Gibeah.

[16]Of all this force, there were seven hundred picked men who were left-handed; every one could sling a stone at a hair, and not miss.

[17]And the Israelites, apart from Benjamin, mustered four hundred thousand armed men, all of them warriors.

---

[15] The spelling of the tribal name is different in the New Revised Standard Version of the Bible than in other versions.

> [18]The Israelites proceeded to go up to Bethel, where they inquired of God, "Which of us shall go up first to battle against the Benjaminites?" And the LORD answered, "Judah shall go up first."(Judges 20:14-18 NRSV)

The Benjamites were very skilled warriors. Defeating them would not be easy. Israel did not engage in this war without consulting with the Lord. They asked God for help with their battle plan. God instructed them to send the tribe of Judah into battle first. God did not tell the Israelites not to fight the Benjamites. He instead supported what the Israelites were about to do. By raping this woman, the Benjamites had broken God's law. It didn't matter that the woman who was raped had committed adultery. The crime of rape against her was still punishable by death. Her past sexual indiscretions were not held against her. She was still considered important enough in God's eyes for him to endorse Israel's plan to go to war against their own brothers, the Benjamites, because of the wicked thing the Benjamites supported by not giving up the men who defiled her.

Certainly a chauvinistic God would not have supported the nation of Israel in its decision to make war against one of its own tribes and certainly not in order to avenge the gang rape and murder of whom some would describe as a "mere woman." Moreover, a "mere woman" who was also an adulterer and a secondary wife at that.[16] But God looked upon the concubine as a woman who deserved justice and he did not deny her the justice she deserved simply because of her gender. Nor did God take her past indiscretions or lower social status into account. And even though this concubine has remained nameless in the text, God knew who she was and he knew her name. She was no less a child of God than any other Israelite. The concubine was a woman who had been grossly mistreated and therefore God instructed the Israelites as to how to strategically come against the Benjamites. Let's continue with the account:

> [19]Then the Israelites got up in the morning, and encamped against Gibeah. [20]The Israelites went out to battle against Benjamin; and the Israelites drew up the

---

[16] See Chapter 11.

battle line against them at Gibeah. ²¹The Benjaminites came out of Gibeah, and struck down on that day twenty-two thousand of the Israelites. ²²The Israelites took courage, and again formed the battle line in the same place where they had formed it on the first day. ²³The Israelites went up and wept before the LORD until the evening; and they inquired of the LORD, "Shall we again draw near to battle against our kinsfolk the Benjaminites?" And the LORD said, "Go up against them."

²⁴So the Israelites advanced against the Benjaminites the second day. ²⁵Benjamin moved out against them from Gibeah the second day, and struck down eighteen thousand of the Israelites, all of them armed men. ²⁶Then all the Israelites, the whole army, went back to Bethel and wept, sitting there before the LORD; they fasted that day until evening. Then they offered burnt offerings and sacrifices of well-being before the Lord. (Judges 20:19-26 NRSV)

The Israelites lost their first battle against the Benjamites and had become discouraged. They asked the Lord whether or not they should continue to fight against the Benjamites. But the Lord did not hesitate in instructing the Israelites to keep fighting. The account goes on to tell us that on the second day of battle the Israelites lost an additional eighteen thousand men. They sought the instruction of the Lord once more, but this time all the people of Israel wept before the Lord, fasted, and presented burnt offerings. The account continues:

²⁷And the Israelites inquired of the LORD (for the ark of the covenant of God was there in those days, ²⁸and Phinehas son of Eleazar, son of Aaron, ministered before it in those days), saying "Shall we go out once more to battle against our kinsfolk the Benjaminites, or shall we desist?" The LORD answered, "Go up, for tomorrow I will give them into your hand." (Judges 20:27-28 NRSV)

The final victory would belong to the Israelites with the help of God. God was about to orchestrate things so that the Benjamite Israeli tribe would loose the war although they had won certain battles. In the end the Israelites slew fifty thousand and one hundred Benjamite soldiers.[17] Only six hundred Benjamite men survived the war as attested to in the following verses of scripture:

> [46] So all who fell that day of Benjamin were twenty-five thousand arms-bearing men, all of them courageous fighters. [47]But six hundred turned and fled toward the wilderness to the rock of Rimmon, and remained at the rock of Rimmon for four months. [48]Meanwhile, the Israelites turned back against the Benjaminites, and put them to the sword—the city, the people, the animals, and all that remained. Also the remaining towns they set on fire. (Judges 20:46-48 NRSV)

The account goes on to tell us that only six hundred Benjamites survived this civil war and that the Israelites eventually grieved for their Benjamite brothers. Since all of the remaining Benjamite cities, towns, people, and even the animals that belonged to the people, had been slain by the soldiers of the Israelite tribes, there were no more Benjamite women and children because they had all been killed as a result of this war. If the Benjamite men did not remarry and have more children, the entire tribe would have eventually become non-existent because the Benjamite men would have had no way in which to carry on their bloodline. The Israelites knew this and did not want one of their own to become extinct. The following verses of scripture continue the account:

> [6]But the Israelites had compassion for Benjamin their kin, and said, "One tribe is cut off from Israel this day. [7]What shall we do for wives for those who are left, since we have sworn by the LORD that we will not give them any of our daughters as wives? (Judges 21:6-7 NRSV)

---

[17] The rest of the historical account of this battle is found in Judges 20:29-46 (See Appendix)

Earlier, the Israelites had taken an oath declaring that they would execute anyone from any of the tribes of Israel whose military men had not gathered with them before the Lord at Mizpah. They talked among themselves to inquire about which one of the tribesmen may not have been present.[18] They soon discovered that none of the men from Jabesh Gilead had participated in the assembly at Mizpah. Therefore, they targeted these men for execution. The account goes on to inform us that twelve thousand Israeli soldiers were sent to Jabesh Gilead to kill all of the tribes people living there except for the virgin women. There were four hundred virgin women in Jabesh Gilead. They took these women captives, brought them to the camp at Shiloh and gave them to the remaining Benjamite men. But there were not enough women. The account goes on as follows:

> [15]The people had compassion on Benjamin because the LORD had made a breach in the tribes of Israel. [16]So the elders of the congregation said, "What shall we do for wives for those who are left, since there are no women left in Benjamin?" [17]And they said, "There must be heirs for the survivors of Benjamin, in order that a tribe may not be blotted out from Israel. [18]Yet we cannot give any of our daughters to them as wives." For the Israelites had sworn, "Cursed be anyone who gives a wife to Benjamin." [19]So they said, "Look, the yearly festival of the LORD is taking place at Shiloh, which is north of Bethel, on the east of the highway that goes up from Bethel to Shechem, and south of Lebonah." [20]And they instructed the Benjaminites, saying, "Go and lie in wait in the vineyards, [21]and watch; when the young women of Shiloh come out to dance in the dances, then come out of the vineyards and each of you carry off a wife for himself from the young women of Shiloh, and go to the land of Benjamin. [22]Then if their fathers or their brothers come to complain to us, we will say to them, 'Be generous and allow us to have them; because we did not capture in battle a wife for each man. But

---

[18] For the account of the decision made regarding Jabesh Gilead, read Judges 21:8-12 (see your Bible).

neither did you incur guilt by giving your daughters to them.'" [23]The Benjaminites did so; they took wives for each of them from the dancers whom they abducted. Then they went and returned to their territory, and rebuilt the towns, and lived in them. [24]So the Israelites departed from there at the time by tribes and families, and they went out from there to their own territories.

[25]In those days there was no king in Israel; all the people did what was right in their own eyes. (Judges 21:15-25 NRSV)

The Benjamite men abducted the women of Shiloh and forced them to be their wives. The women who were captured at Jabesh Gilead were also forced to become wives of the Benjamites. This is almost no less disturbing than the gang rape of the concubine. Women today would label these abductions and forced marriages as rape also. However, it appears that the Israelites may not have seen it that way and that the practices of the time frequently clouded the fact that women were being mistreated. It was not uncommon for marriages to be arranged during those times and since the fathers and brothers of the abducted women from Shiloh agreed to the marriages, despite the unusual circumstances surrounding the marriages, more than likely, these marriages were considered no less arranged than any other arranged marriage. On the other hand, all the men, children, and non-virgin women of Jabesh Gilead were slain in order that the virgin women there may have been taken as wives. These women were left without men to remarry just as the Benjamite men were left without women to remarry. Overall, the thinking was that as long as the Benjamites married the abducted women, the honor of the women was preserved. Consequently, any trauma these women may have suffered from being abducted and forced into marriage was probably overlooked.

As verse 25 tells us, the Israelites had no king at the time and therefore did what was right in their own eyes, but this does not mean that they did what was actually right. God did not instruct the Israelites to abduct the women from Jabesh Gilead and Shiloh and force them into marriage. The Israelites did this on their own in order to preserve the tribe of Benjamin.

The main focus here is that through the instruction and hand of God an entire Israeli tribe (the Benjamites) was nearly annihilated because of the rape and murder of one Israelite woman. Again, all this was done for a concubine. God did not think she was unimportant because she was a secondary wife. Her past indiscretions were not even brought into question. God did not say that because she committed adultery "that's what she gets." God did not say, "well if she hadn't have committed adultery and ran away in the first place, this would never have happened." God did not blame the victim but instead endorsed the Israelites' quest to bring the perpetrators to justice. The fact that the Benjamites were tribesmen brothers to the other Israelites did not give them immunity from the wicked act committed against the concubine. Apparently, the rape of this concubine was more abominable than the two brotherly tribes declaring war against one another. Clearly then, God had not acted chauvinistically.

Lot and his daughters

There is a similar account of an incident that almost led to the rape of the daughters of a man named Lot. Lot was a nephew of Abraham. Lot and his family traveled with Abraham and his family. Both men settled down in the land of Bethel, but the herdsmen who worked for Abraham and the herdsmen who worked for Lot did not get along with one another.[19] So Abraham suggested to Lot that the two of them live separately from one another. Lot agreed and chose to move his family to the Jordan Valley. The city of Sodom, where Lot and his family ultimately lived, was one of the cities located in the Valley. Because the Jordan Valley was rich in natural resources, it not only attracted herdsmen but also attracted heathen aristocrats. Eventually certain kings went to war against the city of Sodom in order to seize the city and gain control of it. They succeeded in their quest and Lot was taken prisoner. When Abraham heard that Lot had been taken prisoner he organized an army and rescued Lot from his captors. However, Lot continued to live in Sodom.

The Lord decided to destroy the cities of Sodom and Gomorrah because of the wickedness of the people who lived in those cities.[20] But Lot was not aware of this. Abraham had pleaded with the Lord to spare the city of Sodom because Lot still resided there. God acknowledged

---

[19] Genesis chapter 13 holds this account of Lot and Abraham (see your Bible).

[20] Genesis 18:17-33 (see your Bible).

Abraham's plea and promised Abraham that if there were as little as ten righteous people living in Sodom, he would not destroy the city. The account of Lot continues in the 19th chapter of Genesis. Let's take a look:

> [1]It was evening when the two angels came to Sodom's [city] gate. Seeing them, Lot rose up to meet them and bowed to the ground.
> [2]And he said, My lords, turn aside, I beg of you, into your servant's house and spend the night and bathe your feet. Then you can arise early and go on your way. But they said, No, we will spend the night in the square.
> [3][Lot] entreated and urged them greatly until they yielded and [with him] entered his house. And he made them a dinner [with drinking] and had unleavened bread which he baked, and they ate.
> [4]But before they lay down, the men of the city of Sodom, both young and old, all the men from every quarter, surrounded the house.
> [5]And they called to Lot and said, Where are the men who came to you tonight? Bring them out to us, that we may know (be intimate with) them. (Genesis 19:1-5 Amp.)

Once again we have come across a biblical historical account whereby a group of men saw unfamiliar men[21] in the public square and decided that they wanted to have sex with them. Let's continue with the account:

> [6]And Lot went out of the door to the men and shut the door after him
> [7]And said, I beg of you, my brothers, do not behave so wickedly.
> [8]Look now, I have two daughters who are virgins; let me, I beg of you, bring them out to you, and you can do as you please with them. But only do nothing to

---

[21] Or what they thought were men. These men were really angels of the Lord.

these men, for they have come under the protection of my roof. (Genesis 19:6-8 Amp.)

The fact that Lot offered up his daughters does not mean that it was the right thing to do. Although customary hospitality at the time required that a man protect his guests under all circumstances, this did not mean that Lot was forced to put the safety of his guests before the safety of his family. There were two other alternatives that Lot could have considered just as there were two other alternatives that the Levite man and the old man could have considered when the gang of men from Gibeah wanted to rape the Levite man. Lot could have sacrificed himself instead of sacrificing his daughters or he could have tried to fight. Of course the latter alternative would have certainly resulted in his defeat unless God intervened. Therefore there was only one real noble alternative, and that was for him to sacrifice himself to the mob in order to spare his daughters and his houseguests. But just as the Levite man was willing to sacrifice his wife instead of sacrificing himself, Lot was also willing to sacrifice his daughters instead of sacrificing himself. Let's look further:

> [9]But they said, Stand back! And they said, This fellow came in to live here temporarily, and now he presumes to be [our] judge! Now we will deal worse with you than with them. So they rushed at and pressed violently against Lot and came close to breaking down the door.
> [10]But the men [the angels] reached out and pulled Lot into the house to them and shut the door after him.
> [11]And they struck the men who were at the door of the house with blindness [which dazzled them], from the youths to the old men, so that they wearied themselves [groping] to find the door.
> [12]And the [two] men asked Lot, Have you any others here—sons-in-law or your sons or your daughters? Whomever you have in the city, bring them out of this place,
> [13]For we will spoil and destroy [Sodom]; for the outcry and shriek against its people has grown great before the Lord, and He has sent us to destroy it. (Genesis 19:9-13 Amp.)

The mob of men became angry at the fact that Lot offered them his daughters instead of the two male strangers who were in his house. The two strangers are identified as angels. The angels appeared as men but were actually heavenly beings. God had sent them to the city of Sodom to destroy the city. Once the mob rushed the house, the angels pulled Lot inside and then the angels struck the entire mob with blindness. The angels did not grab the women and throw them out. They instead fought the mob. These angels were angels of the Lord. They were God's angels. If the noblest thing to do would have been to give the women up to the mob then it follows that the angels would have done just that. But instead the angels fought to protect the entire household. The account goes on to inform us that the Lord did indeed destroy the cities of Sodom and Gomorrah.[22]

In the case of the gang rape of the concubine, an entire Jewish tribe was almost wiped out forever because of the crime of rape committed against this woman. And synonymously, in the case of the homosexual activity of an entire city and the near gang rape of two women, God destroyed two cities, Sodom and Gomorrah, and the inhabitants within those cities.

The rape of Tamar

The account of the rape of Tamar is found in the 13th chapter of 2nd Samuel. Tamar was one of the daughters of King David. She was raped by her half brother Amnon. Let's take a look at the account:

> [1]After this Absalom the son of David had a lovely sister, whose name was Tamar; and Amnon the son of David loved her.
> [2]Amnon was so distressed over his sister Tamar that he became sick; for she was a virgin. And it was improper for Amnon to do anything to her.
> [3]But Amnon had a friend whose name was Jonadab the son of Shimeah, David's brother, Now Jonadab was a very crafty man.
> [4]And he said to him, "Why are you, the king's son, becoming thinner day after day? Will you not tell me?"

---

[22] Genesis 9:14-29 has the rest of the account (see your Bible).

Amnon said to him, "I love Tamor, my brother Absalom's sister."

[5]So Jonadab said to him, "Lie down on your bed and pretend to be ill. And when your father comes to see you, say to him, 'Please let my sister Tamar come and give me food, and prepare the food in my sight, that I may see it and eat it from her hand.'"

[6]Then Amnon lay down and pretended to be ill; and when the king came to see him, Amnon said to the king, "Please let Tamar my sister come and make a couple of cakes for me in my sight, that I may eat from her hand." (2 Samuel 13:1-6 NKJV)

Verse 4 says that Amnon loved Tamar but, as we will see, he loved her only as far as he could have sex with her. His desire to have sex with her was a violation of the Law that God had handed down to Moses. Incest was (and still is) a sin.[23] And the punishment for incest was for the perpetrator to be cut off from the people of Israel. A person guilty of incest, if found out, would have to go into exile.[24] Amnon knew he was wrong for wanting to have sex with his sister, but his perversion consumed him to the point where he wasn't eating and thus he conspired with Jonadab to create a situation whereby he'd be able to seduce her. Let's continue:

[7]And David sent home to Tamar, saying, "Now go to your brother Amnon's house, and prepare food for him."

[8]So Tamar went to her brother Amnon's house; and he was lying down. Then she took flour and kneaded it, made cakes in his sight, and baked the cakes.

[9]And she took the pan and placed them out before him,

---

[23] "No one is to approach any close relative to have sexual relations. I am the Lord." (Leviticus 18:6 NKJV)

"Do not have sexual relations with your sister, either your father's daughter or your mother's daughter, whether she was born in the same home or elsewhere." (Leviticus 18:9 NKJV)

[24] Everyone who does any of these detestable things—such persons must be cut off from their people. (Leviticus 18:29 NKJV)

but he refused to eat. Then Amnon said, "Have everyone go out from me." And they all went out from him.

[10]Then Amnon said to Tamar, "Bring the food into the bedroom, that I may eat from your hand." And Tamar took the cakes which she had made, and brought them to Amnon her brother in the bedroom.

[11]Now when she had brought them to him to eat, he took hold of her and said to her, "Come, lie with me, my sister."

[12]But she answered him, "No, my brother, do not force me, for no such thing should be done in Israel. Do not do this disgraceful thing!

[13]And I, where could I take my shame? And as for you, you would be like one of the fools in Israel. Now therefore, please speak to the king; for he will not withhold me from you."

[14]However, he would not heed her voice; and being stronger than she, he forced her and lay with her. (2 Samuel 13:7-14 NKJV)

Amnon's original plot was to seduce Tamar into having sex with him. He actually thought that she would be interested in him as a sexual partner. To his dismay, his perversion belonged to him alone. When Tamar did not submit to his desires he raped her. Before she was raped Tamar begged her brother not to do such a despicable thing. She was desperate and tried to convince him that the king would allow the two of them to get married. However, the king would have never allowed such a thing because as we have seen, incestuous relationships were against the Law of God. But Tamar was trying anything to get Amnon to stop from raping her. Unfortunately, her pleas fell on deaf ears and he defiled her anyway. The scriptures go on to inform us that as soon as Amnon raped Tamar he hated her. Let's take a look:

[15]Then Amnon hated her exceedingly, so that the hatred with which he hated her was greater than the love with which he had loved her. And Amnon said to her, "Arise, be gone!"

361

¹⁶So she said to him, "No, indeed! This evil of sending me away is worse that the other that you did to me." But he would not listen to her. (2 Samuel 13:15-16 NKJV)

The account goes on to inform us that Tamar took refuge in her brother Absalom's house and that Absalom hated Amnon for what he did to Tamar and did not speak to him. After two years had past Absalom plotted to kill Amnon because he had raped Tamar. The scriptures do not inform us as to why Absalom waited two years. He may have been waiting for an opportune moment. The verses of scripture below tell of how Absalom avenged the rape of his sister by having Amnon killed.

²³Two years later, when Absalom's sheep were being sheared at Baal-hazor near Ephraim, Absalom invited all the king's sons to come to a feast. ²⁴He went to the king and said, "My sheep-shearers are now at work. Would the king and his servants please come to celebrate the occasion with me?"

²⁵The king replied, "No, my son. If we all came, we would be too much of a burden on you." Absalom pressed him, but the king wouldn't come, though he sent his thanks.

²⁶"Well, then," Absalom said, "if you can't come, how about sending my brother Amnon instead?"

"Why Amnon?" The king asked. ²⁷But Absalom kept on pressing the king until he finally agreed to let all his sons attend, including Amnon.

²⁸Absalom told his men, "Wait until Amnon gets drunk, then at my signal, kill him! Don't be afraid. I'm the one who has given the command. Take courage and do it!" ²⁹So at Absalom's signal they murdered Amnon. Then the other sons of the king jumped on their mules and fled.

³⁰As they were on the way back to Jerusalem, this report reached David: "Absalom has killed all your sons; not one is left alive!" ³¹The king jumped up, tore his robe, and fell prostrate on the ground. His advisers also tore their clothes in horror and sorrow.

³²But just then Jonadab, the son of David's brother Shimea, arrived and said, "No, not all your sons have been killed! It was only Amnon! Absalom has been plotting this ever since Amnon raped his sister Tamar. ³³No, your sons aren't all dead! It was only Amnon." ³⁴Meanwhile Absalom escaped.

Then the watchman on the Jerusalem wall saw a great crowd coming toward the city from the west. He ran to tell the king, "I see a crowd of people coming from the Horonaim road along the side of the hill."

³⁵"Look!" Jonadab told the king. "There they are now! Your sons are coming, just as I said." ³⁶They soon arrived, weeping and sobbing, and the king and his officials wept bitterly with them. ³⁷And David mourned many days for his son Amnon.

Absalom fled to his grandfather, Talmai son of Amnihud, the king of Geshur. ³⁸He stayed there in Geshur for three years. ³⁹And David, now reconciled to Amnon's death, longed to be reunited with his son Absalom. (2 Samuel 13:23-39 NLT)

After killing Amnon, Absalom fled to the land of Geshur and lived there three years. Verse 39 says that King David longed to see Absalom and had ceased mourning the death of Amnon. The 14ᵗʰ chapter of 2ⁿᵈ Samuel goes on to tell us that King David eventually forgave Absalom for killing Amnon.[25] God did not punish Absalom for having Amnon killed and once again, the rape of a woman was avenged.

RAPE AND WAR

There are those who believe that the Bible supports the rape of women in instances of war. However, when taking into consideration the biblical accounts of rape and the repercussions suffered by the rapists, it is apparent that God does not condone the rape of women, nor the rape men for that matter. Despite this fact, some may be prone to misinterpret

---

[25] The entire account of the rape of Tamar and its aftermath is found in 2 Samuel Chapters 13 and 14 (see your Bible).

certain verses of scripture that pertain to rape inside of war. We will take a look at a couple of passages that address this:

> ¹The LORD will have his day. And when it comes, everything that was ever taken from Jerusalem will be returned and divided among its people. ²But first, he will bring many nations to attack Jerusalem—homes will be robbed, women raped, and half of the populations dragged off, though the others will be allowed to remain.
>
> ³The LORD will attack those nations like a warrior fighting in battle. ⁴He will take his stand on the Mount of Olives east of Jerusalem, and the mountain will split in half, forming a wide valley that runs from east to west. ⁵Then you people will escape from the LORD's mountain, through this valley, which reaches to Azal. You will run in all directions, just as everyone did when the earthquake struck in the time of King Uzziah of Judah. Afterwards, the LORD my God will appear with his holy angels.
>
> ⁶It will be a bright day that won't turn cloudy. ⁷And the LORD has decided when it will happen—this time of unending day.
>
> ⁸In both summer and winter, life-giving streams will flow from Jerusalem, half of them to the Dead Sea in the east and half to the Mediterranean Sea in the west. ⁹Then there will be only one LORD who rules as King and whose name is worshiped everywhere on earth. (Zechariah 14:1-9 CEV)

The verses of scripture just cited are prophetic verses. Some theologians believe that the prophecies have already been fulfilled and others believe that the prophecies have yet to be fulfilled. The stronger arguments are in favor of the latter.

Although end time prophecy is too vast a subject for a detailed discussion here, certain things need to be pointed out in order to understand more fully the scriptural text quoted from the book of Zechariah.

The day of the Lord refers to the Second Coming of Jesus Christ. At his Second Coming the battle of Armageddon will take place, a new Jerusalem will be established, and the Lord will fight against those nations who have fought against his people. The following verses of scripture speak of the New Jerusalem:

> [1]I saw a new heaven and a new earth. The first heaven and the first earth had disappeared, and so had the sea. [2]Then I saw New Jerusalem, that holy city, coming down from God in heaven. It was like a bride dressed in her wedding gown and ready to meet her husband. [3]I heard a loud voice shout from the throne:
>
>> God's home is now with his people. He will live with them, and they will be his own. Yes, God will make his home among his people. [4]He will wipe all tears from their eyes, and there will be no more death, suffering, crying, or pain. These things of the past are gone forever.
>
> [5]Then the one sitting on the throne said:
>
>> I am making everything new. Write down what I have said. My words are true and can be trusted. [6]Everything is finished! I am Alpha and Omega, the beginning and the end. I will freely give water from the life-giving fountain to everyone who is thirsty. [7]All who win the victory will be given these blessings. I will be their God, and they will be my people. (Revelation 21:1-7 CEV)

Those who have confessed that Jesus is Lord and have believed that he rose from the dead will be with Jesus as he reigns on earth in New Jerusalem.[26] The Second Coming of Christ is the day of the Lord. In

---

[26] Romans 10:9 (see your Bible)

getting back to our text that was cited in Zechariah, verses 1 and 2 are our main focus. Let's take a look at those verses again:

> ¹See, a day is coming for the LORD, when the plunder taken from you will be divided in your midst. ²For I will gather all the nations against Jerusalem to battle, and the city shall be taken and the houses looted and the women raped; half the city shall go into exile, but the rest of the people shall not be cut off from the city. (Zechariah 14:1-2 NRSV)

Some theologians believe that just before the actual Second Coming of Christ occurs, (before the Armageddon battle and during the tribulation period[27]), nations will fight against Jerusalem and God will deliver Jerusalem into the hands of those nations. The defeat will include the capture of the city, the ransacking of homes, and the rape of women. This does not mean that God condones the ransacking of homes and the rape of women. It only shows us that men do vile things in the name of war and that God allows wars to take place. But the ransacking of homes and the rape of women is a description of what takes place during war and is not a God-ordained formula for war. Unfortunately, because of the brutality of war and its inhumanity, rape will no doubt be a part of war unless men erect laws against it.

There is no verse of scripture that gives a soldier a license from God to rape a woman under the banner of war. And although God allows negative things to happen, he does not condone evil actions. Rape is a sexual sin no matter if it is done during war or during peacetime, rape is still sin.

In the book of Isaiah, the prophecy against the city of Babylon gives us another example of rape during wartime. Babylon was a city that existed during Old Testament times in the southern region of Mesopotamia. It consisted of people who worshipped many false gods. The Babylonians persecuted the people of Jerusalem. The prophet Isaiah gives a divine prophecy regarding Babylon. This particular prophecy fits into our discussion on rape and war. Let's take a look:

---

[27] The Bible speaks of a great time of tribulation that will last for seven years near the end times. This is a time when the antichrist will rule and when those who refuse to take his mark (666) will be beheaded for their belief in Christ.

> [9] The day of the LORD is coming—that cruel day of his fierce anger and fury. The earth will be made a wilderness, and every sinner will be destroyed. [10] Every star and every constellation will stop shining, the sun will be dark when it rises and the moon will give no light. (Isaiah 13:9-10 GNT)

Again, there is reference to the day of the Lord. It is a day in which God will show his anger and his power. It is a time of judgement and could be referring to the end times Armageddon war or specifically to the prophetic destruction of Babylon. Let's look further:

> [11] The Lord says, "I will bring disaster on the earth and punish all wicked people for their sins. I will humble everyone who is proud and punish everyone who is arrogant and cruel.
> [12] Those who survive will be scarcer than gold. [13] I will make the heavens tremble, and the earth will be shaken out of its place on that day when I, the LORD Almighty, show my anger.
> [14] The foreigners living in Babylon will run away to their homelands, scattering like deer escaping from hunters, like sheep without a shepherd. [15] Anyone who is caught will be stabbed to death. [16] While they look on helplessly, their babies will be battered to death, their houses will be looted, and their wives will be raped."
> [17] The Lord says, "I am stirring up the Medes to attack Babylon. They care nothing for silver and are not tempted by gold. [18] With their bows and arrows they will kill the young men. They will show no mercy to babies and take no pity on children. [19] Babylonia is the most beautiful kingdom of all; it is the pride of its people. But I, the LORD, will overthrow Babylon as I did Sodom and Gomorrah! [20] No one will ever live there again. No wandering Arab will ever pitch a tent there, and no shepherd will ever pasture a flock there. [21] It will be a place where desert animals live and where owls build their nests. Ostriches will live there, and wild

goats will prance through the ruins. [22]The towers and palaces will echo with the cries of hyenas and jackals. Babylon's time has come! Her days are almost over!" (Isaiah 13:11-22 GNT)

God destroyed Babylon just as he destroyed Sodom and Gomorrah. However, his method of destroying Babylon was different from the method he used to destroy Sodom and Gomorrah. In the case of the destruction of Sodom and Gomorrah, God caused burning sulfur to rain down from the sky on both cities.[28] All of the people of the city were destroyed.

In the case of the city of Babylon, God used mankind to destroy the city. Instead of raining burning sulfur down on the city from the sky, God gave the Medes the power to overthrow the city. However, in cases of war, men can be brutal. In the process of capturing and overthrowing Babylon, the Medes sliced babies to pieces with the sword and raped all of the women. God does not condone the killing of innocent children just as he does not condone the rape of women. The fact that God gave the Medes the power to overthrow Babylon doesn't mean he instructed them in their inhumanities. God allowed this cruelty, but he did not authorize it. The Medes did not have to be cruel in order to overthrow the Babylonians because God had already given the Medes the power to overthrow them. The Medes chose to be cruel all on their own. The Medes were not instructed by God to tear children to pieces with the sword or to rape women. God only gave Isaiah the vision of what would happen so that Isaiah could prophesy about the destruction of Babylon. The people of Babylon were aware of Isaiah's prophecy and they chose to continue to turn their faces against God anyway. Therefore, God destroyed Babylon by means of war because the people living there worshipped idol gods and refused to correct their ways.

SUMMARY

As we have seen, the Bible does not teach that God condones the rape

---

[28] "Then the LORD rained down burning sulfur on Sodom and Gomorrah—from the LORD out of the heavens. Thus he overthrew those cities and the entire plain, including all those living in the cities—and also the vegetation in the land." (Genesis 19:24-25 NIV)

of women regardless of circumstances or situations. However, there are some radical religious people that have misused and misinterpreted the Bible to say otherwise. One historical example of this misuse has to do with the atrocities that occurred in the country of Bosnia Hercegovina, specifically in the city of Kosovo. In 1991 Bosnia and Hercegovina declared independence from Yugolsavia. Both Serbian and Bosnian peoples occupied Yugoslavia. Under the new government the Serbians moved in to overtake quite a bit of the Yugoslavian land. There was much fighting between the Serbs and the Bosnians.

The Serbs are Christians while the Bosnians are mostly Muslim. The Serbs forced thousands of Muslims from their homes as a part of what they called "ethnic cleansing." The Serbs specifically went after the ethnic Albanian population. Eventually this "ethnic cleansing" turned into inhumanity against man and included mass killings, detentions, executions, the confiscating of pieces of identification, and the systematic rape of women. This "ethnic cleansing" was most wide spread in the city of Kosovo in 1999. NATO forces moved in to neutralize the situation. Because they were fighting a civil war, the Serbs apparently felt that they had the right to rape the women of the opposing people. They may have felt that the Bible condoned it. But as we have clearly seen, they had no biblical right to do so. What they did by systematically raping women was a sin under the eyes of God.

Any kind of fornication is a sin. This includes rape. The Bible does not justify the rape of women. However, there are accounts in which God foretold of the rape of certain women because God was about to hand the nation these certain women belonged to over to captors who would in turn rape them. But God never instructed any captors to rape any women. Therefore, no one can correctly use the Bible to justify the rape of women. Rape was punishable by death during Old Testament times and is considered a sin and a crime in this dispensation of Grace. As we have seen, the rape of the concubine and near rape of Lot's daughters, were avenged with God's sanction.

11.

ON THE ISSUE OF POLYGAMY

Polygamy is the practice in which an individual is married to several people at one time. In a polygamous marriage, all partners in the marriage have agreed to the multiple marriage. Polygamy is usually associated with a man having multiple wives, although the term itself can be applied to a situation where a woman has multiple husbands. There are many examples of polygamous relationships that are spoken of in the Bible. All of the historical accounts of polygamy that are presented in the Bible are of men being married to more than one woman. Because of this, there are many women, as well as men, who believe that God condones polygamy. But although God allowed polygamous practices during the dispensation of the Law,[1] he clearly speaks against it during this dispensation of Grace[2] and, it is plainly indicated in the scriptures that when it comes to marriage, God's ultimate will is for a man to be married to no more than one woman. Let's take a look:

> [14]When you come to the land which the LORD your God is giving you, and possess it and dwell in it, and say, 'I will set a king over me like all the nations that are around me.'
> [15]"you shall surely set a king over you whom the LORD your God chooses; one from among your brethren you shall set as king over you; you may not set a foreigner over you, who is not your brother.
> [16]"But he shall not multiply horses for himself, nor cause the people to return to Egypt to multiply horses, for the LORD has said to you, 'You shall not return that way again.'
> [17]"Neither shall he multiply wives for himself, lest his heart turn away; nor shall he greatly multiply silver and gold for himself. (Deuteronomy 17:14-17 NKJV)

---

[1] See Introduction.
[2] See Introduction.

The commands given above regarding setting a king over Egypt are part of a long list of commands, statutes, and judgments that God gave Moses to give to the Jews when they were led out of Egypt from slavery. Whoever was to be in charge of the land was not to have multiple wives. This was a commandment from God. The king was to live up to a higher standard than the rest of the men in Israel. Therefore, it can safely be concluded that it was more holy and more righteous for a man to have only one wife during those times.

Some might argue that in commanding that the king not multiply wives to himself (verse 17), God was not saying that it was unacceptable for the king to have a *few* wives (two or three), but just that he could not have *many* wives (more than two or three). As a matter of fact, there are some English translations of the Bible that translate the command in verse 17 that says, *"neither shall he multiply wives to himself"* to *"the king shall not have many wives."* To most people, not having many of something doesn't mean that you can't have a few of that something and therefore certainly doesn't mean that you can only have just one. However, the word *multiply* is translated from the Hebrew word *rabah*. This Hebrew word means *to increase in any way*. Consequently, an increase of one, even in the least of ways, is at least two. Therefore, the king was not to increase the number of his wives in any way meaning that he could not have more than one wife and still be respected as king.

The prime example of what God wants in a marriage is revealed when taking into consideration the account of Adam and Eve:

> [21] And the LORD God caused a deep sleep to fall on Adam, and he slept; and He took one of his ribs, and closed up the flesh in its place.
> [22] Then the rib which the LORD God had taken from man he made into a woman, and He brought her to the man.
> [23] And Adam said:
>
> "This is now bone of my bones
> And flesh of my flesh;
> She shall be called Woman,
> Because she was taken out of Man."
>
> [24] Therefore a man shall leave his father and mother and be joined to his wife, and they shall become one flesh.

371

²⁵And they were both naked, the man and his wife, and were not ashamed. (Genesis 2:21-25 NKJV)

When God made the woman (whom Adam later named Eve), God immediately joined Adam and Eve together as husband and wife. God considered them to be as one. God only made one woman for Adam, not multiple women. Adam was only given one wife, not multiple wives. Therefore, one wife to one husband and one husband to one wife is how God set the foundation of marriage from the very beginning.

God's foundational marriage teaches us that two people who are married to one another are to remain married to one another until one of them dies. Through the initial marriage of Adam and Eve came the eventual population of the world. Adam lived to be 930 years old. There is no indication in the Bible that he ever had any other wife in all his life besides Eve. There is also no indication that Eve ever had any other husband during her lifetime besides Adam. And there is also no indication that either of them ever committed adultery. Let's take a look at Adam's final years:

> ²⁵Adam lay with his wife again, and she gave birth to a son and named him Seth, saying, "God has granted me another child in place of Abel, since Cain killed him." (Genesis 4:25 NIV)

> ¹This is the written account of Adam's line.

> When God created man, he made him in the likeness of God. ²He created them male and female and blessed them. And when they were created, he called them "man."
> ³When Adam had lived 130 years, he had a son in his own likeness, in his own image; and he named him Seth. ⁴After Seth was born, Adam lived 800 years and had other sons and daughters. ⁵Altogether, Adam lived 930 years, and then he died. (Genesis 5:1-5 NIV)³

---

³ The word *man* used in verses 1 and 2 is translated from the Hebrew word *adam* which is used interchangeably in chapters one through five of Genesis to

Adam and Eve continued to procreate long into their lives. Adam held on to the wife of his youth. The Bible teaches that men should revere the wives of their youth and hold on to them. Let's take a look:

> [15] Drink water from your own well--share your love only with your wife.
> [16] Why spill the water of your springs in public, having sex with just anyone? [17]You should reserve it for yourselves. Don't share it with strangers.
> [18]Let your wife be a fountain of blessing for you. Rejoice in the wife of your youth. [19]She is a loving doe, a graceful deer. Let her breasts satisfy you always. May you always be captivated by her love. [20]Why be captivated, my son, with an immoral woman, or embrace the breasts of an adulterous woman?
> [21]For the Lord sees clearly what a man does, examining every path he takes. [22]An evil man is held captive by his own sins; they are ropes that catch and hold him. [23]He will die for lack of self-control; he will be lost because of his incredible folly. (Proverbs 5:15-23 NLT)

Although the above verses of scripture are mainly teaching against adultery, verse 18 also implies that a man should stay with the first woman he married when he was young. He should always be captivated by her love no matter how old she gets. He should always strive to see her as sexually attractive ("let her breasts satisfy you always") despite the fact that she is aging and that her body is changing as she grows older. Nothing in the above verses says that a woman must weigh a certain amount, look a certain way, dress a certain way, and so on, in order to maintain the sexual interests of her husband.[4]

The instruction to continue to love one's spouse into and through old age (and therefore changed appearances) is directed towards men. A God who instructs a man to remain true to his wife, to continue to love his wife emotionally and sexually no matter how old she gets and no matter

---

mean *mankind* (human beings as a whole) or *the first man, Adam*. In this case the word *man* means *mankind, people, human beings*.

[4] See Chapter 7.

how her body ages, to share his love only with his wife, and to stay with the woman he married when he was young (indicating that he is to stay with the first woman he married) is by no means a chauvinistic God. This is a God who is instead, protecting the emotional interests and well-being of women.

God appealed to the men of Israel to be faithful to the wives of their youth. This, of course, means that God no longer allowed polygamy at that time. Polygamy was a short-lived privilege for men. It was allowed from the dispensation of Conscience[5] through the dispensation of the Law. God's protection of the interests of women and his further directive to the men of Israel to be faithful to the wives of their youth is further attested to in the following verses of scripture:

> [13] And this you do as well: You cover the LORD's altar with tears, with weeping and groaning because he no longer regards the offering or accepts it with favor at your hand. [14]You ask, "Why does he not?" Because the LORD was a witness between you and the wife of your youth, to whom you have been faithless, though she is your companion and your wife by covenant. [15]Did not one God make her? Both flesh and spirit are his. And what does the one God desire? Godly offspring. So look to yourselves, and do not let anyone be faithless to the wife of his youth. [16]For I hate divorce, says the LORD, the God of Israel, and covering one's garment with violence, says the LORD of hosts. So take heed to yourselves and do not be faithless. (Malachi 2:13-16 NRSV)

The Lord gave Israel the above message through Malachi, the prophet. There is no question that God's tolerance for the previous polygamous practices of the Jews was over. A man was expected and obligated to stay with the first woman he married. God was no longer lenient toward the act of polygamy. Men could no longer take on more than one wife without repercussion. God made it clear that he wanted men to remain faithful to their wives and not divorce them. The Israelite men at that time had a tendency to divorce their wives in order to marry

---

[5] See Introduction.

other women that attracted their eye. But God specifically told the Israelites that he hates divorce and he specifically instructed the men to stay with the wives of their youth. Such a strong admonishment against adultery and polygamy could certainly not come from a God who is a chauvinist.

With this said, it should be understood that although God allowed polygamy to take place from the dispensation of Conscience through the dispensation of the Law, it was not his original plan for men to have more than one wife. As we have seen, the foundation that God set for marriage is one wife to one man for as long as the two shall live. But, in order to present a complete examination concerning this, we need to take a look at some of the rules God set forth when he tolerated polygamy. Let's take a look:

> [2]If you buy a Hebrew slave, he must remain your slave for six years. But in the seventh year you must set him free, without cost to him. [3]If he was single at the time you bought him, he alone must be set free. But if he was married at the time, both he and his wife must be given their freedom. [4]If you give him a wife, and they have children, only the man himself must be set free; his wife and children remain the property of his owner.
>
> [5]But suppose the slave loves his wife and children so much that he won't leave without them. [6]Then he must stand beside either the door or the doorpost at the place of worship, while his owner punches a small hole through one of his ears with a sharp metal rod. This makes him a slave for life.
>
> [7]A young woman who was sold by her father doesn't gain her freedom in the same way that a man does. [8]If she doesn't please the man who bought her to be his wife, he must let her be bought back. He cannot sell her to foreigners; this would break the contract he made with her. [9]If he selects her as a wife for his son, he must treat her as his own daughter.
>
> [10]If the man later marries another woman, he must continue to provide food and clothing for the one he bought and to treat her as a wife. [11]If he fails to do any

of these things, she must be given her freedom without cost. (Exodus 21:2-11 CEV)

The verses of scripture cited above, particularly pertain to Hebrews (the Israelites) enslaving other Hebrews. In ancient Hebrew society, men could sell themselves into slavery in order to pay a debt or even to barter. A man could also be sold from one master to another. Men and women could also be born into slavery. A father could sell his daughter into slavery, but the slave master had to marry her. However, taking a person by force (kidnapping) and selling him or her was a sin in the eyes of God and punishable by death.[6]

If a man was married when he became enslaved then his wife was to be enslaved with him. The two were to be enslaved together. Hebrew slave masters were commanded to free other Hebrew slaves in the seventh year of the slave's servitude (verse 2). If a man became a slave while he was married then both he and his wife had to be set free after the sixth year of servitude. However, if during his enslavement, a man was given a wife, and granted his freedom afterwards, his wife could only be set free along with him if she and her husband were childless. But if he and his wife had parented children, then the slave master was at liberty to keep the wife and children and only set the man free. This was because the slave woman originally belonged to the slave master. Therefore, any children she bore would belong to the master and the mother was needed to care for her children. But if the man loved his wife, as he should have, then he would refuse to be free without her and he would agree to serve the master forever, along with his wife. It should be understood that any slave, whether male or female, had the option to runaway from the master at any time, without fear of retribution.[7]

Verses 7 through 11 tell us what was to happen when a man sold his daughter. Hebrew men who were poor could sell their daughters into slavery with the hope that the slave masters would marry their daughters when they became women. This was one way that a Hebrew man who

---

[6] "If a man is caught kidnapping one of his brother Israelites and treats him as a slave or sells him, the kidnapper must die. You must purge the evil from among you." (Deuteronomy 24:7 NIV)

[7] "If slaves should escape from their masters and take refuge with you, do not force them to return. Let them live among you in whatever town they choose, and do not oppress them." (Deuteronomy 23:15-16 NLT)

lived in poverty could provide for his daughter. Although it seems strange to us today, the customs and regulations surrounding the enslavement of one Israelite to another made for a more tolerable atmosphere in the realm of servitude. It was understood that mistreatment of slaves was forbidden and therefore slavery wasn't necessarily looked upon as a bad thing.[8] A man who gave his slave girl to his son to be married had to honor her as his daughter once she was married. She'd gain familial status above that of a slave.

If a slave master married his slave woman and then married another woman afterwards, he could not treat the first woman that he married any different from the second. He had to provide just as sufficiently for the first wife as for the second. He could not deprive the first wife of any necessities and he also could not deprive her sexually. If he deprived her then she was free to leave without her father having to pay any money to the slave master to redeem her.

Upon first looking at this it seems unfair that any man would be allowed a second wife. However, in ancient Jewish society, it was very important for a woman to marry, since marriage was her main means of having financial security aside from living in her father's house. A woman's status also rose according to how many children she had. So, the pressure to marry was immense. Polygamy was therefore, not only accepted by men but accepted by women as well.

Although God allowed for polygamous marriages during the dispensation of the Law, he knew that in such arrangements favoritism of one wife over another was bound to happen. 1st Timothy 5:21 forbids partiality and favoritism among Christians. It says, *"I charge you, in the sight of God and Christ Jesus and the elect angels, to keep these instructions without partiality, and to do nothing out of favoritism."* The instructions that Paul was speaking of were the instructions he had given to the church. However, the instruction not to practice favoritism also applies in general. This application is evident in the following verses of Old Testament scripture whereby the Law was in effect:

> [15]Suppose a man has two wives, but he loves one
> and not the other, and both have given him sons. And

---

[8] For a comprehensive look at the issue of slavery and the Bible, suggested reading includes the book titled, "What the Bible really says about Slavery," written by this same author.

suppose the firstborn son is the son of the wife he does not love. [16]When the man divides the inheritance, he may not give the larger inheritance to his younger son, the son of the wife he loves. [17]He must give the customary double portion to his oldest son, who represents the strength of his father's manhood and who owns the rights of the firstborn son, even though he is the son of the wife his father does not love. (Deuteronomy 21:15-17 NLT)

A man with two wives was directed not to favor the second wife over the first. The son that a man fathered through his first wife was due to get what was his regardless as to whether or not the man's love had waned for that son's mother. God would not and does not tolerate favoritism. Therefore he did not tolerate a man favoring one wife over another.

As stated before, although God allowed Polygamy during the dispensation of the Law, he no longer tolerates it today, during the dispensation of Grace.[9] We see this when taking another look at the verses below found in Matthew:

[1]When Jesus had finished saying these things, he left Galilee and went into the region of Judea to the other side of the Jordan. [2]Large crowds followed him, and he healed them there.

[3]Some Pharisees came to him to test him. They asked, "Is it lawful for a man to divorce his wife for any and every reason?"

[4]Haven't you read," he replied, "that at the beginning the Creator 'made them male and female,' [5]and said, 'For this reason a man will leave his father and mother and be united to his wife, and the two will become one flesh? [6]So they are no longer two, but one. Therefore what God has joined together, let man not separate."

[7]"Why then," they asked, "did Moses command that a man give his wife a certificate of divorce and send her away?"

---

[9] See Introduction

> [8]Jesus replied, "Moses permitted you to divorce your wives because your hearts were hard. But it was not this way from the beginning. [9]I tell you that anyone who divorces his wife, except for marital unfaithfulness, and marries another woman commits adultery."
>
> [10]The disciples said to him, "If this is the situation between a husband and wife, it is better not to marry."
>
> [11]Jesus replied, "Not everyone can accept this word, but only those to whom it has been given. [12]For some are eunuchs because they were born that way; others were made that way by men; and others have renounced marriage because of the kingdom of heaven. The one who can accept this should accept it." (Matthew 19:1-12 NIV)

When taking into consideration the first part of the answer Jesus gave the Pharisees as to their inquiry (verse 9), it is obvious that the Pharisees asked Jesus about divorce because many of them were interested in divorcing their wives so that they could marry other women.[10] If Jesus had condoned polygamy then instead of telling the Pharisees that any one who divorces his wife and marries another commits adultery, he would have instead instructed them to marry a second wife if they were dissatisfied with the first one. But Jesus did not advise them to marry more than one woman, which indicates to us that biblically, polygamy is no longer allowed. The reason why the Pharisees were so concerned about the issue of marriage and divorce is because they knew that a man could only have one wife, and history teaches us that many of the Pharisees who lived during the era of Christ were divorcing their wives for miniscule reasons in order to marry their mistresses.

Not only is a man only to have one wife, but a woman is only to have one husband, as the following verses of scripture attest to:

> [10]When they were in the house again, the disciples asked Jesus about this. [11]He answered, "Anyone who divorces his wife and marries another woman commits adultery against her. [12]And if she divorces her husband

---

[10] For a more detailed discussion of this, see Chapter 8.

and marries another man, she commits adultery."
(Mark 10:10-12 NIV).

Of course, as discussed in Chapter 8, this is not an absolute. There
are exceptions to the rule. However, in general, divorce is a sin when
there are no acceptable grounds for it. From what Jesus taught, it is clear
that marriage is a lifetime commitment between a man and a woman.
Polygamy, then, is clearly against the will of God. Let's look further.

> [1]This is a faithful saying: If a man desires the position
> of a bishop, he desires a good work.
> [2]A bishop then must be blameless, the husband of one
> wife, temperate, sober-minded, of good behavior,
> hospitable, able to teach;
> [3]not given to wine, not violent, not greedy for
> money, but gentle, not quarrelsome, not covetous;
> [4]one who rules his own house well, having his
> children in submission with all reverence
> [5](for if a man does not know how to rule his own
> house, how will he take care of the church of God)?
> (1 Timothy 3:1-5 NKJV)

> [12]Let Deacons be the husbands of one wife, ruling
> their children and their own houses well. (1 Timothy
> 3:12 NKJV)

Our emphasis is on verse 2 and 12. A bishop is one who oversees the
church, a pastor. A deacon assists the pastor and is considered to be one
of the highest officials in the local church.[11] However, 1st Corinthians
12:28[12] teaches us that God's hierarchy of status in the church as a whole
(the body of Christ) is first apostles, secondly preachers/prophets, thirdly
teachers, then those who work miracles, those who heal, those who help
others, those with administrative know-how, and those who speak in
tongues.

Neither a pastor nor a deacon is to have more than one wife. Some
will read this and misinterpret the verses to mean that men who are not

---

[11] See Chapter 5 for a detailed discussion.
[12] See your Bible.

pastors or deacons can therefore have more than one wife and that the limit of one wife to a man only applies to high officials in the church. But if this were the case then it would never have made sense for the Pharisees to ask about divorce and remarriage. Jesus himself is recorded in Matthew 5:28 (NKJV) as saying that *"whoever looks at a woman to lust for her has already committed adultery with her in his heart."* A man usually does not consider marrying a woman unless he has looked at her with some lust in his heart. This may be why the word of God commands a man to marry a woman whom he is engaged to.[13] If he does not marry her, the two will eventually commit fornication. It will only be a matter of time. Lust is only considered by God to be a sin, if the one lusting is not married to the one whom he or she is lusting after.

With these things in mind, the command for a pastor or deacon to be the husband of but one wife, does not indirectly give other men the go-ahead to engage in polygamy, but instead tells us that a man who has divorced and remarried a woman other than his first wife should not be allowed to serve in the position of a pastor or deacon unless his divorce from his first wife was for just cause.[14] A man can be the husband of more than one wife in his lifetime by simply marrying, divorcing, and remarrying. The meaning of the scripture is made clearer in the New Revised Standard Version of the Bible (with special emphasis on verse 2) which says:

> [1]The saying is sure: whoever aspires to the office of bishop desires a noble task. [2]Now a bishop must be above reproach, married only once, temperate, sensible, respectable, hospitable, an apt teacher, [3]not a drunkard, not violent but gentle, not quarrelsome, and not a lover of money. [4]He must manage his own household well, keeping his children submissive and respectful in every way—[5]for if someone does not know

---

[13] "Now I say to those who aren't married and to widows—it's better to stay unmarried just as I am. But if they can't control themselves, they should go ahead and marry. It's better to marry than to burn with lust." (1 Corinthians 7:8-9 NLT)

[14] See Chapter 8 on the issue of Christians and divorce under the subheading "Till death do us part."

how to manage his own household, how can he take
care of God's church? (1 Timothy 3:1-5 NRSV)

[12]A deacon must be faithful to his wife, and must
manage his children and household well.
(1 Timothy 3:12 NLT)

Being faithful to one's wife means resisting any temptation to commit
adultery and doing so can tie in to a man being married to only one
woman for a lifetime. As stated earlier, not all men who remarry have
done so in error, but to those who have and to those where no just cause
can be found for their divorce, they are not eligible to be an elder or
pastor in the church. This also applies if a man has been divorced by a
woman in which she had just cause to divorce him.

SUMMARY

It is evident when looking at the New Testament scriptures
surrounding marriage and divorce that there is no indication that
polygamy is allowed in today's time. Furthermore, the verses of
scripture that were quoted from the Old Testament books of Proverbs
and Malachi instruct men to be faithful to the wife of their youth.

During the era in which polygamy was allowed, it was easy for
favoritism to creep into polygamous marriages. But the scripture tells us
that favoritism is a sin and men were instructed not to take anything
away from the first wife upon marrying the second. A man who married
more than one woman still had to be able to care for the first wife just as
well as he did before ne married the second. Moreover, he could not
decrease his love making towards the first wife. Consequently, the more
wives a man had, the less able he was to fulfill his sexual obligations to
all of them, since all men have physical limitations when it comes to
sexual endurance. But God instructs those who are married not to
deprive one another sexually unless both agree, and then just for a time,
so that neither of them will be tempted towards adultery. Let's take a
look:

[1]Now about the questions you asked in your letter.
Yes it is good to live a celibate life. [2]But because there
is so much sexual immorality, each man should have his

own wife, and each woman should have her own husband. ³The husband should not deprive his wife of sexual intimacy, which is her right as a married woman, nor should the wife deprive her husband. ⁴The wife gives authority over her body to her husband, and the husband also gives authority over his body to his wife. ⁵So do not deprive each other of sexual relations. The only exception to this rule would be the agreement of both husband and wife to refrain from sexual intimacy for a limited time, so they can give themselves more completely to prayer. Afterward they should come together again so that Satan won't be able to tempt them because of their lack of self-control. ⁶This is only my suggestion. It's not meant to be an absolute rule.
(1 Corinthians 7:3-6 NLT)

Notice verse 2 says that each man should have his own wife and each wife her own husband. The verse steadfastly implies that a man should be married to no more than one woman just as it implies that a woman should be married to no more than one man. The verse does not say that a man should have his own *wives* (plural) while a woman should have her own husband (singular). Both men and women are instructed to marry singularly, not in plurals.

Verses 3 and 4 go on to instruct married people not to deprive each other of sex. Again, there is no question, that the more wives a man has the more difficult it would be for him to fulfill his sexual obligations to all of his wives continuously. Someone would get "the short end of the stick." This is not God's plan. Furthermore, Jesus specifically stated that when a man and a woman are joined together in marriage, they are joined together in one flesh. How can a man be joined with one woman in the flesh if he joins himself with other women as well? The joining of man and wife in one flesh indicates in and of itself that multiple marriages fall short of being an example of holiness. As documented in Genesis, only one woman was assigned to become Adam's wife, and that was Eve. And, as stated earlier, there is no indication that Adam ever had a wife other than Eve. And there is certainly no indication that he was married to more than one woman at a time. It is quite evident that God laid the foundation of marriage by using the marriage of Adam and Eve as the prime example. Even Jesus, in his response to the Pharisees' questions regarding divorce, quoted from the verses of scripture in Genesis with respect to Adam and Eve that says, *"therefore a man shall leave his father and mother and be joined to his wife, and they shall become one flesh.* "[15] Neither Jesus nor the verses of scripture in Genesis said that a man shall leave his father and mother and be joined to his *wives* and he shall become one flesh with all of his *wives*.

Polygamy is clearly, in today's time, a practice that goes against the word of God. Again, God only allowed it during the dispensation of Conscience through the dispensation of the Law. One can only speculate as to why God allowed or tolerated it then, but we know for certain that it is a sin to engage in polygamy now. Therefore there is no chauvinism on God's part when considering the subject of polygamy. It is a dead issue.

---

[15] Genesis 2:24 (NKJV)

12.

GOD'S VALIDATION OF SINGLE WOMEN

For generations, women have validated themselves based upon whether or not they have a man in their lives. Before the women's liberation movement of the sixties, an unmarried woman usually stayed at home until she was married. Her whole existence and sense of well-being centered on the prospect of becoming a bride. An unmarried woman over the age of thirty was considered an "old maid." This phrase was indeed a negative term and implied that the woman to whom it was referring was somehow unfit to be married or that no man wanted her. In Western society, before the sixties, it was generally expected of a woman to get married and have children. Taking these things into account, it is no wonder that many young women of past generations validated themselves and other women by their marital status.

Unfortunately, this sort of validation continues today, if not overtly and consciously, then covertly and unconsciously. Single people, especially women, often times find themselves explaining why they are not married. People want to know whether or not theirs is a conscious choice or if they just haven't found the right mate yet. A woman who doesn't want children is often times labeled as selfish or is frowned upon, particularly by men.

There are still those who believe that a woman has not really fully met the demands of life and done everything she is supposed to do unless she has had at least one child. Of course, in the Christian arena, this means that she must marry. There are also those women who are being pressured, by their parents, to get married and have children. Their parents want to become grandparents because unfortunately, that is where a great amount of validation lies for many of them. But let's take a look at what the word of God has to say about being single:

> [1]Now for the matters you wrote about: It is good for a man not to marry. [2]But since there is so much immorality, each man should have his own wife, and

385

each woman her own husband. ³The husband should fulfill his marital duty to his wife, and likewise the wife to her husband. ⁴The wife's body does not belong to her alone but also to her husband. In the same way, the husband's body does not belong to him alone but also to his wife. ⁵Do not deprive each other except by mutual consent and for a time, so that you may devote yourselves to prayer. Then come together again so that Satan will not tempt you because of your lack of self-control. ⁶I say this as a concession, not as a command. ⁷I wish that all men were as I am. But each man has his own gift from God; one has this gift, another has that. (1 Corinthians 7:1-7 NIV)

In verse 1, Paul says that it is good for a man *not* to marry. It appears upon first glance, that Paul is contradicting what God is quoted as saying in the following verses taken from the book of Genesis, with particular attention to verse 18 which many have misquoted as saying "it is not good for man to be alone." But the Bible is not contradicting itself in this respect. God created Eve because he saw that it was not good for *Adam* to be alone. Let's take a careful look at what the book of Genesis actually says about this:

¹⁵The LORD God took the man and put him in the Garden of Eden to work it and take care of it. ¹⁶And the LORD God commanded the man, "You are free to eat from any tree in the garden; ¹⁷but you must not eat from the tree of the knowledge of good and evil, for when you eat of it you will surely die."
¹⁸The LORD God said, "It is not good for the man to be alone. I will make a helper suitable for him."
¹⁹Now the LORD God had formed out of the ground all the beasts of the field and all the birds of the air. He brought them to the man to see what he would name them; and whatever the man called each living creature, that was its name. ²⁰So the man gave names to all the livestock, the birds of the air and all the beasts of the field.

386

> But for Adam no suitable helper was found. [21]So the
> LORD caused the man to fall into a deep sleep; and
> while he was sleeping, he took one of the man's ribs
> and closed up the place with flesh. [22]Then the LORD
> God made a woman from the rib he had taken out of
> the man, and he brought her to the man. (Genesis 2:15-
> 22 NIV)

It was not until Adam could not find a suitable helper to assist him in
tending the Garden that God caused Adam to go into a deep sleep so that
he could remove one of Adam's ribs to create Eve.

Many theologians also generalize, to all men, what was Adam's
succinct situation. They say that it is not good for *any* man to be alone.
However, it was not good for Adam ("the man"), specifically, to be
alone. The predicament of Adam's unique existence in the Garden
specifically applied to Adam. And Adam was more specifically *all* alone.
There were no other human beings besides him. Therefore, the remedy
given for Adam's solitude does not necessarily apply to all men.
Furthermore, the Bible does not give a definitive reason as to why it was
not good for Adam to be alone. The closest inference the Bible gives is
that Adam needed help tending the garden. Eve was the remedy for the
dilemma that *Adam* was experiencing.

After Eve's creation, Adam considered Eve to be his wife as
indicated by what Adam is quoted as saying in the following verses of
scripture:

> [23]And Adam said:
>
> "This is now bone of my bones
> And flesh of my flesh;
> She shall be called Woman,
> Because she was taken out of Man."
>
> [24]Therefore a man shall leave his father and mother and
> be joined to his wife, and they shall become one flesh.
> [25]And they were both naked, the man and his wife, and
> were not ashamed. (Genesis 2:23-25 NKJV)

Adam and Eve were the first man and woman[1] and the first example of husband and wife. When Adam described Eve as "bone of my bones and flesh of my flesh" he meant this in a literal way since Eve had literally been created from his bones and flesh.

It appears that during the dispensation of Innocence,[2] before the fall and curse of man, marriage was overall a good thing. The marital partnership between Adam and Eve became the order of things. There is no indication that their marriage prevented either of them from serving the Lord to their fullest potential. However, after the fall, things changed. Because of Adam's transgressions, men were cursed to have to work hard for the fruits of their labor. Women were cursed twofold because of Eve's transgression. Their pain in childbirth would be increased and their husbands would rule over them.[3] No doubt this would put a strain on any marriage. Increasingly marriage, although still a good thing, became something that was not the best thing for people to engage in if they wanted to serve the Lord as diligently as they possibly could. As we will see further along in our discussion, the decrease in opportunity to serve the Lord more frequently when married as opposed to the increase in opportunity to serve the Lord more frequently in a single status, is the reason Paul says that it is good for a man *not* to marry.

In going back to look at the verses of scripture quoted in 1st Corinthians at the beginning of the chapter where Paul says *"it is good for a man not to marry"* we see that Paul also said the following: *"But since there is so much immorality, each man should have his own wife, and each woman her own husband."* Paul was saying that although it is good to be single, there are those who should go ahead and get married because if they don't they will not be able to withstand sexual temptation. Most men and women cannot resist the strong urge of wanting to have sexual intercourse. If they are not married, no doubt they will be tempted to behave in immoral sexual ways, especially if they are engaged or

---

[1] Some theologians believe that there was a "pre-adamic race" meaning that God created people before he created Adam and Eve. However, the argument in favor of Adam and Eve being the first human beings that God created, is a strong one and aligns itself with the creation account presented in the book of Genesis as well as with the beliefs of Orthodox Christianity.

[2] See Introduction.

[3] See Chapter 3.

dating. Sexual temptation is difficult to resist. Therefore, if a person finds it difficult to resist sexual temptation, then that person should get married. Because it is only within marriage that God allows sex. Let's look further.

> ⁸But I say to the unmarried and to the widows: It is good for them if they remain even as I am;
> ⁹but if they cannot exercise self-control, let them marry. For it is better to marry than to burn with passion. (1 Corinthians 7:8-9 NKJV)

As we have seen Paul had already addressed men earlier (1ˢᵗ Corinthians 7:1) in which he says that it is good for a man not to marry. He again addresses men as well as women when referring to the "unmarried" in the above verses of scripture. There is no question that he is referring to women when speaking of widows. Paul is referring to all single men and women which would include those women who have never been married, those women who are divorced and those women whose husbands have died (widows). Paul is actually saying that it is good for a woman not to get married and he is addressing himself to virgins and non-virgins alike. He makes the same concession for women in regards to marriage that he does for men. There's no getting around this. Paul goes on to explain that although it is good for women not to marry, if they cannot control their sexual behavior, then it is better for them to get married than to struggle with sexual urges. This is not to say that if they have sexual urges they should get married. Having sexual urges and controlling one's behavior in response to those sexual urges are two different things. These verses of scripture imply that the sexual urges are present and whether or not a woman stays single or gets married has to do with how well she is able to abstain from sex despite the urges that she experiences. The same applies to men.

A chauvinistic God would not have inspired Paul to write verses of scripture that are in favor of women remaining single. A chauvinistic God would have instead inspired writings that teach that a woman is incomplete without a man. Paul continues:

> ²⁵Now about virgins: I have no command from the Lord, but I give a judgment as one who by the Lord's mercy is trustworthy. ²⁶Because of the present crisis, I

think that it is good for you to remain as you are. [27]Are you married? Do not seek a divorce. Are you unmarried? Do not look for a wife. [28]But if you do marry, you have not sinned; and if a virgin marries, she has not sinned. But those who marry will face many troubles in this life, and I want to spare you this. (1 Corinthians 7:25-28 NIV).

In Paul's time, the definition of a virgin not only included women who had never had sex but also included women who had never been married. It was automatically assumed that a woman, who had never been married, also had never had sex (unless she was a known prostitute or had been caught in the act of fornication or adultery). It was clearly understood that sex should be reserved for marriage. The same applied for men. The scriptures indicate that this is the way God wants things to be. However, it should be emphasized that a person, who is single that has had sexual experiences in the past, is no less single than a single virgin is. Both are legitimately single. Both have the same restraint instructions placed upon them by the word of God. God permits neither of them to engage in sex.

In verse 26 Paul suggests that virgins stay as they are. By suggesting this, he was encouraging them to remain unmarried. A virgin woman who remains unmarried is never supposed to have sex (the same applies for virgin men). Consequently, she is never supposed to have children. How could she if she is never to have sex? Therefore verse 26 refutes any argument that says a woman's primary obligation in life is to get married and have children. This is not to say that there are no women called of God to have children. Certainly, there are. Eve is referred to in the Bible as the mother of all living.[4] We can therefore safely surmise that the major calling upon her life was to have children in order that the earth would be populated. And, as we saw in Chapter 2, both the Virgin Mary and Elizabeth were called to have children, Jesus and John the Baptist, respectively. Inarguably then, there are women who are called of God to have children. But it is not *every* woman's calling to have children. If childbearing were every woman's primary obligation, then Paul, most assuredly, would not have encouraged women, especially

---

[4] "And Adam called his wife's name Eve; because she was the mother of all living." (Genesis 3:20)

virgins, to remain single. He would have instead said the opposite. He would have encouraged all women to get married and have babies. Certainly a chauvinistic God would not have inspired Paul to write anything that might prompt some women to remain single (and thus be the head of their own homes)[5] and childless.

This brings us to the following verses of scripture (with particular attention to verse 15):

> [11]Let a woman learn in silence with full submission. [12]I permit no woman to teach or to have authority over a man; she is to keep silent. [13]For Adam was formed first, then Eve; [14]and Adam was not deceived, but the woman was deceived and became a transgressor. [15]Yet she will be saved through childbearing, provided they continue in faith and love and holiness, with modesty. (1Timothy 2:11-15 NRSV)

For a commentary of verses 11 through 14, see Chapter 5. Our focus here is on verse 15. Verse 15 says that a woman will be saved through childbearing. However, we just examined a passage of scripture that teaches us that it is all right with God if a woman remains unmarried and therefore childless. It seems as if one verse of scripture contradicts the other. However, a woman's salvation is not based on whether or not she has a baby but instead on whether or not she has confessed Jesus as Lord and believes in her heart that he rose from the dead.[6] If a woman cannot be saved unless she bears children, then all barren women would be bound for hell and all fertile women would have to get married and bear at least one child. Could this be what Paul really meant when he said, "women will be saved though childbearing?" Do all women have to bear at least one child in order to reap salvation? If the answer is yes, then this contradicts all the other teachings in the Bible regarding salvation and it would seem that Paul certainly would not have encouraged women to remain single, but instead to get married. Clearly then, the answer is no. But then the question becomes, what does it mean?

---

[5] See Chapter 3.

[6] "...if you confess with your mouth, 'Jesus is Lord,' and believe in your heart that God raised him from the dead, you will be saved. (Romans 10:9 NIV)

Theologians have explained verse 15 in many various ways. But there are only two basic explanations of the passage that would not be contrary to the doctrine of salvation. The first explanation rests upon the fact that during the time of Paul many women died during childbirth. Therefore the verse could mean that through faith and love in God, a woman can survive the life threatening moments of childbirth and therefore be saved from death. The New American Standard Bible translates the verse as such, "*but women shall be preserved through the bearing of children if they continue in faith and love and sanctity with self-restraint.*" The word *preserved* is used instead of the word *saved*, which gives the text a different meaning and indicates that the text is actually referring to a woman being preserved from death during childbearing. The verse before it (verse 14) speaks of Eve falling into transgression. We know that increased pain in childbirth was one of the curses she had to endure (and all women afterwards) because of her transgression. So if we connect verse 14 with verse 15 we see that what Paul could have been saying was that although Eve sinned and therefore childbirth is painful and possibly deadly, a woman who continues in the faith of the Lord Jesus Christ will be preserved through the pain of childbearing. She will make it through unscathed.

The second explanation is based on the fact that in the Greek, verse 15 actually reads like this, "But *she* will be saved through *the* childbearing, if they remain in faith and love and sanctification with good moral judgment." Most translators use the word *women* instead of the Greek pronoun *she* that is actually there. They feel it makes more sense. They also take out the article *the* before the word *childbearing*. The phrase "but women will be saved through childbearing" is marginally different from how it actually reads in the Greek: "but she will be saved through *the* childbearing." However, this marginal difference makes a big difference in interpretation. In making these slight changes away from the actual Greek, the tone of the scripture does not necessarily remain the same. We can safely assume that the pronoun *she* does indeed refer to the word *woman* in verse 11 ("Let a woman") which we know is referring to women in general. Therefore to put the word *women* in the place of the pronoun *she* seems accurate. However, when looking at the Greek, the word *childbearing* becomes less generalized because the article *the* is added in front of it, giving it specification. *The childbearing* therefore points to *a specific* childbearing and the specific childbearing which has brought salvation to all is the one in which Mary bore Jesus. Therefore all women (and men for that matter) will be saved through the childbearing of Christ if they remain in the faith. Paul not only emphasized the point that women are included among those who can be saved through faith in Christ, but also indirectly emphasized that a woman's role in Christ's ministry is essential, for it was a woman who bore Jesus.

In getting back to the scriptures being discussed in 1st Corinthians 7:25-28, we'll take a look at those verses of scripture once more:

> [25]Now about virgins I have no command from the Lord, but I give a judgment as one who by the Lord's mercy is trustworthy. [26]Because of the present crisis, I think that it is good for you to remain as you are. [27]Are you married? Do not seek a divorce. Are you unmarried? Do not look for a wife. [28]But if you do marry, you have not sinned; and if a virgin marries, she has not sinned. But those who marry will face many troubles in this life, and I want to spare you this. (NIV)

Since Paul kept emphasizing that it is good to remain single, he apparently knew that it was also wise to emphasize that it is not a sin to get married. He knew that there were those who might take things to the extreme and teach that marriage is sinful since, as will be pointed out in scripture during our discussion, being single is a better state to be in than being married if one wants to serve the Lord more diligently. Again, Paul emphatically states that although being single is good, it is not a sin for single people to get married. But by getting married, they make trouble for themselves.

Just as it is not a sin to get married, it is not a sin to remain single either. However, there are those that treat singleness as if it were a sin. Many good intentioned people in the church often times hound single people about getting married. Many mothers and fathers hound their children about getting married, especially their daughters. Things are changing in Western society, but for the most part, it is expected that children will grow up, get married, and have children. And although the tide has been changing, it has been a longstanding unspoken societal rule to criticize women more harshly than men if women decide not to get married and not to have children.

The phrase "do not look for a wife" (verse 27) is inarguably addressed to men and the phrase "if a virgin marries, she has not sinned" (verse 28) is inarguably addressed to women. Again, in looking at the scriptural text, we can plainly see that the word *virgin* is synonymous with one who is unmarried. Paul emphasizes that he does not have a command from the Lord regarding those who are unmarried but has an opinion about the unmarried. Paul is quick to note that his opinion (or judgment) regarding the matter is a trustworthy one since he has obtained the Lord's mercy in these matters. This coincides with what he said in 2nd Timothy 3:16 which tells us that "all scripture is given by inspiration of God." So, it doesn't matter if Paul had no direct command from God concerning these things. What he said is part of scripture and therefore was inspired of God anyway.

In verse 26, Paul instructed the Christians of that time to remain as they were. In other words, if they were virgins, meaning if they were unmarried, then they were to stay unmarried. Paul gave this instruction "because of this present crisis." Theologians have speculated about what the crisis may have been that prompted Paul to instruct the singles to stay single, but they admit that no one knows for sure. It is possible that the "present crisis" may have had to do with the high rate of divorce that apparently existed during that time. Matthew 19:1-12 indicates that divorce may have been very prevalent then. Let's take a look:

> [1]When Jesus had finished saying these things, he left Galilee and went into the region of Judea to the other side of the Jordan. [2]Large crowds followed him, and he healed them there.
>
> [3]Some Pharisees came to him to test him. They asked, "Is it lawful for a man to divorce his wife for any and every reason?
>
> [4]"Haven't you read," He replied, "that at the beginning the Creator 'made them male and female,' [5]and said, "for this reason a man will leave his father and mother and be united to his wife, and the two will become one flesh? [6]So they are no longer two, but one. Therefore what God has joined together, let man not separate."

[7]"Why then," they asked, "did Moses command that a man give his wife a certificate of divorce and send her away?"

[8]Jesus replied, "Moses permitted you to divorce your wives because your hearts were hard. But it was not this way from the beginning. [9]I tell you that anyone who divorces his wife, except for marital unfaithfulness, and marries another woman commits adultery."

[10]The disciples said to him, "If this is the situation between a husband and wife, it is better not to marry."

[11]Jesus replied, "Not everyone can accept this word, but only those to whom it has been given. [12]For some are eunuchs because they were born that way; others were made that way by men; and others have renounced marriage because of the kingdom of heaven. The one who can accept this should accept it." (NIV)

The Pharisees decided that it was better not to marry since they could not divorce their wives for just any reason (verse 10). As explained in Chapter 8, this in itself tells us that men were divorcing women for frivolous reasons in order to marry other women they were attracted to, which means that there must have been a high rate of divorce during that time. These men figured that they could divorce their wives to marry their mistresses. This way they figured they'd avoid the sin of adultery. But Jesus didn't let them get away with this and told them that a man who divorces his wife to marry another would still be guilty of adultery unless his wife had been guilty of marital unfaithfulness herself. Consequently, men couldn't get away with divorcing their wives to marry their mistresses. This greatly incited the Pharisees against marriage. But what Jesus said to them protected the women who would have otherwise been thrown away after their husbands tired of them. The men could not righteously throw their wives away (divorce them) unless their wives had done something that justifiably called for a divorce.

Just as there was probably a high rate of divorce during the time of Paul, there is a high rate of divorce today as compared to 40 or so years ago.[7] There is no question that marriages, Christian marriages included, are in crisis. And when considering today's present crisis when it comes to the high divorce rate, it would seem that Paul's advice for a Christian not to marry, is advice that would apply today.

The Pharisees decided that it was better not to marry since they could not divorce their wives for just any trivial reason. In response, Jesus did not dispute their conclusion that it is better not to marry and taught that those who can accept the fact that it is better not to marry should accept that fact for their own lives. Apparently, there are only three categories of people that can accept not being married. According to Jesus, they are the following: those who were eunuchs from birth, those who were made eunuchs by other men, and those who have consciously chosen to remain single in order that they might be better able to serve the Lord.

Eunuchs are men who were born without male genitalia or who have been castrated in order to serve other men as slaves.[8] With this being the case, what Jesus was teaching us when he gave us the three categories of people that can accept not being married is that much of a person's desire to marry has to do with a desire to have sex. If a man is born without testicles or a penis or a woman is born without a vagina or more specifically a clitoris, then the issue of marriage for them, according to Jesus, is mute because the biological makings that are responsible for sexual urges are not there. They are eunuchs from birth and therefore they can do without sex. They can therefore also do without marriage since the primary factor that drives people into marriage according to what Jesus and Paul taught, is an insatiable desire to engage in sexual intercourse. Eunuchs don't necessarily care for marriage because they don't necessarily have a sexual need driving them to wed. This is not to say that they would not or could not get married. Instead, this is just to emphasize that the main trigger that drives most people into marriage (sexual drive) does not biologically exist for them.[9]

---

[7] The divorce rate in America has increased from under 1% to roughly 12% since 1960 and is steady rising.

[8] During the time of Jesus and before, many men were castrated at birth in order that they might serve other men without being sexually distracted. The definition of a eunuch technically applies to men, however, the concept of a eunuch also applies to women who are born without female genitalia or have been victims of genital mutilation.

[9] However, it still may exist psychologically.

On the other hand, a person who has decided not to marry is not necessarily a person who never feels any sexual urges, as some may think. Christians who have decided not to marry are usually people who experience regular sexual urges just as anyone else does, but choose not to satisfy those urges in order that they may be able to serve God more diligently by remaining single. They have actually made a conscious decision, maybe for just a little while, or maybe for a lifetime, to remain single in order to be free to serve Jesus without the interruption of married life.

Again, Jesus gave three categories of people to whom he has given the fortitude not to marry: the eunuch at birth, the man-made eunuch, and those who have renounced marriage (thereby turning away from their sexual desires) for the sake of the kingdom of heaven (to more diligently serve him). Jesus did not say that this third category of person had no sexual desires. In looking at what Jesus has said about the matter, we can safely say that in order for a person to be void of sexual desire he or she would have to be born without genitalia or would have to be a victim of castration or genital mutilation.

Jesus' third category of those "who can accept this" is a category different from those who would desperately like to get married but are having a difficult time finding a mate. Not getting married is a difficult thing for people to accept if they are not eunuchs and/or if it is not their intention to deny themselves and renounce marriage for the "kingdom of Heaven." Even if a person has the intention of denying himself sexually for the sake of the kingdom of heaven (and therefore not marrying) he will not be able to carry out those intentions unless it is given to him (or her) by God to do so.

Jesus taught that the only people who can successfully remain single, besides eunuchs, are those to "whom it is given," meaning those whom God helps. This indicates that God gives a certain wherewithal or ability to abstain from marriage and sex to those that he wills. This ability is what some refer to as the gift of singleness. Of course, not all people have this gift of singleness, which is why Paul teaches that if a man cannot control his sexual urges towards his fiancé then he should marry her before he falls into sexual sin. Although it is better to remain single, it is not given to all to accept being single. Some Christians may try very hard to be single only to realize that it is very difficult for them to live without sexual passion. They should therefore marry. However, there are also those people to whom God has given the ability to resist sexual passion who reject their gift of singleness and seek to get married anyway. There are probably many Christians to whom God has given a gift of singleness, who fight against this gift or won't accept the fact that they may be in possession of it. It can be safely assumed that this resistance exists partly as a result of the church's tendency, as a whole, to glorify marriage and undervalue singleness. Many Christians who God has given the gift of singleness to end up believing that they would be happier being married, instead of believing what the Bible teaches on these things, which is that they would be happier being single. But the word of God also teaches us that God will not tempt us beyond what we can bear. So those whom God has given a gift of singleness, can bear everything that comes along with the gift, including any temptation towards sexual sin. But if they refuse to accept this, then they will essentially be turning their backs on the gift that God has given them. There are those Christians for whom singleness is God's will for their lives.

The New Living Translation of the Bible translates 1st Corinthians 7:7 in these words: *"I wish everyone could get along without marrying, just as I do. But we are not all the same. God gives some the gift of marriage, and to others he gives the gift of singleness."* Therefore, being single is certainly not for everyone. Jesus taught and emphasized this. But for those who can accept being single, and to those to whom it is given to be single, it is a very good thing because as Jesus said, "they have renounced marriage because of the kingdom of heaven." This means that they have sacrificed a large part of themselves for the sake of the kingdom of God. They have consciously chosen to deny sexual gratification in order to serve God more completely and without the distraction of marriage. God has given them the willpower to resist sexual urges. With this said, it cannot be emphasized enough that to be single is as much of a gift from God as to be married and that married women are no more favored of the Lord than single women.

Some say that in order for a man or a woman to deny sex and marriage for the kingdom of heaven, he or she must have a "gift of celibacy." They believe that those who have this gift never experience sexual temptation or urges. But the Bible doesn't say this. Again, from what Jesus taught, it is safe to say that those with the gift to remain single may indeed experience sexual urges but are able to deny themselves sexually, with God's help, for the sake of the kingdom of God. If there is a gift in operation then the gift is the willpower God has given them to resist sexual urges, not the elimination of these urges. The message of Jesus and Paul concerning these things seems clear: if a person has the ability to deny his or herself sexual pleasures, then he or she should remain single in order to have the freedom to serve God more diligently. Those who can live without being married, should.

In moving along with our discussion, certain emphasis must be put on 1st Corinthians 7:27 which reads, *"Are you married? Do not seek a divorce. Are you unmarried? Do not look for a wife."* Men and women should not seek a divorce unless they have sound biblical justification to do so. Although Paul stated that it is good to remain single, by instructing Christians not to seek a divorce,[10] he was telling them that although being single is a good thing, one cannot divorce his or her spouse just because they'd like to be single again. Interestingly, Paul also instructed single men not to look for a wife. This must be focused upon because there are those Christians who, when discussing these matters, point to and emphasize Proverbs 18:22 in an attempt to support their position that it's all right for a man to overtly search for a wife. The scripture reads, *"whoso findeth a wife findeth a good thing, and obtaineth favour of the LORD."* Many preachers and ministers of the gospel use this verse to encourage men to actually look for a wife as well as use it to discourage women from looking for a husband. They mistakenly equate the term *findeth* with the phrase *looketh for*. However, according to the verse of scripture just cited in Corinthians, a man is not supposed to look for a wife ("do not look for a wife") any more than a woman is supposed to look for a husband. A person can *find* something or someone that he or she was not necessarily looking for. The Hebrew for the word *findeth* that is used in the text is *matsa* and it means to *appear, exist, attain, find, acquire, to occur, meet, befall, catch*. All of these meanings give the implication that something occurred by happenstance, so to speak. So, if a man finds a wife, then according to what Paul said, he should have done so without looking for her. Otherwise, 1st Corinthians 7:27 contradicts Proverbs 18:22.

If a man (as well as a woman) happens to meet someone he wants to marry, then that is a good thing. However, according to 1st Corinthians 7:27 which instructs a single man not to look for a wife and 1st Corinthians 7:26 that encourages single women ("virgins") to remain unmarried, single Christian men and women should not seek to get

---

[10] For a more detailed discussion on divorce, see Chapter 8.

married. Neither gender should run around looking for a mate. As we will see, Paul has emphasized that although marriage is a good thing, it is not the best thing. Therefore, Paul basically advises against getting married and only advises marriage for those who cannot control their sexual passions.[11]

Besides "the present crisis" being the reason Paul gave for discouraging marriage, he also warned (as we discussed earlier in this chapter) in 1st Corinthians 7:28 that those who marry will face great troubles in life and he wanted to spare the saints these troubles. Paul is not saying that single people will not have any troubles in life. What he is saying is that married people will have more troubles in life than single people (of course, this is not applicable to singles that live unholy lives). Marriage is usually accompanied by children, in-laws, differences in opinion on a myriad of important issues such as money matters, sex, religious matters, how to raise the children, friends, career goals, housework, and the like. Single people are ideally not supposed to have these concerns and are therefore supposed to be able to concentrate more on serving the Lord. The following verses of scripture support this:

> [29]Now let me say this, dear brothers and sisters. The time that remains is very short, so husbands should not let marriage be their first concern. [30]Happiness or sadness or wealth should not keep anyone from doing God's work. [31]Those in frequent contact with the things of the world should make good use of them without becoming attached to them, for this world and all it contains will pass away. [32]In everything you do, I want you to be free from the concerns of this life. An unmarried man can spend his time doing the Lord's work and thinking how to please him. [33]But a married man can't do that so well. He has to think about his earthly responsibilities and how to please his wife. [34]His interests are divided. In the same way, a woman who is no longer married or has never been married can be more devoted to the Lord in body and in spirit, while the married woman must be concerned about her

---

[11] See 1st Corinthians 7:8, earlier in the chapter. This goes hand in hand with the newlywed sexual passion expressed in the *Song of Songs*. See Chapter 7.

earthly responsibilities and how to please her husband.
(1 Corinthians 7:29-35 NLT)

In verse 29 Paul tells Christians that the time is short and therefore, those who are married should not make their marriage their first priority. The implication is that they should put serving God above their marriage because one day, in the not too distant future, Christ will return, and Christians must strive to proclaim the gospel and serve the Lord as much as they can before time runs out and the Lord comes back. Not only should married Christians place their service to God above their marriage, but also, neither happiness, nor sadness, nor wealth should ever keep them from doing God's work.

This is not readily taught in the church today. Instead it is taught that Christians who are married are supposed to make sure to "balance" their responsibilities to their spouses equally with their responsibilities to God. But the word of God says differently. It implies a certain imbalance, not the kind of imbalance where a spouse is neglected, but the kind of imbalance that says the priority for a married Christian is to put serving God before serving one's spouse and one's children. If there is to be an imbalance, then the imbalance should be on the side of God and not on the side of the marriage. Of course, this "imbalance" must be within reason. But even the New International Version of the Bible translates verse 29 as saying *"those who have wives should live as though they had none."* Of course, this doesn't mean that married Christian men should go about committing adultery or neglecting their wives. It does, however, mean that they should try to serve the Lord (as much as they can within the boundaries of their marriage) as diligently as they would if they were single. Married women should do the same. They should serve the Lord as diligently as they would if they were single.

Paul goes on to explain himself further concerning these issues. He includes additional reasons as to why he believes single people should remain unmarried. In verses 32 and 33, Paul says that a single man concerns himself with how he can please the Lord while a married man concerns himself with the affairs of the world and how he can please his wife. He says the same thing about married women, that they concern themselves with how they can please their husbands while single women concern themselves with how they can please the Lord. In other words, being married gets in the way of serving God to one's fullest potential. If one is married, he or she must always consider how ministering for the

Lord will effect his or her spouse, how it will effect the children, and how it will effect his or her marriage. This does not mean that it is wrong to get married. This simply means that it is not wrong to remain single. Marriage is a blessing for many. However, a person who is single can do anything he or she wishes to do for the Lord without being limited by the emotional, physical, or financial needs of a spouse.

Some will argue that in serving her husband, a wife is thereby serving the Lord (especially if her husband is serving the Lord) since, in marriage, the man is the head of the wife, and Christ is the head of the man. However, there is nothing specifically in scripture that supports this type of thinking. If by serving one's husband a woman is serving the Lord, then it would stand to reason that Paul would have never differentiated between a woman serving the Lord and serving her husband. Paul would have seen them as one in the same. But he indeed differentiated between the two which is evident in verse 34 which again reads, *"in the same way, a woman who is no longer married or has never been married can be more devoted to the Lord in body and in spirit, while the married woman must be concerned about her earthly responsibilities and how to please her husband."* Serving the Lord and serving one's husband are therefore two different functions. A woman who is serving her husband is serving her husband, not the Lord. The word of God does not make serving one's husband synonymous with serving the Lord, and therefore neither should we. To further the point, as stated earlier, the Bible clearly teaches that serving one's husband gets in the way of serving the Lord, just as serving one's wife gets in the way of serving the Lord. Let's look further:

> [36]If anyone thinks he is acting improperly toward the virgin he is engaged to, and if she is getting along in years and he feels he ought to marry, he should do as he wants. He is not sinning. They should get married. [37]But the man who has settled the matter in his own mind, who is under no compulsion but has control over his own will, and who has made up his mind not to marry the virgin—this man also does the right thing. [38]So then, he who marries the virgin does right, but he who does not marry her does even better.
> (1 Corinthians 7:36-38 NIV)

In verse 36 Paul makes it clear again that it is not a sin to marry. This must be emphasized since he has stated that it is actually better for Christians to remain single (verse 38). According to Paul, marriage is a good thing but, when it comes to serving the Lord, it is not the best thing. Verse 36 instructs engaged Christian men who are acting improperly towards their fiancés, not to hesitate in getting married. The phrase "acting improperly" means that the man is attempting to have sexual intercourse with his fiancé before marriage. If he is doing this and his fiancé is getting along in years, then he should marry her. He should not keep her waiting and he should not keep trying to seduce or coerce her into having sex before marriage. Sex is only reserved for the marriage bed. Otherwise, Paul would not insist for men, who have difficulty controlling their sexual behavior, to marry.

Verse 37 moves on to say that a man who has control over his sexual desires (not that he doesn't have any sexual desires) and has made up his mind not to marry, does the right thing. In other words, he should call off the engagement so he can fully concentrate on serving the Lord. However, Paul also says that a man who marries his fiancé does the right thing as well. Then Paul says *"but he who does not marry her does even better."* Again, with this said, Paul is teaching us that it is better to remain single than to get married.

These things are rarely mentioned in the pulpit, if at all. Many men are prone to preach entire sermons about a woman's submissive role in a marriage and barely touch upon the doctrine that says that ultimately, it is better for a woman to remain single and that she'd be happier if she did (see the following scripture quote). Many women are just as prone to rank marriage above singleness. Christian women will often ask single women whether or not they are "believing God for a husband" as if whether or not a woman is married has to do with how much she believes that God will give her a husband. The Bible teaches us that God will give us what we want but only according to his will.[12] Therefore, if it is God's will for a woman to be married then at some point in her life, she will have the opportunity to do so. But there are also those women whom God has given to remain single. No doubt there are many of these women who marry out of God's will.

---

[12] "Now this is the confidence that we have in Him, that if we ask anything according to His will, He hears us." (1 John 5:14 NKJV)

Although it is better for Christians to remain single, being single does not make a Christian any holier or more righteous than his or her married sister or brother in the Lord. What it does, however, is make them more available to be used by God.

When looking at how the Bible compares married life to the single life, being single is simply a better state to be in for a Christian if he or she wants to serve the Lord better. This does not mean that a married Christian cannot steadfastly serve the Lord but only that their service has limitations because they are married. Paul also says the following in regards to single women:

> [39]A wife should stay married to her husband until he dies. Then she is free to marry again, but only to a man who is a follower of the Lord. [40]However, I think I am obeying God's Spirit when I say she would be happier to stay single. (1 Corinthians 7:39-40 CEV)

Paul teaches us again and again that it is better for a woman to remain single; not just for the sake of the Lord, but for her own sake as well; for her own happiness. He says that widows are free to marry, but that in his judgment, a widow will be happier if she remains single. But this seems to contradict the following verses of scripture concerning widows:

> [3]Give proper recognition to those widows who are really in need. [4]But if a widow has children or grandchildren, these should learn first of all to put their religion into practice by caring for their own family and so repaying their parents and grandparents, for this is pleasing to God. [5]The widow who is really in need and left all alone puts her hope in God and continues night and day to pray and to ask God for help. [6]But the widow who lives for pleasure is dead even while she lives. [7]Give the people these instructions, too, so that no one may be open to blame. [8]If anyone does not provide for his relatives, and especially for his immediate family, he has denied the faith and is worse than an unbeliever.

⁹No widow may be put on the list of widows unless she is over sixty, has been faithful to her husband, ¹⁰and is well known for her good deeds, such as bringing up children, showing hospitality, washing the feet of the saints, helping those in trouble and devoting herself to all kinds of good deeds.

¹¹As for younger widows, do not put them on such a list. For when their sensual desires overcome their dedication to Christ, they want to marry. ¹²Thus they bring judgment on themselves, because they have broken their first pledge. ¹³Besides, they get into the habit of being idle and going about from house to house. And not only do they become idlers, but also gossips and busybodies, saying things they ought not to say. ¹⁴So I counsel younger widows to marry, to have children, to manage their homes and to give the enemy no opportunity for slander. (1 Timothy 5:3-14 NIV)

During Paul's time it was the duty of the church to take care of widows because women were basically not able to make a living as they are able to do today. In Paul's time, the financial security of a woman depended on whether or not she was married. Women who were not married remained at home under the care of their parents until they were married and those women who were married depended on their husbands for income. Rarely did a woman provide for herself without the assistance of a husband or of her immediate family. It is certainly a good thing that today's Western society allows for the financial independence of women. It is a blessing in large part, because a woman who wishes to remain single is at liberty to do so without worrying about her own financial security.

Because financial independence of women went against the customs of Paul's time, the church was left with the responsibility of taking care of widows. Apparently the churches of Paul's time had a widow's list and those women who were on the list were guaranteed lifetime living provisions from the church. However, Paul instructed the immediate family members of all widows to take care of the widows in their families so that the church could be relieved of the burden. There were also certain qualifications that were required in order for the name of a widow to be placed on the church's widow list. One of those qualifications was that the widow be at least 60 years old. This is because it was felt that younger widows (59 years of age and under) would eventually be overcome with sexual desires and want to marry again.

Church support for widows then, was to only be used as a lifetime means of support for those widows of whom it was suspected would never marry again, did not have any family to help them, and had done good deeds in the Lord during their marriage, such as raising children, being hospitable to others (probably especially to those ministers of the gospel who were traveling from city to city preaching the word), washing the feet of the saints,[13] and helping those who were in trouble. Church support was not to be used, as a temporary financial means of support for widows of whom it was suspected would remarry some day.

Scholars are not sure what is meant in verse 12 when it says that by remarrying, the younger widows would have brought judgment upon themselves because they would have broken their first pledge. This could not have been referring to the marital pledge they had made with their husbands, because, as we have seen earlier, they were automatically free to marry when their husbands died. Therefore, theologians believe that there may have been some kind of widow's pledge that Paul was speaking of here. It is speculated by some theologians that the pledge had to do with a promise not to remarry should their husbands die, thereby allowing the opportunity to devote time to Christ persistently.

Our particular focus here however, is Paul's counsel that the younger widows remarry (verse 14). This is the verse in particular that seems to contradict his earlier counsel in 1st Corinthians 7:39-40 in which he says that he believes a widow would be happier if she didn't remarry. The difference between the two instructions is that in 1st Corinthians Paul is actually emphasizing the point that women would be happier if they did not get married. However, no matter how much he says it, there will be women who feel that they would be happier if they were married. Just as Jesus taught that only certain people are able to accept being single, Paul knew that most women (and men for that matter) are not willing to remain single and when their "sensual desires overcome their dedication to Christ" they marry. Furthermore, as we have seen when looking at

---

[13] Sandals were worn during the time of Jesus. Often times a person's feet would become dusty from walking in sandals. Foot washing was a common practice, usually performed by servants. However, Jesus taught a lesson in humility and hospitality when he washed the feet of the apostles (see Chapter 3).

what Jesus said in Matthew 19:11-12, singleness is only for those to whom it is given. So, if a widowed woman cannot control her sexual desires then she is commanded to marry just as a man is who cannot control his sexual desires towards his fiancé.

Thus, when Paul instructs widows to marry in 1st Timothy 5:14, he is not contradicting what he said earlier about it being better not to marry. He is instead addressing the fact that although he knows a woman would be happier if she were not to get married, he understands that most women don't realize this and are not willing to give up their sensual desires for the cause of Jesus (just as most men are not). And therefore, they should marry.

But in regards to happiness, studies have shown that married women suffer from depression substantially more than married men do. This might be due to the fact that many husbands expect their wives to be the perfect homemaker as well as work outside of the home.[14] Most women cannot do both well, simultaneously. Consequently, most married women who work outside the home have a difficult time living up to the expectations of their husbands when it comes to their duties inside the home. This can be a great cause for depression. In addition, raising children is a 24-hour job. This is something that many men don't seem to understand very well. Raising children and taking care of the home is very demanding even if the woman doing it is not working the traditional "9 to 5" outside of the home. We must remember that the most virtuous of wives had nannies, servants, and slaves to help her take care of her household.[15] Most men do not provide any housekeeping help for their wives in the home and only pitch in once in a while themselves with the housework and caring for the children. It is very difficult for women to live up to the expectations of their husbands without some help in the home. But the days of the extended family are virtually over. Most housewives are forced to meet the demands of taking care of the home and raising the children all on their own. This is simply not the way it was during biblical times. Women had help in the home. Lots of help. That help is not here today. However, there are those husbands who still expect their wives to meet the demands of homemaker and caretaker despite the fact that they have not provided any help for their wives in the home. Many men do not believe that women need any help. But

---

[14] See Chapter 6.

[15] See Chapter 6.

when looking at how women handled their households during biblical times, it is obvious that they do. This homemaker/caretaker demand that a woman is faced with in the marital home with little assistance from her husband is also great cause for a woman's depression in a marriage. When the honeymoon is over, for many women, it is unfortunately over forever.

Moreover, when a Christian woman gets married, she greatly compromises her ability to chose her options in life, while her husband, although he has put himself in a position where he should be willing to compromise, is not nearly risking as much in marrying his wife as she is in marrying him, since he is the head of the house and his final decision about a matter stands. A married woman's happiness greatly depends on how much her husband is willing to sacrifice his wants and desires for hers and is greatly dependent on whether or not her husband rules over her harshly. Moreover, happiness is a very subjective thing. A man might not feel as if he is ruling over his wife harshly while his wife may feel that he is.

To cite a couple of examples: if a man wants more children and his wife doesn't, his wife is obligated to have them. However, if a woman wants more children and her husband doesn't, she is obligated not to have them. If a man wants to move out of town and his wife doesn't, his wife is obligated to move thus leaving all of her friends and family. However, if a woman wants to move out of town and her husband doesn't, she must learn to be content with where she is living. In marriage a woman's options can easily disappear, while a man's options remain in tact. No wonder Paul said that a woman is happier if she remains single. A woman's happiness is truly dependent on whether or not her husband shows her the kind of sacrificial love that Paul spoke of when he instructed husbands to love their wives as Christ loved the church. If a man operates in this kind of love, then his wife's options remain open. But this is a big if. However, God's word instructs men to love their wives in this sacrificial way. Therefore, we can safely surmise that the "sacrificial love" instruction exists in order to limit the cursedness of a husband's rule. The problem is that many men do not love their wives sacrificially and by not doing so, cause much more trouble in their marriages and more distress for their wives than need be.

When writing to the Philippians, Paul also taught that Christians should remain content in whatever circumstance they are in. Let's take a look:

¹²I know what it is to have little, and I know what it is
to have plenty. In any and all circumstances I have
learned the secret of being well-fed and of going
hungry, of having plenty and of being in need. ¹³I can
do all things through him who strengthens me.
(Philippians 4:12-13 NRSV)

Paul is saying that Christians should learn to be content in any and
every circumstance. Being single is a circumstance (just as being married
is). Some Christians are upset because they are single and they long to
get married. But if a Christian is single and desires to be married, he or
she should strive to be content with being single.

There is an example of a man whom God instructed to remain single
for a certain period of time. The man was the prophet Jeremiah. Let's
take a look:

¹The word of the LORD came to me: ²You shall not take
a wife, nor shall you have sons or daughters in this
place. ³For thus says the LORD concerning the sons and
daughters who are born in this place, and concerning
the mothers who bear them and the fathers who beget
them in this land: ⁴They shall die of deadly diseases.
They shall not be lamented, nor shall they be buried;
they shall become like dung on the surface of the
ground. They shall perish by the sword and by famine,
and their dead bodies shall become food for the birds of
the air and for the wild animals of the earth.
    ⁵For thus says the LORD: Do not enter the house of
mourning, or go to lament, or bemoan them; for I have
taken away my peace from this people, says the LORD,
my steadfast love and mercy. ⁶Both great and small
shall die in this land; they shall not be buried, and no
one shall lament for them; there shall be no gashing, no
shaving of the head for them. ⁷No one shall break bread
for the mourner, to offer comfort for the dead; nor
shall anyone give them the cup of consolation to drink
for their fathers or their mothers. (Jeremiah 16:1-7
NRSV)

> ¹⁰When you tell the people all these things, they will ask, 'Why has the LORD decreed such terrible things against us? What have we done to deserve such treatment? What is our sin against the LORD our God?' ¹¹Tell them that this is the LORD's reply: It is because your ancestors were unfaithful to me. They worshipped other gods and served them. They abandoned me. They did not keep my law. ¹²And you are even worse than your ancestors! You stubbornly follow your own evil desires and refuse to listen to me. ¹³So I will throw you out of this land and send you into a foreign land where you and your ancestors have never been. There you can worship idols all you like—and I will grant you no favors. (Jeremiah 16:10-13 NLT)

Jeremiah was a prophet during King Josaiah's thirteenth year of reign. Jeremiah was the son of a Jewish priest. He prophesied against those Israelites who were in the cities of Jerusalem and Judah, which were often referred to together as the city of Judea. Judea was a province that included Jersualem and the regions surrounding Jerusalem. The word Judea itself means *Jewish*. Apparently, those in the city of Jerusalem and the nation of Israel had once again turned against God, by worshipping false gods as their ancestors did.¹⁶

Jeremiah was called to proclaim judgment on Israel. This was no easy task. In order to adhere to his calling, Jeremiah had to live in Judea. God instructed Jeremiah not to get married or have children in Judea because the land of Judea was full of famine and disease. Since Jeremiah's ministry in Judea was to be a lifelong task, God's instruction for Jeremiah not to marry or have children was a lifelong instruction. So, Jeremiah never married and he never had children. This is not to say that he didn't want to, but he was heeding the call of God and abiding by God's instruction. If then Jeremiah was never to marry and never to have children, then it follows that he was never to have sex. Certainly, God gave him the fortitude to carry out his mission without fretting over marriage and sex. But the emphasis here is that Jeremiah was instructed not to marry (and therefore not to be sexually active), not that he didn't

---

¹⁶ Jeremiah also prophesied against the city of Babylon. Babylon conquered and destroyed Jerusalem in the year 587. B.C.

want to. Apparently, if Jeremiah were to have married, then the burdens of marriage would have gotten in the way of the assignment that God had given him to do in life. As we can see when examining the life of the prophet Jeremiah, not all people are supposed to get married. There are those who are supposed to stay single, if but for a certain period of time, to do a special work for the Lord. And as we have learned through the teachings of Paul, it is possible for women as well as men to be called of God into a life of singleness in order that they may serve the Lord better or in order that they might heed to a specific calling. The greatest example of this is Jesus. He was single. In the natural, he never married nor did he have children.

A Christian who is single but does not want to be single, is often struggling with sexual urges, intense feelings of loneliness, societal stigmas associated with being single, an unfulfilled desire to have children, the feeling that they are lacking in physical and emotional affection, and a host of other frustrating issues which should not be minimized by satisfied singles and those who are married. A Christian who is single but does not want to be single has a serious matter to contend with. But they must still strive to be content in their situation. This doesn't mean that they have to like the situation they are in, but only that they must accept it and learn to live with it because there is a reason that God has them in a state of singleness. And as we have seen, singleness is no less an honorable state to be in than marriage. Furthermore, the word of God teaches us that God will not tempt us beyond what we can bear.[17] So those Christians who are single, can apparently bear it.

To take matters further, not only does the Bible teach that being single (for Christians at least) is a better state to be in than being married, but it also emphasizes the point by teaching that marriage is merely an earthly endeavor. There is no marriage in heaven now and there will be no marriage in heaven ever. The following verses of scripture attest to this:

> [27]Some Sadducees, those who say there is no resurrection, came to him [28]and asked him a question,

---

[17] "...And God is faithful; he will not let you be tempted beyond what you can bear. But when you are tempted, he will also provide a way out so that you can stand up under it." (1 Corinthians 10:13 NIV)

> "Teacher, Moses wrote for us that if a man's brother dies, leaving a wife but no children, the man shall marry the widow and raise up children for his brother. [29]Now there were seven brothers; the first married, and died childless; [30]then the second [31]and the third married her, and so in the same way all seven died childless. [32]Finally the woman also died. [33]In the resurrection, therefore, whose wife will the woman be? For the seven had married her."
>
> [34]Jesus said to them, "Those who belong to this age marry and are given in marriage; [35]but those who are considered worthy of a place in that age and in the resurrection from the dead neither marry nor are given in marriage. [36]Indeed they cannot die anymore, because they are like angels and are children of God, being children of the resurrection. (Luke 20:27-36 NRSV)

Jesus made it clear that none of the men that the woman was married to during her earthly life could claim her during her heavenly everlasting life. The marriages she was involved in would no longer matter once she was in heaven. Marriages will become a shadow of things past once Christians enter the kingdom of heaven. The resurrection of the dead that is spoken of is what Christians refer to as the rapture. The rapture is a catching away of Christians, dead and alive, at the Second Coming of Jesus Christ. The scriptures teach us that at the return of Christ, all those who believed on the name of Jesus and accepted him as Lord and Savior will be caught up in the air (the "rapture") to meet him. The scriptures also teach that, at the time when the church will be caught up in the air, Christians who have died (the dead in Christ) will rise first (from the dead) and then those Christians who are still living will then rise. The occurrence of the dead rising in Christ is referred to as the resurrection of the dead.[18]

If there is no marriage in heaven then there is no sex in heaven. If there is no sex in heaven then there will be no desire for sex in heaven. If there is no desire for sex in heaven then it stands to reason that the citizens of heaven might be without gender. But the latter is just speculation. One thing is for sure, there will be no marriage in heaven

---

[18] 1 Thessalonians 4:16 and John 11:24 (see your Bible).

and therefore there will be no sex in heaven. Marriage among humans is an earthy matter, not a heavenly one. It is for this age. It is for this dispensation.[19] But once Christians are living in the eternal heavenly age, marriage will be a thing of the past and singleness will be the rule of thumb just as it was in the beginning when God first created man. Initially, Adam was single. God's ultimate plan (which was represented in the singleness of Adam when he first created him) is that we will all live a single life (in heaven) thereby serving him without distraction. Those who live single in this dispensation of Grace and those who have lived single before us, are earthly examples of a heavenly life.

In spite of the verses of scripture in the Bible that teach that it is better to be single as opposed to being married, there will always be those who try to minimize the message in those verses of scripture. Ecclesiastes 4:9 is one of the verses of scripture some will use to try to prove that it is better for people, in general, to be married than for them to be single. It says, the following:

> [7]I observed yet another example of meaninglessness in our world. [8]This is the case of a man who is all alone, without a child or a brother, yet who works hard to gain as much wealth as he can. But then he asks himself, "Who am I working for? Why am I giving up so much pleasure now?" It is all so meaningless and depressing.
> [9]Two people can accomplish more than twice as much as one; they get a better return for their labor. [10]If one person falls, the other can reach out and help. But people who are alone when they fall are in real trouble. [11]And on a cold night, two under the same blanket can gain warmth from each other. But how can one be warm alone? [12]A person standing alone can be attacked and defeated, but two can stand back-to-back and conquer. Three are even better, for a triple-braided cord is not easily broken. (Ecclesiastes 4:7-12 NLT)

These verses in Ecclesiastes are specifically referring to people whose main focus on life is getting rich. In order to do so, they have put aside

---

[19] See Introduction

413

everything else, including family, friends, the prospect of getting married and the prospect of having children. They have become workaholics in an attempt to achieve their goal of being rich. They have not only decided not to marry, but in their quest to get rich they have alienated all of the people around them including their family and friends. These people are literally alone and if they get in trouble there will be no one there to help them. This is different from what the Bible says about women and men remaining single. Just because a person is single, this does not mean that they don't have any family and friends to lean on in times of trouble. Singleness is not a synonym for loneliness as some would like to think. But, according to the verses cited in Ecclesiastes, the love of money is.

Verse 11 goes on to say that on a cold night it is better if two are under the blanket, because it is hard for one person to keep warm alone. Because of our culture, we might automatically assume that this verse is talking about a husband and wife. But this is not necessarily the case. When looking at verse 12, it is suggested that three people working together are even better than two are. Certainly then, the writer of the book of Ecclesiastes is not really speaking of marriage when expressing his view that two people can accomplish twice as much as one, because he said that even three people can accomplish more. Thus, he cannot be speaking of marriage if he is indirectly saying that it is better for three people to be under the blanket (verse 12), for as we have seen polygamy is not allowed and the marriage bed should have in it no more than two. Therefore, we can safely surmise that these scriptures are not encouraging people to get married or teaching that it is better to be married but are instead encouraging teamwork, in general.

SUMMARY

No matter how successful a marriage is, a married Christian is simply not as free to serve the Lord as a single Christian is. In the case of married Christians, there will be things that come up in their marriages that they must always consider and often times these things will be put ahead of God, even though Paul taught not to do so. Despite this, there are still certain responsibilities in marriage that must be fulfilled. For example, Paul instructed married couples not to separate for long periods of time because a long separation can trigger the temptation of adultery.[20] Paul went on to say that both the wife and husband must agree as to how long any separation between them will be. Therefore, if one spouse has a ministry that requires out of town travel for a time and his or her spouse is despondent in regards to the length of this time, then the one with the ministry must compromise his or her ministry in order to appease his or her spouse. Single Christians do not have to worry about such things. They are free to serve God as often and as long as they like, without spousal interference.

When looking categorically at single women, Paul specifically said that a single woman can more easily devote herself to the Lord when compared to a woman who is married. Paul goes on to say that single Christians, in general, are able to give undivided devotion to the Lord. Paul unequivocally said that it is better for women as well as men to be single and that marriage brings along with it lots of trouble. Certainly, a chauvinistic God would not encourage a woman to remain single.

No matter how difficult it is for some who are in the church to accept this, when considering what has been discussed in this chapter, it is an undeniable truth that the scriptures teach that it is all right with God if a woman chooses not to get married and therefore not to have children. Not only does scripture teach this but scripture goes one step further and teaches that a woman is better off emotionally, as well as in her ability to serve the Lord, if she remains single.

Certainly a chauvinistic God would have instead said that it is better for a man to remain single in order that he may serve the Lord but better for a woman to get married in order for her to serve man. But God did not say this. He does not make a difference between the sexes when it comes to serving him. Marriage divides the attention of both men and women away from God. No difference is made between the sexes when it comes to the benefits of being single. Single men are given no special privileges as opposed to single women. Furthermore, single women are no less valid to God than married women are. God has not set any doubles standards here.

---

[20] Corinthians 7:3-5 (see Appendix)

13.

SOME "FEMINIST" CONCERNS

Feminism is any organized activity that defends the rights of women and says that women should have the same political, economic, social and religious opportunities that a man does, in any society. Feminism, in its purist form is not necessarily a bad thing. The women's suffrage movement led to women getting the vote (1920) and was a historical feminist battle (although not referred to as feminism in that day) that needed to be fought. There was also a time when women, who performed the same work as men on the job, were paid less. But because of the women's liberation movement of the sixties, which was spearheaded by many feminists of that day, women now make the same pay as men if they are working the same jobs as men.

Both men and women can have feminist views and therefore be considered feminists. However, a woman with feminist views is more likely to be labeled a feminist, whereas a man with feminist views is more likely to be labeled a liberal. There are certain popularized concerns that many feminists have when it comes to the topic of God. In this chapter, we will discuss some of these concerns.

REFERENCE TO GOD IN THE MALE VERNACULAR

There are conservative feminists and liberal feminists. Most liberal feminists believe that God can be thought of in the female vernacular as well as in the male vernacular. Many of these feminists refer to God as "she" and refuse to embrace the Bible because the Bible speaks of God in masculine terms. But although the Bible does indeed reference God in the male vernacular, God is neither a man nor a woman, but is a spirit, as the following verses of scripture attest to:

> [23]But the hour is coming, and now is, when the true worshipers will worship the Father in spirit and truth; for the Father is seeking such to worship Him.
> [24]God is Spirit, and those who worship Him must worship in spirit and truth. (John 4:23-24 NKJV)

> Now the Lord is the Spirit; and where the Spirit of the
> Lord is, there is Liberty. (2 Corinthians 3:17 NASB)

John 4:24 teaches us that God is a Spirit. This means that his being is best described in spiritual terms. However, as explained in the Introduction, There is only one God, and this one God represents himself in three persons or personages: The Father, the Son (who once came in the person of Jesus Christ), and the Holy Ghost (God's spirit). Normally, when we think of a person we think of a human being. But the meaning of the word *person* when used in defining who God is, is wider in scope and is synonymous with the words *soul, personage, life,* and *being.* Therefore, although God is a spirit, he is a person as well, because a spirit is a being and a being is a person. And as the scripture says, "where the Spirit of the Lord is, there is Liberty."

The terminology of *Father* and *Son* is masculine. Consequently, God is spoken of in masculine terms. Furthermore, Jesus, in his earthly form, came as a man. Jesus is the second person of the Godhead.[1]

In the Bible, God is identified in the male vernacular. But despite the fact that God is referenced in the masculine, he is no less the God of women than he is the God of men. And both men and women were created in God's image. Let's take a look:

> [26]Then God said, "Let Us make man in Our image, according to Our likeness; and let them rule over the fish of the sea and over the birds of the sky and over the cattle and over all the earth, and over every creeping thing that creeps on the earth."
> [27]And God created man in His own image, in the image of God He created him; male and female He created them. (Genesis 1:26-27 NASB)

God made women in his image just as he made men in his image. Therefore, in light of the teaching that God is Spirit, the reference of God in the masculine does not necessarily denote a sexual being. If then men and women are both made in the image of God, then metaphorically, men and women are humanly the same, although physically very different. Since, both men and women are a reflection of

---

[1] See Introduction for more detailed information

417

God's image, women are as much a representation of God as men. And therefore, men and women were made equal.

Accordingly, we can say without hesitation that God represents women no less than he represents men. This in no way suggests that God should therefore be referenced in the female vernacular, it only suggests that it should not matter if he isn't.

The reference to God as *He* does nothing to minimize or change the fact that the Bible teaches that both men and women were made in the image of God on equal grounds. The reference to God as *He* does not make men superior to women or connote any special favor God has towards men over women. And the reference to God as *He* does not lessen the reality that both men and women are equally created in the image of God. God being referenced in the male vernacular simply does not take anything away from women.

With that said, it is important to make note of a biblical feminine reference to God that is virtually rarely spoken of, if spoken of at all, in the church today. This feminine reference has to do with the Hebrew word that the writers of the Old Testament used for the word *Spirit* when referring to the Spirit of God. In the Old Testament, the Hebrew word *ruwach* is used for the word *Spirit* each time the Spirit of God was spoken of. The word *ruwach* is a feminine word.

Some languages specify words as masculine, feminine, or neutral. Hebrew and Greek are two of those languages, but generally, English is not. Therefore, it may be difficult for those who speak English to understand the significance of a word written or spoken in the feminine or masculine, since the English language does not identify its nouns as masculine, feminine, or neutral. But those who speak English *do* understand *nouns* as masculine, feminine, or neutral when it comes to names. Thus the following example is presented to emphasize the point: *Robert*, which is a masculine name becomes *Roberta* in the feminine, and *Pat* is a neutral name that can be given to a man or a woman. Most people wouldn't name their daughters Robert and they wouldn't name their sons Roberta. Therefore the feminine version of *Robert* (which is *Roberta*) can be safely said to represent a female, just as the masculine version of *Roberta* (which is *Robert*) can be safely said to represent a male.

The Spirit of God is the same as the Holy Spirit of God. The third person of the Godhead, the Holy Spirit, is spoken of in the feminine in the Hebrew (*ruwach*). However, the New Testament Greek word that is used for the *Spirit* of God is *pneuma*. *Pneuma* is a neutral word, meaning it has no masculine or feminine connotation. On the other hand, Jesus specifically speaks of the Holy Spirit in the masculine in the following verses of scripture:

> [16]And I will ask the Father, and he will give you another Counselor to be with you forever—[17]the Spirit of truth. The world cannot accept him, because it neither sees him nor knows him. But you know him, for he lives with you and will be in you. (John 14:16-17 NIV)

> But the Counselor, the Holy Spirit, whom the Father will send in my name, will teach you all things and will remind you of everything I have said to you. (John 14:26 NIV)

And again in the King James:

> [26] But the Comforter, which is the Holy Ghost, whom the Father will send in my name, he shall teach you all things, and bring all things to your remembrance, whatsoever I have said unto you. (John 14:26)

The Spirit that Jesus refers to is the Spirit of truth. The Spirit of truth and God's Holy Spirit are synonymous. The pronoun *he* that Jesus associates with the Spirit (the Counselor) is translated from the Greek masculine pronoun *ekeinos*. There is no question then that Jesus refers to the Holy Spirit in masculine terms. Consequently, most biblical translators follow suit when applying the male vernacular to the Holy Spirit in the New Testament.

One might ask how the Spirit of God could be referenced in the feminine in the Hebrew language of the Old Testament and then referenced in the masculine in the Greek language of the New Testament. One explanation may lie in looking at functionality as opposed to position. The theologians responsible for the New International Version of the Bible compare the Holy Spirit (Counselor, Comforter) to that of a helper (by teaching and bringing all things to remembrance the Holy

Spirit is helping). The Greek word for Comforter that is used in John 14:26 is *parakletos* and is a verb, which literally means to give aid to or to stand by the side of another, to help. Eve, a female, was created as a helper to Adam. Therefore the function of a helper (Counselor, Holy Spirit) may be defined in feminine terms whereas the actual position (status, place) of the helper may be defined in masculine terms. But, this is only theory.

God is who he is and he has a right to identify himself whichever way he chooses. And although there is Old Testament reference to the Spirit of God in feminine terms, this does not give license to refer to God as "she" for Jesus refers to the Holy Spirit as "he" and it is obvious that the Father and the Son are masculine terms. However, the fact that the Hebrew feminine term *ruwach* is used in the Old Testament when referring to the Spirit of God is not something that should be minimized or overlooked. It is, after all, a feminine noun used throughout the Old Testament to refer to a personage of the Godhead. This is a fact that would be difficult to explain away and a fact that cannot be erased. Certainly a chauvinistic God would have never inspired any of the biblical authors to ever make reference to any personage of him in any way by using a feminine derivative of a word. But as we see, he did. *Ruwach* is a Hebrew feminine word and was used extensively to refer to God's Spirit in the Old Testament.

NONE OF THE BIBLICAL BOOKS WERE WRITTEN BY WOMEN...OR WERE THEY?

There are 66 books in the Bible. Each book is either categorized as an Old Testament book or a New Testament book. There are 39 books of the Old Testament which include the following books: Genesis, Exodus, Leviticus, Numbers, Deuteronomy, Joshua, Judges, Ruth, 1st Samuel, 2nd Samuel, 1st Kings, 2nd Kings, 1st Chronicles, 2nd Chronicles, Ezra, Nehemiah, Esther, Job, Psalms, Proverbs, Ecclesiastes, Song of Songs, Isaiah, Jeremiah, Lamentations, Ezekiel, Daniel, Hosea, Joel, Amos, Obadiah, Jonah, Micah, Nahum, Habakkuk, Zephaniah, Haggai, Zechariah, and Malachi.

There are 27 books of the New Testament which include the following books: Matthew, Mark, Luke, John, Acts, Romans, 1st Corinthians, 2nd Corinthians, Galatians, Ephesians, Philippians, Colossians, 1st Thessalonians, 2nd Thessalonians, 1st Timothy, 2nd

Timothy, Titus, Philemon, Hebrews, James, 1st Peter, 2nd Peter, 1st John, 2nd John, 3rd John, Jude, and Revelation.

The Old Testament was written before the birth of Jesus Christ between 1400 B.C. and 400 B.C., and foretold his coming and his ministry. The New Testament was written between 45 and 95 A.D. and documented the teachings and ministry of the Gospel of Jesus Christ.

Theological scholars unanimously agree that Moses wrote the first five books of the Bible. According to the New International Version of the Bible translators, there is uncertainty as to who the final author and editor was of the book of Joshua.

Most biblical scholars believe that Solomon wrote the book of Judges, but there is no real proof that he did. There is speculation that Solomon may have gathered together written accounts that were already available during the period of judges and assisted in putting those accounts together that eventually led to the Book of Judges. There is also speculation that the prophets Nathan and Gad may have assisted in this compilation and even in the editing of the material. However, this is only speculation.

Scholars agree that it is virtually unknown who the author of Ruth is. Jewish tradition has assigned Samuel as the author but the majority of theologians believe that Samuel could not have been the author because reference to David in the book of Ruth dates the writing of the book later than when Samuel could have actually written it.

Scholars are also not certain of the authorship of the books of 1st and 2nd Samuel. Although many theologians in times past believed Jeremiah to be its author, most theological scholars today would agree that it is more probable than not that the prophet Jeremiah was not the author. Instead, scholars agree that the books of 1st and 2nd Samuel were written by an individual who took much of his information from individual sources and compiled the information into one book. There is some speculation that Zabud may have written the books of Samuel. Zabud was a son of the prophet Nathan, and was also an advisor to King Solomon. However, no solid evidence exists that Zabud authored the text.

The authorship of 1st and 2nd Kings is questionable in the same way as the authorship of 1st and 2nd Samuel. The Committee on Bible Translation responsible for the New International Version of the Bible has this to say about the authorship of 1st and 2nd Kings:

There is little conclusive evidence as to the identity of the author of 1,2, Kings. Although Jewish tradition credits Jeremiah, few today accept this as likely. Whoever the author was, it is clear that he was familiar with the book of Deuteronomy—as were many of Israel's prophets. It is also clear that he used a variety of sources in compiling his history of the monarchy. Three such sources are named: "the book of the annals of Solomon: (11:41), "the book of the annals of the kings of Israel (14:19), "the book of the annals of the kings of Judah" (14:29). It is likely that other written sources were also employed.

Although some scholars have concluded that the three sources specifically cited in 1,2, Kings are to be viewed as official court annals from the royal archives in Jerusalem and Samaria, this is by no means certain. It seems at least questionable whether official court annals would have included details of conspiracies such as those referred to in 16:20; 2Ki 15:15. It is also questionable whether official court annals would have been readily accessible for public scrutiny, as the author clearly implies in his references to them. Such considerations have led some scholars to conclude that these sources were probably records of the reigns of the kings of Israel and Judah compiled by the succession of Israel's prophets spanning the kingdom period. 1,2 Chronicles makes reference to a number of such writings: "the records of Samuel the seer, the records of Nathan the prophet and the records of Gad the seer" (1Ch 29:29), "the prophecy of Ahijah the Shilonite" and "the visions of Iddo the seer" (2Ch 9:29), "the records of Shemaiah the prophet" (2Ch 12:15), "the annals of Jehu son of Hanani" (2Ch 20:34), "the annotations on the book of the kings" (2Ch 24:27), the "events of Uzziah's reign...recorded by the prophet Isaiah son of Amoz" (2Ch 26:22; see also 2Ch 32:32)—and there may have been others. It is most likely, for example, that for the ministries of Elijah and Elisha the author depended on a prophetic source (perhaps from the eighth century) that had drawn up an account of those two prophets in which they were already compared with Moses and Joshua.[2]

In similar fashion scholars cannot be absolutely certain as to who authored the following books of the Bible: 1st Chronicles, 2nd Chronicles, Ezra, Nehemiah, Esther, Job, many of the Psalms, some of the Proverbs, Ecclesiastes, Lamentations, Jonah, Malachi, and Hebrews.

In spite of the fact that there is some uncertainty about the identity of the authors of the books of the Bible cited in the preceding paragraph, there is no uncertainty about the authenticity of the godly messages contained within their pages. All scripture contained in the Bible is inspired by God, as attested to in the following verse of scripture:

> [16]All Scripture is inspired by God and profitable for teaching, for reproof, for correction, for training in righteousness;
> [17] that the man of God may be adequate, equipped for every good work. (2 Timothy 3:16-17 NASB)

Jesus endorsed the scriptures. And since he endorsed the scriptures and he is the second person of the Godhead, then it stands to reason that all scripture is inspired of God. Let's take a look at some of what Jesus said about the scriptures:

> [44]And he said unto them, These are the words which I spake unto you, while I was yet with you, that all things must be fulfilled, which were written in the law of Moses, and in the prophets, and in the psalms, concerning me.
> [45]Then opened he their understanding, that they might understand the scriptures. (Luke 24:44-45)

Moses, the prophets, and those who wrote the Psalms, are responsible for the Old Testament writings of the Bible. Jesus separates

---

[2] *The NIV Study Bible 10th Anniversary Edition*, Kenneth Baker, General Editor, copyright ©1995 by The Zondervan Corporation, pp. 459-460, used by permission of Zondervan.

the writings of the prophets from the psalms in that some of the psalms were written by prophets and some of the psalms were not necessarily written by prophets but were still credible in the eyes of Jesus. Jesus quotes from many of the books in the Old Testament which adds to their credibility.

Paul, the apostle wrote most of the books of the New Testament. It is basically agreed that the apostle Matthew wrote the book of Matthew. The apostle John wrote the books of John, 1st John, 2nd John, 3rd John, and Revelation. Paul, the apostle wrote Romans, 1st Corinthians, 2nd Corinthians, Galatians, Ephesians, Philippians, Colossians, 1st Thessalonians, 2nd Thessalonians, 1st Timothy, 2nd Timothy, Titus, and Philemon. It is believed that James, the brother of Jesus (not James the apostle) wrote the book of James. The apostle Peter wrote 1st Peter and 2nd Peter. It is widely believed that Jude[3] wrote the book of Jude. Luke was not an apostle. He was an assistant to Paul and wrote the gospel[4] of Luke and the book of Acts. Mark was not an apostle, but was an assistant to Peter and wrote the gospel of Mark. As stated earlier, scholars are not certain who wrote the book of Hebrews. The author identifies himself only as a man. Some believe Barnabus or Apollos are possibilities, while others believe that the apostle Paul wrote the book of Hebrews.

Overall the Bible was written by roughly 40 different authors at different times spanning 1500 years on 3 different continents, those being: Africa, Asia, and Europe. Miraculously, no verse of scripture contradicts another.

Although it is clear that the Bible was written mainly by men, it is not clear whether or not women had any involvement in any of its writings. Some would say that since Jesus referred to Moses and "the prophets" and not to "the prophets and prophetesses" when speaking about scripture, that the elimination of the female vernacular proves that only men, not women, were responsible for writing scripture. But there are those translations that refer to female prophets as prophets, not prophetesses. And Jesus also referred to the psalms separately, giving

---

[3] The Hebrew form of this name is Judas (not Judas Iscariot). One of Jesus' brothers was named Judas. It is believed that this is the Judas that wrote the book of Jude.

[4] The gospels are the first four books of the New Testament and contain direct quotes of Jesus.

indication to the already known fact that other people besides the prophets wrote psalms. After all, for the most part, the psalms are lyrics to songs.

We can be fairly certain that men wrote all of the New Testament. But this is not to absolutely say that women had no part in editing it or in somehow assisting in its writing. However, there are several books of the Old Testament in which there is no absolute certainty as to authorship. There is also nothing in the Bible that teaches us that women were forbidden to write psalms, proverbs, or any spiritual text. Theologians and scholars are very careful not to dogmatically assert that no women ever wrote a verse of scripture. They cannot assert this because there is simply no proof of it. Women were endowed with the gift of prophecy just as men were. As discussed in Chapter 5, there were women of the Old Testament who were prophets. Moreover, The Old Testament prophet Joel makes reference to women prophesying.[5]

Since there is no absolute proof that women never wrote a verse of scripture, we cannot absolutely say that no woman ever had a hand in writing, editing, or assisting in the writing of the Holy Scriptures contained within the pages of the Bible.

THE DRESS CODE

Another point of contention that many women have when it comes to the Bible is the command that women are to dress modestly. Let's take a look:

> [8]So wherever you assemble, I want men to pray with holy hands lifted up to God, free from anger and controversy. [9]And I want women to be modest in their appearance. They should wear decent and appropriate clothing and not draw attention to themselves by the way they fix their hair or by wearing gold or pearls or expensive clothes. (1 Timothy 2:8-9 NLT)

---

[5] "And it shall come to pass afterward, that I will pour out my spirit upon all flesh; and your sons and your daughters shall prophesy, your old men shall dream dreams, your young men shall see visions:" Joel 2:28-29

Paul was basically instructing women on how to dress while they are in attendance at church assembly. He directed women not to dress in a way that would draw attention to themselves. He instructed women to wear clothing that is decent and appropriate, thereby dressing modestly. Paul then goes on to define what he means by dressing in modest fashion. Wearing anything elaborate, including over the top hairdos, excessive jewelry, or even expensive clothes that defy humility is the opposite of dressing modestly. So, if a woman attends church wearing an expensive suit, a fur coat, expensive jewelry, carrying an expensive handbag, and the like, then she has not dressed modestly and is in violation of the above of directive.

But Paul's instruction for modest dress does not only apply to women, as some may think, but also applies to men. The following quote from the words of Jesus attests to this:

> [19]Do not store up for yourselves treasures on earth, where moth and rust consume and where thieves break in and steal; but store up for yourselves treasures in heaven, where neither moth nor rust consumes and where thieves do not break in and steal. [21]For where your treasure is, there your heart will be also. (Matthew 6:19-21 NSRV)
> [25]Therefore I tell you, do not worry about your life, what you will eat or what you will drink, or about your body, what you will wear. Is not life more than food, and the body more than clothing? (Matthew 6:25 NRSV)
> [31]Therefore do not worry, saying, 'What will we eat?' or 'What will we drink?' or 'What will we wear?' [32]For it is the Gentiles who strive for all these things; and indeed your heavenly Father knows that you need all these things. [33]But strive first for the kingdom of God and his righteousness, and all these things will be given to you as well. (Matthew 6:31-33 NRSV)

No Christian should ever worry about clothing. This is not to say that a Christian should not be concerned if he or she has hardly any clothing, but instead, Jesus is saying that no Christian should fret over clothes or food. Christians, men and women, should be satisfied with the clothes and the food that they have. They should not endeavor to dress the best. They should not worry about wearing designer clothes. The pagans were concerned about these things. They were always concerned about how they looked and how others perceived them, which is why the pagan nations of the time labored to dress elaborately, because for them it was validating. In this sense, Jesus was saying what Paul would eventually say, and that is that Christians are to dress with humility. Again, men are not exempt from this directive.

Although men and women are to dress humbly, there are some, especially some men, who are apt to take the directive to an extreme when it comes to women. Taking the directive to an extreme is most notably seen when looking at how some Muslim women are made to dress. In many fundamentalist Islamic areas of the Middle East and even in some places in the West, Muslim women are expected to wear clothing that covers their entire bodies including their face. They are only allowed to show their eyes, so that they can see. This kind of dress is not a symbol of humility but it is instead a symbol of oppression, power, and control.

There is no verse of scripture in the Bible that commands a woman to cover her face and her entire body while she is in public. There are verses of scripture that encourage women to wear head coverings during worship at church, but only then in light of the customs of that certain era.[6]

Biblically, modest dressing is to be done within reason and without oppression. The fundamentalist Muslims who force women to dress in oppressive ways defend themselves by saying it is done so that a man will not gaze lustfully upon a woman. But Jesus said if your eye offends you, pluck it out. He didn't say if your eye offends you, cover up that which you gaze upon. The person that must pay the price is the offender (the man in this instance), not the one offended (the woman in this instance). Let's take a look:

> [27]You have heard that it was said, 'Do not commit adultery. [28]But I tell you that anyone who looks at a woman lustfully has already committed adultery with her in his heart. [29]If your right eye causes you to sin, gouge it out and throw it away. It is better for you to

---

[6] See Chapters 3 and 5.

> lose one part of your body than for your whole body to
> be thrown into hell. [30]And if your right hand causes you
> to sin, cut it off and throw it away. It is better for you
> to lose one part of your body than for your whole body
> to go to hell. (Matthew 5:27-30 NIV)

Jesus is fair about this thing. He makes the man accountable for his own lusts. He does not make the woman accountable for the lusts of a man. This is why there is no command from Jesus for a woman to cover her body from head to toe. It is unreasonable for a woman to be made to cover herself from head to toe in order to curtail the lust of men. Instead, men are instructed not to look lustfully at women. Plain and simple. But Jesus goes further than that. He says that if a man finds himself looking lustfully at another man's wife, he should pluck his eyes out in order to rid himself of this sin. According to Jesus, instead of women being subjected to wearing oppressive coverings in order not to incite the stares of lustful men, men who look at women with lust in their eyes should be stumbling around with gouged eyes.[7] This certainly doesn't sound like a chauvinistic God. God faults the man who is lusting after a woman and not the woman who is being lusted after.

Another reason given as to why women should seek to dress modestly has to do with God's directive for women not to be concerned about beauty.[8] Let's take a look:

> [3]Don't be concerned about the outward beauty that
> depends on fancy hairstyles, expensive jewelry, or
> beautiful clothes. [4]You should be known for the beauty
> that comes from within, the unfading beauty of a gentle
> and quiet spirit, which is so precious to God.
> (1 Peter 3:3-4 NLT)

God does not want women to be concerned about outer beauty.[9] Although society puts many pressures on women to be beautiful, God doesn't want Christian women to succumb to the pressure. Instead he wants Christian women to concern themselves with the things of God

---

[7] This applies figuratively, not literally.
[8] See Chapter 7.
[9] See Chapter 7.

rather than their looks. This is another reason the scriptures instruct women to dress modestly.

Although dressing modestly is frequently associated with not dressing seductively, the two are different. As we have seen, to dress modestly means not to wear flashy clothes, flashy hairstyles, and flashy jewelry. Dressing in a non-seductive way means something a little different. Let's take a look:

> [6]From the window of my house, I once happened to see [7]some foolish young men.
>
> [8]It was late in the evening, sometime after dark.
>
> [9]One of these young men turned the corner and was walking by the house of an unfaithful wife.
>
> [10]She was dressed fancy like a woman of the street with only one thing in mind.
>
> [11]She was one of those women who are loud and restless and never stay at home,
>
> [12]who walk street after street, waiting to trap a man.
>
> [13]She grabbed him and kissed him, and with no sense of shame, she said:
>
> [14]I had to offer a sacrifice, and there is enough meat left over for a feast.
>
> [15]So I came looking for you, and here you are!
>
> [16]The sheets on my bed are bright-colored cloth from Egypt.
>
> [17]And I have covered it with perfume made of myrrh, aloes, and cinnamon.
>
> [18]"Let's go there and make love all night.
>
> [19]My husband is traveling, and he's far away.
>
> [20]He took a lot of money along, and he won't be back home before the middle of the month."
>
> [21]And so, she tricked him with all of her sweet talk and her flattery.
>
> [22]Right away he followed her like an ox on the way to be slaughtered, or like a fool on the way to be punished [23] and killed with arrows. He was no more than a bird rushing into a trap, without knowing it would cost him his life.
>
> [24]My son, pay close attention to what I have said.

²⁵Don't even think about that kind of woman or let yourself be misled by someone like her.
²⁶Such a woman has caused the downfall and destruction of a lot of men.
²⁷Her house is a one-way street leading straight down to the world of the dead. (Proverbs 7:6-27 CEV)

Although, the woman seduced this young man, he was still responsible for his actions and was instructed not to be misled by her (verse 25). Not only was he accountable (Just as David was responsible in his actions towards Bathsheba[10]) but the young man is described as being like a fool. In other words, he wasn't very bright to have stumbled into her snare. Thus, this is what the word of God has to say about any man who stumbles into fornication as described: that he is simpleminded and that he doesn't have common sense.

Certainly a chauvinistic God would not make a man accountable for a woman's seduction. But as we see in the pages of the Bible, men have been accountable for falling into the seductive hands of women, since the beginning of time. We have but to consider Adam and Eve. Adam was punished for being seduced by Eve. Even though Adam tried to blame Eve for his weakness, God made Adam pay for his fault just as he made Eve pay for hers. The whole burden didn't rest on Eve alone.

When considering what the verses in Proverbs had to say about the seduction of women, we become aware that women are not only instructed to dress modestly, but women are also indirectly instructed not to dress seductively. There are times that women don't want to admit that they are dressing seductively when in actuality they are. Deciding what is seductive and what is not, is an objective task and often times depends on the society in which one lives. However, it can be said that certain ways of dressing are universally considered seductive. Let's face it, tight fitting clothes that accentuate the structure of a woman's body can be very seductive to a man. Women dressed in skimpy clothing can also be very seductive to a man. Shorts and mini skirts are questionable at best. Even painted fingernails and painted toenails are seductive to some men. High heels and a great pair of legs can be very seductive to a man. It doesn't take much. So women must make sure to dress modestly without becoming prisoners of an extreme view of what dressing modestly is.

---

[10] See Chapter 2.

Interestingly, when it comes to modest dressing, men have a tendency to examine women much more closely than they examine themselves or other men. But Just as it can be said that Jesus' directive to pluck one's eye out if that eye causes one to sin, applies to women as well as it applies to men, it can be said that Paul's instruction to dress modestly applies to men as it does to women.

Women are apt to lust after men no less frequently than men are apt to lust after women. Therefore, men should be careful in their dress as well. In the West, there are those men who frequently dress seductively by wearing muscle revealing attire, tight fitting T-shirts, tight jeans, and the like. Some men walk the streets with no shirt on at all. Since this is legal in Western society, the church rarely speaks against it. But a man who walks around with no shirt on is literally half-naked. There is no modesty in being half-naked.

Finally, Old Testament law commanded women not to wear men's clothing and also commanded men not to wear women's clothing. Let's take a look:

> A woman must not wear men's clothing, nor a man
> wear women's clothing, for the LORD your God detests
> anyone who does this. (Deuteronomy 22:5 NIV)

Although the directive for both men and women not to dress in one another's clothing is an Old Testament law, it can be safely surmised that God feels the same way about these things today. In today's society there are men who like to dress in women's clothing and women who like to dress in men's clothing. They are called cross-dressers. However, such behavior is symbolic of homosexual behavior, and the Bible has clearly stated that homosexuality is a sin.[11] Therefore, God has expressed that cross-dressing is inappropriate for a man or a woman. The Contemporary English Version of the Bible translates verse 5 as such, *"Women must not pretend to be men, and men must not pretend to be women. The LORD is disgusted with people who do that."* Women are to dress in feminine ways and men are to dress in masculine ways. God expects women to dress like women just as God expects men to dress like men. God does not want women to dress like men, just as God does not want men to

---

[11] See Chapter 9.

dress like women. To do so is a perversion for both genders. God makes no difference between men and women on this issue.

NAME CHANGES IN MARRIAGE

What's in a name? Quite a bit. One's identity is associated with one's name. Depending on how a person lives his or her life, a name can be associated with goodness or it can be associated with evil.

Take the name Lucifer for example. Even though Lucifer was the name of the Devil (Satan) before he became God's adversary and ultimately was thrown out of heaven, Lucifer means "day star." Before his fall, Satan, whose name was then Lucifer, covered the glory of God. He was doing a good service to God and his name meant something good. However, once he decided to turn against God he became God's adversary and was henceforth called Satan. Consequently, even the good name he once had is now associated with evil. Other names associated with evil are Delilah, Jezebel, Judas, Hitler, Dracula, and so forth. The Bible talks about the importance of having a good name. Let's take a look:

> A good name is more desirable
> than great riches;
> to be esteemed is better than silver
> or gold. (Proverbs 22:1 NIV)

It is important to have a good name. To have a good name means to have a good reputation. It usually takes time to build up a good reputation. It takes very little time, however, to hurt one's reputation or hurt the reputation of another. The Bible teaches that people who have confessed Jesus as Lord and Savior and believe that Jesus has risen from the dead will be saved and therefore their names are written in the book of life.[12] Let's continue:

> [16]My followers, whoever listens to you
> is listening to me. Anyone who says
> "No" to you is saying "No" to me.

---

[12] "If anyone's name was not found written in the book of life, he was thrown into the lake of fire." (Revelation 20:15 NIV)

And anyone who says "No" to me is
really saying "No" to the one who sent
me.
[17]When the seventy-two followers returned, they were
excited and said, "Lord, even the demons obeyed when
we spoke in your name!"
[18]Jesus told them:

I saw Satan fall from heaven like a flash
of lightning. [19]I have given you the
power to trample on snakes and
scorpions and to defeat the power of
your enemy Satan. Nothing can harm
you. [20]But don't be happy because evil
spirits obey you. Be happy that your
names are written in heaven!
(Luke 10:16-20 CEV)

In the above verses of scripture, Jesus was speaking to 72 of his
disciples (verse 17). They had returned from proclaiming the word of
God. Jesus encouraged them by basically telling them that he would give
them great fortitude in order that they might carry out their mission for
the Lord (verse 19). He told them to be happy because their names were
written in heaven. All Christians have their names written in heaven.
Let's take a look:

[1]This is what you must write to the angel of the church
in Sardis:
I have the seven spirits of God and
the seven stars. Listen to what I say. I
know what you are doing. Everyone
may think you are alive, but you are
dead. [2]Wake up! You have only a little
strength left, and it is almost gone. So
try to become stronger. I have found
that you are not completely obeying
God. [3]Remember the teaching that you
were given and that you heard. Hold
firmly to it and turn from your sins. If

you don't wake up, I will come when
you least expect it, just as a thief does.

⁴A few of you in Sardis have not
dirtied your clothes with sin. You will
walk with me in white clothes, because
you are worthy. ⁵Everyone who wins
the victory will wear white clothes.
Their names will not be erased from
the book of life, and I will tell my
Father and his angels that they are my
followers.

⁶If you have ears, listen to what the
Spirit says to the churches. (Revelation
3:1-6 CEV)

Those who truly belong to the church of Jesus Christ will have their
names written in the Book of Life. So there is a lot in a name. To have a
good name in the Lord means that one belongs to the body of Christ and
has his or her name written in the Lamb's Book of Life that leads to
heaven.

Although God knows our names no matter how many times we
might change it, it is not easy for a person to change his or her name
once they have established that name and especially if there is good
reputation attached to the name. This brings us to the issue of name
changes for women in marriage.

Tradition in Western society dictates that a woman legally change
her surname to that of her husband's surname when she gets married.
However, although men and women become one flesh when they get
married and the man is the head of the house, there is simply no biblical
mandate or command that says a woman must change her surname to
that of her husband's once she is married. The pressure for a woman to
change her surname to that of her husband in Western society, is not
pressure that comes from any biblical command, but instead pressure
that comes from cultural tradition.

Social mores are loosening a bit in this area. Men are beginning to
realize how difficult it is for a woman to change her surname, especially
for a woman who has established herself in society and therefore has
established her name and is well recognized by that name. A woman
who changes her name must begin all over again in building her identity.

While a man has no loss of identity at all when he marries, a woman looses her identity to that of her husband's when she marries and changes her name. However, it is rare for a man in Western society not to insist that his wife carry his name. A hyphenated surname that includes the wife's maiden name and her married name, is therefore a fair compromise. And a man who loves his wife as God has commanded him to will sacrifice his pride in order to please his wife if she desires to hyphenate. There are even those men who allow their wives to keep their maiden names altogether. But these men are usually married to women who have made a career name for themselves and consequently, these men understand the importance of allowing their wives to keep their identities.

When looking at marriage in Old Testament times and during the time of Jesus' ministry, we see that women still kept their identities despite the fact that they were married. Despite the fact that surnames were used, there is no indication that women were mandated to change their surnames once married. In the genealogy[13] of Jesus, which is found in the first chapter of Matthew, men and women of the genealogy are referenced by their first names. Joseph is referenced as "the husband of Mary" and Mary[14] is referenced as "of whom was born Jesus."[15] Matthew 1:15 says, *"and to Jacob was born Joseph the husband of Mary, by whom was born Jesus, who is called Christ."* The latter reference is certainly more reverencing than the former. Certainly a chauvinistic God would not have inspired Matthew to reference a man as merely the husband of a woman and then have him reference that same woman as the mother of the Messiah, savior of the world.

Mary's identity is not lost in the fact that she married Joseph. And Mary's surname is not used in the Bible to identify her. Although it is known that Mary was Joseph's wife, Mary's reputation and long lasting identity comes with the fact that she was the mother of Jesus and not with the fact that she was married to Joseph. She has an identity of her own, aside from Joseph. She was also identified as a virgin,[16] and as highly favored.[17] The Bible establishes Mary's identity more by what she

---

[13] Matthew 1:1-16 (see Appendix)

[14] See Chapter 2 for more on Mary.

[15] NIV

[16] Matthew 1:23 (see your Bible)

[17] Luke 1:28 (see your Bible)

did to serve the Lord, and less by the man she was married to. We see the same phenomenon when looking at the lives of Deborah and Huldah.[18] Although Mary married Joseph, she was able to hold on to her name and to her identity. Therefore, there is nothing wrong with a woman wanting to do the same today.

Again, name changing in marriage, just like wearing a wedding ring, is not a command of God, but only a cultural tradition in Western society. As we have seen, a woman who wants to hold on to a piece of her identity once she gets married is not wrong for wanting to. Her desire to keep her name does not mean she is less spiritually mature than is a woman who decides to give up her last name. In wanting to keep her name, she may be resisting a cultural tradition, but she is not defying God.

THE PRO-CHOICE ISSUE

The question is not whether or not God is pro-choice. God always gives us a choice. We have the choice to accept him or not. We have the choice to worship him or not. We have the choice to believe in God's word or not. We have the choice to live holy or not. We have the choice to commit sin or not. God did not create robots. He created human beings and gave us a will and the freedom to choose. Therefore, in this respect, God is pro-choice.

The argument over whether or not abortion is a sin becomes the most decisive issue. In order to affirm that abortion is a sin, one must prove it is murder. In order to disaffirm that abortion is a sin, one must prove that it isn't murder and that it isn't against the will of God in any way. Since this book focuses mainly on what God has to say about things, as opposed to what mankind has to say, it will do no less when it comes to the issue of abortion.

Pro-life advocates argue that no woman should have the legal right to get an abortion unless (some argue) her pregnancy is the result of an incestuous relationship, rape, or is life threatening. They argue that the fetus is a living soul at the time of conception.

Pro-choice advocates argue that a woman should have a legal choice to abort the embryo/fetus she is carrying and that an embryo is not really a human being until a certain time has passed after conception. They also

---

[18] See Chapters 1 and 2.

argue that a woman should have the right to do with her body what she wants. But what does God say? Let's take a look:

> Before I formed you in the womb I knew you,
> Before you were born I sanctified you;
> I ordained you a prophet to the nations.
> (Jeremiah 1:5 NKJV)

In the above scriptural quote, God was speaking to the prophet Jeremiah. God knew Jeremiah before he was formed in the womb. This is not to say that Jeremiah existed before his earthly birth but that God's purpose for Jeremiah was set before he was even born. Since God is all knowing, he knows ahead of time who will chose to carry out his will and who will not. Since God knew Jeremiah before he formed him in the womb then God knew us all before he formed us in the womb. If a person has a calling before he or she is ever conceived, then how can we say that an embryo/fetus has no soul? Embryos are indeed conceived. If God knew us before conception (before we were embryos) then he certainly knew us when we were embryos. How then can we say that an embryo is a non-person? The embryo/fetus is the formation of the person that God knew before conception. How can a non-person have a calling of God? God called Jeremiah to be a prophet before Jeremiah was ever conceived in the womb. Of course, Jeremiah still had the choice to accept or turn away from God. He still had the choice of whether or not to accept the calling. But God knew him before he was born. There are more scriptures that refute the notion that an embryo or a fetus is a non-person. Let's take a look:

> [13]For you created my inmost being;
>   you knit me together in my
>   mother's womb.
> [14]I praise you because I am fearfully
>   and wonderfully made;
>   your works are wonderful,
>   I know that full well.
> [15]My frame was not hidden from you
>   when I was made in the secret
>   place.
> When I was woven together in the

437

> depths of the earth,
> [16]your eyes saw my unformed body.
> All the days ordained for me
> were written in your book
> before one of them came to be.
> (Psalms 139:13-16 NIV)

King David wrote the above Psalm as a prayer to God. The Psalm teaches us that as human beings, before we were born, God himself wove us together in the womb (verse 13). Verse 15 says we were woven together in the "depths of the earth." The phrase, *depths of the earth,* is referring to a woman's womb. Verse 16 declares that God's eyes were upon us while he was forming us in the womb. Not only this, but David speaks about his "unformed body" in the womb thereby validating the unformed body as something important. It is unformed but it is still a living body being formed. Then he says that before his days as a human being even began, they were ordained and written down in God's book.

When looking at things from a biblical perspective, there can certainly be no argument against the fact that embryos and fetuses are human beings that are in a phase of existence in which they are being shaped by God. With this being so, then from the time of conception, human beings have souls. Conclusively then, to abort an embryo or fetus, is to kill an innocent human being which is a living body in the process of being formed, whom God has ordained, and whom God knows. The following scripture supports this view:

> [22]If men who are fighting hit a pregnant woman and she gives birth prematurely but there is no serious injury, the offender must be fined whatever the woman's husband demands and the court allows. [23]But if there is serious injury, you are to take life for life, eye for eye, tooth for tooth, hand for hand, foot for foot, burn for burn, wound for wound, bruise for bruise. (Exodus 21:22-24 NIV)

The scripture applies the rule of an *eye for an eye* to the serious injury of either the mother or her unborn baby, no matter if she has just become pregnant or if she has been pregnant for a while. The scripture does not differentiate between a short period between time of conception and loss of the baby and a long period between time of conception and loss of the baby. Since the scripture does not differentiate, then we are not at liberty to do so either. A pregnant woman is a pregnant woman and she is no less pregnant at day one of her pregnancy than she is in the ninth month of her pregnancy.

Although the rule of *an eye for an eye* is Old Testament law and does not apply today,[19] it still gives us a great deal of indication as to how God feels about the disturbing of a woman's pregnancy. Even if there was no serious injury to the unborn child (verse 22) a fine had to be paid and some kind of litigation was eminent. If the unborn child was seriously injured then the same injury was to be inflicted upon the perpetrator. Verse 22 teaches that a person had to be punished for harming an unborn child even if the harm was accidental. Verse 23 teaches that if two men were fighting each other and in the midst of the fight accidentally hit a pregnant woman, then the two men had to be put to death if the woman's unborn baby died as a result of the injury. Indeed if accidental injury to an unborn child invoked the wrath of God, surely intentional injury would provoke more wrath and is against the will of God. The following scripture attests to this:

> [13]Thus says the Lord:
>
> For three transgressions of the people of Ammon,
> and for four,
> I will not turn away its punishment,
> Because they ripped open the women with child
> in Gilead,
> That they might enlarge their territory,
> [14] But I will kindle a fire in the wall of Rabbah,
> And it shall devour its palaces,
> Amid shouting in the day of battle,
> And a tempest in the day of the whirlwind.
> [15]Their king shall go into captivity,
> He and his princes together
> Says the LORD.
> (Amos 1:13-15 NKJV)

---

[19] See "Biblical argument against capital punishment" under Chapter 13 subheading in the Appendix.

Amos was called of God to pronounce judgement on Northern Israel because of their immorality. The Ammonites, which occupied Northern Israel at the time, were descendants of Noah's son Shem, whom Abraham also descended from. Therefore, the Ammonites are considered to be an ancient Semitic nation. Through the prophet Amos, God declared that there were four transgressions the Ammonites were guilty of, and that because of these transgressions they would be punished. God specifically focused upon the fact that the Ammonites had ripped open the wombs of pregnant women while in Gilead. For this, God would allow the city of Ammon (Rabbah) to be taken in battle and for its king to go into captivity.

The Ammonites ripped open the women with child in an attempt to put and end to the next generation of Gileadites. Both the woman and the unborn child died in these instances. Notice, however, that the emphasis is placed on the fact that the women were pregnant. If we don't consider an embryo or fetus to be a human being, the Ammonites surely did. Otherwise, they would not have imposed such barbaric measures to stop the birth of these unborn children.

Man has no right to disturb the fruit of a woman's womb. The legality of abortion in today's world does not negate God's law against such things. If God has clearly indicated that man has no right to disturb the forming of an unborn child then indeed it can follow that a woman has no right to do so either. The argument many women embrace by saying, "it's my body and I should be able to do what I want with it" does not apply here. A woman who is carrying a baby is doing just that. She is carrying another human being *within* her body. However, the body she is carrying is not *her* body, if that were the case then the fetus would remain in her body forever. The body that a woman is carrying within her body, when she is pregnant, belongs to God. Just as her body belongs to God. Let's look further:

> [16]These six things the LORD hates,
> Yes, seven are an abomination to Him:
> [17]A proud look,
> A lying tongue,
> Hands that shed innocent blood,
> [18]A heart that devises wicked plans,
> Feet that are swift in running to evil,
> [19]A false witness who speaks lies,

And one who sows discord among brethren.
(Proverbs 6:16-19 NKJV)

Particular attention is paid to verse 17, which says that God hates the shedding of innocent blood. As we have seen, Exodus 21:22-23 teaches us that, during Old Testament times, men who unintentionally caused the death of a woman's unborn child had to pay with his life. This means that God considers an unborn child to be a living being and not to be something that has no life. Therefore to kill it means to shed innocent blood. There can be no human being that is more innocent than a embryo/fetus. The embryo/fetus has not yet had the opportunity to sin. Therefore, we have no choice but to put the shedding of the innocent blood of any fetus, in the category of murder.

God is not biased when it comes to prohibiting people from killing the offspring of a woman's womb. As we have seen, a man could be held responsible for causing a woman to miscarry even if he didn't intend to. Therefore, we can safely assume that a man (or a woman for that matter), who intentionally encourages a woman to get an abortion, or intentionally pays for an abortion, shares in her accountability in the eyes of God for the abortion. Of course, a man who performs an abortion is directly guilty of the murder himself.

Much of this seems unfair to many women. A woman who is unmarried, had consenting sex, and unintentionally becomes pregnant is usually left with the brunt of the pregnancy, unless the man who impregnated her decides to marry her.[20] In carrying the baby to term, she will experience drastic bodily changes, what could be months of nausea, bloating, swelling, and many times public disgrace. Unless the woman is financially secure and prepared for the extraordinary financial burden that accompanies the birth of a child, statistics show that she may very well become destitute and have to apply for some kind of government financial aid. There is no guarantee that she will have any one to help her or that the man who impregnated her will have enough resources to help or even if he will be willing to help. Unfortunately, at least in America, many women who find themselves in this situation also find themselves

---

[20] Even at that, she might not want to marry him. Furthermore, there is no biblical mandate that says she must marry him because she is carrying his child. The biblical mandate forbade the sex she had outside of marriage. See Chapter 9.

garnering the assistance of the law to help them get what is due to them in child support.

When faced with the reality of all of this, the idea of abortion may be a temptation difficult for a woman to fight, especially if the man who impregnated her is encouraging her to get one. In doing so, he's giving her more than enough indication that he might not willingly support her and the child should the she carry the baby to term.

Even more distressing is the plight of the girl or woman who has been the victim of incest or has been raped and becomes pregnant as a result. The temptation to abort the child is understandably overwhelming for a girl or woman who finds herself living either of these horrible scenarios. If a woman has been impregnated due to being raped and she is married, there is no doubt that her husband will have just as much of an overwhelming temptation to urge her to get an abortion. What man wants his wife carry the baby of a man who raped her? However, as difficult as it would be for a girl or a woman to carry to term a baby conceived by incest or rape, and as easy as it would be to understand and excuse any girl or woman who opted to abort a baby that she conceived in her womb as the result of an act of incest or rape, the child conceived as the result of an incestuous act or a rape is no less innocent and no less of a person than a child conceived as a result of consenting sex (whether inside or outside of a marital relationship). And therefore, killing the embryo/fetus would no less be murder. Moreover, as far as God is concerned, incest and rape is no greater a sin of fornication than pre-marital sex and adultery. Therefore, a child conceived as a result of rape or incest has no less of a right to life, than a child conceived during any other act of fornication, say pre-marital sex or adultery in which the woman consented.

Pro-life advocates who make exception for rape victims, victims of incest, or for women who are in danger of dying if they carry the baby to term,[21] are really pro-choice advocates. The difference is that they are

---

[21] The argument here is that it should be up to God whether or not the mother lives or the baby lives. The question becomes whether or not the mother has the right to abort the baby she is carrying, in order to save her own life, if the baby still has a chance of surviving even if she (the mother) were to die in childbirth. Jesus himself said that, "the greatest way to show love for friends is to die for them"(John 15:13 CEV). So, we can conclude that dying for the sake of another

pro-choice advocates for a certain population of women while general pro-choice advocates are pro-choice for all women. Either way you look at it, both positions are pro-choice. A true pro-life position is one in which no woman is allowed an abortion under any circumstances... period. The only conceivable exception would be if both the mother and her unborn baby were at great risk of not surviving the pregnancy.

The stigma of having had an abortion is great, especially for those women in the church who have had one. A woman who has had an abortion, even if she had the abortion several years ago, is not only often times haunted by the guilt of having had had one, but is also haunted by the possibility that someone in the church congregation might find out. Although Christians often times feel free to talk about how they used to fornicate or use drugs or party a lot before they came to know Jesus, Christian women who have had abortions in the past do not feel free to discuss their experiences or feelings about it. It is something that is kept in the closet. And although society says that adoption is a better option than getting an abortion, the societal stigma that comes with giving a child up for adoption is much worse than the societal stigma of getting an abortion.

Despite the fact that there is a stigma surrounding abortion that does not exist with certain other sins, it should be emphasized that God will forgive a woman (no less than he will forgive others who have committed other sins) who has had an abortion as long as she is in the Lord and as long as she repents of her sin. This is what the Bible says about sin and forgiveness:

> [5]This is the message we have heard from him and proclaim to you, that God is light and in him there is no darkness at all. [6]If we say that we have fellowship with him while we are walking in darkness, we lie and do not do what is true; [7]But if we walk in the light as he himself is in the light, we have fellowship with one another, and the blood of Jesus his Son cleanses us from all sin. [8]If we confess our sins, he who is faithful and just will forgive us our sins and cleanse us from all unrighteousness. [10]If we say that we have not sinned,

is an honorable thing. Certainly then it would be no less honorable if a woman were to risk her life for the sake of her unborn child.

we make him a liar, and his word is not in us. (1 John 1:5-10 NSRV)

[1]My little children, I am writing these things to you so that you may not sin. But if anyone does sin, we have an advocate with the Father, Jesus Christ the righteous; [2]and he is the atoning sacrifice for our sins, and not for ours only but also for the sins of the whole world. [3]Now by this we may be sure that we know him, if we obey his commandments. [4]Whoever says, "I have come to know him," but does not obey his commandments, is a liar, and in such a person the truth does not exist; [5]but whoever obeys his word, truly in this person the love of God has reached perfection. By this we may be sure that we are in him: [6]whoever says, "I abide in him," ought to walk just as he walked. (1 John 2:1-6 NSRV)

SUMMARY

In this chapter we have explored several issues ranging from the referencing of God in the male vernacular, to examining whether or not it is a possibility that women had anything to do with the writing of the Bible, to looking at the commands given in the Bible as to how women should dress, to the Western tradition of having a woman change her last name when she gets married, and on through a discussion centering on the pro-choice issue.

The concerns that feminists have are many and to try to cover them all would constitute a book in itself. However, when considering the issues that were discussed, the following conclusions can be made: although God is basically referred to in the male vernacular, he is a God of both men and women, and does not deem either sex superior to the other. Even though there is no direct proof that women had part in writing, editing, or assisting in writing the Bible, there is no direct proof against it. Although women are told to dress modestly this does not give men a license to dress immodestly. There is no sin in a woman keeping her maiden name when she gets married. And although God is against abortion and considers it murder, if asked, God will forgive a woman who has had an abortion no less than he will forgive any one else of their sins. God is merciful and just.

14.

HOW JESUS TREATED WOMEN

If God is a chauvinist then Jesus would have to be one too, since Jesus is the second person of the Godhead.[1] During his earthly ministry, Jesus often times spoke to and instructed women. He even used women as examples in many of his parables. Therefore, any chauvinism on Jesus' part would have been clearly apparent in the historical accounts of how he treated women and how he referred to women in his parables. However, as we will soon see, the historical accounts of Jesus' treatment of women and reference to them distinctly indicate that he made no chauvinistic statements or commands and that nothing he said implicated any chauvinism on his part. As a matter of fact, Jesus' treatment of women helped to curtail the chauvinism against women that already existed during his time. Let's take a look:

> [1]And it came soon about afterwards, that He began going about from one city and village to another proclaiming and preaching the kingdom of God; and the twelve were with Him,
> [2]and also some women who had been healed of evil spirits and sickness: Mary who was called Magdalene, from whom seven demons had gone out,
> [3]and Joanna the wife of Chuza, Herod's steward, and Susanna, and many others who were contributing to their support out of their private means (Luke 8:1-3 NASB)

Verse 2 tells us that Jesus permitted women to travel with him during his evangelistic ministry in which he went from city to city proclaiming the gospel along with the twelve apostles. Three of these women are

---

[1] See Introduction

mentioned by name. They are Mary Magdalene, Joanna, and Susanna. Mary Magdalene was the woman whom Jesus cast seven devils out of.[2] Afterwards, she became a devout follower of Christ.

Joanna is mentioned as having been married during the time she traveled with Jesus. The fact that Joanna was married did not prevent Jesus from allowing Joanna to travel with him. Certainly if Jesus had been chauvinistic he would not have allowed a married woman to travel with him. He would have instead instructed her to stay home and tend to her husband. We don't know how long Joanna journeyed with Jesus. For all we know, her husband Chuza may have accompanied her. However, the scriptures don't say either way. The point here is that Jesus did not see it as improper to include a married woman among those who participated with him in traveling from city to city "proclaiming and preaching the kingdom of God." To further emphasize the point, Jesus did not see it as improper to include women, as a whole, in his ministry. Many of the apostles had wives and their wives traveled with them on their missionary journeys.[3]

Joanna is also identified as one of the women who (along with Mary Magdalene,[4] and Mary the mother of James) was among the first to talk to the two angels who were at the tomb of Jesus after his resurrection. Therefore Joanna was one of the first human beings among mankind to hear the good news of Jesus' resurrection.

Verse 3 tells us that the women were among "many others that were contributing to their support out of their private means." This tells us that many of the women who accompanied Jesus and the apostles while they evangelized from city to city, helped to lessen some of the financial burdens of the travel by providing them with the resources they needed. It is safe to say that these provisions were not just limited to finances, but may have also included food, clothing, and other necessities that are important to sustain one who is endeavoring on a long journey. And although the scripture emphasizes that the women provided necessary support, there is no indication that the women themselves were not

---

[2] See Chapter 1

[3] Paul asked, "Don't we have the right to take a believing wife along with us, as do the other apostles and the Lord's brothers and Cephas? Or is it only I and Barnabus who must work for a living? (1 Corinthians 9:5-6 NIV)

[4] See Chapter 1

involved somehow in the evangelism that was taking place. Let's continue:

> [1]After these things the Lord appointed seventy others also, and sent them two by two before His face into every city and place where He Himself was about to go.
> [2]Then He said to them, "The harvest truly is great, but the laborers are few; therefore pray the Lord of the harvest to send out laborers into His harvest.
> [3]Go your way; behold, I send you out as lambs among wolves.
> [4]Carry neither money bag, knapsack, nor sandals; and greet no one along the road.
> [5]But what ever house you enter, first say, 'Peace to this house.'
> [6]And if a son of peace is there, your peace will rest on it; if not, it will return to you.
> [7]And remain in the same house, eating and drinking such things as they give, for the laborer is worthy of his wages. Do not go from house to house.
> [8]Whatever city you enter, and they receive you, eat such things as are set before you.
> [9]And heal the sick there, and say to them "The kingdom of God has come near you.'
> [10]But whatever city you enter, and they do not receive you, go out into its streets and say,
> [11]The very dust of your city which clings to us we wipe off against you. Nevertheless know this, that the kingdom of God has come near you.'
> [12]But I say to you that it will be more tolerable in that Day for Sodom than for that city." (Luke 10:1-12 NKJV)

Verse 1 tells us that Jesus appointed seventy of his followers to go out into the cities in pairs to proclaim the gospel. He described them as "lambs among wolves" and told them to proclaim the gospel and wipe the dust of the city off of themselves whose people reject the message that they were bringing. It stands to reason that women were probably included among these seventy disciples since scripture tells us that women traveled with Jesus during his evangelistic ministry. Let's look further:

> [38]As Jesus and his disciples were on their way, he came to a village where a woman named Martha opened her home to him. [39]She had a sister called Mary, who sat at the Lord's feet listening to what he said. [40]But Martha was distracted by all the preparations that had to be made. She came to him and asked, "Lord, don't you care that my sister has left me to do the work by myself? Tell her to help me!"
> [41]Martha, Martha, the Lord answered, you are worried and upset about many things, [42]but only one thing is needed. Mary has chosen what is better, and it will not be taken away from her." (Luke 10:38-42 NIV)

The account does not tell us exactly how many disciples were with Jesus when he came to Martha's home. But apparently there were enough people with Jesus to trigger some anxiety in Martha.[5] It appears that Martha was trying to get her house in order for Jesus and those of the disciples who were with him at the time. Since her home was not prepared to take in visitors, one could conclude that Martha may have invited Jesus and his disciples at the spare of the moment. The account does not tell us the things that Martha was doing to prepare her home for Jesus and his disciples, but it is clear when reading the scriptures that Martha was scurrying around trying to prepare things while Jesus and his disciples were present in her home. It can be assumed that she may have been preparing a meal for the travelers or getting her house in order so that those that were there could lodge comfortably. At any rate, as Martha was scurrying about, her sister Mary, sat at Jesus' feet and listened to all he had to say. One can surmise that Jesus was either teaching or giving his disciples some instruction.

Martha became perturbed at Mary because Mary was not helping her clean up the house and prepare the food. Martha even complained to

---

[5] John 11:15 talks about how Jesus loved Martha and how he had a special relationship with she and her siblings, Lazarus and Mary (see your Bible).

Jesus about this and asked him to tell Mary to join in and help her. However, Jesus' response was not a typical male response. He did not reprimand Mary for not helping Martha with the housework. He instead reprimanded Martha by telling her that she was worried about many things but that Mary chose what was important. In other words, it was more important for Mary to sit at Jesus' feet and listen to what he was teaching than for her to help Martha with the housework. The tone of the account gives the impression that Martha was fretting over nothing and that the housework was not important enough for Jesus to command Mary to leave his side so that Mary could go about assisting Martha in doing it. As a matter of fact, Jesus made it clear to Martha that what Mary had chosen to do was better than Martha choosing to do the housework and that he would not take away from Mary her decision to listen to God's word for the sake of housework. Certainly then, Jesus is not a chauvinist. A chauvinist would have most definitely agreed with Martha. A chauvinist would have insisted that Mary rise up immediately and help Martha with the housework.

This has great implications because when taking Jesus' response to Martha into account, one can safely presume that it would not be very spiritual for a man to insist that his wife put housework before the study of the word of the Lord. A man should not detain his wife at home with menial chores if it interferes with her work for the Lord. Household chores should take a back seat to God's instruction. Furthermore, the fact that Jesus told Martha that the chores weren't important enough for him to insist that Mary do them tells us how Jesus viewed women. Jesus does not see women as many men do. He sees them much more than just housekeepers. He sees them instead as equal co-partners with men in the furthering of the gospel. It was just as important for a woman to learn all she could about the gospel as it was a man, even if that meant that the housework didn't get done.

During the time of Jesus' ministry, women were often times treated as second class citizens by Jewish society. But Jesus denounced the customs and mores that were instrumental in oppressing women. The following account is an example of this:

> [7]A woman of Samaria came to draw water. Jesus said
> to her, "Give me a drink."
> [8]For His disciples had gone away into the city to buy
> food.

> 9Then the woman of Samaria said to Him, "How is it that You, being a Jew, ask a drink from me, a Samaritan woman?" For Jews have no dealings with Samaritans. (John 4:7-9 NKJV)

The city of Samaria was forty-two miles north of Jerusalem and was later identified as part of Palestine. The Samaritans were those who lived in the city of Samaria. The Samaritans were known for worshipping false gods. Furthermore, many of God's prophets had been executed in the city of Samaria. Because of these things, there was a great rift between the Samaritans and the Jews. Even when traveling, the Jews would inconvenience themselves by taking a longer route than necessary in order to avoid crossing into the city of Samaria. The existence of strained relations between the Samaritans and the Jews was the reason the Samaritan woman was surprised that Jesus, a Jew, took the time to speak to her. Let's continue with the account:

> 10Jesus answered and said to her, "If you knew the gift of God, and who it is who says to you, 'Give Me a drink,' you would have asked Him, and He would have given you living water."
> 11The woman said to Him, "Sir, You have nothing to draw with, and the well is deep. Where then do You get that living water?
> 12Are You greater than our father Jacob, who gave us the well, and drank from it himself, as well as his sons and his livestock?"
> 13Jesus answered and said to her, "Whoever drinks of this water will thirst again.
> 14But whoever drinks of the water that I shall give him will never thirst. But the water that I shall give him will become in him a fountain of water springing up into everlasting life." (John 4:10-14 NKJV)

Jesus told the woman (verse 10) that if she knew who was speaking to her, she'd turn the tables around and ask *him* for a drink of *living* water. The woman was perplexed and responded to Jesus by pointing out that Jesus didn't have anything with him with which to draw from the well.

She asked for further explanation concerning this "living water" that Jesus was speaking of.

Little did the woman know that she was being personally witnessed to by the Messiah himself, Jesus Christ. Verse 12 reveals that the woman was trying to get clarification as to who Jesus was. She still focused on the physical well and asked if Jesus was greater than her earthly father, Jacob, who had given her the well and drank from it himself. Jesus explained to her that those who drink from the well of water that she was talking about (the actual physical well of water) will eventually become thirsty again, but those who drink from the water that he supplies will never be thirsty again because the water that Jesus supplies leads to everlasting life. Jesus used the terminology of water metaphorically and metaphorically speaking, the living water that Jesus spoke of was the gospel, the word of God. It appears as if the woman may have begun to realize that Jesus was talking about spiritual matters, as is evidenced by her following response:

> [15]The woman said to Him, "Sir, give me this water, that I may not thirst, nor come here to draw."
> [16]Jesus said to her, "Go, call your husband, and come here."
> [17]The woman answered and said, "I have no husband." Jesus said to her, "You have well said, 'I have no husband,'
> [18]for you have had five husbands, and the one whom you now have is not your husband; in that you spoke truly."
> [19]The woman said to Him, "Sir, I perceive that You are a prophet." (John 4:15-19 NKJV)

Although it appears that the woman realized that Jesus was talking about spiritual matters, it looks as if she still may not have realized that Jesus was speaking metaphorically in regards to the water because she continued to associate the water with not having to draw it from the well. However, Jesus was very willing to explain things further to her. But before he began to explain further, he told her to call her husband so that he could talk with both of them. Jesus knew that she really had no husband. Some theologians believe that she was, however, involved with a man whom she referred to as her husband.

The woman told Jesus that she did not have a husband. She could have lied but she chose not to. It is evident that this woman had been lying to others by saying that she had a husband when she really didn't, because Jesus told her that she did well to say that she did not have a husband.

Jesus went on to tell the woman that she answered truthfully, as if she had not answered truthfully when approached with the question by others. He also told her about herself stating to her that she had five husbands before she had become involved with the man she was currently involved with and that this current man was not her husband. Since Jesus told her about herself, the woman perceived that he was a prophet, but she still had not come to the realization that he was much more. So, Jesus continued to witness the good news of the gospel to this woman as attested to in the following verses of scripture:

> [20]Our fathers worshipped on this mountain, and you Jews say that in Jerusalem is the place where one ought to worship."
>
> [21]Jesus said to her, "Woman, believe Me, the hour is coming when you will neither on this mountain, nor in Jerusalem, worship the Father.
>
> [22]You worship what you do not know; we know what we worship, for salvation is of the Jews.
>
> [23]But the hour is coming, and now is, when the true worshipers will worship the Father in spirit and truth; for the Father is seeking such to worship Him.
>
> [24]God is spirit, and those who worship Him must worship in spirit and in truth.
>
> [25]The woman said to Him, "I know that Messiah is coming" (who is called Christ). "When He comes, He will tell us all things."
>
> [26]Jesus said to her, "I who speak to you am He."
>
> [27]And at this point His disciples came, and they marveled that He talked with a woman; yet no one said, "What do You seek?" Or, "Why are You talking with her?"
>
> [28]The woman then left her waterpot, went her way into the city, and said to the men,

²⁹Come, see a Man who told me all things that I ever
did. Could this be the Christ?"
³⁰Then they went out of the city and came to Him.
(John 4:20-30 NKJV)

As the woman continued to talk with Jesus, she questioned him in her
own way. She talked to him about how the Jews were saying that people
should worship in Jerusalem. But Jesus prophesied to her telling her that
the time will come when people will neither worship on the mountain in
Samaria or in Jerusalem. In saying this he was essentially telling her that
where worship takes place doesn't matter as long as it *does* take place.
Jesus expounded further by telling the woman that she worships what she
does not know. In other words, she worships false gods. One cannot
know a false god, because a false god is just that...false. Jesus told the
woman that salvation is of the Jews. Jesus was a Jew. Salvation comes
through Jesus. This is what Jesus meant when he said that salvation is of
the Jews. And the Bible tells us that true Jews are those who have
confessed Jesus as Lord.[6]

Jesus went on to tell the woman that a time is coming when true
worshippers will worship God in spirit and in truth. The woman
immediately understood what Jesus was talking about and told him that
she knew the Messiah was coming and that when he comes he will teach
new things. However, she did not realize that the one whom she was
speaking to was indeed the Messiah. Jesus then identified himself as the
Messiah.

The main point in our examination of Jesus' conversation with the
Samaritan woman comes at verse 27 after Jesus identifies himself. Again
the verse reads as such: *"And at this point His disciples came, and they
marveled that he talked with a woman; yet no one said, "What do You
seek?" or "Why are You talking with her?"*

Jesus told a woman, a Samaritan woman at that, about the good news
of the gospel. He personally witnessed to her so that she might be saved.
But when the disciples saw him talking to her, they marveled at the fact

---

[6] "For you are not a true Jew just because you were born of Jewish parents or
because you have gone through the Jewish ceremony of circumcision. No, a true
Jew is one whose heart is right with God and true circumcision is not a cutting
of the body but a change of heart produced by God's Spirit...." (Romans 2:28-
29 NLT)

that Jesus would even talk to a woman.[7] Even though they marveled at this, they dared not to ask the woman what she wanted from Jesus, and they dared not to ask Jesus why he was talking to her. It appears from the tone of the text that although the disciples did not ask these questions, they certainly wanted to. The disciples looked down upon this woman. They did not really feel that Jesus should be talking to her, because Jewish custom forbade it. But Jesus did not hold back his message from her. He talked to her anyway. By doing so, he was giving a firm message that women are not second class citizens and that women need the gospel proclaimed to them just as any man does. This is certainly not a chauvinistic Jesus.

After Jesus identified himself, the woman left her waterpot and went into the city and encouraged the men of the city to follow her back to where Jesus was so that they could meet a man that told her everything she ever did. From the tone of scripture it sounds as if she was excited and rushed to the city to tell the men. It is also interesting to note that God used a woman to go to the men of the city, (where they worshipped false gods), and tell them about Jesus. If Jesus were a chauvinist, he certainly would not have used a woman to bring the good news of the gospel to an entire city of men.

The following verses of scripture go on to inform the reader that this woman's testimony made a huge impact in the city and because of the testimony of this woman, many of these men that came from the city to meet Jesus and to hear his word were ultimately saved. Let's take a look:

> [39]And many of the Samaritans of that city believed in Him because of the word of the woman who testified, "He told me all that I ever did."
> [40]So when the Samaritans had come to Him, they urged Him to stay with them; and He stayed there two days.
> [41]And many more believed because of His own word.
> [42]Then they said to the woman, "Now we believe, not because of what you said, for we ourselves have heard Him and we know that this is indeed the Christ, the Savior of the world. (John 4:39-42 NKJV)

---

[7] During that era, Jewish religious leaders rarely spoke to women in public.

Verse 39 tells us that there were those who believed in Jesus because of what the woman told them and then verse 42 says that there were others who believed because they eventually heard him for themselves. Either way, the woman was instrumental in bringing many of the Samaritans to the Lord. A chauvinistic God would have never used a woman for such a noble deed.

Not only did Jesus talk to women when other men would not have, he also defended women when other men did not. Let's look further:[8]

> [1]But Jesus went to the Mount of Olives.
>
> [2]Now early in the morning He came again into the temple, and all the people came to Him; and He sat down and taught them.
>
> [3]Then the scribes and Pharisees brought to Him a woman caught in adultery. And when they had set her in the midst,
>
> [4]they said to Him, "Teacher, this woman was caught in adultery, in the very act.
>
> [5]Now Moses, in the law, commanded us that such should be stoned. But what do You say?"
>
> [6]This they said, testing Him, that they might have something of which to accuse Him. But Jesus stooped down and wrote on the ground with His finger, as though He did not hear.
>
> [7]So when they continued asking Him, He raised Himself up and said to them, "He who is without sin among you, let him throw a stone at her first."
>
> [8]And again He stooped down and wrote on the ground.
>
> [9]Then those who heard it, being convicted by their conscience, went out one by one, beginning with the oldest even to the last. And Jesus was left alone, and the woman standing in the midst.
>
> [10]When Jesus had raised Himself up and saw no one but the woman, He said to her, "Woman, where are those accusers of yours? Has no one condemned you?"

---

[8] John 8:1-11 is not found in the earliest available manuscripts.

[11]She said, "No one, Lord." And Jesus said to her, "Neither do I condemn you; go and sin no more." (John 8:1-11 NKJV)

According to God's Law of the Old Testament, those caught in the act of adultery were to be put to death. Let's take a look:

If a man commits adultery with another man's wife— with the wife of his neighbor—both the adulterer and the adulteress must be put to death. (Leviticus 20:10 NIV)

If a man is found sleeping with another man's wife, both the man who slept with her and the woman must die. You must purge the evil from Israel. (Deuteronomy 22:22 NIV)

It is interesting to note that the men who brought this adulterous woman to the Lord neglected to also bring the man whom she was guilty of committing adultery with. She was caught in the very act of adultery, so it is not as if this man's identity was a mystery. If the woman was to be stoned, then the same plight should have awaited the man.

Not only did these men neglect to bring the man to Jesus, but they also neglected to keep in mind the sins that they themselves had committed. Certainly many of the sins they had committed during their lifetime, according to Mosaic Law, were punishable by death. But although these men neglected to bring the man forth and to examine the sins that they themselves had gotten away with, Jesus did not neglect to bring their past sins to their attention. When Jesus did so, all of them walked away and left the woman alone. No doubt, many of them had probably been guilty of adultery themselves.[9]

It appears that these men held women to a higher standard of Christian living than they held themselves to. However, Jesus held the same standard for the men as he did for the woman. Jesus did not dabble in double standards. He was not going to allow these men to put this

---

[9] More than likely, we have all done something in our pasts in which, as far as God is concerned, we deserved to die for. This is attested to in the verses of scripture contained in Romans 1:18-32 (see your Bible).

woman to death when they themselves were no less guilty of sin than she was. Jesus protected this woman from the societal chauvinism of the time. Certainly then, Jesus was not a chauvinist.

Despite the fact that there is quite a bit of scripture that lends argument to the position that Jesus was not a chauvinist and did not substantially treat women any differently than he treated men, there is one account that could easily be misconstrued as contradicting this claim. The following is the account. Let's examine it:

> [21] And going away from there, Jesus withdrew to the district of Tyre and Sidon.
>
> [22] And behold, a woman who was a Canaanite from that district came out and, with a [loud, troublesomely urgent] cry, begged, Have mercy on me, O Lord, Son of David! My daughter is miserably and distressingly and cruelly possessed by a demon!
>
> [23] But He did not answer her a word. And His disciples came and implored Him, saying, Send her away, for she is crying out after us.
>
> [24] He answered, I was sent only to the lost sheep of the house of Israel.
>
> [25] But she came and, kneeling, worshipped Him and kept praying, Lord, help me!
>
> [26] And He answered, It is not right (proper, becoming, or fair) to take the children's bread and throw it to the little dogs.
>
> [27] She said, Yes, Lord, yet even the little pups (little whelps) eat the crumbs that fall from their [young] master's table.
>
> [28] Then Jesus answered her, O woman, great is your faith! Be it done for you as you wish. And her daughter was cured from that moment. (Matthew 15:21-28 Amp.)

This Canaanite woman[10] was not a Jew. Jesus was basically telling her that his message and ministry was for the Jews.[11] However, the

---

[10] Although there existed a land of Canaan during Old Testament times, Canaan was no longer a country or a nation during New Testament times. Mark 7:26

gospel was also meant for the Gentiles (those who are not Jews) as well, which becomes very clear when reading Acts 11:1-18.[12] Jesus brought the message to the Jews first, but, the Gentiles were granted repentance unto life as well. This has also been emphasized in Romans 3:29-30 when Paul says, *"Is God the God of Jews only? Is he not the God of Gentiles too? Yes, of Gentiles too, since there is only one God, who will justify the circumcised[13] by faith and the uncircumcised through that same faith."* (NIV)

When Jesus began his earthly ministry, his focus was on the Jews. However, although Jesus sent his twelve apostles to the Israelites (the Jews) to preach about the kingdom of heaven, he did so knowing that the apostles, who would eventually be brought before the courts, *"would be a testimony to them and to the Gentiles."*[14] The fact that the apostles were to be a testimony to the Gentiles gives credibility to the position that the gospel was as much for the Gentiles as it was for the Jews. Earlier, we examined the account of Jesus speaking with the Samaritan woman. She was not a Jew, but a Gentile. Still, Jesus told her about the living water of eternal life. The Canaanite woman, whose daughter Jesus cast the demon from, was also a gentile.

The problem comes with how Jesus responded to the Canaanite woman in verse 26 when he said to her, *"It is not right (proper, becoming, or fair) to take the children's bread and throw it to the little dogs."* Many take this to mean that Jesus was calling this woman a dog and that he was saying to her that she was not good enough to receive for herself and for her daughter, the miracles of God. But it appears as if what Jesus was really doing was testing her to see how strong her belief in him was. The term *dog* was not specific to her, but it is indicative of

---

(see your Bible) is more exact in describing the woman as a "Greek born in Syrian Phoenicia" (NIV). Theologians have assessed that at one time Canaan was a part of Phoenicia and that therefore the reference to the woman as a Canaanite denotes the usage of a cultural idiom at the time when referring to those from Phoenicia.

[11] Matthew 10:2-23 (see your Bible)

[12] See Appendix

[13] During Old Testament times every Hebrew (Jew) male infant had to be circumcised at eight days old. However, circumcision was no longer required during Jesus' ministry.

[14] Matthew 10:17-18 (see your Bible and previous footnote citing Matthew 10:2-23)

how the Jews felt about the Gentiles in general. Jesus used the terms of the day to test her faith and to get his point across. If it had been a Gentile man that had approached him with the same request, it follows that Jesus would have responded to him in the same way he responded to the Canaanite woman.

The Jews looked upon the Gentiles with much contempt. They looked upon them with such contempt that they referred to the Gentiles as dogs. Jesus therefore used an example of the Jews' own contempt to teach them a lesson. The Canaanite woman wanted her daughter to be healed of demon possession. She knew who to go to. She went to Jesus. Furthermore, there was no doubt in the Canaanite woman's mind as to who Jesus was. Jesus used the derogatory term *dog* to make a point to the Jews. When Jesus told the woman that it is not proper to give the food that is prepared for the children to the dogs, the children metaphorically represented the Israelites while the dogs metaphorically represented the Gentiles.

The woman responded to Jesus as follows: *"Yes, Lord, yet even the little pups (little whelps) eat the crumbs that fall from their [young] master's table."* In other words, the food that Jesus was speaking of was the gospel of salvation. The crumbs also represent the food of the gospel, because crumbs, of course, come from food. Therefore, just as the dogs take hold of the crumbs of food, so was she taking hold of the word of God, which was proper for her to do as a believer and a human being. It did not matter that she was a Gentile. She knew who Jesus was and believed in him and she therefore also knew that she should benefit from even the very smallest "crumb" of the word of God. Because of her faith and her belief in him, Jesus blessed her by healing her child (verse 28). This was also a lesson to those who were around to witness this. As attested to in verse 23, the disciples wanted Jesus to send the woman away. But just like he did with the Samaritan woman at the well, Jesus engaged in a conversation with this Canaanite woman, and blessed her as he would have blessed any Jew.

SUMMARY

From our studies we can see that the men during the days of Jesus were often very critical of women. The apostles did not believe Mary Magdalene, Joanna, and Mary the mother of James when they told them that Jesus had been resurrected.[15] The scriptures indicate that they thought the women were speaking nonsense. It was probably difficult for them to believe that God would appoint women as the first to actually witness the evidence of the resurrection of Christ. The disciples marveled that Jesus would even talk to a woman, when they found him talking to the Samaritan woman. However, Jesus persisted in talking to her to the point where the woman believed in him and testified of him to the men in the city of Samaria, many of which eventually believed in Jesus. They believed in Jesus as a result of a woman's testimony. In another incident, the disciples wanted a Canaanite woman, who needed a demon to be cast out of her daughter, to be sent away. However, despite the fact that the Jews looked upon the Canaanites with contempt and referred to them as dogs, Jesus got rid of the demon anyway. In yet another incident, the teachers of the Law and the Pharisees brought a woman to Jesus who was caught in the act of adultery in order that they might stone her. But, Jesus instructed only those men without sin to stone her. Of course, none of the men stoned her because they knew that they were just as guilty of sin as she was. When taking all of these things and more into account, there is no doubt that Jesus is not and never was a chauvinist.

---

[15] Luke 24:1-12 (see Appendix)

EPILOGUE

When considering all of the information presented in this book, one would be hard pressed to hold on to the position that the Bible is a chauvinistic/sexist book and that God is a chauvinist. There are simply too many strong arguments against such opinion.

We've seen that God has used women just as greatly as he has used men. Deborah was a judge over all of Israel. She was also the Commander in chief of Israel's entire military during the time she served as judge. Esther rescued her people from certain death and annihilation just as Moses rescued his people from slavery and destruction. Jesus commemorated Mary of Bethany for anointing his feet with expensive oil while others scorned and criticized her. He memorialized her for her act of humility. There was no other person that Jesus memorialized during his ministry on earth. Rahab, a prostitute, was rewarded for helping the Israelites defeat the city of Jericho. She and her family were spared and she lived among the Israelites, married an Israelite man, and became part of the lineage of Jesus on the side of Joseph. Jesus healed the hemorrhaging woman of a disease that caused her to bleed vaginally for twelve years. Ruth was rewarded for her loyalty to her mother-in-law and was also eventually included as part of the lineage of Jesus on the side of Joseph. The Shunammite woman was rewarded for her hospitality. Elisha worked two miracles for her through the help of the Lord. He healed her of her barrenness and she conceived a son. When the boy became ill and died, he raised him from the dead.

God has used women as apostles, preachers, prophets, deacons, teachers, and so forth. Miriam, Deborah, Huldah, and Anna were all prophets. Phoebe was a deacon in the church. Junias was an apostle.

The Virgin Mary carried Jesus in her womb and gave birth to him. Jesus Christ (the Messiah, the Savior of the world, the second part of the Godhead, God in the flesh), was therefore born of a woman. Pregnancy, is an honorable thing and the vessel used to initially bring Jesus into the world was the womb of a woman.

Although women are commanded to submit to their husbands, husbands are commanded to love their wives as Christ loved the church and to honor their wives. If they do not do so, God will not hear their prayers. Therefore, husbands have the greater charge. God will turn away from a man who does not honor his wife the way he ought to. There is no scripture that says that God will turn away from a woman

461

who does not submit to her husband the way she ought to. And if a man truly loves his wife as Christ loved the church then his wife will rarely feel the brunt of the curse of his rule because he will sacrifice his wants and desires for her sake just as Jesus sacrificed himself on the cross for everyone's sake.

Although wives are commanded to submit to their husbands, they do not have to submit to anything that they believe is a sin or that is actually a sin. And although some men may be quite legalistic when it comes to the submission scriptures, God is not. A woman is commanded to obey God rather than man, just as a man is. Ultimately, she is to put God first.

Women are equal to men. Genesis 1:27 tells us that women have been made in the image of God just as men have been.[1] Galatians 2:28 takes it a step further[2] by teaching us that in Christ there really is no gender, but that men and women are the same under Christ. They are equal. The most defining role difference that God makes between men and women is seen in his directive to wives to submit to their husbands, and some argue that even that particular role directive exists as the result of a curse.

The word of God teaches that women would be happier if they were not married. God says that it is better for a woman to remain single so that she can serve the Lord more diligently. There is no mandate from God for women to get married and have children. In the Bible, marriage is not glorified the way it is in the church. The word of God instead teaches that staying single is better than being married for those who want to serve the Lord more attentively. With this said, the Bible essentially teaches that a woman is complete without having a man in her life and that she doesn't need to get married or have children in order to be valid in the eyes of God.

When looking at the physical makeup of women. Men are no cleaner than women are. If we are to take the Old Testament Laws into account, the menstrual blood of a woman is no more unclean than the semen is of a man. Both discharges are just as unclean as the other.

The virtuous wife spoken of in the book of Proverbs was "kept" well by her husband. Her husband gave her everything (including maids and servants) that she needed to be comfortably able to do what she needed to do around the house. We can safely assume that it was her husband who

---

[1] See chapter 3
[2] See chapter 3

supplied her with the start-up funds she needed to begin her own business. Although this woman was married with children, she was taken care of so well by her husband that she happily went about being an entrepreneur. If men make comparison to this virtuous wife when looking at their own wives, then they must also compare themselves with her husband. God never said that a woman must do all the housework without any help from her husband or servants. God makes it clear in his word, that the husband is the one who is supposed to support his family, if necessary, single-handedly, and that he is to provide for his wife adequately so that all of her needs are sufficiently met. It is all right for a man's wife to work, but God has not made it mandatory for her to work. God has made it mandatory for the husband to work. Therefore, if a man's wife does not want to work, then her husband should not force her to do so, but should instead himself seek to find additional employment if he is struggling to pay the bills. The man was the one cursed to work by the sweat of his brow, not the woman.

God never said that a woman has to be physically beautiful or endowed with a certain shape or figure in order to be appreciated as a woman. God's word repeatedly teaches that a woman's real beauty is measured by her character not her curves. Although men may favor beautiful women over average looking women, God does not. God uses who he will, despite his or her looks.

God speaks against rape, polygamy, abuse of women, domestic violence and the like. Furthermore, Jesus treated women contrary to the way the men of the time thought he ought to. Women were allowed to be disciples. They traveled with him during his ministry just as men did. Jesus talked to women and proclaimed the gospel to them just as he did any man, even when it was against custom to speak to a woman.

As evidenced in this book, God uses women for his work no less than he uses men. When it comes to issues of singleness, marriage, sex, polygamy, church service, and the like, there are no double standards with God. The rules are basically the same for men as they are for women. Women have no less of an opportunity to serve the Lord than men do. Women are no more obligated to get married and have children than men are. The same restrictions placed on women when it comes to sex are placed on men. Pregnancy is honorable. A woman does not have to submit to her husband in absolutely everything. Women have just as many privileges as men do. Women were not put on earth to be subservient to men. Beauty really *does* come from within. And men are commanded to love their wives as Christ loved the church...to sacrifice their wants and desires, and their lives if necessary, for the sake of their wives. Therefore, in light of everything that has been discussed, it is clearly and undeniably evident, that God is not a chauvinist.

APPENDIX

INTRODUCTION

John 1:1-14

[1]In the beginning was the Word, and the Word was with God, and the Word was God.
[2]He was in the beginning with God.
[3]All things came into being by Him, and apart from Him nothing came into being that has come into being.
[4]In Him was life, and the life was the light of men.
[5]And the light shines in the darkness, and the darkness did not comprehend it.
[6]There came a man, sent from God, whose name was John.
[7]He came for a witness, that he might bear witness of the light, that all might believe through him.
[8]He was not the light, but came that he might bear witness of the light.
[9]There was the true light which, coming into the world, enlightens every man.
[10]He was in the world, and the world was made through Him, and the world did not know Him.
[11]He came to His own, and those who were His own did not receive Him.
[12]But as many as received Him, to them He gave the right to become children of God, even to those who believe in His name,
[13]who were born not of blood, nor of the will of the flesh, nor of the will of man, but of God.
[14]And the Word became flesh, and dwelt among us, and we beheld His glory, glory as of the only begotten from the Father, full of grace and truth. (NASB)

CHAPTER 1

Genesis 12:1-7

[1]Now the LORD had said unto Abram, Get thee out of thy country, and from thy kindred, and from thy father's house, unto a land that I will shew thee:
[2]And I will make of thee a great nation, and I will bless thee, and make thy name great; and thou shalt be a blessing:
[3]And I will bless them that bless thee, and curse him that curseth thee: and in thee shall all families of the earth be blessed.
[4]So Abram departed, as the LORD had spoken unto him; and Lot went with him: and Abram was seventy and five years old when he departed out of Haran.
[5]And Abram took Sarai his wife, and Lot his brother's son, and all their substance that they had gathered, and the souls that they had gotten in Haran; and they went forth to go into the land of Canaan; and into the land of Canaan they came.

Appendix

[6] And Abram passed through the land unto the place of Sichem, unto the plain of Moreh. And the Canaanite was then in the land.

[7] And the LORD appeared unto Abram, and said, Unto thy seed will I give this land: and there builded he an altar unto the LORD, who appeared unto him.

Exodus 3:4-10

[4] And when the LORD saw that he turned aside to see, God called unto him out of the midst of the bush, and said, Moses, Moses. And he said, Here am I.

[5] And he said, Draw not nigh hither: put off thy shoes from off thy feet, for the place whereon thou standest is holy ground.

[6] Moreover he said, I am the God of thy father, the God of Abraham, the God of Isaac, and the God of Jacob. And Moses hid his face; for he was afraid to look upon God.

[7] And the LORD said, I have surely seen the affliction of my people which are in Egypt, and have heard their cry by reason of their taskmasters; for I know their sorrows;

[8] And I am come down to deliver them out of the hand of the Egyptians, and to bring them up out of that land unto a good land and a large, unto a land flowing with milk and honey; unto the place of the Canaanites, and the Hittites, and the Amorites, and the Perizzites, and the Hivites, and the Jebusites.

[9] Now therefore, behold, the cry of the children of Israel is come unto me: and I have also seen the oppression wherewith the Egyptians oppress them.

[10] Come now therefore, and I will send thee unto Pharaoh, that thou mayest bring forth my people the children of Israel out of Egypt.

Judges 4:17-24

[17] Howbeit Sisera fled away on his feet to the tent of Jael the wife of Heber the Kenite: for there was peace between Jabin the king of Hazor and the house of Hebor the Kenite.

[18] And Jael went out to meet Sisera, and said unto him, Turn in, my lord, turn in to me; fear not. And when he had turned in unto her into the tent, she covered him with a mantle.

[19] And he said unto her, Give me, I pray thee, a little water to drink; for I am thirsty. And she opened a bottle of milk, and gave him drink, and covered him.

[20] Again he said unto her, Stand in the door of the tent, and it shall be, when any man doth come and enquire of thee, and say, Is there any man here? that thou shalt say, No.

[21] Then Jael Heber's wife took a nail of the tent, and took an hammer in her hand, and went softly unto him, and smote the nail into his temples, and fastened it into the ground: for he was fast alseep and weary. So he died.

Appendix

[22] And, behold, as Barak pursued Sisera, Jael came out to meet him, and said unto him, Come, and I will shew thee the man whom thou seekest. And when he came into her tent, behold, Sisera lay dead, and the nail was in his temples.
[23] So God subdued on that day Jabin the king of Canaan before the children of Israel.
[24] And the hand of the children of Israel prospered, and prevailed against Jabin the king of Canaan, until they had destroyed Jabin king of Canaan.

Matthew 1:1-16

[1] The book of the genealogy of Jesus Christ, the son of David, the son of Abraham.
[2] To Abraham, was born Isaac; and to Isaac, Jacob; and to Jacob, Judah and his brothers.
[3] and to Judah were born Perez and Zerah by Tamar; and to Perez was born Hezron; and to Hezron, Ram;
[4] and to Ram was born Amminadab; and to Amminadab, Nahshon; and to Nahshon, Salmon;
[5] and to Salmon was born Boaz by Rahab; and to Boaz was born Obed by Ruth; and to Obed, Jesse;
[6] and to Jesse was born David the king.
And to David was born Solomon by her who had been the wife of Uriah;
[7] and to Solomon was born Rehoboam; and to Rehoboam, Abijah; and to Abijah, Asa;
[8] and to Asa was born Jehoshaphat; and to Jehoshaphat, Joram; and to Joram, Uzziah;
[9] and to Uzziah was born Jotham; and to Jotham, Ahaz; and to Ahaz, Hezekiah;
[10] and to Hezekiah was born Manasseh; and to Manasseh, Amon; and to Amon, Josiah;
[11] and to Josiah were born Jeconiah and his brothers, at the time of the deportation to Babylon.
[12] And after the deportation to Babylon, to Jeconiah was born Shealteil; and to Shealtiel, Zerubbabel;
[13] and to Zerubbabel was born Abiud; and to Abiud, Eliakim; and to Eliakim, Azor;
[14] and to Azor was born Zadok; and to Zadok, Achim; and to Achim, Eliud;
[15] and to Eliud was born Eleazar; and to Eleazar, Matthan; and to Matthan, Jacob;
[16] and to Jacob was born Joseph the husband of Mary, by whom was born Jesus, who is called Christ. (NASB)

Appendix

CHAPTER 2

Leviticus 15:19-26

[19]When a woman has her monthly period, she remains unclean for seven days. Anyone who touches her is unclean until evening. [20]Anything on which she sits or lies during her monthly period is unclean. [21-23]Any who touch her bed or anything on which she has sat must wash their clothes and take a bath, and they remain unclean until evening. [24]If a man has sexual intercourse with her during her period, he is contaminated by her impurity and remains unclean for seven days, and any bed on which he lies is unclean.

[25]If a woman has a flow of blood for several days outside her monthly period or if her flow continues beyond her regular period, she remains unclean as long as the flow continues, just as she is during her monthly period. [26]Any bed on which she lies and anything on which she sits during this time is unclean. (GNT)

Deuteronomy 17:14-17

[14]When thou art come unto the land which the LORD thy God giveth thee, and shalt possess it, and shalt dwell therein, and shalt say, I will set a king over me, like as all the nations that are about me:
[15]Thou shalt in any wise set him king over thee, whom the LORD thy God shall choose: one from among thy brethren shalt thou set king over thee: thou mayest not set a stranger over thee, which is not thy brother.
[16]But he shall not multiply horses to himself, nor cause the people to return to Egypt, to the end that he should multiply horses: forasmuch as the LORD hath said unto you, Ye shall henceforth return no more that way.
[17]Neither shall he multiply wives to himself, that his heart turn not away: neither shall he greatly multiply to himself silver and gold.

John 9:1-3

[1]As Jesus was walking along, he saw a man who had been born blind. [2]His disciples asked him, "Teacher, whose sin caused him to be born blind? Was it his own or his parents' sin?"
[3]Jesus answered, "His blindness has nothing to do with his sins or his parents' sins. He is blind so that God's power might be seen at work in him. (GNT)

468

Appendix

CHAPTER 3

1 Timothy 4:1-5

[1]The Spirit says clearly that some people will abandon the faith in later times; they will obey lying spirits and follow the teachings of demons. [2]Such teachings are spread by deceitful liars, whose consciences are dead, as if burnt with a hot iron. [3]Such people teach that it is wrong to marry and to eat certain foods. But God created those foods to be eaten, after a prayer of thanks, by those who are believers and have come to know the truth. [4]Everything that God has created is good; nothing is to be rejected, but everything is to be received with a prayer of thanks, [5]because the word of God and the prayer make it acceptable to God. (GNT)

Mark 12:13-17

[13]Some Pharisees and some members of Herod's party were sent to Jesus to trap him with questions. [14]They came to him and said, "Teacher, we know that you tell the truth, without worrying about what people think. You pay no attention to anyone's status, but teach the truth about God's will for people. Tell us, is it against our Law to pay taxes to the Roman Emperor? Should we pay them or not?

[15]But Jesus saw through their trick and answered, "Why are you trying to trap me? Bring a silver coin, and let me see it."

[16]They brought him one, and he asked, "Whose face and name are these?" "The Emperor's," they answered.

[17]So Jesus said, "Well, then, pay to the Emperor what belongs to the Emperor, and pay to God what belongs to God."

And they were amazed at Jesus. (GNT)

CHAPTER 4

Matthew 3:1-6

[1]In those days came John the Baptist, preaching in the wilderness of Judaea,
[2]And saying, Repent ye: for the kingdom of heaven is at hand.
[3]For this is he that was spoken of by the prophet Esaias, saying, The voice of one crying in the wilderness, Prepare ye the way of the Lord, make his paths straight.
[4]And the same John had his raiment of camel's hair, and a leathern girdle about his lions; and his meat was locusts and wild honey.
[5]Then went out to him Jerusalem, and all Judaea and all the region round about Jordan,

Appendix

[6]And were baptized of him in Jordan, confessing their sins.

Genesis 17:3-8

[3]And Abram fell on his face: and God talked with him, saying,

[4]As for me, behold, my covenant is with thee, and thou shalt be a father of many nations.

[5]Neither shall thy name any more be called Abram, but thy name shall be Abraham; for a father of many nations have I made thee.

[6]And I will make thee exceeding fruitful, and I will make nations of thee, and kings shall come out of thee.

[7]And I will establish my covenant between me and thee and thy seed after thee in their generations for an everlasting covenant, to be God unto thee, and to thy seed after thee.

[8]And I will give unto thee, and to thy seed after thee, the land wherein thou art a stranger, all the land of Canaan, for an everlasting obsession; and I will be their God.

2 Corinthians 12:6-10

[6]Should I desire to boast, I shall not be a witless braggart, for I shall be speaking the truth. But I abstain [from it] so that no one may form a higher estimate of me than [is justified by] what he sees in me or hears from me.

[7]And to keep me from being puffed up and too much elated by the exceeding greatness (preeminence) of these revelations, there was given me a thorn (a splinter) in the flesh, a messenger of Satan, to rack and buffet and harass me, to keep me from being excessively exalted. [Job. 2:6.]

[8]Three times I called upon the Lord and besought [Him] about this and begged that it might depart from me;

[9]But He said to me, My grace (my favor and loving-kindness and mercy) is enough for you [sufficient against any danger and enables you to bear the trouble manfully]: for My strength and power are made perfect (fulfilled and completed) and show themselves most effective in [your] weakness. Therefore, I will all the more gladly glory in my weaknesses and infirmities, that the strength and power of Christ (the Messiah) may rest (yes, may pitch a tent over and dwell) upon me!

[10]So for the sake of Christ, I am well pleased and take pleasure in infirmities, insults, hardships, persecutions, perplexities and distresses; for when I am weak [in human strength], then am I [truly] strong (able, powerful in divine strength). (Amp.)

470

Appendix

CHAPTER 9

Acts 13:4-12

[4]Having been sent by the Holy Spirit, Barnabas and Saul went to Seleucia and sailed from there to the island of Cyprus. [5]When they arrived at Salamis, they preached the word of God in the synagogues. They had John Mark with them to help in the work.

[6]They went all the way across the island to Paphos, where they met a certain magician named Bar-Jesus, a Jew who claimed to be a prophet. [7]He was a friend of the governor of the island, Sergius Paulus, who was an intelligent man. The governor called Barnabas and Saul before him because he wanted to hear the word of God. [8]But they were opposed by the magician Elymas (that is his name in Greek), who tried to turn the governor away from the faith. [9]Then Saul—also known as Paul—was filled with the Holy Spirit; he looked straight at the magician [10]and said, "You son of the Devil! You are the enemy of everything that is good. You are full of all kinds of evil tricks, and you always keep trying to turn the Lord's truths into lies! [11]The Lord's hand will come down on you now; you will be blind and will not see the light of day for a time."

At once Elymas felt a dark mist cover his eyes, and he walked around trying to find someone to lead him by the hand. [12]When the governor saw what had happened, he believed; for he was greatly amazed at the teaching about the Lord. (GNT)

John 8:42-47

[42]Jesus said unto them, If God were your Father, ye would love me: for I proceeded forth and came from God; neither came I of myself, but he sent me. [43]Why do ye not understand my speech? even because ye cannot hear my word. [44]Ye are of your father the devil, and the lusts of your father ye will do. He was a murderer from the beginning, and abode not in the truth, because there is no truth in him. When he speaketh a lie, he speaketh of his own: for he is a liar, and the father of it. [45]And because I tell you the truth, ye believe me not. [46]Which of you convinceth me of sin? And if I say the truth, why do ye not believe me? [47]He that is of God heareth God's words: ye therefore hear them not, because ye are not of God.

Mark 7:14-23

[14]Then Jesus called the crowd to him once more and said to them, "Listen to me, all of you, and understand. [15]There is nothing that goes into you from the

outside which can make you ritually unclean. Rather, it is what comes out of you that makes you unclean.

[17]When he left the crowd and went into the house, his disciples asked him to explain this saying. [18]"You are no more intelligent than the others," Jesus said to them. "Don't you understand? Nothing that goes into you from the outside can really make you unclean, [19]because it does not go into your heart but into your stomach and then goes on out of the body." (In saying this, Jesus declared that all foods are fit to be eaten).

[20]And he went on to say, "It is what comes out of you that makes you unclean. [21]For from the inside, from your heart, come the evil ideas which lead you to do immoral things, to rob, kill, [22]commit adultery, be greedy, and do all sorts of evil things; deceit, indecency, jealousy, slander, pride, and folly—[23]all these evil things come from inside you and make you unclean. (GNT)

Matthew 26:36-42

[36]Then commeth Jesus with them unto a place called Gethsemane, and saith unto the disciples, Sit ye here, while I go and pray yonder.

[37]And he took with him Peter and the two sons of Zebedee, and began to be sorrowful and very heavy.

[38]Then saith he unto them, My soul is exceeding sorrowful, even unto death: tarry ye here, and watch with me.

[39]And he went a little farther, and fell on his face, and prayed, saying, O my Father, if it be possible, let this cup pass from me: nevertheless not as I will, but as thou wilt.

[40]And he cometh unto the disciples, and findeth them asleep, and saith unto Peter, What could ye not watch with me one hour?

[41]Watch and pray, that ye enter not into temptation: the spirit indeed is willing, but the flesh is weak.

[42]He went away again the second time, and prayed, saying, O my Father, if this cup may not pass away from me, except I drink it, thy will be done.

CHAPTER 10

Judges 20:29-46

[29]And Israel set liers in wait round about Gibeah.

[30]And the children of Israel went up against the children of Benjamin on the third day, and put themselves in array against Gibeah, as at other times.

[31]And the children of Benjamin went out against the people, and were drawn away from the city; and they began to smite of the people, and kill, as at other times, in the highways, of which one goeth up to the house of God, and the other to Gibeah in the field, about thirty men of Israel.

³²And the children of Benjamin said, They are smitten down before us, as at the first. But the children of Israel said, Let us flee, and draw them from the city unto the highways.

³³And all the men of Israel rose up out of their place, and put themselves in array at Baaltamar: and the liers in wait of Israel came forth out of their places, even out of the meadows of Gibeah.

³⁴And there came against Gibeah ten thousand chosen men out of all Israel, and the battle was sore: but they knew not that evil was near them.

³⁵And the LORD smote Benjamin before Israel: and the children of Israel destroyed of the Benjamites that day twenty and five thousand and an hundred men, all these drew the sword.

³⁶ So the children of Benjamin saw that they were smitten: for the men of Israel gave place to the Benjamites, because they trusted unto the liers in wait which they had set beside Gibeah.

³⁷And the liers in wait hasted, and rushed upon Gibeah; and the liers in wait drew themselves along, and smote all the city with the edge of the sword.

³⁸Now there was an appointed sign between the men of Israel and the liers in wait, that they should make a great flame with smoke rise up out of the city.

³⁹And when the men of Israel retired in the battle, Benjamin began to smite and kill of the men of Israel about thirty persons: for they said, Surely they are smitten down before us, as in the first battle.

⁴⁰But when the flame began to arise up out of the city with a pillar of smoke, the Benjamites looked behind them, and, behold, the flame of the city ascended up to heaven.

⁴¹And when the men of Israel turned again, the men of Benjamin were amazed; for they saw that evil was come upon them.

⁴²Therefore they turned their backs before the men of Israel unto the way of the wilderness; but the battle overtook them; and them which came out of the cities they destroyed in the midst of them.

⁴³Thus they inclosed the Benjamites round about, and chased them, and trode them down with ease over against Gibeah toward the sunrising.

⁴⁴And there fell of Benjamin eighteen thousand men; all these were men of valour.

⁴⁵And they turned and fled toward the wilderness unto the rock of Rimmon: and they gleaned of them in the highways five thousand men; and pursued hard after them unto Gidom, and slew two thousand men of them.

⁴⁶So that all which fell that day of Benjamin were twenty and five thousand men that drew the sword; all these were men of valour.

CHAPTER 13

Matthew 1:1-16
Documented on page 467 of this Appendix.

Appendix

Biblical Argument against Capital Punishment

In Matthew 5:21-22 Jesus, during his talk to the multitude on the Mount, talks about murder and says that long ago it was commanded that people should not murder and that anyone who did so was subject to judgment. Then he says that it now goes deeper than that and anyone who is angry with his brother is subject to judgment. Let's take a look:

> [21]"You have heard that people were told in the past, 'Do not commit murder; anyone who does will be brought to trial. [22]But now I tell you: if you are angry with your brother you will be brought to trial, if you call your brother 'You good-for-nothing!' you will be brought before the Council, and if you call your brother a worthless fool you will be in danger of going to the fire of hell." (GNT)

Jesus continues (verse 27) by instructing his listeners not to commit adultery. The following is what he said:

> [27]"You have heard that it was said, 'Do not commit adultery. [28]But now I tell you: anyone who looks at a woman and wants to possess her is guilty of committing adultery with her in his heart. (Matthew 5:27 GNT)

Jesus taught the same lesson regarding adultery that he taught regarding murder, which was, that both sins can be committed in the heart of someone although they never actually physically commit the sin. Jesus taught that having anger in one's heart for someone is just as bad as murdering him or her and he also taught that having lust in one's heart is just as bad as committing adultery. Anyone who looks lustfully at a woman has committed adultery in his heart. Leviticus 20:10[1] says a man must be put to death for committing adultery. Leviticus 24:17[2] says that if anyone takes the life of another he must be put to death. Leviticus 24:20 breaks it down even further and says that there should be an "eye for eye, and a tooth for a tooth." Then in Matthew 5:38 Jesus says that it was said "an eye for an eye, and tooth for a tooth," but now we must turn the other cheek.

In this talk on the Mount that we see in Matthew 5, Jesus puts murder and adultery in the same league. Both murder and adultery were punishable by death in the Old Testament. Both murder and adultery are discussed in similar ways in

---

[1] See your Bible
[2] See your Bible

Matthew 5. This puts murder and adultery in the same category. Paul does the same in Romans 13:9-10. He lumps murder and adultery together along with stealing and says that loving one's neighbor is the fulfillment of not murdering and not committing adultery. Let's take a look:

> [9]The commandments, "do not commit adultery; do not commit murder; do not steal; do not desire what belongs to someone else"—all these, and any others besides, are summed up in the one command, "Love your neighbor as you love yourself." [10]If you love others, you will never do them wrong; to love, then, is to obey the whole Law. (GNT)

James 2:8-11 lumps murder and adultery together again and goes much further by telling us that in breaking one law one is guilty of breaking all of it. So one who commits adultery is no less guilty of one who murders and one who murders is no guiltier than one who commits adultery. Let's take a look:

> [8]You will be doing the right thing if you obey the law of the Kingdom, which is found in the scripture, "Love your neighbor as you love yourself." [9]But if you treat people according to their outward appearance, you are guilty of sin, and the Law condemns you as a lawbreaker. [10]Whoever breaks one commandment is guilty of breaking them all. [11]For the same one who said, "Do not commit adultery," also said, "Do not commit murder." Even if you do not commit adultery, you have become a lawbreaker if you commit murder." (GNT)

What James is saying is that if a person commits murder but doesn't commit adultery, that person is still guilty of adultery because by committing murder that person has broken the entire Law of God. If then this is the case then it follows that the reverse is true also, that being, that if a person commits adultery but doesn't commit murder, that person is still guilty of murder because by committing murder he has broken the entire Law of God.

Verse 13 goes on to say that judgment without mercy is not a good thing and that mercy should triumph over judgment. Jesus showed this type of mercy to the adulterous woman who was brought to him (John 8:1-11). Mercy triumphed over judgment. She was guilty of adultery and by Mosaic Law was to be executed. But Jesus basically instructed the people not to execute her, and by doing so, he taught the people the *better* way. Let's take a look:

> [1]Then everyone went home, but Jesus went to the Mount of Olives. [2]Early the next morning he went back to the Temple. All the people gathered around him, and he sat down and

began to teach them. [3]The teachers of the Law and Pharisees brought in a woman who had been caught committing adultery, and they made her stand before them all. [4]"Teacher," they said to Jesus, "this woman was caught in the very act of committing adultery. [5]In our Law Moses commanded that such a woman must be stoned to death. Now, what do you say?" [6]They said this to trap Jesus, so that they could accuse him. But he bent over and wrote on the ground with his finger. [7]As they stood there asking him questions, he straightened up and said to them, "Whichever one of you has committed no sin may throw the first stone at her. [8]Then he bent over again and wrote on the ground. [9]When they heard this, they all left, one by one, the older ones first. Jesus was left alone, with the woman still standing there. [10]He straightened up and said to her, "Where are they? Is there no one left to condemn you?"

[11]No one, sir," she answered.

"Well, then," Jesus said, "I do not condemn you either. Go, but do not sin again." (GNT)

If one who commits adultery is just as guilty as one who murders, and if Jesus basically taught against executing the adulterer ("those of you without sin throw the first stone"), then it stands to reason that Jesus was also teaching against executing the murderer. It is therefore safe to assume that if a murderer had been brought to Jesus instead of an adulterer, Jesus' response would have been the same. In the eyes of God, murder is no greater a sin than adultery. In teaching us against executing the adulterer, Jesus also taught us against executing the murderer. By doing this, he was letting us know that we are all worthy of death since if we commit just one sin, we are guilty of them all. Therefore, it behooves us to be merciful towards others.

CHAPTER 14

Acts 11:1-18

[1]The apostles and the other believers throughout Judea heard that the Gentiles also had received the word of God. [2]When Peter went to Jerusalem, those who were in favor of circumcising Gentiles criticized him, saying, [3]"You were a guest in the home of uncircumcised Gentiles, and you even ate with them?" [4]So Peter gave them a complete account of what had happened from the very beginning:

[5]While I was praying in the city of Joppa, I had a vision. I saw something coming down that looked like a large sheet being lowered by its four corners

Appendix

from heaven, and it stopped next to me. [6]I looked closely inside and saw domesticated and wild animals, reptiles, and wild birds. [7]Then I heard a voice saying to me, 'Get up, Peter; kill and eat?' [8]But I said, 'Certainly not, Lord! No ritually unclean or defiled food has ever entered my mouth.' [9]The voice spoke again from heaven, 'Do not consider anything unclean that God has declared clean.' [10]This happened three times, and finally the whole thing was drawn back up into heaven. [11]At that very moment three men who had been sent to me from Caesarea arrived at the house where I was staying. [12]The Spirit told me to go with them without hesitation. These six fellow believers from Joppa accompanied me to Caesarea, and we all went into the house of Cornelius. [13]He told us how he had seen an angel standing in his house, who said to him, 'Send someone to Joppa for a man whose full name is Simon Peter. [14]He will speak words to you by which you and all your family will be saved.' [15]And when I began to speak, the Holy Spirit came down on them just as on us at the beginning. [16]Then I remembered what the Lord had said: 'John baptized with water, but you will be baptized with the Holy Spirit.' [17]It is clear that God gave those Gentiles the same gift that he gave us when we believed in the Lord Jesus Christ; who was I, then, to try to stop God!"

[18]When they heard this, they stopped their criticism and praised God, saying, "Then God has given to the Gentiles also the opportunity to repent and live! (GNT)

Luke 24:1-12

[1]Very early on Sunday morning the women went to the tomb, carrying the spices they had prepared. [2]They found the stone rolled away from the entrance to the tomb, [3]so they went in; but they did not find the body of the Lord Jesus. [4]They stood there puzzled about this, when suddenly two men in bright shining clothes stood by them. [5]Full of fear, the women bowed down to the ground, as the men said to them, 'Why are you looking among the dead for one who is alive? [6]He is not here; he has been raised. Remember what he said to you while he was in Galilee: [7]The Son of Man must be handed over to sinners, be crucified, and three days later rise to life."

[8]Then the women remembered his words, [9]returned from the tomb, and told all this to the eleven disciples and all the rest. [10]The women were Mary Magdalene, Joanna, and Mary the mother of James; they and the other women with them told these things to the apostles. [11]But the apostles thought that what the women said was nonsense, and they did not believe them. [12]But Peter got up and ran to the tomb; he bent down and saw the grave cloths but nothing else. Then he went back home amazed at what had happened. (GNT)

BIBLIOGRAPHY

Bristow, John Temple, *What Paul really said about Women*, New York, New York, HarperSanFrancisco 1988

Butler, Trent C., Ph.D., *Holman Bible Dictionary*, Nashville, Tennessee, Holman Bible Publishers, 1991

Evans, Patricia, *The Verbally Abusive Relationship*, Holbrook Massachusetts: Adams Media Corparation 1992, 1996

Goodrick, Edward W., John R. Kohlenberger III, James A. Swanson (Associate Editor), *Zondervan NIV Exhaustive Concordance*, Grand Rapids Michigan, Zondervan Publishing House, 1999.

Hsu, Albert Y,.*Singles at the Crossroads,* Downers Grove Illinois, Intervarsity Press, 1997

Kaiser Jr., Walter C., Peter H. Davids, F.F. Bruce, Manfred T. Brauch, *Hard Sayings of the Bible*, Downers Grove, Illinois, Intervarsity Press, 1996

Lockyer, Herbert, *All the Women of the Bible*, Grand Rapids Michigan, Zondervan Publishing House

Reuben M.D, David, *Everything you always wanted to know about Sex*, New York, New York, St. Martin's Press, 1999

Strong, James,. LL.D., S.T.D. *The Strong's Exhaustive Concordance of the Bible* , Nashville, Tennessee, Thomas Nelson Publishers , 1995, 1996

Thomas, Robert L.TH.D., *New American Standard Exhaustive Concordance of the Bible Hebrew, Aramaic, and Greek Dictionaries,* Anaheim California, The Lockman Foundation 1981, Foundation Publications

Vine, W.E., *Vine's Complete Expository Dictionary*, Nashville, Tennessee: Thomas Nelson Publishers 1984, 1996

The Bethany Parallel Commentary, Minneapolis MN: Bethany House Publishers 1985

The Holy Bible, *African American Jubilee Edition, Contemporary English Version*, New York, New York: American Bible Society 1995, 1999

The Holy Bible, *Good News Translation*, Grand Rapids Michigan, Zondervan Publishing House 1992

The Holy Bible, *King James Version*, 1611

The Holy Bible, *New American Standard Bible*, Nashville, Tennessee: Thomas Nelson Publishers and the Lockman Foundation, 1985

The Holy Bible, *New King James Version*, Nashville, Tennessee, Thomas Nelson, Inc., 1982

The Holy Bible, *New Living Translation*, Wheaton, Illinois, Tyndale House Publishers, Inc., 1997

The Holy Bible, *The Access Bible, New Revised Standard Version*, New York, New York, Oxford University Press, 1999

The Holy Bible, *The Amplified Bible*, Grand Rapids, Michigan, Zondervan Publishing House, 1987

The Holy Bible, *The NIV Study Bible, 10th Anniversary Edition*, Grand Rapids Michigan, Zondervan Publishing House, 1995

NAME INDEX

NAME INDEX